SECRECY IN US

*For my parents, Koki and Mieko Komine,
and my brother, Yukihiko Komine*

Secrecy in US Foreign Policy
Nixon, Kissinger and the Rapprochement with China

YUKINORI KOMINE
Miyazaki International College, Japan

LONDON AND NEW YORK

First published 2008 by Ashgate Publishing

2 Park Square, Milton Park, Abingdon, Oxon OX14 4RN
711 Third Avenue, New York, NY 10017, USA

Routledge is an imprint of the Taylor & Francis Group, an informa business

First issued in paperback 2016

Copyright © 2008 Yukinori Komine

Yukinori Komine has asserted his moral right under the Copyright, Designs and Patents Act, 1988, to be identified as the author of this work.

All rights reserved. No part of this book may be reprinted or reproduced or utilised in any form or by any electronic, mechanical, or other means, now known or hereafter invented, including photocopying and recording, or in any information storage or retrieval system, without permission in writing from the publishers.

Notice:
Product or corporate names may be trademarks or registered trademarks, and are used only for identification and explanation without intent to infringe.

British Library Cataloguing in Publication Data
Komine, Yukinori
  Secrecy in US foreign policy : Nixon, Kissinger and the
  rapprochement with China
  1. Nixon, Richard M. (Richard Milhous), 1913-1994
  2. Kissinger, Henry, 1923- 3. United States - Foreign
  relations - China 4. China - Foreign relations - United
  States 5. United States - Foreign relations - 1969-1974
  6. China - Foreign relations - 1949-1976
  I. Title
  327.7'3'051'09047

Library of Congress Cataloging-in-Publication Data
Komine, Yukinori.
 Secrecy in US foreign policy : Nixon, Kissinger, and the rapprochement with China / by Yukinori Komine.
  p. cm.
  Includes bibliographical references and index.
 1. United States--Foreign relations--China. 2. China--Foreign relations--United States. 3. Nixon, Richard M. (Richard Milhous), 1913-1994. 4. Kissinger, Henry, 1923- 5. United States--Foreign relations--1969-1974. 6. United States--Foreign relations--Decision making. 7. Executive privilege (Government information)--United States. 8. Official secrets--United States. I. Title.

E183.8.C5K64 2008
327.73051--dc22

2007041407

ISBN 13: 978-0-7546-7272-2 (hbk)
ISBN 13: 978-1-138-26628-5 (pbk)

Contents

Acknowledgements	*vii*
List of Abbreviations	*ix*
A Note on Transliteration of Chinese Terms	*xi*
Introduction	1

PART I   THE FOUNDATIONS OF FOREIGN POLICY DECISION-MAKING

1	The Nixon-Kissinger Leadership for a New China Initiative	15
2	Foreign Policy Decision-Making Machinery for the US Rapprochement with China	41

PART II   THE EVOLUTION OF THE RAPPROACHEMENT POLICY

3	The Development of Policy Options from January to July 1969	71
4	The Reassessment of the China Policy from July to November 1969	91
5	The Resumption of the Warsaw Ambassadorial Talks from December 1969 to May 1970	115
6	The Development of Backchannel Communications from June 1970 to July 1971	135

PART III   DIRECT TALKS

7	Kissinger's Trips to Beijing in July and October 1971	159
8	Nixon's Trip to China in February 1972	197
Epilogue		229
Conclusion		241
Appendix		*251*
Bibliography		*255*
Index		*279*

Acknowledgements

During the research for and writing of this book for almost a decade, I have benefited from assistance and generosity of a number of people in America, Britain, and Japan.

I would like to express my appreciation to the former and present members of the Department of Politics and International Relations at Lancaster University, Britain. I am indebted to Professor Ian Bellany, Mr. Gordon Hands, Professor Gerd Nonneman, and Dr. Peter Wilkin for their comments on the manuscripts. I would like to record my gratitude to Miss Becky Richards for proof-reading the manuscripts and for offering me invaluable suggestions.

I would like to express my appreciation to Dr. Paul Stares, then the Director of Research and Studies Program, the United States Institute of Peace, who provided me a crucial opportunity of consultation which materialized a series of interviews with former US officials. I am indebted to Dr. Gareth Davies, St Anne's College, Oxford University, who has given me a number of advices for archival research in Washington DC.

I owe a special debt of gratitude to the following academic experts and former US officials for their cooperation for interviews and correspondences: Professor Saki Dockrill, Professor Rosemary Foot, Dr. Evelyn Goh, Dr. Morton Halperin, Mr. Charles Kennedy, Ambassador Winton Lord, Mr. Peter Rodman, Professor David Shambaugh, Ambassador Richard Solomon, Professor Nancy Bernkopf Tucker, and Professor Allen Whiting.

I would like to express my thanks to the support of a number of archivists and librarians in the following institutes: The National Archives, Archives II, Maryland; The Manuscript Division, The Library of Congress, Washington DC; The Special Collection Division, The Lauinger Library, Georgetown University, Washington DC; and The inter-library loans, Lancaster University Library.

My editors at Ashgate Publishing Limited have provided an excellent assistance and continuing encouragement throughout the review and editing of this book. My gratitude goes to: Ms. Carolyn Court, Nikki Dines, Aimée Feenan, Kirstin Howgate, and Margaret Younger.

I am grateful to my colleagues and friends in Miyazaki International College, Japan. I have received useful comments, help and encouragement from Professors Bern Mulvey, Mundoli Narayanan, Edward Rummel, and Amy Szarkowski. Amy generously read the entire manuscript and offered a number of significant suggestions.

I have benefited from the support and encouragement given by my old friends and colleagues. My thanks go to: Cem Birsay, John Boyle, Jim Bowey, Estevao Cabral, Tom Colombino, John Elder, Stewart Fraser, Ozge Girit, Juan Hall, Radhika

Kanchana, Githadethevi Kanisin, Philipe Larcher, Al Lawson, Luis Lobo-Guerrero, Vince Miller, Rob Moore, Beth Rempe, Athanasia Rodaki, Tracy Sartin, Graham Smith, Chris Shelhorse, Lee Smith, Ghulam Yar.

Finally, a special word of thanks must be reserved for my parents, Koki and Mieko Komine, and my brother, Yukihiko Komine, for their support over the last twelve years in America, Britain, China, and Japan.

Yukinori Komine
Washignton DC
August 2007

List of Abbreviations

ADST	Association of Diplomatic Studies and Training
CF	Country Files
CIA	US Central Intelligence Agency
Chicom	Chinese Communists
CWIHP	Cold War International History Project, Woodrow Wilson Center for Scholars
DOD	US Department of Defense
FAOHC	Foreign Affairs Oral History Collection
FPF	For the President's Files
FPF/Lord	For the President's Files (Winston Lord)
FRUS	*Foreign Relations of the United States*
Haig-File	Alexander M. Haig, Jr. Special File
HAK	Henry A. Kissinger
HAK-ASF	Henry A. Kissinger Administrative and Staff Files
HAKOF	Henry A. Kissinger Office Files
INR	Bureau of Intelligence and Research, US Department of State
Memcon	Memorandum of Conversation
MemforP	Memoranda for the President
NA	US National Archives and Records Administration, Archives II, College Park, Maryland
NF	Name Files
NPMS	Nixon Presidential Materials Staff
NSA	National Security Archive, George Washington University, Washington DC
NSC	US National Security Council
NSCF	National Security Council Files
NSCIF	National Security Council Institutional Files
NSCP-OHR	The National Security Council Project, Oral History Roundtables, The Brookings Institute and Center for International and Security Studies, Maryland, Virginia
NSDM	National Security Decision Memorandum
NSSM	National Security Study Memorandum

P/HAK Memcons	Presidential/Henry A. Kissinger Memorandum of Conversations
POF	President's Office Files
PPF	President's Personal Files
PPS	Policy Planning Staff
PRC	People's Republic of China
PSF	President's Speech Files
PTF	President's Trip Files
RG 59	Record Group 59, General Records of the US Department of State
RN	Richard M. Nixon
ROC	Republic of China
ROM	Records of Meetings
SALT	Strategic Arms Limitation Talks
SF	Subject Files
SNF	Subject-Numeric Files
STATE	US Department of State
Telcon	Telephone Conversation
WHCF	White House Central Files
WHSF	White House Special Files
WSAG	Washington Special Action Group

A Note on Transliteration of Chinese Terms

In general, this book has used the Pinyin system of transliteration of most Chinese names and places. It uses the original forms regarding Wade-Giles spelling in direct quotations from primary documents. For example, the declassified transcripts and policy analysis papers wrote "Peking," "Mao Tse-tung," and "Chou En-lai," which the Pinyin transliteration system has rendered as "Beijing," "Mao Zedong," and "Zhou Enlai," respectively.

Introduction

[A general] must be able to mystify his officers and men by false reports and appearances, and thus keep them in total ignorance. By altering his arrangements and changing his plans, he keeps the enemy without definite knowledge. By shifting his camp and taking circuitous routes, he prevents the enemy from anticipating his purpose.

Sun Tzu, *The Art of War*

Secrecy is the very soul of diplomacy.

François de Callières, 1716

1. Setting the Scene: Secrecy and the Nixon-Kissinger Diplomatic Coup

On July 15, 1971, US President Richard M. Nixon announced his decision to accept the invitation from the Chinese leaders to visit the People's Republic of China at appropriate time before May 1972, resulting from the confidential talks between Dr. Henry A. Kissinger and Premier Zhou Enlai in Beijing to open the door for more normalized relations between the United States and China. His briefly televised announcement astonished and delighted a large number of the American and international audiences. The diplomatic breakthrough in US-China relations also shocked America's allies as well as its adversaries in the world. In short, the Nixon-Kissinger diplomacy of surprise dramatically ended the two decades of mutual hostilities between Washington and Beijing since the establishment of the People's Republic of China in October 1949 and the outbreak of the Korean War in June 1950, which caused the "Loss of China" to the Communists and the development of Sino-Soviet alliance. Nixon's historic journey to a newly-emerging but still mysterious Middle Kingdom and the spectacle of his meeting with the prominent revolutionary leader, Chairman Mao Zedong, also formed romanticism in the American public symbolizing the entry of the world into the era of negotiations. In particular, the US rapprochement with China transformed the structure of the international system from US-Soviet bipolar military rivalry to US-Soviet-China diplomatic triangle, in which the US played the pivotal role of being a balancer in the deepening Sino-Soviet rift. Simultaneously, by opening to China, which US officials once viewed as an expansive threat causing America's prolonged involvement into the Vietnam War, Nixon and Kissinger attempted to put pressure and isolate North Vietnam. Prior to the Nixon announcement, there had been Washington's public and private communications with Beijing over a two-and-half year period, based on a highly complex bureaucratic maneuvering between the Nixon-Kissinger White House and the State Department.

This book examines the pursuit of strict secrecy by President Richard M. Nixon and the National Security Adviser Henry A. Kissinger in foreign policy decision-making as a principal characteristic in the US rapprochement with China in the early 1970s.[1] It was Nixon's presidential leadership that drove the new China initiative, along with Kissinger's contributions as a skilful negotiator and strategic thinker. Together, Nixon and Kissinger re-activated the National Security Council as the President's principal forum for foreign policy decision-making, namely a multi-level system with the Council at the highest, the Kissinger-led Review and Operational Groups in the middle and the Interdepartmental Groups at the bottom. Nixon wanted a formal and systematic NSC, which moved authority from the departments to the White House; Kissinger designed the systematic control of policy study papers within the NSC that enabled the development of a full range of policy options for presidential consideration and decision.

In a broader sense, therefore, this study perceives the centralization of power in the White House and the exclusion of the State Department from the direct decision-making process as a "diplomatic coup" by Nixon and Kissinger. While the so-called "rational actor model" perceives the government as a unitary actor with agreed-upon goals to be attained, the alternative "bureaucratic politics model" emphasizes government as the representative of diverse interests to be bargained.[2] On the basis of the rational actor model or the so-called realist model, the conventional interpretation of the US rapprochement with China emphasizes the importance of

---

1   "Rapprochement" is a term of French origin, which implies: a coming together again in friendship of former enemies; and the reconciliation, restoration, and renewal of relations, especially between states. *Longman Dictionary of Contemporary English*, New edition. (New York: Pearson Longman, 2003). In particular, the term "rapprochement" is often used to describe the US opening to China, namely the development of US initial diplomatic contact with China from January 1969 to June 1971, which resulted in Kissinger's trips to Beijing in July and October 1971, and Nixon's trip to China in February 1972. "Normalization" implies a much longer political process toward the establishment of US official diplomatic relations with the People's Republic of China in January 1979.

2   Allison examines the decision-making process of the 1962 Cuban Missile Crisis as a case study in crisis management. He suggests three models for the analysis of foreign and defense policy decision-making analysis: 1) the rational actor model – an examination of purposive and reasonable actions by a unified national government; 2) the organizational model – an exploration of the pattern and operating procedure of organizational behavior; and 3) the bureaucratic politics model – an analysis of a resultant of various bargaining process among players within national government. See Graham Allison and Philipe Zelikow, *Essence of Decision: Explaining the Cuban Missile Crisis*, Second edition. (New York: Longman, 1999). Halperin and Clapp, with Kanter, analyze the roles played by government departments, agencies and individual officials with a set of interests to preserve and promote. Those priorities and their occasional conflicts influence the formulation and implementation of foreign policy. See Morton H. Halperin and Priscilla Clapp with Arnold Kanter, *Bureaucratic Politics and Foreign Policy*, Second edition. (Washington DC: The Brookings Institution Press, 2007). Chapter 2 of this book examines the bureaucratic politics model within the context of the revitalization of the National Security Council system by Nixon and Kissinger.

the strategic and geopolitical calculations for the US's leverage in the Sino-Soviet rift and the subsequent development of the triangular balance of power between the United States, the Soviet Union, and China.³ On the other hand, adhering most closely to the bureaucratic politics model, this book examines how the pursuit of strict secrecy by Nixon and Kissinger affected the interactions between the White House and the State Department over the devising and implementing of the new China initiative; and how Nixon and Kissinger personalized diplomacy and held secret talks with the Chinese leaders regarding the reduction of direct threat from the respective sides.⁴

The present introduction briefly outlines the following: 1) the evolution of the conception of rapprochement; 2) the aspects of the search for secrecy by Nixon and Kissinger in the implementation of rapprochement; and 3) the major security issues which Nixon and Kissinger sought to discuss with the Chinese leaders during their highly confidential talks. At the same time, it also demonstrates how this book seeks to fill the gaps in focus and coverage left by the existing accounts of the Nixon-Kissinger diplomacy toward a new China policy.

Despite the respective claims by Nixon and Kissinger for the historical breakthrough which shifted the balance of power in the international system from military bipolarity to political multipolarity, the US rapprochement with China was not necessarily an original political notion of the two decision-makers. In reality, beneath the Nixon-Kissinger initiative, there was a long-term development of a variety of concepts for US reconciliation with China during the pre-Nixon-Kissinger era, such as American domestic debate on China during the mid-1960s, Sino-US ambassadorial talks from 1955 to 1968, and the middle-rank level bureaucratic policy studies during the Kennedy and Johnson administrations.⁵ From the mid 1960s,

---

3   See, for example, Raymond L. Garthoff, *Détente and Confrontation*, Revised edition. (Washington DC: The Brookings Institution, 1994); James H. Mann, *About Face: A History of America's Curious Relationship with China, from Nixon to Clinton* (New York: Alfred Knopf, 1999); and Patrick E. Tyler, *A Great Wall: Six Presidents and China, An Investigative History* (New York: Public Affairs, 1999). As for the main arguments in the existing literature on the Kissinger years, see, for example, Jussii M. Hanhimaki, "'Dr. Kissinger' or 'Mr. Henry'? Kissingerrogy, Thirty Years and Coming," *Diplomatic History*, Vol. 27, No. 5 (November 2003).

4   Secrecy in politics and diplomacy can be defined as the practice of sharing information only among a group of key officials, as small as one individual, while concealing it from others, such as other members of governments, leaders of political parties, foreign governments, journalists and the public. Secrecy is considered to be "necessary to enable governments that have taken extreme positions in public to compromise in private and to be protected against the consequences of disclosure until the terms of agreement are final and can be defended successfully against domestic critics." See Charles W. Freeman Jr., *The Diplomat's Dictionary*, Revised edition. (Washington DC: United States Institute of Peace Press, 2006), p. 264.

5   See, for example, Rosemary Foot, "Redefinition: The Domestic Context of America's China Policy in the 1960s," and Steven M. Goldstein, "Dialogue of the Deaf: The Sino-American Ambassadorial-Level Talks, 1955–1970" in Robert Ross and Jiang Changbin (eds), *Re-examining the Cold War: US-China Diplomacy, 1954–1973* (Cambridge, Massachusetts: Harvard University Press, 2001); and Evelyn Goh, *Constructing the Rapprochement with*

China experts in academia held a series of public debates on US China policy in order to raise awareness among the American public of the importance of reversing a rigid policy of containment and isolation and reducing tensions with China, which formulated a firm political and social foundation for the new China initiative by Nixon and Kissinger. The Warsaw ambassadorial talks played a vital role as a crisis management channel between the US and China in order to prevent miscalculation of the respective intentions during the escalation of the Vietnam War. In the 1960s, State Department officials at mid-level ranks continuously assessed China's military, political, economic and ideological power resources; they came to conclude that the threat from Beijing was not as serious as it had previously been estimated within the US government since the founding of the People's Republic of China in October 1949 and the outburst of the Korean War in June 1950.[6]

Within the historical context of those long-term bureaucratic assessments and public debates, this book compares the development of Nixon's and Kissinger's conceptions on US policy toward China, *viz.* the evolution of Nixon's personal interest in China as Vice President in the Eisenhower administration during the 1950s and as a private citizen during the 1960s; and Kissinger's views on China prior to 1969 as well as the possible influence of bureaucratic and academic expertise on Kissinger's interpretations of the Sino-Soviet differences.[7] While maintaining his long-term public reputation as an anti-Communist cold warrior toward the threat from Communist China, Nixon privately assessed China's short-term weakness in the Sino-Soviet rift as well as its long-term potential strength as a nuclear-armed state being outside the regular diplomatic interactions of the international community. On the other hand, Kissinger originally perceived China as a revolutionary power which was much more aggressive than the Soviet Union and thus was skeptical about any quick opening to China in the earlier period of the Nixon administration. When, why and how did Nixon and Kissinger come to convince themselves of the *necessity* and *possibility* of the rapprochement with China? What differences and similarities were there between their respective views on US China policy? While the existing accounts examine the breadth of US-China relations (from the late 1940s to the early 1970s), this book takes a deeper look into the most dynamic stage of the Nixon-Kissinger initiative (January 1969–February 1972).

China, 1961–1974: From 'Red Menace' to 'Tacit Ally' (Cambridge: Cambridge University Press, 2005).

6   Foot emphasizes the importance of a much wider conceptual framework in the US attempt to integrate China into the international community through the practice of "structural power" – the establishment of multiple international interactions with China strategically, commercially, intellectually, and militarily. Rosemary Foot, *The Practice of Power: US Relations with China since 1949* (Oxford, New York: Clarendon Press, 1995).

7   In his memoirs, Kissinger creates the impression that he independently came to realize the necessity and possibility of the opening to China during the early period from 1968 to 1969. See Henry A. Kissinger, *White House Years* (Boston, Little Brown, 1979), pp. 163–167. Yet, it seems likely that because of his original specialization in European power politics, Kissinger's interest, knowledge, and experience regarding China were still limited in early 1969. This subject is discussed in detail in Chapter 1, Section 2 (pp. 30–37) of this book.

Upon assuming the office, Nixon and Kissinger centralized power and operated foreign policy from the White House, because of their personal distrust of the Washington bureaucracy and their excessive sensitivity to the danger of leakages (especially by the State Department and also by US allies), which might undermine a new China initiative. They were also afraid of the conservative backlash by the pro-Chinese Nationalist lobby in Congress against any new initiative toward the Communist regime in Beijing. Following the two decades of mutual hostility, the only formal communication between the United States and China was via the ambassadorial talks in Warsaw. Thus, in parallel to the sending of a number of public signals (official statements which expressed the US's willingness to resume a diplomatic dialogue with China as well as the lifting of trade and travel restrictions), Nixon and Kissinger privately explored and utilized the so-called "back-channel" – "a direct negotiation through White House communications, bypassing regular diplomatic channels and forums" – through third parties, such as Pakistan and Romania, to communicate with the Chinese leaders.[8] In essence, Nixon and Kissinger valued the speed of these back-channel communications for the transformation of US policy toward China from containment and isolation to engagement and co-existence. This book examines the political-diplomatic process of the US's opening to China, namely how Nixon and Kissinger designed and sent public signals to the Chinese leaders and simultaneously sought to install and develop backchannels, while the State Department, without knowing the real intensions of the White House, continued to seek the resumption of the Warsaw ambassadorial talks.

Nixon and Kissinger operated within a certain time frame; they wanted to see the realization of rapprochement with China before the presidential election in November 1972.[9] They sought to obtain credit for an historic breakthrough, dramatically ending prolonged hostility with Beijing. Nixon envisioned that the presidential trip to China in February 1972, which he described as a "journey for peace," would earn him international credit as a peace-maker, and thus significantly enhance his domestic political support for re-election.[10] At the same time, after his secret trip to Beijing in July 1971, Kissinger attempted to establish international prestige as a great diplomat and statesman in an era of negotiation.[11] Together, Nixon and Kissinger wanted

---

8   Henry A. Kissinger, *Years of Renewal* (Boston: Little Brown, 1999), p. 79. In the third volume of his memoirs, Kissinger presents his latest reflections on the Nixon presidency, including the development of the National Security Council system and the China initiative. See ibid., chapters 2 and 5.

9   The political time frame started in January 1969.

10   Reeves sought to create a detailed chronological description to "reconstruct the Nixon presidency as it looked from the center." Richard Reeves, *President Nixon: Alone in the White House* (New York: Simon & Schuster, 2001), p. 13. MacMillan describes Nixon's visit to China as a great ceremonial occasion for the media and public to maximize the dramatic effect of historical opening. Margaret MacMillan, *Seize the Hour: When Nixon Met Mao* (London: John Murrey, 2006).

11   Hanhimaki conducted a comparative analysis of Kissinger on the one hand as a skilful diplomat and on the other as a bureaucratic manipulator obsessed with secrecy. Jussi Hanhimaki, *The Flawed Architect: Henry Kissinger and American Foreign Policy* (New York: Oxford University Press, 2004).

the China breakthrough to come as a "great headline," calculating that "public excitement would sweep away a lot of the uncertainty, suspicion, hostility, [and] criticism that might otherwise have accrued."[12] Finally, the historical and dramatic opening to China became a highly personal issue of ego and jealousy between Nixon and Kissinger. On the one hand, the new China policy symbolized the height of the Nixon-Kissinger secret diplomacy making the two decision-makers privately compete for credit and publicity. On the other hand, the excessive secrecy itself remained within the Nixon presidency, sowing the seeds of the Watergate scandal.[13] While the existing biographical accounts of the Nixon-Kissinger relationship assessed the political careers of the respective leaders in a broad international and domestic political context of the 1960s and 1970s, the present book focuses on the China initiative to re-assess the nature of the Nixon-Kissinger leadership.

In his memoirs, Nixon stressed the need for secrecy because "the more we had to put things into words, the less freedom of movement we would have in our dealings with the Chinese."[14] Kissinger also explained that owing to the "delicacy of the event," the "uniqueness of the opportunity," and the unforeseeable outcome, it was essential for the United States to be in control of the presentation of the China initiative. "[W]e did not want to risk inflating expectations, generating pressures, and forcing the two sides to take public positions before the results were known."[15] Thus, the pursuit of secrecy for the China initiative was necessary for Nixon and Kissinger and could be justified because of the danger of leaks, possible conservative opposition, and finally bureaucratic pressure to seek concessions.[16]

In reality, however, Nixon and Kissinger, because of their highly personalized use of the foreign policy decision-making machinery, also caused unnecessary confusion and friction within the bureaucracy. At the operational level, the re-vitalized NSC system was "very secretive at the top."[17] Nixon did not share some information even with Kissinger. Together, Nixon and Kissinger did not share their intentions and

---

12 Paul Kreisberg (Director, Office of Asian Communist Affairs, Policy Planning, Department of State, 1965–81), Oral History Interview, p. 11, in *A China Reader*, Vol. III, January 1995, Foreign Affairs Oral History Collection, Association for Diplomatic Studies and Training, Lauinger Library, Georgetown University.

13 Dallek examines the Nixon-Kissinger partnership as the two most powerful but compelling and contradictory policy-makers whose complex personal relationship influenced both collaboration and rivalry. Robert Dallek, *Nixon and Kissinger: Partners in Power* (New York: HarperCollins, 2007).

14 Richard M. Nixon, *RN* (New York: Grosset & Dunlap, 1978), p. 555.

15 Kissinger, *White House Years*, pp. 762–763.

16 See, for example, William Bundy, *A Tangled Web: The Making of Foreign Policy in the Nixon Presidency* (New York: Hill and Wang A Division of Farrar, Staus and Giroux, 1998), p. 233, and pp. 244–245; and Walter Isaacson, *Kissinger: A Biography* (New York: McGraw-Hill, 1992), pp. 342–343, and pp. 347–348. Hanhimaki interprets that secrecy was a "means to a broader bureaucratic end" for Kissinger to secure his "personal reserve" of US China policy. Hanhimaki, *The Flawed Architect*, p. xvii, and p. 118.

17 Allen Whiting, interview with the author, October 19, 2003.

agenda with other senior officials within the administration.[18] Kissinger's NSC staff was "closely held."[19] For example, former NSC staff member, Morton H. Halperin, recalls that Kissinger "manipulated" the NSC staff and "dealt with each one separately and instructed them not to tell anyone else what they were doing. Often he had two people working on the same issue without telling them."[20] Kissinger used the NSC staff for "what he thought they were good at." The problems arose further as Nixon and Kissinger "wanted to operate without talking to the cabinet members."[21] On the other hand, though he was the dominant intellectual on the NSC staff, Kissinger was less at home as an administrator. Thus, while Nixon preferred to avoid face-to-face meetings with other senior officials and used memoranda extensively, Kissinger greatly benefited from his Deputy Alexander M. Haig Jr.'s bureaucratic experience as well as from the White House Chief of Staff H.R. Haldeman's role as intermediary in dealing with the State Department.[22]

At policy planning level, despite the deliberate and systematic exclusion of the State Department from the decision-making process, Nixon and Kissinger still relied on bureaucratic expertise, especially that of the Bureau of East Asian and Pacific Affairs, headed by Assistant Secretary Marshall Green in order to develop policy options in the National Security Study Memoranda (NSSMs) papers from 1969 to 1971.[23] Hence, senior State Department officials, regional experts, and intelligence officers contributed to the formulation of the new China initiative without knowing

---

18   In early 1971, Nixon told the White House Chief of Staff, H.R. Haldeman, that he needed a record of his decision-making to protect himself in the eyes of history. Nixon wanted Oval Office and Cabinet Room meetings recorded on tape. Hence, the Technical Services Division of the US Secret Service installed a voice-activated system in the Oval Office and a switch-activated system in the Cabinet Room starting on February 16, 1971. The entire system, which was completed during the next four months, recorded conversations between President Nixon, his staff, and visitors at locations in the Oval Office; the President's Executive Office Building hideaway office; the Cabinet Room; various White House telephones in the Oval Office and the Lincoln Sitting Room; and at various Camp David locations. *History of the Nixon White House Tapes*, Audiovisual Research Room, National Archives, Archive II, College Park, Maryland.

19   Whiting, interview with the author, October 19, 2003.

20   Morton H. Halperin, Correspondence with the author, May 11, 2004.

21   Ibid.

22   Haldeman was often present when Nixon and Kissinger held private discussions about US China policy. Thus, Haldeman's handwritten notes and diaries provide very useful records about precisely when Nixon and Kissinger discussed China policy. Specific examples are examined in Part II (Chapters 3–6).

23   As for the reassessment of the operational process of US rapprochement with China by former US officials, see, for example, Alexander M. Haig Jr. (with Maccarry Charles), *Inner Circles, How America Changed the World: A Memoir* (New York: Warner Books, 1992); H.R. Haldeman, *The Haldeman Diaries: Inside the Nixon White House* (New York: G.P. Putnam's Sons, 1994); Marshall Green, John H. Holdridge, and William N. Stokes, *War and Peace with China: First-Hand Experiences in the Foreign Service of the United States* (Maryland: Dacor-Bacon House, 1994); and John H. Holdridge, *Crossing the Divide: An Insider's Account of the Normalization of US-China Relations* (Boulder, New York, Oxford: Rowman & Littlefield Publishers, INC., 1997).

the real intentions of Nixon and Kissinger. On the other hand, while maintaining a low profile, NSC staff members, such as Winston Lord and Peter Rodman, played a crucial role as a mini-bureaucracy in the day-to-day operation of highly secretive US China policy. NSC staff regional experts, such as John Holdridge, Richard Smyser and Richard Solomon also provided expertise in policy option studies and situational analyses as well as NSC briefing papers for Nixon and Kissinger prior to the July and October 1971 trips and February 1972 trip.

In particular, the evidence presented in the chapters that follow shed a new light on the resumption of the Warsaw Ambassadorial talks in January and February 1970 as the first major breakthrough during the US opening to China, which officially clarified the US intention to promote a new dialogue with the People's Republic of China. Ironically, however, Nixon and Kissinger introduced a number of ideas without sufficiently attempting to "discover the kinds of policies toward China that had [previously] been advocated."[24] Hence, the bureaucratic preparation for the Warsaw talks also revealed the difference between the White House (especially the Kissinger-NSC staff) and the State Department (especially its Bureau of East Asian and Pacific Affairs) regarding the timing and agenda for the new China initiative. In comparison, while the White House wanted to operate faster and was principally interested in improving relations with its adversaries, namely China and the Soviet Union, the State Department remained cautious and was concerned more about coordinating US relations with its allies, especially the Republic of China (commonly referred to as Taiwan) and Japan. On the one hand, Nixon and Kissinger tended to impose the simplified global framework of a US-Soviet-China strategic triangle on complex and subtle regional issues, such as the handling of Taiwan's status, Japan's role in East Asia, and the India-Pakistan rivalry in South Asia. On the other hand, because of their pursuit for strict secrecy, Nixon and Kissinger under-estimated the importance of the US's regular diplomatic channels with its allies.

Hence, Nixon and Kissinger did not sufficiently use the multiple intelligence sources from the State Department to more effectively implement China policy, especially after the US's military operation in Cambodia in May 1970 and the subsequent ending of Warsaw ambassadorial talks. Consequently, Nixon and Kissinger failed to understand the subtle and symbolic signals that China was sending in the attempt to promote a new dialogue.[25] Moreover, as the following chapters will show in detail, there was bureaucratic rivalry among US officials with different views on the priority of issues in the US relations with China. For example, there was difference between the NSC staff and State Department officials over the method, timing, and agenda of a new China initiative, and also between China experts and Soviet experts within the State Department over the pros and cons about the resumption of a diplomatic dialogue with China.[26] Finally, as already suggested, the inadequate communication between the White House and the State Department increased the perception gap between them over a new China policy.

---

24 Rosemary Foot, interview with the author, July 13, 2004.
25 Specific examples are examined in Chapter 6.
26 Specific examples are examined in Chapters 3, 4, and 5.

In military-security terms, Nixon and Kissinger sought to restore the US centrality in the international system. On the global level, through secret diplomacy and private negotiations, Nixon and Kissinger estimated that because of the deepening Sino-Soviet rift since the late 1950s and the early 1960s, the opening to Beijing would make Moscow become more cooperative with Washington in arms control talks and thus enhance détente – the easing of tensions between the two superpowers. Repeatedly stressing the importance of *Realpolitik* and the balance of power, it is Kissinger who criticizes China experts (both in the bureaucracy and in academia) and the liberals who failed to recognize sufficiently the opportunity for the US to exercise leverage within the Sino-Soviet rivalry.[27] On the regional level, with the announcement of the Nixon Doctrine to promote Vietnamization, which increased pressure on America's Asian allies to further build up their defense capabilities, Nixon and Kissinger sought to explore the opportunity to use China's influence on North Vietnam to promote a negotiated settlement in the Vietnam War. Consequently, as Kissinger often stressed, the US rapprochement with China thus marked the beginning of a new relationship, the so-called "strategic triangle" between the United States, the Soviet Union, and China. More particularly, as this book examines in greater detail, during the behind-the-scene talks in July and October 1971, and February 1972, Nixon and Kissinger gave a private assurance to the Chinese leaders of the US withdrawal from Taiwan in accordance with the easing of tensions in Indochina. Simultaneously, Nixon and Kissinger sought to persuade the Chinese leaders that the remaining US military presence in Asia would serve China's security interests in order to counter-balance other states, not only the Soviet Union, but also Japan and India.[28] This book thus perceives the rapprochement as the beginning of a long political and diplomatic process to pursue pragmatic co-existence between the United States and China, not as new friends or as old enemies, but as the two unsentimental calculators of self-interests.

The purpose of this book, then, is a detailed and systematic analysis of the evolution process of the rapprochement policy, with particular attention to the pursuit of secrecy by Nixon and Kissinger. In doing so, the focus is on the three major stages in the US rapprochement with China:

---

27 Kissinger, *White House Years*, p. 165. Kissinger's views on the balance of power in theory and practice are examined in Chapter 1, Sub-sections 2.2 and 2.3 (pp. 31–35) of this book.

28 Recent publications examine Chinese motivations for the rapprochement with the United States and a series of internal policy studies as well as discussions among the Chinese leaders. Shambaugh recognizes that Zhang Baijia, the son of Zhang Wenjin, former Foreign Minister [1971–1972], is a very important historian in the Chinese Communist Party's Party Research Office in Beijing. David Shambaugh, interview with the author, October 15, 2003. See, for example, Zhang Baija and Jia Qingguo, "Steering Wheel, Shock Absorber, and Diplomatic Probe in Confrontations: Sino-American Ambassadorial Talks Seen from the Chinese Perspective," and Li Jie, "Changes in China's Domestic Situation in the 1960s and Sino-US Relations," in Robert Ross and Jiang Changbin (eds), *Re-examining the Cold War: US-China Diplomacy, 1954–1973* (Cambridge, Massachusetts, and London: Harvard University Press, 2001); and Chen Jian, *Mao's China and the Cold War* (Chapel Hill, NC: University of North Carolina Press, 2001), chapter 9.

- *Conception*: The similarities and differences between Nixon's and Kissinger's views on China, the presidential leadership and the revitalization of the NSC system as the principal foreign policy decision-making body.
- *Implementation*: The development of policy option studies and the public and private signal exchange from January 1969 to June 1971, and the pattern of bureaucratic rivalry between the Nixon-Kissinger White House (including the National Security Council staff) and the State Department (especially its Bureau of East Asian and Pacific Affairs) regarding the timing and issues of US negotiations with China.
- *Direct talks*: The major security issues during the "behind-the-scene" talks in Kissinger's trips to Beijing in July and October 1971 and Nixon's trip to China in February 1972.

2. A Note on Sources

Underpinning this book is the substantial use of new archival materials in the Nixon Presidential Materials Staff and the State Department files in the National Archives and private papers of former US officials in the Library of Congress.[29] Equally important, the study makes extensive use of the updated transcripts of the Foreign Affairs Oral History Collection (FAOHC) in the Association for Diplomatic Studies and Training (ADST)[30] as well as the National Security Council Project in the Brookings Institution, which has conducted a series of oral history roundtables with former NSC staff members and State Department officials.[31] Finally, the work

---

29 The year 1997 marked the 25th anniversary of Nixon's trip to China in February 1972. Therefore, historians anticipated that US official documents on the rapprochement with China would be declassified in the following years. This study, which started in October 1997, has thus examined both newly-declassified archival documents and recently-published documents.

30 The Foreign Affairs Oral History Program was established in 1985 and housed in the Special Collections Room at the Lauinger Library of Georgetown University and at the Foreign Service Institute, Arlington, Virginia. Tucker explains that one of the main reasons why the Foreign Affairs Oral History Collection was established was because a former State Department official, Marshall Green, was "bitter" about Kissinger's underestimation of other officials' contributions to the Nixon foreign policy. Green thus provided some of the funding for the ADST to develop a collection which would help to advance a more balanced understanding of important initiatives, including the opening to China. Nancy Bernkopf Tucker, Interview with the author, October 1, 2003. Significantly, the collection of interviews has been added to and updated every year.

31 *The Nixon Administration National Security Council* (published online December 8, 1998) <http://www.brookings.org/fp/research/projects/nsc/transcripts/19981208.htm>, accessed October 15, 2003. *The Roles of the National Security Adviser* (published online October 25, 1999) <http://www.brookings.org/fp/research/projects/nsc/transcripts/19991025.htm>, accessed October 15, 2003. *China Policy and the National Security Council* (published online November 4, 1999) <http://www.brookings.org/fp/research/projects/nsc/transcripts/19991104.htm>, accessed October 15, 2003. The National Security Council Project (NSCP), Oral History Roundtables (OHP), The Brookings Institution and Center for

is also based on the author's interviews with former US officials, and with senior scholars on US-China relations, as well as declassified on-line documents, memoirs and diaries of former US officials, and newspaper articles. Mining these sources made it possible to shed new light on the complexity and dynamism of the evolution of the new China initiative and to demonstrate the existence of a range of policy options and different perspectives among US officials.

3. Organization

The book is organized in three major parts. Part I (Chapters 1 and 2) examines the conception of US rapprochement with China. Chapter 1 reassesses how Nixon and Kissinger developed their respective perceptions of the China policy before they entered office. Chapter 2 analyzes the revitalization of the National Security Council system during the transition period from November 1968 to January 1969. It examines the advantages and disadvantages of the highly secretive and centralized foreign policy decision-making machinery. In particular, the chapter compares the respective roles in the new China initiative played by the NSC staff and State Department officials. Finally, it investigates the geopolitical perception gap between the White House and the State Department.

Part II (Chapters 3–6) examines the implementation of the US rapprochement with China. The process of Washington's resumption of diplomatic communication with Beijing is divided into four major stages. Chapter 3 analyzes the initial development of strategic perspectives and policy options for a new China initiative that emerged in the first half of 1969, including Nixon's directive for the review of US China policy, and the NSC's and State Department's investigation of the outbreak of Sino-Soviet border clashes. Chapter 4 explores the continuing reassessments of the US China policy in the latter half of 1969, including Nixon's installing of the Pakistani and Romanian backchannels to launch private communications with the Chinese leaders, the NSC's and State Department's policy option studies toward the escalation of Sino-Soviet border conflicts, the rifting of trade restrictions, and the Chinese representative issue in UN. Chapter 5 examines the resumption of the Warsaw Ambassadorial talks from December 1969 to January and February 1970, and their collapse as a result of the Cambodian military operation in May 1970. In particular, the chapter investigates the widening gap between the White House and the State Department regarding the method, timing and agenda for a new dialogue with the Chinese leaders. Chapter 6 analyzes the development of back-channel communications with the Chinese via Pakistan and Romania from June to December 1970, and also the breakthrough from April to June 1971 in terms of the further pursuit of strict secrecy by the White House in order to completely cut off the State Department from direct decision-making process.

Part III (Chapters 7 and 8) then turns to the direct talks between the US and the Chinese leaders. Chapter 7 begins by examining the development of policy option

---

International and Security Studies at Maryland. The author would like to show his gratitude to Mr. Winston Lord who suggested the inclusion of these crucial sources into the research for the present book.

studies for Kissinger's secret trip to Beijing in July 1971, including the NSC staff briefing papers for Kissinger and the Nixon-Kissinger private talks. The main body of the chapter analyses the five major security issues which arose during the Kissinger-Zhou talks in July and October 1971: the Taiwan issue; the conflicts in Indochina; Japan's future role; the India-Pakistan rivalry; and the growth of the Soviet military threat. Finally, it examines how Nixon and Kissinger assessed the implications of a new China initiative in briefing meetings with Cabinet officials, Congressional leaders, and foreign leaders from July to December 1971. Chapter 8 begins by examining the final preparations for the Nixon trip, such as Haig's advance trip to China in January 1972 and the NSC staff and State Department briefing papers for the President. The chapter mainly investigates how Nixon and the Chinese leaders discussed the five major security issues in February 1972. Finally, it analyses how Nixon and Kissinger assessed the implications of the China summit in briefing meetings with Cabinet officials and Congressional leaders.

The Epilogue picks up on the trends exposed in the foregoing chapters, to show how US officials continued to discuss the remaining conflicting issues with the Chinese leaders through the mid-1970s – including the conflicts in Indochina, Japan's future role, the Soviet military threat, and the treatment of Taiwan's status. The Conclusion evaluates the major issues raised in this work and assesses what the US rapprochement with China in the early 1970s achieved, and what it left unresolved. The evidence unearthed in these chapters made for a fascinating period of research. It is hoped that the resulting account and analysis might prove equally fascinating reading – and perhaps challenge some view and assumptions in the process.

PART I
The Foundations of Foreign Policy Decision-Making

Chapter 1

The Nixon-Kissinger Leadership for a New China Initiative

The first chapter of Part I begins by investigating both the similarities and differences between Nixon and Kissinger regarding their respective views on US policy toward China. The first half of this chapter examines the development of Nixon's view on China from the late 1940s to the late 1960s. While maintaining a "cold warrior" public image against the threat of Communist China, Nixon privately spent many years to develop his more pragmatic view to open a new dialogue with the Chinese leaders. The latter half of this chapter analyses the development of Kissinger's view on the balance of power both in theory and in practice. It also examines how Kissinger developed his view on the China policy. Kissinger sought to exploit the Sino-Soviet rift and enhance US leverage within the US-Soviet-China strategic triangle. Finally, this chapter assesses the Nixon-Kissinger leadership for the opening to China. It was Nixon who set the overall directive for a new China initiative, while Kissinger provided a philosophical framework for the Nixon administration's foreign policy.

1. Richard M. Nixon as the Architect of US Rapprochement with China

1.1 The development of Nixon's early view on China

This book perceives Richard Nixon as the architect of the US opening to China. Richard Solomon, a former NSC staff member, and China expert, emphasizes the importance of distinguishing between Nixon as a politician and Kissinger as an academic.[1] Nixon had "a lot more exposure to Asia and foreign policy decision-

---

[1] Richard Solomon, interview with the author, September 24, 2003. Since his death on April 22, 1994, there have been a number of reassessments on Nixon's influence in re-shaping US foreign policy and American society. See, for instance, Joan Hoff, *Nixon Reconsidered* (New York: Perseus Books, 1994); Michael Barone, "Nixon's America," *US News and World Report*, September 20, 1999; William Bundy, *A Tangled Web: The Making of Foreign Policy in the Nixon Presidency* (New York: Hill and Wang S Division of Farrar, Straus and Giroux, 1998); Melvin Small, *The Presidency of Richard Nixon* (Kansas: University Press of Kansas, 1999); and Richard Reeves, *President Nixon: Alone in the White House* (New York: Simon & Schuster, 2001). Kissinger reassesses Nixon's presidency, foreign policy style, and personal character in his third memoirs, *Years of Renewal* (Boston: Little Brown, 1999). As for the controversial dark characteristic aspects of Nixon, see Anthony Summers with Robbyn Swan, *The Arrogance of Power: The Secret World of Richard Nixon* (London: Victor Gollancz, 2000).

making than Kissinger did." Solomon argues that because of his life-long involvement in politics, Nixon was an "'expert' by virtue of his long-term exposure to China as a political issue." It is thus important to take into consideration the self-confidence of successful politicians – the ability to understand the political dynamics of the international situation.[2]

The development of Nixon's view on China needs to be re-examined within the broader context of change and continuity in the US relations with China. There are three major angles in America's historical view on China from the mid-19th century to the mid-20th century:

- From an idealistic point of view, to transform China into a friendly nation in Asia,
- From a realist point of view, to re-build China as a central political force to maintain stability in Asia,
- From a commercial point of view, to foresee China as a potentially huge market in Asia.[3]

The origins of Nixon's interest in China policy can be traced back to his political career in the late 1940s and the early 1950s.[4] During his early career as congressman, Nixon built up his political reputation as a strong anti-Communist cold warrior by criticizing the Truman administration's "Loss of China" to the Communists.[5] It was a result of the establishment of the People's Republic of China in October 1949, the

---

2 Ibid.

3 Allen Whiting, interview with the author, October 19, 2003. Shambaugh uses the term "paternalism" to describe the US approach to China prior to the Second World War. Paternalism means "co-optation, hegemonic power and patron-client relationship," in which the US intended to transform China in its own image from a Christian ideological standpoint. David Shambaugh, interview with the author, October 8, 2003.

4 Regarding Nixon's view on China in his pre-presidential era, see, for example, Irwin Gellman, *Richard Nixon: The Congress Years, 1946–1952* (New York: Diane Pub Co, 1999); Philipe Pope, "Foundation of Nixonian Foreign Policy: The Pre-Presidential Years of Richard Nixon, 1946–1968," PhD thesis University of Southern California, August 1988; and Glenn Speer, "Richard Nixon's Position on Communist China, 1949–1960: The Evolution of a Pacific Strategy," PhD thesis, City University of New York, 1992; and Evelyn Goh, *Constructing the Rapprochement with China, 1961–1974: From 'Red Menace' to 'Tacit Ally'* (Cambridge: Cambridge University Press, 2005), chapter 5. The author would like to show his gratitude to Dr. Goh for her advice regarding the pre-presidential Nixon materials.

5 In spring 1949, the Truman Administration published the so-called "White Paper," which claimed the inevitable course of the fall of the mainland under the control of the Chinese Communists. Nixon accused Secretary of State, Dean Acheson of heading a "Cowardly College of Communist Containment." See US Department of State, *United States Relations with China* (Washington DC: Government Printing Office, 1949); and Richard M. Nixon, *RN: The Memoirs of Richard Nixon* (New York: Grssett & Danlap, 1978), p. 110. During his campaign for a Senate seat in 1950, Nixon declared: "All that we have to do is to take a look at a map and we can see that if Formosa falls the next frontier is the coast of California." A Speech by Richard M. Nixon during the California Senate Campaign, September 18, 1950, in *China and US Foreign Policy* (Washington DC: Congressional Quarterly, 1971), p. 19.

formulation of the Sino-Soviet alliance in February 1950, the outbreak of the Korean War in June 1950, and Chinese volunteer troops' entry into the war in October 1950.[6] Within the United States, while the pro-Nationalist China Lobby exerted heavy pressure on Congress and influenced public opinion, the State Department was under sharp criticism.[7] The United States pursued an open-ended containment policy towards the monolithic threat from Communism without clarifying a distinction between vital and peripheral interests.[8] The main elements of US policy toward Beijing during the two decades of mutual hostility were the following:

- Military containment of Chinese Communist expansionism embodied in the renewed support for the Chinese Nationalists on Taiwan, the stationing of the Seventh Fleet in the Taiwan Straits, and the maintenance of a web of military security treaties with non-Communist Asian states.
- Political isolation of the Beijing regime in the international community as reflected in the sustained US effort to keep the People's Republic of China from membership in the United Nations and associated agencies.
- Economic embargo imposed by the United States on any trade with Communist China.[9]

During the 1950s, as the Vice President in the Eisenhower administration, Nixon publicly maintained his firm political attitude towards the threat of Communist China. In the late spring of 1953, Nixon took his first official trip to Asia, which became a highly "educational" influence on Nixon's thinking, establishing the basis of his foreign policy experience.[10] In particular, the trip gave him a crucial opportunity to "assess" Asian attitudes toward the "emerging colossus" of Communist China.[11] Nixon concluded that Communist China was the "major new and unfathomable

---

While running for Vice President in 1952, Nixon charged that: "China wouldn't have gone Communist – if the Truman Administration had had backbone." Ibid.

6 On the question of the "Lost Chance" of Sino-US diplomatic relations in the late 1940s, see Warren I. Cohen, 'Symposium: Rethinking the Lost Chance in China: Introduction: Was there a "Lost Chance" in China?' *Diplomatic History*, Vol. 21, No. 1, Winter 1997; and Nancy Bernkopf Tucker, *Patterns in the dust: Chinese-American Relations and the Recognition Controversy, 1949–1950* (New York: Columbia University Press, 1983).

7 See Robert S. Ross, *After the Cold War: Domestic Factors and US-China Relations* (New York: M.E. Sharpe, 1998); and Ross Koen, *The China Lobby in American Politics* (New York: Macmillan, 1960).

8 This subject is discussed by John Lewis Gaddis, *Strategies of Containment* (Oxford: Oxford University Press, 1982).

9 These policies are comprehensively analysed in Rosemary Foot, *The Practice of Power: US Relations with China since 1949* (Oxford, New York: Clarendon Press, 1995). Armstrong interprets the US attempts to pressure China as the process of socializing it in "the norms" of the international community. David Armstrong, *Revolution and World Order: The Revolutionary State in International Society* (Oxford: Claredon Press, 1993), p. 177.

10 Nixon, *RN*, p. 134. Nixon recalls that throughout his political career, as Vice President, as a private citizen, and as President, he often dealt with people whom he had already met during his early trips, including the 1953 trip.

11 Ibid., p. 119.

factor" in Asia, and that its influence was already "spreading throughout the area."[12] During the NSC meeting on December 23, 1953, Nixon emphasized that there was "very little chance" for the US policy of "containment and economic blockade" of the Beijing regime on the basis of the hope of "overthrowing the government from within instead of from without."[13] Nixon suggested the alternative "to continue the policy of containment and isolation but to allow trade," which could be a "good cover" without necessarily recognizing Beijing.[14] Nixon concluded that although it was important to preserve Formosa [Taiwan] as a "symbol," the United States should tell Chinese Nationalists that "they can't go back to the mainland."[15]

The US Government publicly maintained its policy of nuclear deterrence against any aggression from Communists.[16] On March 17, 1955, Vice President Nixon argued in Chicago that: "tactical atomic weapons are now conventional and will be used against the targets of any aggressive force."[17] During the Taiwan Straits Crises in 1954–1955 and in 1958–1959, Nixon continued to suggest firm response to pressure and contain the expansionism of Chinese Communists. For example, on September 12, 1955, in the National Security Council meeting, Nixon insisted on paying close attention to any sign of miscalculation from Beijing. Nixon suggested that the only practical choice would be to "play poker" in order to "keep the Communists guessing" and to "take a chance on the possible consequences."[18]

On the other hand, Vice President Nixon suggested the easing of trade and travel sanctions on Communist China as means of unwinding its political and ideological rigidity. During an NSC meeting on August 18, 1954, Nixon argued that Communist

---

12   Ibid., p.136.

13   Memorandum of Discussion at the 177th Meeting of the National Security Council, Washington, December 23, 1953, *Foreign Relations of the United States (FRUS), 1952–54, Vol. XIV, China and Japan (1of2)* (Washington DC: Government Printing Office, 1985), p. 348.

14   Ibid., p. 349. On the other hand, in December 1953, Vice President Nixon already privately expressed his interest in Communist China: "Someday I'll go to China ... mainland China." In 1960, Nixon sought to obtain the permission to visit the People's Republic of China. This was refused by the State Department. Summers with Swan, *The Arrogance of Power*, p. 163.

15   Ibid.

16   On the more realistic aspects of the Eisenhower-Dulles policy toward China, see Nancy Bernkopf Tucker, "A House Divided: The United States, the Department of State, and China," in Warren I. Cohen and Akira Iriye (eds), *Great Powers in East Asia, 1953–1960* (New York: Columbia University, 1990); and John L. Gaddis, "The American Wedge Strategy, 1949–1958," in Harry Harding and Yuan Ming (eds), *Sino-American Relations, 1945–1955: A Joint Reassessment of a Critical Decade* (Wilmington, Del.: Scholarly Resources Inc., 1989).

17   *The New York Times*, March 17, 1955.

18   Memorandum of Discussion at the 214th Meeting of the National Security Council, Denver, September 12, 1954, *FRUS, 1952–1954, Vol. XIV*, pp. 622–623. On the US policy toward the two Taiwan Strait Crises, see Ronald W. Pruessen, "Over the Volcano: The United States and the Taiwan Strait Crisis, 1954–1955," and Robert Accinelli, "'A Thorn in the Side of Peace': The Eisenhower Administration and the 1958 Offshore Islands Crisis,' in Robert Ross and Jiang Changbin (eds), *Re-examining the Cold War: US-China Diplomacy, 1954–1973* (Cambridge, Massachusetts, and London: Harvard University Press, 2001).

China was "the key problem" for the US policy in Asia.[19] Nixon remained cautious, suggesting that any decision to change the policy of containment and isolation towards Communist China "should be postponed for the time being."[20] Nixon presented three specific points to consider: 1) how much the US was willing to trade with Communist China; 2) whether the US would recognize China; and 3) whether and when Communist China would be admitted to the United Nations.[21] Nixon claimed that the US would have to face the final decision whether to adopt "a hard or a soft policy" toward Communist China.[22] He went on to suggest that the US should explore "an area of action between war and appeasement" because in the long run, the Soviet Union and Communist China "can and must be split apart."[23] Thus, Nixon entered into the policy debate on the possibility of a rift between China and the Soviet Union. Foot argues that Nixon was "less influenced by the ideological tenor" of the Beijing government, and "more concerned about power issues – the balance of power issue – even in those days."[24]

During the presidential debate in October 1960, while condemning the Eisenhower-Dulles team for their "brinksmanship" in the Taiwan Strait crises, Democratic candidate John F. Kennedy insisted that the small offshore islands of Quemoy and Matsu were "not strategically defensible" or "essential to the defense of Formosa [Taiwan]."[25] Nixon sought to defend the Eisenhower administration's handling of the offshore island crisis of 1958 by emphasizing that if the United States drew a line at the island of Formosa itself, it would lead to a "chain reaction" of aggression by Chinese Communists.[26] On October 13, Nixon emphasized Communist China's expansionist threat: "Now what do the Chinese Communists want? They don't want just Quemoy and Matsu. They don't want just Formosa. They want the world."[27]

Importantly, Nixon became "very fascinated with China": his main concern was the Soviet threat, and his interest in the China issue grew out of the Quemoy-Matsu discussion during the campaign debates.[28] Solomon emphasizes the long-term importance of the Nixon-Kennedy debate in 1960 on the Quemoy-Matsu crisis of 1958, which "set off some interesting trends that took over a decade to fully play themselves out."[29]

---

19   Memorandum of Discussion at the 211th Meeting of the National Security Council, Washington, August 18, 1954, *FRUS, 1952–1954 Vol. XIV*, p. 529.
20   Ibid.
21   Ibid., p. 535.
22   Ibid.
23   Ibid. p. 536.
24   Rosemary Foot, interview with the author, July 13, 2004.
25   Robert W. Barnett, Oral History Interview, March 2, 1990, p. 9, Foreign Affairs Oral History Collection (FAOHC), Association for Diplomatic Studies and Training, Lauinger Library, Georgetown University. See also Richard M. Nixon, *Six Crises* (New York: Doubleday & Company, Inc., 1962), p. 345.
26   Ibid. See also Nixon, *RN*, p. 220.
27   *China and US Foreign Policy*, Second edition. (Washington DC: Congressional Quarterly, 1973), p. 1.
28   Richard H. Solomon, Oral History Interview, September 13, 1996, p. 18, FAOHC.
29   Ibid.

1.2 Changes and developments of the China issue during the 1960s

The development of Nixon's view on China took place within the context of the gradual development of academic and bureaucratic discussion on relaxation and subsequent reconciliation with Beijing.

From the late 1950s to the early 1960s, a fragmentation emerged in Sino-Soviet relations. One of the major causes of the split was the Soviet attempt to seek détente with the West, which was against China's anti-capitalist united front strategy.[30] Hence, the Chinese were "competing against" the Russians, "making a deliberate, direct challenge for the leadership of the world communist movement."[31]

Since the first nuclear explosion in October 1964, which was a major symbol of her self-reliance, China pursued a revolutionary dual strategy towards the two superpowers.[32] Throughout the 1960s, however, Chinese leaders had an increasing sense that they were surrounded by hostile enemies. In the north, the Soviet Union, with its satellite state, Mongolia, increased hostilities along the long disputed border areas with China. In the east, China faced the US network of allied relations with Japan and South Korea with their extensive bases. Moreover, the regular US navy patrolling in the Taiwan Straits indicated Washington's continuing support for the Chinese Nationalists in Taiwan. In the southwest, after the Sino-Indian border conflict in October 1962, there was a continuing increase of tension between Beijing and New Delhi leading India to move towards the Soviets. In the southeast, US military intervention in Indochina increased tension in China's southern hemisphere. Thus, Beijing came to face with the danger of full "encirclement" – being surrounded by the hostile neighbors.[33] In 1966, Mao launched the Great Proletarian Cultural Revolution, terminating all diplomatic relations with other states (except with Egypt) and bringing about China's political isolation.

During the 1960s, the Cold War still "hindered the whole image of China as a positive element in the international community."[34] Public opinion polls in the US showed that some 90 percent of Americans still had a negative image of China, and approximately 70 percent saw China as the greatest threat to the world peace. Within the US government, the China threat was "seen in a domino sense."[35] Thus, there was a "huge debate" about the question of "whether China would intervene in

---

30 See Chen Jian, *Mao's China and the Cold War* (Chapel Hill, NC: The University of North Carolina Press, 2001); Gordon H. Chang, *Friends and Enemies: The United States, China, and the Soviet Union, 1948–1972* (Stanford, California: Stanford University Press, 1990).

31 John Holdridge (Interviewed by Marshall Green), Oral History Interview, in *A China Reader*, Vol. II, p. 22, January 1995, FAOHC.

32 On US policy toward China's nuclear capabilities, see, for example, Foot, *The Practice of Power*, chapter 7; and Electric Briefing Book No. 1, *The United States, China and the Bomb*; and *The United States and the Chinese Nuclear Program, 1960–1964*, The National Security Archive, George Washington University.

33 Chen, *Mao's China and the Cold War*, p. 240.

34 Whiting, interview with the author, October 19, 2003.

35 Ibid.

the Vietnam War."[36] Equally important, there were "heated and bitter" arguments about the Sino-Soviet rift. On the one hand, a group of opinion insisted that the Chinese had very deep "anti-foreign feelings," especially toward the West, and that they would move back toward the Soviet Union if it suited their national purposes.[37] However, another school of thought insisted that China was "not aggressive" as previously estimated, and could be a "bulwark" against the Soviet Union, and thus the United States should "open up relations" with China.[38]

On a bureaucratic level, since the early 1960s, State Department officials had discussed the beginning of a "task force" approach on the "broad-scale rethinking exercise" of China policy.[39] By the mid 1960s, although Secretary of State, Dean Rusk, "resisted very strongly" any moves toward China, a change in China policy was "debated in bureaucracy."[40] Rusk was also "extremely reluctant to acknowledge" the Sino-Soviet split because he emphasized the monolithic threat from the Sino-Soviet alliance to "rationalize the deeper engagement in Vietnam."[41] There still remained

---

36   Solomon, interview with the author, September 24, 2003. Solomon argues further that what the US government did not fully understand at that time was that Mao needed the army within China to support the Cultural Revolution politically, rather than to send it off to fight in Vietnam.

37   James R. Lilley (CIA station, Hong Kong, 1969–1970), Oral History Interview, pp. 61–62, 1996, FAOHC.

38   Ibid.

39   Robert W. Komer to McGeorge Bundy, "Quick Thought on China," March 1, 1961, *FRUS, 1961–63, Vol. XXII, China; Korea; Japan* (Washington DC; Government Printing Office, 1996). A China expert in the Policy Planning Staff, Edward Rice, prepared a detailed paper on possible initiatives toward China, including the lifting of the trade embargo and the promotion of the Warsaw Talks. "US Policy Toward China," October 26, 1961, *FRUS, 1961–63, Vol. XXII*, pp.162–167. For bureaucratic reassessment of US China policy during the 1960s, see James C. Thomson, Jr. "On the Making of US China Policy, 1961–1969: A Study in Bureaucratic Politics," China Quarterly, 50 (April–June 1972); Rosemary Foot, "Redefinition: The Domestic Context of America's China Policy in the 1960s," in Ross and Jiang (eds), *Re-examining the Cold War*; and Goh, *Constructing the Rapprochement with China, 1961–1974*, chapters 2–4.

40   William H. Gleysteen, JR. (career Foreign Service officer, 1951–1981), "China Policy and the National Security Council," p. 5, The National Security Council Project (NSCP), Oral History Roundtables (OHR), Center for International and Security Studies at Maryland and the Brookings Institution, November 4, 1999. For Rusk's rigidity on China policy, see also Foot, "Reflections," p. 283.

41   Paul Kreisberg (Director, Office of Asian Communist Affairs, Policy Planning, Department of State, 1965–1981), Oral History Interview, p. 3, in *A China Reader*, Vol. III, January 1995, FAOHC. The creation of the Office of Asian Communist Affairs in 1965 – the separation of the ROC from the mainland led to turn the focus of policy attention much more on the People's Republic. Ibid. Moscow supplied more advanced weaponry to Hanoi than Beijing, which could only advise the pursuit of guerrilla warfare and provide rifles and bullets. However, Hanoi had no intention of being Moscow's puppet, and exploited Sino-Soviet hostility, obtaining military aid from both, but taking sides with neither. Qiang Zhai, *China and the Vietnam Wars, 1950–1975* (Chapel Hill, NC: The University of North Carolina Press, 2000), pp. 3–5.

rigidity at the top level of the foreign policy decision-making machinery, while middle rank officials in the State Department were reassessing US China policy.

During the twenty years of mutual hostility, despite harsh rhetorical exchanges in public, Washington and Beijing attempted to develop and preserve a communication line at the Ambassadorial level, firstly in Geneva from 1955 to 1957, and then in Warsaw from 1958 to 1968.[42] Although the talks did not reconcile profound political and ideological differences, the two sides continued to communicate in order to prevent any misunderstanding of the degree of threat in the case of crisis. As a former State Department official, Donald Anderson, recalls, US officials kept informing the Chinese in Warsaw that "we seek no wider war in Vietnam," which was intended as an "assurance" that the United States did not intend to invade North Vietnam.[43] Anderson argues further that State Department officials also attempted to "promote some sort of informal non-official contact," such as to get journalists into China in order to "improve the atmosphere" and "lower the tension levels" between the two sides.[44]

Overall, the State Department officials in the Kennedy and Johnson administrations prepared a list of policy items to move towards a "civil dialogue with China," in an attempt to "open up travel and trade."[45] In reality, however, the possible flexibility of the Johnson administration's policy in East Asia was tied down by the combination of the escalation of the Vietnam War, the Chinese refusal to ease tension with three major adversaries, the United States, the Soviet Union and India, and the outbreak of Cultural Revolution.[46]

During the 1960s, it was academic experts who led the public argument about the need to move toward China.[47] For example, during the height of the Cultural Revolution, William Bundy, then the Assistant Secretary of State for Far Eastern Affairs of the Johnson administration, "set up sort of a Wise Men's Group of some academic scholars," such as A. Doak Barnett, Alexander Eckstein, John King

---

42 "A Resume of the Warsaw Talks, 1955–1970," October 12, 1971, Secret-Sensitive, Box 2189, Subject-Numeric Files (SNF), General Records of the Department of State, Record Group 59 (RG59), National Archives. See also Steven M. Goldstein "Dialogue of the Deaf: The Sino-American Ambassadorial-Level Talks, 1955–1970," in Ross and Jiang (eds), *Re-examining the Cold War*; and Kenneth T. Young, *Negotiating with the Chinese Communists: The United States Experience, 1953–1967* (New York: McGraw-Hill, 1968).

43 Donald Anderson (China Desk/Warsaw talks, Department of State, 1966–1970), Oral History Interview, p.12, in *A China Reader*, Vol. III, January 1995, FAOHC.

44 Ibid.

45 Ralph Clough (Deputy Chief of Mission American Embassy Taipei, Taiwan, 1961–1965), Oral History Interview, p. 19, in *A China Reader*, Vol. III, January 1995, FAOHC.

46 Foot, *The Practice of Power*, pp. 262–263; and Robert D. Schulzinger, "The Johnson Administration, China, and the Vietnam War," in Ross and Jiang (eds), *Re-examining the Cold War*. President Johnson remarked that "lasting peace" could never come to Asia, "as long as 700 million people of mainland China are isolated by their rulers from the outside world." *The New York Times*, March 14, 1966.

47 As for academic activities on the re-assessment of China policy during the 1960s, see Foot, "Redefinition," pp. 278–279, and Idem, *The Practice of Power*, pp. 93–103.

Fairbank, Lucian W. Pye, and Robert Scalapino, to discuss periodically "whither China"[48] In reality, however, Whiting points out that the Vietnam War had "broken the sense of community" in America, and thus, there was no "academic community" as a whole.[49] Thus, there had to be "some public form that could legitimise the consideration of China as a normal power."[50]

From March 8 to 30, 1966, the Hearings for the Senate Foreign Relations Committee entitled "US Policy with Respect to Mainland China" broadcasted a number of views of China experts as well as International Relations experts in academia.[51] A. Doak Barnett urged the shift of America's China policy from "containment plus isolation" to "containment without isolation."[52] John King Fairbank advocated an open policy to promote "international contact with China on many fronts," in order to encourage its leaders to reshape their worldview and to bring China into the international order.[53] Thus, the Hearings provided the most comprehensive discussion of China policy ever given to the American people. In essence, US China policy debate during the mid 1960s was a crucial turning point which promoted the American domestic political attitude of the necessity of new relations with China. The American public came to realize that the existence of Communist China was a fact of life. Foot suggests that a broad "consensus" of opinion emerged in America regarding the integration of China; and this consensus became a powerful "inheritance" for Nixon and Kissinger to take an initiative toward China.[54]

Nixon, as a private citizen, paid close attention to the US policy and public opinion toward China during the 1960s. In public, Nixon maintained his anti-Communist hardliner stance by describing the Vietnam War as a manifestation of Communist China's expansionism, namely a "confrontation" between the US and China.[55] In private, however, there were signs of development in Nixon's view on China. During his private trip to Europe in June 1963, Nixon met French President

---

48 Anderson, Oral History Interview, p.15, in *A China Reader*, Vol. III, January 1995, FAOHC.

49 Whiting, interview with the author, October 19, 2003. Whiting explains further that among academic experts on China, A. Doak Barnett was the "foremost progressive speaker" who was a "cautious, optimistic, forward-looking, but he was not advocating any radical move." Robert Scalapino supported the Vietnam War, and "took a lot of abuse because of that." Ibid.

50 Ibid.

51 "US Policy with Respect to Mainland China," Hearings Before the Committee on Foreign Relations, US Senate, 89 Congress, 2nd session, March 8, 10, 16, 18, 21, 28, 30, 1966.

52 A. Doak Barnett statement, ibid., p. 306.

53 John King Fairbank statement, ibid., p. 309.

54 Foot, *The Practice of Power*, p. 85, pp. 112–113.

55 Speech to the Commonwealth Club of California by Richard M. Nixon, *The New York Times*, April 2, 1965. For the Johnson administration, Communist China and North Vietnam were still inevitably "linked." In response to Nixon's recommendation to take a hard line in Vietnam, President Johnson stated that: "China's the problem… We can bomb the hell out of Hanoi and the rest of that damned country, but they've got China right behind, and that's a different story." Nixon, *RN*, pp. 280–281.

Charles De Gaulle and discussed "whether it might not be wise to develop lines of communications with the Soviets and the Chinese."[56] Nixon argued that there was "considerable sentiment" in the US State Department, not only in favor of a "Soviet-US détente" but also of a "lineup of the Soviets, Europe and the US against Chinese." Nixon judged that while this might be a "good short-range policy," it was more important in the longer run to recognize that China and the USSR were "two great powers," and to develop "parallel relationships with them."[57]

In March 1967, Nixon again took a trip to Europe, during which the China issue came up regularly. The West German Chancellor, Konrad Adenauer urged that in order to "counterbalance" the growth of the Soviet military threat, the United States should lean toward China.[58] Nixon's initial reply to Adenauer was that the West should not unilaterally exploit the Sino-Soviet dispute. However, Nixon continued to argue that if the situation developed, the United States might benefit from the expansion of differences between the two communist states. During his talk with the Romanian President, Nicolae Ceauşescu, Nixon expressed his doubt whether any true détente with the Soviet Union could be achieved until "some kind of rapprochement" was reached with Communist China.[59] Nixon felt that if China remained isolated, within twenty years, it could pose a grave threat to world peace. In the short run, Nixon remained cautious, expressing doubt about the possibility of establishing effective communications with China until the Vietnam War had ended. Nixon argued that, following the war, the United States could "take steps to normalize relations" with China.[60]

In April 1967, Nixon took a trip to Asia and consulted with Asian leaders and US diplomats regarding the development of recent changes in the region. Nixon recognized that there was a "growing concern" about China's emergence among Asian leaders who came to agree that some "new and direct" relations between the United States and China were "essential" for the restoration of stability in the post-Vietnam era.[61] In Indonesia, Nixon met the US Ambassador, Marshall Green, with

---

56   During his presidential visit to France in March 1969, Nixon reviewed the China issue of their 1963 talk with De Gaulle. Memcon, Nixon and De Gaulle, March 1, 1969 [Morning session], p. 6, Presidential/HAK MemCons Box 1023, Nixon Presidential Materials Staff (NPMS), National Archives (NA). In his memoirs, however, Nixon fails to mention the specific contents of his private talk with De Gaulle in June 1963. See Nixon, *RN*, p. 248.
57   Ibid.
58   Nixon, *RN*, p. 281.
59   Ibid. See also James H. Mann, *About Face: A History of America's Curious Relationship with China, from Nixon to Clinton* (New York: Alfred Knopf, 1999), p. 17.
60   Ibid., p. 282.
61   Ibid., pp. 282–283. Nixon's speechwriters, Raymond Price and William Safire, recall that Nixon had a great knowledge on foreign affairs. For example, while they were preparing for briefing books for Nixon's trip to Asia in April 1967, Nixon made his own preparation, asking specific questions on leadership and political situation of Asian countries. See William Safire, *Before the Fall: An Inside View of the Pre-Watergate White House* (DaCapo Press, 1975), pp. 367–368.

whom he had a long private conversation on events in East Asia, especially China.[62] Green emphasized the development of new nationalism in Asia and suggested that it would be wise to limit the US presence and promote each Asian country's initiative in dealing with Asian problems. In particular, Green recalls Nixon's much more "realistic" and "strategic" remarks on the development of the Sino-Soviet split: "We must not line up with China or with the Soviet Union against the other; we must always play it even-handed."[63] As Solomon explains, Nixon was assessing "policy alternatives based on domestic concerns" by consulting with many American people and other experts on Asia, Nixon's approach to China policy was driven "primarily by the concerns about the Soviet Union, and secondly by the Vietnam War."[64] Overall, Nixon's trips overseas during the mid-1960s provided crucial opportunities for him to assess geopolitical changes in Asia, especially the re-emergence of China.

1.3 "Asia after Viet Nam" in October 1967

Nixon's article entitled "Asia after Viet Nam" appeared in *Foreign Affairs* of October 1967.[65] As the two decades of containment of China became an increasingly heavy burden for the US, Nixon urged the need to comprehend the reality of China's re-emerging geopolitical dynamism in Asia and the world:

> Taking the long view, we simply cannot afford to leave China forever outside the family of nations ... There is no place on this planet for a billion of its potentially most able people to live in angry isolation ... The world cannot be safe until China changes. Thus our aim, to the extent we can influence the events, shall be to induce change.[66]

Nixon suggested that: 1) in the short term, "a policy of firm restraints of no reward, of a creative counterpressure designed to persuade Peking that its interest can be served only by accepting the basic rules of international activity" and 2) in the long term, "pulling China back into the world community – but as a great and progressing nation, not as the epicenter of world revolution."[67] Reflecting the re-emergence of

---

62 Marshall Green, *Evolution of US-China Policy 1956–1973: Memoirs of An Insider*, p. 25, FAOHC. Nixon "took down notes on key points" and also tape-recorded his talks with Green. Green recalls: "When I asked him what he did with all these notes and tapes, he replied that he had them transcribed, filed and cross-filed for later reference." Green remembers Nixon as the "best informed on foreign affairs" of all the luminaries who visited Jakarta during his four years there. Ibid. However, in his memoirs, Nixon did not mention his conversation with Green.
63 Ibid.
64 Solomon, interview with the author, September 24, 2003.
65 Richard M. Nixon, "Asia after Viet Nam," *Foreign Affairs* (October, 1967). Nixon's speechwriters, Raymond Price and William Safire, assisted the drafting of the article. See Safire, *Before the Fall*, pp. 367–368. On July 29, 1967, Nixon made an informal speech to the Bohemian Club, San Francisco, arguing: "We live in a new world," with new ideas and new leaders, which his *Foreign Affairs* article developed further. It was off the record and received no publicity. Nixon, *RN*, p. 284.
66 Ibid., p. 121.
67 Ibid., p. 123.

Japan and Western Europe as economic great powers, Nixon also urged that the United States should coordinate its relations with its major allies in order to reduce its burden for the open-ended containment of Communism. Finally, Nixon encouraged the US continuing presence in Asia, as an "Asian power," and emphasized that US leadership should be exercised "with restraints," and there was a need for American "subtle encouragement" of the Asian initiatives.[68]

When the *Foreign Affairs* article was first published, it was generally considered as Nixon's political attempt to moderate his anti-Communist image and acquire the nomination for the Republican Presidential Candidacy in 1968.[69] After the announcement of the Nixon Doctrine on July 25, 1969, the article captured public attention as the framework of the Nixon administration's foreign policy. However, the importance of the Nixon article should not be over-stated. Nixon's suggestions were not entirely new because his views reflected the debates which were taking place among Democrats and also among Republicans during the 1960s. In the short run, Nixon still preserved his hard-liner stance, criticizing that the "containment without isolation" covered "only half the problem."[70] In particular, Nixon was still against any short-term change to allow trade with China. He also advocated pressuring China by the build-up of Asian allies' military capabilities. Finally, Nixon implied that it was not the US but China that had to change.

On the other hand, Shambaugh assesses that the article was a "crucial piece of evidence" regarding Nixon's interest in China. Shambaugh emphasizes the importance of Nixon's "intentional" selection of terms in his writing, which avoided direct criticism of China's ideology or expansionist tendency.[71] Nixon clearly had a political intension to present his personal interest in opening a new dialogue with the Chinese leaders. In particular, the phrase of Nixon's article, especially China being "outside the family of nations" suggests that there was a broader and "multitiered conceptualisation" of engaging China "as a society and as an economy, not simply strategically playing it off against the Soviet Union." Finally, Nixon's proposal of integrating China into the world community was an origin of the policy of engagement with China.[72] More particularly, Foot stresses the importance of the US long-term practice of its "structural power" to embrace China into an international pattern of behavior.[73] In the historical perspective, the integration strategy reflects a

---

68   Ibid., p. 124. In this article, Nixon perceived the Soviet Union as a European power.

69   "Nixon Sees Asia Helping Itself," *The New York Times*, September 17, 1967.

70   Nixon, "Asia after Viet Nam," p. 123. For example, in October 1967, Secretary Rusk warned of the danger of billions of Chinese armed with nuclear weapons. See Warren Cohen, *Dean Rusk* (Totowa, New Jersey: Cooper Square, 1980), pp. 283–289.

71   Shambaugh, interview with the author, October 8, 2003.

72   Ibid. See also David Shambaugh, "Containment or Engagement of China," *International Security*, Vol. 21, No. 2 (Fall 1996), p. 182.

73   Foot, *The Practice of Power*, pp. 9–21, pp. 262–265. Foot refers to Nye, who introduces distinctions between "hard" and "soft" power and between "the coercive and visible forms and the consensual and less visible aspects." In particular, "soft" power refers to more indirect ways of getting others to do what one wants by "the attractiveness of one's culture and ideology" or "the ability to manipulate the agenda of political choices." Hence, the issue of legitimacy, drawn from a recognized authority, becomes important to the exercise

very long lasting tradition in the US approach to China, which could be traced back to the end of nineteenth century, namely the idea that the US could "tutor" China to "either protect it or modify it or change it."[74]

Former NSC staff members, such as Lord, Rodman, and Solomon argue that, after his trip to Asia in April 1967, Nixon's views on Asia and China were already quite well developed.[75] Nixon had become aware of the need to shift the course of foreign policy with more restraints of power. By the late 1960s, it was widely recognized that Washington's non-recognition policy to Beijing became largely stalemated because of the major changes in the international situation, such as the Sino-Soviet rift, the US over-involvement in the Vietnam War, and the prolonged Sino-US mutual hostility. Hence, realizing the major shifts in "American conceptions of what needed to be done in terms of China policy," Nixon assessed the political advantage of promoting accommodation with China.[76] In his meeting with Premier Zhou on February 24, 1972, President Nixon remarked:

> [M]y goal is normalization with the People's Republic ... I started down this road in 1967 in an article in Foreign Affairs, with some rhetoric. And now we are trying to follow it with action. The goal of normalization is the one which I alone at the outset initiated and it's my intent to realize this goal.[77]

In essence, Nixon viewed the materialization of diplomatic normalization as the beginning of long and complex process to integrate China into the international system.

1.4 China issue during the 1968 presidential election campaign

During the presidential campaign in 1968, Nixon's public statements on the China issue reflected two contradictory aspects of his view. On the one hand, Nixon continued to maintain a firm attitude towards China's aggression, and thus denied any immediate possibility of recognizing the Beijing regime. In October 1968, Nixon remarked that:

---

of power in normative terms. Joseph Nye, *Bound to Lead: The Changing Nature of American Power* (New York: Basic Book, 1990), p. 267, n. 11, cited in ibid., pp. 3–5.

74 Foot, interview with the author, July 13, 2004.

75 Solomon, interview with the author, September 24, 2003; Winston Lord, interview with the author, October 15, 2003; and Peter Rodman, interview with the author, October 21, 2003.

76 Foot, *The Practice of Power*, p. 103.

77 Memcon, Nixon and Zhou, February 24, 1972, p. 10. Memoranda for the President, "Beginning February 20, 1972," Box 87, President's Office Files (POF), NPMS, NA. During the height of the Cultural Revolution, Chairman Mao had not only already read Nixon's writings, including the October 1967 *Foreign Affairs* article, but also followed a number of America's newspaper accounts of the policy reassessment progressing in the State Department. See Richard H. Solomon, *Chinese Negotiating Behavior: Pursuing Interests Through 'Old Friends'* (Washington DC: United States Institute of Peace, 1999), p. 48; and Chen, *Mao's China*, pp. 238–239.

I would not recognize red China now and I would not agree to admitting it to the UN and I would not go along with those well-intended people that said, 'Trade with them, because that will change them.' Because doing it now would only encourage them, the hardliners in Peking and the hardline policy that they're following. And it would have an immense effect on discouraging great numbers of non-communists elements in Free Asia that are now just beginning to develop their strength and their own confidence.[78]

On the other hand, Nixon expressed the view that, in the long run, Washington should begin a new dialogue with Beijing. On August 9, 1968, after obtaining the nomination for the Republican Presidential candidacy, Nixon stated that: "We must not forget China. We must always seek opportunities to talk with her, as with the USSR ... We must not only watch for changes. We must seek to make changes."[79]

Since the Soviet invasion of Czechoslovakia in August 1968, the tension between Beijing and Moscow increased further along their shared border areas.[80] On September 17, 1968, the United States proposed a resumption of the Warsaw ambassadorial talks. On November 8, New China News Agency (NCNA) article described US election as "cut-throat competition" between various cliques of "Monopoly Capitalism," and all these groups are "jackals of the same lair" and equally incapable of saving US "from fate of utter defeat."[81] On November 15, 1968, the US government proposed postponing the next Warsaw meeting until next February after being unable to obtain any answer from the Chinese on their intentions with respect to the scheduled November 20 meeting. On November 26, 1968, Beijing responded by proposing a Sino-US Ambassadorial talk at Warsaw to

78 *China and US Foreign Policy*, Second edition. (Washington DC: Congressional Quarterly, 1973), p. 89. Quotation marks in original.

79 *US News and World Report*, September 16, 1968, p. 48. Reflecting the policy review within the Johnson administration for "containment without necessarily isolation," Democrat presidential candidate, Herbert Humphrey also advocated such specific moves as 1) the lifting of the ban on exports of non-strategic goods, 2), the promotion of exchange of scholars, journalists, and technicians, and 3) the clarification of the US intention to welcome China's participation in the international community. Herbert Humphrey, Interview with *Asahi Shimbun*, October 22, 1968, Translated and transmitted by American Embassy in Tokyo, October 31, 1968 to Bryce Harlow, Office of President Elect Nixon, The Pierre Hotel, New York, HAK Administrative and Staff Files, Box 1, Transition, November 1968–January 1969, Henry A. Kissinger's Office Files (HAKOF), NSCF, NPMS, NA.

80 As for China's criticism of the Soviet Union after its invasion of Czechoslovakia as a "social-imperialist" state, see Chen, *Mao's China and the Cold War*, pp. 242–243. Shambaugh explains that there are two types of rules in Chinese governance, benevolent rule "Wan" and coercive rule "Ba." The Soviet Union was announced as "Ba" – hegemon. The difference between hegemony and imperialism is that while hegemony is a "type of behavior," imperialism is a "stage of government's governance system." Thus, one can have a "socialist state that is hegemonic." And one can also have a "capitalist state that is hegemonic." However, one cannot have a "socialist state that is imperialist theoretically." Nevertheless, the Chinese called the Soviets "social-imperialists" because when they charged, they realized that the real meaning was "social hegemonism." Shambaugh, interview with the author, October 15, 2003.

81 Telegram, American Consulate General Hong Kong, "Chinese People Told of Nixon Victory," November 9, 1968, p. 1, POL Chicom-US, 1967–69, Box 1972, SNF, RG59, NA.

take place on February 20, 1969. Beijing added a "very significant" statement in the eyes of US officials: "It has always been the policy of the People's Republic of China to maintain friendly relations with all states, regardless of social systems, on the basis of the five principles of peaceful coexistence."[82] Finally, the Chinese urged the United States to "withdraw all its armed forces from China's Taiwan Province and the Taiwan Straits."[83]

During the meeting with Kissinger on November 25, 1968, Nixon mentioned his concern about the "need to re-evaluate" US policy toward China, and urged Kissinger to read the October 1967 *Foreign Affairs* article.[84] Former NSC staff member Winston Lord assesses that China was one of the "three real priorities" of Nixon, along with Vietnam and the Soviet Union.[85] By 1968, Nixon had a personal interest in seeking an opening towards China, though he had not yet formulated the precise methods and timing of a new initiative. It is likely that Nixon tactically manipulated his political image and utilized ideological rhetoric with a practical aim. In reality, although many of its older generation passed away, the China Lobby still had influence, particularly in the Republican Party.[86] Thus, Nixon was still concerned about the "backlash" from pro-Taiwan conservative supporters, such as Anna Chennault, the widow of Claire L. Chennault, who served as an adviser to Chiang Kai-shek during the World War II, Walter Judd, former medical missionary in China and Congressman, and Ray Cline, former CIA officer and CIA station chief in Taipei.[87]

---

82 Holdridge, Oral History Interview in *A China Reader*, Vol. II, pp. 21–22, January 1995, FAOHC. Premier Zhou first brought up the five principles of peaceful coexistence at the Geneva Conference in 1954.

83 Chen, *Mao's China and the Cold War*, p. 245; and Kissinger, *White House Years*, p. 166.

84 Nixon, *RN*, p. 341. In his memoirs, however, Kissinger does not refer to Nixon's suggestion to read his *Foreign Affairs* article. Lord recalls that: "I don't know whether Kissinger talked about China with Nixon during the transition. I suspect they did. Before he took office, Kissinger independently saw the advantages of opening to China. Nixon certainly saw the value of it. And, in fact, they may have talked about it. I would think they would have." Lord, interview with the author, October 15, 2003.

85 Lord, interview with the author, October 15, 2003. After the victory in the presidential election on November 5, 1968, Nixon held private talks and telephone conversations with President Johnson on the succession of the policy issues and options. On December 12, 1968, Johnson and Nixon met alone in the Oval Office – the only occasion during November and December when they met alone. Document 331, *FRUS, 1964–1968 Volume XIV, Soviet Union* (Washington DC: United States Government Printing Office, 2001). Although no official record of the talk is found by the State Department's historians, William Bundy introduces an episode (which presumably took place in their December 12 talk) from his personal files: "Johnson had told Nixon that he was prepared to go ahead with these measures [the resumption of Warsaw Ambassadorial talks and the lifting of travel and trade restrictions] on his own responsibility, but that if Nixon preferred, he would refrain from taking action and simply turn them over to the incoming administration to use as it saw fit. Nixon replied that he preferred the latter course." Bundy, *A Tangled Web*, p. 103. Bundy served as the Assistant Secretary of State for East Asian and Pacific Affairs from March 1964 to May 1969.

86 Solomon, interview with the author, September 24, 2003.

87 Lord, interview with the author, October 15, 2003.

Finally, there is one interesting point, which is related to Nixon's long experience with foreign affairs. During the 1950s and 1960s, Nixon had already met almost all the major political leaders in the world, and he had visited most Asian countries. China remained the only major state which Nixon had not visited, and Mao Zedong and Zhou Enlai were two of the few world leaders whom Nixon had not met yet. Thus, before entering the office, Nixon had developed a strong personal interest in obtaining the sole credit for the historic opening to China.

2. Henry A. Kissinger's Role in US Rapprochement with China

2.1 Kissinger as a theorist for new administration's foreign policy philosophy

Henry A. Kissinger came to office with the experience of being an academic at Harvard over 15 years, as well as having been a consultant to the Kennedy and Johnson administrations during the 1960s. In essence, he provided the fundamental "intellectual framework" for the new administration's foreign policy.[88]

In his early writings, Kissinger defines an international order as "legitimate" if all the major states agree about the "nature of workable arrangements and about the permissible aims and methods of foreign policy"; he defines it as "revolutionary" if one or more of the major dissatisfied states refuses to cope with other states in accordance with the conventional rules of state relations.[89] In a legitimate international order, status quo states are principally concerned with their security, and there is a tendency for the pursuit of equilibrium on the basis of the practice of balance of power. Hence, stability is a consequence of generally accepted legitimacy. A legitimate international order does not prevent conflicts, but it limits the scope of them.

By the late 1960s, owing to the prolonged open-ended containment policy of the monolithic threat of Communism, the United States was in relative military and economic decline. In his article of 1968, a year before he entered the government, Kissinger presented his perspective on the newly emerging political multipolarity in world politics. He argued that military bipolarity caused rigidity: "A bipolar

---

88 See, for example, Walter Isaacson, *Kissinger: Biography* (New York: McGraw-Hill, 1992); Jussi M. Hanhimaki, *The Flawed Architect: Henry Kissinger and American Foreign Policy* (New York: Oxford University Press, 2004); and Idem, '"Dr. Kissinger" or "Mr. Henry"? Kissingerology, Thirty Years and Counting,' *Diplomatic History*, Vol. 27, No. 5 (November 2003).

89 Henry A. Kissinger, *A World Restored* (Boston: Houghton Mifflin, 1957), pp. 1–2; and Idem, *Nuclear Weapons and Foreign Policy* (New York: Harper & Brothers, 1957), pp. 316–321. On Kissinger's intellectual base as an academic, see, for example, Coral Bell, *The Diplomacy of Détente: The Kissinger Era* (London: Martin Robertson, 1977), chapters 2 and 3; Robert L. Beisner, "History and Henry Kissinger," *Diplomatic History*, 14 (Fall 1990); Richard Weitz, "Henry Kissinger's Philosophy of International Relations," *Diplomacy and Statecraft*, Vol. 2, No. 1 (March 1991); John Lewis Gaddis, "Rescuing Choice from Circumstance: The Statecraft of Henry Kissinger," in Gordon A. Craig and Francis L. Loewenheim (eds), *Diplomats 1939–1979* (Princeton: Princeton University Press, 1994).

world loses the perspective for nuance; a gain for one side appears as an absolute loss for the other. Every issue seems to involve a question of survival."[90] Political multipolarity would not necessarily guarantee stability, but it would reduce rigidity and provide greater opportunities for developing "an agreed concept of order" in the international system.[91] The great powers had to exercise power with restraint, and also restrain the actions of less cooperative states in order to maintain the stabilizing equilibrium of the system. Kissinger believed that although the two superpowers would remain powerful with their overwhelming military strength, a more pluralistic world was in the long-term interest of the United States.

In order to re-adjust US power resources to a new international situation, Kissinger urged a pragmatic conception of foreign policy, namely the re-assessment of the national interests in military, political, economic, and psychological terms. Accordingly, the Nixon administration advocated that America's new initiative should be based on "a realistic assessment of our and others' interests," proclaiming: "Our interests must shape our commitments, rather than the other way around."[92] The Nixon administration sought to promote "mutual self-restraint" among states to accommodate conflicting national interests "through negotiation rather than confrontation."[93] It was this particular issue of self-restraint that was the fundamental requirement for the balance of power among states.

2.2 Kissinger's balance of power in theory

Kissinger has often explained the US opening to China in terms of maintaining a balance of power: "It was not to collude against the Soviet Union but to give us a balancing position to use for constructive ends – to give each Communist power a stake in better relations with us. Such an equilibrium could assure stability among the major powers."[94] He argues that the traditional criteria of balance of power were territorial; military power was considered as the final recourse.[95] However, he maintains that in a nuclear age, power cannot automatically be translated into influence, and it is difficult to use power diplomatically.[96] Managing a military

---

90   Henry A. Kissinger, "Central Issues of American Foreign Policy," in *American Foreign Policy: Three Essays* (New York: W.W. Norton & Company, Inc., 1969), pp. 56–58.

91   Ibid., p. 57.

92   Richard M. Nixon, "United States Foreign Policy for the 1970s: A Strategy for Peace," A Report to Congress, Vol. 1, February 18, 1970 (Washington DC: Government Printing Office, 1970), p. 119.

93   Richard M. Nixon, "US Foreign Policy for the 1970s: The Emerging Structure of Peace," A Report to the Congress, Vol. 3, February 9, 1972, in *Public Papers of the Presidents of the United States, Richard M. Nixon, 1972* (Washington DC: Government Printing Office, 1972), pp. 345–346.

94   Henry A. Kissinger, *White House Years* (Boston: Little Brown, 1979), p. 192; Idem, *Years of Upheaval* (Boston: Little Brown, 1982), p. 54. Idem, *Diplomacy* (London: Simon & Schuster, 1994), pp. 722–723; Idem, *Years of Renewal* (New York: Little Brown, 1999), p. 140. See also Gaddis, *Strategies of Containment*, pp. 279–282, and pp. 295–298.

95   Kissinger, "Central Issues," pp. 9–60.

96   Ibid., pp. 61–62.

balance of power required vigilance on two levels: "being strong enough not only strategically with nuclear power but also locally with conventional arms."[97]

In theory, Kissinger's concept of balance of power evolved from the intellectual base of the traditional/classical realist school.[98] Realists perceive states as the main actors in international relations, and the international system as the most important level of analysis. On the international level, the most crucial factor is the permanent existence of the struggle for power among states. In the absence of any central authority maintaining order, states seek to maintain and enhance power, especially militarily, to secure their survival. States also practice balance of power in order to prevent the emergence of a predominant state in the international system.

Hans Morgenthau suggests that the balance of power takes four forms: 1) a policy aimed at certain state affairs, 2) an actual state of affairs, 3) an approximately equal distribution of power, and 4) any distribution of power.[99] Balance of power functions only when states recognize "the same rules of the game" and act "for the same limited stakes" in order to achieve "international stability and national independence."[100] Finally, it is necessary to distinguish between the balance of power as a policy of a state to prevent the emergence of predominant power and the balance of power as a system within which the state interactions prevent the predominance of any one state.[101]

Reflecting the diffusion of power resources and the emergence of economic interdependence among states from the late 1960s and the early 1970s, the neo-realist school advanced the analysis of balance of power by emphasizing "structure."[102]

---

97   Kissinger, *White House Years*, p. 62.

98   Hans J. Morgenthau and Kenneth Thompson, *Politics Among Nations: The Struggle For Power and Peace*, Sixth edition (Brief edition). (New York: Harper & Knopf, 1993); George F. Kennan, *American Diplomacy 1900–1950* (Chicago: University of Chicago Press, 1985); Paul R. Viotti and Mark V. Kauppi, *International Relations Theory: Realism, Pluralism, Globalism*, Second edition. (New York: Macmillan Publishing Company, 1993), p. 575. Morgenthau suggests nine major elements which determine the national power of a state: geography, natural resources, industrial capability, military preparedness, population, national character, national morale, the quality of diplomacy, and the quality of government. Ibid., pp. 124–165.

99   Morgenthau, *Politics Among Nations*, p. 186. Haas presents eight meanings of balance of power. See Ernst B. Haas, "The Balance of Power: Prescription, Concept or Propaganda?" *World Politics*, Book V (July 1953), pp. 442–477, in James E. Dougherty and Robert L. Pfaltzgraff, Jr., *Contending Theories of International Relations: A Comprehensive Survey*, Third edition. (New York: HarperCollins Publishers, Inc., 1990), pp. 30–31. Wight clarifies the nine meanings of balance of power. See Martin Wight, "The balance of power" in H. Butterfield and Martin Wight (eds), *Diplomatic Investigations: Essays in the Theory of International Politics* (London: Allen and Unwin, 1966), p. 151.

100 Ibid., pp. 189–190.

101 Ibid.

102 Kenneth Waltz, *Theory of International Politics* (New York: McGraw-Hill, Inc., 1979); Robert O. Keohane (ed.), *Neorealism and its Critics* (New York: Columbia University Press, 1986); and Barry Buzan, *The Logic of Anarchy: Neorealism to Structural Realism* (New York: Columbia University Press, 1993). Waltz argues that the bipolar system is less likely to be the subject of rapid transformation than multipolar system.

Structure is defined as the interrelationship of states composing the international system. The international political system is defined by anarchy and differentiated by the distribution of power capabilities in military, political, and economic terms among sovereign states. There is a strong tendency towards balance within the system, and the expectation is that balance, once disrupted, will be restored in one way or the other. A state thus reacts to the emergence of a more powerful state by counterbalancing – either to enhance its own power or to align itself with an opposing state or group of states. Structure imposes constraints on states' behavior.

In sum, the balance of power is a rule-based system, inseparable from diplomatic practice as a policy, which restrains the sources of instability, limits the scope of conflicts, and brings relative stability in which no single state or group of states would be in a permanent position to determine the fate of others. Kissinger's concept of balance of power system evolved as a central characteristic of the loosening military bipolarity and the emerging political multipolarity from the late 1960s to the early 1970s. Kissinger's concept of balance of power regarding the US rapprochement with China can be defined as the application of realist logic to exploit the deepening Sino-Soviet hostility, which led to the development of triangular relations between the US, USSR, and China. Accordingly, Kissinger's practice of balance of power policy toward US rapprochement with China needs to be clarified.

2.3 Kissinger's balance of power in practice

Kissinger has been quite critical of academic experts on China. For example, during the transitional period after the November 1968 presidential election, a group of academic experts from Harvard and Massachusetts Institute of Technology sent a memorandum to President-Elect Nixon.[103] These experts examined the implications of the US-Soviet-China relations:

> Implicit in the foregoing suggestions is the hope that the new Administration will attempt to view Sino-American relations as a separate problem from Soviet-American problem, though inevitably a related problem. The Sino-Soviet split provides us with an opportunity to treat each party separately and to scrutinize our national interests in each relationship with care. We urge that the new Administration, in its proper concern with the bilateral super-power balance, avoid judgments about China and its development that derive from Moscow's views of Peking. A Soviet-American alliance against Peking may serve Russian's interests; but it may not automatically serve US national interests.[104]

The academic experts therefore warned the new administration of the danger of a possible US-Soviet collusion against China. Kissinger criticizes that these academics missed the geopolitical perspective "with respect to the Soviet Union that the Chinese might have an incentive to move toward us *without* American concessions but *their*

---

103 "Memorandum for President-Elect Nixon on US relations with China," November 6, 1968, Re-produced in "Communist China Policy," Hon. John Rousselot, The House of Representatives, August 6, 1971, pp. 30765–30767.

104 Ibid., p. 30765.

need for American counterweight to the Soviet Union."[105] In other words, Kissinger condemned their proposal for its failure to explore the linkage among the three states and the possible US leverage within the context of Sino-Soviet hostility.

In October 1969, Kissinger's NSC staff assessed that the diffusion of independent political activity among states had encouraged the loosening of Cold War military bipolarity. For example, Western Europe and Japan, sought much more independence from the superpowers in policies and national will. However, this diffusion had not yet taken the "form of the emergence of significant new centers of military power," such as the destruction of alliances, major realignments or the consolidation of new groupings among states.[106] The only notable exception, the Sino-Soviet alliance, had become a deep rivalry and created a "tripolar relationship" in which (a) the US, USSR, and the PRC respectively had an interest in preventing the other two states cooperating (b) the Soviets had parallel interests with the US in containing China (c) the US ability to achieve closer relations with China and to exploit Moscow's fear of a US-Chinese rapprochement was limited. Within a broader framework of political multipolarity in the world, there was a possibility for the development of US-Soviet-China triangular relationship.

The most comprehensive explanation of the multipolar balance of power came from President Nixon during his interview with *Time* magazine in January 1972:

> We must remember the only time in the history of the world that we have had any extended periods of peace is when there has been balance of power. It was when one nation becomes infinitely more powerful in relation to its potential competitor that the danger of war arises. So I believe in a world in which the United States is powerful. I think it will be a safer world and a better world if we have a strong, healthy United States, Europe, Soviet Union, China, Japan each balancing the other, not playing one against the other, an even balance.[107]

---

105 Kissinger, *White House Years*, p. 165. Italic in original. Despite his personal antipathy toward academia, Kissinger was still "interested in what the scholars thought" on China. Levin, "China Policy and the National Security Council," p. 9, NSCP-OHR. For example, in April 1969, Kissinger and the NSC staff organized a meeting with 48 scholars. As for the options for China policy, a NSC staff member Richard L. Sneider sought to obtain expertise view on: 1) what the long-range US objective on dealing with China should be; and 2) what concrete steps the US might take toward these objectives. Memo from Sneider to Kissinger, "Tentative Schedule for April 12 Meeting," April 9, 1969, p. 1, Box H–299, NSC Vol. II, 4/1/69–5/30/69 [2 of 2], NSCIF, NPMS, NA.

106 Kissinger to Nixon, "Analysis of changes in international politics since World War II and their implications for our basic assumption about US foreign policy," October 20, 1969, Agency Files, NSC 1969–1971, National Security Council Files (NSCF), NPMS, NA.

107 President Richard M. Nixon, interview with *Time*, January 3, 1972, p. 3. As Secretary of State, Kissinger came to realize the emergence of the balance of power at different levels: "In the military sphere, there are two superpowers. In economic terms, there are at least five major groupings. Politically, many more centers of influence have emerged." Henry A. Kissinger, Address to the Pacem in Terris III Conference, Washington, October 8, 1973, cited in Gaddis, *Strategies of Containment*, p. 282.

On February 14, 1972, three days before Nixon's departure to China, Kissinger provided his assessment of the future role of China within the triangular diplomacy:

> For the next 15 years we have to lean the Chinese against the Russians. We have to play this balance of power game totally unemotionally. Right now, we need the Chinese to correct the Russians, and to discipline the Russians ... Our concern with China right now, in my view Mr. President, is to use it as a counterweight to Russia, not for its local policy. ... The fact that it doesn't have a global policy is an asset to us, the fact that it doesn't have global strength yet – and to prevent Russia from gobbling it up. If Russia dominates China, that would be a fact of such tremendous significance.[108]

In sum, Kissinger's practice of the balance of power policy toward the US rapprochement with China can be defined as the diplomatic practice of using the weaker China as a counterweight against the stronger Soviet Union in the Sino-Soviet rivalry, while publicly seeking to create an appearance of taking an even-handed political approach toward the two communist giants. Accordingly, it should be examined how Kissinger developed his view on US policy toward China prior to 1969.

2.4 Kissinger's early views on China

Kissinger was originally not an Asia or China expert, and thus he approached China "from his experience as a specialist in European politics."[109] In his memoirs, although admitting: "China had not figured extensively in my own writings," Kissinger still emphasizes the importance of his role in the composition of the draft of Nelson Rockefeller's presidential campaign speech of May 1, 1968 which proposed "a dialogue with Communist China."[110] In particular, the speech suggested the possible development of a "subtle triangle" of relations between Washington, Beijing, and Moscow: "we improve the possibilities of accommodation with each as we increase our options toward both."[111] Former NSC staff memberRodman perceives Kissinger's suggestion as "independent of Nixon's."[112]

---

108 Conversation between Nixon and Kissinger, February 14, 1972, 4:09–6:19pm, Oval Office, OVAL 671–1, White House Tapes, NA.

109 Solomon, interview with the author, September 24, 2003.

110 Nelson Rockefeller, Speech to the World Affairs Council of Philadelphia, May 1, 1968, *The New York Times*, May 1, 1968.

111 Kissinger, *White House Years*, p. 165; and Idem, *Diplomacy*, p. 721. The intellectual origins of Kissinger's policies toward Sino-Soviet relations, what was to be known as the triangular diplomacy on the basis of the balance of power concept, can be traced back to his early writings. In a study of the European balance of power after the Napoleonic upheavals, Kissinger praised Metternich for placing Austria in a position among its rivals where it served as "the pivotal state" so that "the differences of the major powers among each other were greater than their respective differences with Austria." Henry A. Kissinger, *A World Restored*, p. 247. Kissinger also analyzed Bismarck's proposal to "manipulate the commitments of the other powers so that Prussia would always be closer to any of the contending parties than they were to each other." Henry A. Kissinger, "White Revolutionary: Reflections on Bismarck," *Daedelus*, XCVII (Summer 1968), pp. 912–913.

112 Rodman, interview with the author, October 21, 2003.

In reality, however, Kissinger's early writings failed to show depth on the changing nature of the Sino-Soviet relations, and America's China policy was never discussed independently. In the late 1950s, Kissinger considered China as a "revolutionary" power along with the Soviet Union.[113] He referred to the US primary task of "dividing" the Sino-Soviet alliance: the Sino-Soviet relations might become "cooler," if the US sought to pressure the two communist states to take risks where only one stood to benefit.[114] In the early 1960s, Kissinger cautiously argued that the possibility of a "rift" between Communist China and the USSR "must not be overlooked."[115] He hinted only that "if it [a rift] occurs we should take advantage of it rather than force the erstwhile partners into a new alliance through intransigence. Our diplomacy cannot have as a goal what we can only treat as a fortunate event."[116] Therefore, Kissinger had failed to explore sufficiently the seriousness and complexity of Sino-Soviet hostility. By the mid-1960s, Kissinger acknowledged the fact of a Sino-Soviet split; he suggested that it was "insoluble" owing to the two parties' conflicts over doctrinal issues.[117] It was De Gaulle who sought to play off the weaker Communist China as a "counterweight" to the stronger Soviet Union.[118] However, Kissinger still tended to regard China as an "objective threat" to US "global responsibilities." In his memoirs, Kissinger argues that there was a tendency in the new administration to view China as an aggressive power:

> Originally, we had not thought reconciliation possible. We were convinced that the Chinese were fanatic and hostile. But even though we could not initially see a way to achieve it, both Nixon and I believed in the importance of an opening to the People's Republic of China.[119]

However, the above statement is misleading, because as previously suggested, it was Nixon who came to suggest the importance of opening a dialogue with China by 1967. In Solomon's re-assessment, Nixon estimated that the Soviet Union was a much greater threat than China.[120] Moreover, Nixon was coming to power at the time when the country was torn apart by Vietnam. And he did "not want to fall into the trap where Lyndon Johnson was trapped, and his presidency was destroyed by the Vietnam conflict." Thus, when Nixon was talking about the secret plan for ending the Vietnam War, a critical element of that was including the relations with

---

113 Kissinger, *Nuclear Weapons and Foreign Policy*, chapter 10.
114 Ibid., pp. 148–149.
115 Kissinger, *The Necessity for Choice* (New York: Harper & Brothers, 1961), p. 202.
116 Ibid.
117 Henry A. Kissinger, *The Troubled Partnership: A Reappraisal of the Atlantic Alliance* (New York: McGraw-Hill, 1965), p. 198, and pp. 201–202.
118 Ibid., pp. 59–60. On January 27, 1964, France became the first Western state which officially recognized the People's Republic of China. See Stephen Erasmus, "General de Gaulle's Recognition of Peking," *The China Quarterly*, No. 18 (April–June, 1964), pp. 195–200.
119 Kissinger, *White House Years*, p. 163.
120 Solomon, interview with the author, September 24, 2003.

China. On the contrary, Kissinger saw China as a real threat to the US and regarded the Vietnam War as a "trap drifting resources and political attentions away from the Soviet problem." Thus, Solomon concludes that: "Nixon was several years ahead of Kissinger."[121] On February 21, 1972, Kissinger admitted to Mao and Zhou that: "We thought all socialist/communist states were the same phenomenon. We didn't understand until the President came to the office the different nature of revolution in China and the way revolution developed in other socialist states."[122] Thus, in 1968 and 1969, Kissinger still viewed China as much more aggressive than the Soviet Union.

Kissinger claims that, despite some differences in opinion, he and Nixon came to realize that the development of triangular relations between the United States, the Soviet Union and China would provide "a great strategic opportunity for peace."[123] Lord argues that: "Each one came to office, considering the benefits of opening to China with respect to primarily the Soviet Union and Vietnam, and Asia in general."[124] In actuality, however, Kissinger was not initially interested in China, and remained skeptical about any quick move toward China during the early months of the new administration. Kissinger perceived the China issue in terms of its short and mid term relationship to Sino-Soviet rift. Thus, for Kissinger, China policy was initially a part of a much broader Soviet policy. On the other hand, Nixon believed that "ending the isolation of 800 million Chinese itself removed a great threat to peace."[125] Thus, Nixon was convinced that, even without the growing Soviet military threat, it was still "essential" to open towards China, while China was still physically weak rather than waiting until later when China would have less need of a relationship with the United States.[126] Overall, it was Nixon's determination that drove the initiative, and Kissinger brought the initiative to fruition and fit into a triangular global balance framework.

3. The Nixon-Kissinger Leadership

One of the main reasons why the opening to China was conducted "very secretly and very quietly" was because Nixon and Kissinger were afraid that if it became public, the "domestic public and political reaction could have killed off the initiative before it began."[127] Paradoxically, it was Nixon's life long background as a "staunch anti-Communist" that provided a strong basis within the US domestic political context to open a new dialogue with Communist China.[128] On the other hand, Kissinger

---

121 Ibid.
122 Memcon, Mao, Zhou, Nixon, and Kissinger, February 21, 1972, p. 8, CHINA – President's Talks with Mao and Chou En-lai, February 1972, Box 91, Country Files – Far East, HAKOF, NSCF, NPMS, NA.
123 Kissinger, *White House Years*, p. 164.
124 Lord, interview with the author, October 15, 2003.
125 Kissinger, *White House Years*, p. 164.
126 Richard M. Nixon, *Beyond Peace* (New York: Random House, 1994), p. 130.
127 Solomon, interview with the author, September 24, 2003.
128 Ibid; and Lord, interview with the author, October 15, 2003.

admits the relative weakness of his position in the early period: "I did not have the political strength or bureaucratic clout to pursue such a fundamental shift of policy on my own."[129] Moreover, as the briefing books for his October 1971 trip to Beijing indicated, Kissinger came to anticipate that domestic political reactions to a new China initiative would be "manageable."[130] With his past credentials and his following from the right and center, Nixon was "much less vulnerable to attack than would be more leftist figures" in American society. Thus, the President was probably the "only leader who could carry through this policy."[131] Kissinger explained to Zhou in October 1971 that Nixon asked him to "reaffirm in the strongest terms his personal commitment" to the improvements in relations between the US and China.[132] Finally, during the Nixon-Mao meeting in February 1972, Kissinger admitted that: "It was the President who set the direction and worked out of the plan."[133]

Regarding the actual policy operational process, Kissinger emphasizes that once the President set "a policy direction," he left it to the National Security Adviser "to implement the strategy and manage the bureaucracy."[134] Ambrose evaluates Kissinger's role "as agent, tool, and sometimes adviser, not as a generator of ideas": "The basic thrust of Nixon's innovations came from the President, not the National Security Adviser."[135] Haig assesses Nixon as a "strategic thinker of historic dimensions" and Kissinger as a "brilliantly gifted diplomatic tactician carrying Nixon's ideas forward."[136] Edgar Snow, an American journalist, interviewed Premier Zhou. Interestingly, that interview revealed that the Chinese knew about Kissinger through their intelligence system and through reading of his writings. "Kissinger?" Zhou said, "There is a man who knows the language of both worlds – his own and ours. He is the first American we have seen in his position. With him, it should be

---

129 Kissinger, *White House Years*, p. 163.

130 Opening Meeting, HAK Talking Points, p. 6, Briefing book for HAK's October 1971 trip POLO II [Part I], For the President's Files (Winston Lord) – China Trip/Vietnam, Box 850, NSCF, NPMS, NA.

131 Ibid.

132 Memcon, Kissinger and Zhou, October 20, 1971, 4:40–7:10pm, p. 3, HAK visit to PRC October 1971 Memcons – originals, For the President's Files – China/Vietnam Negotiations, Box 1035, NSCF, NPMS, NA.

133 Memcon, February 21, 1972, p. 3, CHINA – President's Talks with Mao and Chou En-lai February 1972, Box 91, Country Files – Far East, HAKOF, NSCF, NPMS, NA.

134 Kissinger, *White House Years*, p. 163. See also Kissinger, *Years of Renewal*, p. 47, pp. 61–62.

135 Stephen E. Ambrose, *Nixon, Volume II: The Triumph of a Politician 1962–1972* (London: Simon and Schuster, 1989), p. 655. Former Soviet Ambassador to America, Anatoly Dobrynin, assesses that Kissinger was a "good tactician" in both direct and behind-the-scenes negotiations in Soviet-American relations. Anatoly Dobrynin, *In Confidence: Moscow's Ambassador to America's Six Cold War Presidents (1962–1986)* (New York: Times Books, A Division of Random House, Inc, 1995), p. 195.

136 Alexander M. Haig Jr. (with Maccarry Charles), *Inner Circles, How America Changed the World: A Memoir* (New York: Warner Books, 1992), p. 204.

possible to talk."[137] Finally, during a meeting with Zhou in February 1972, President Nixon described Kissinger's role:

> I think that one thing which Dr. Kissinger has greatly contributed in his services to my administration is his philosophic views. He takes the long view, which is something I try to do also, except sometimes my schedule is so filled with practical matters and decisions on domestic and foreign policy that I don't have as much time to take the long term view as he does.[138]

In Winston Lord's assessment, Nixon and Kissinger "divided labor very skillfully; Nixon was providing fundamental guidance. Kissinger was a skillful negotiator and an operator, as well as a strategist."[139] Isaacson gives credit to both Nixon and Kissinger in terms of the speed of transformation in the US-China relations.[140] Based on his vision, Nixon held ultimate authority, making the final decision for a new initiative. Kissinger was a dynamic theorist and tactician, skillfully conducting a series of crucial negotiations. In reality, however, Nixon and Kissinger still needed the foreign policy decision-making system and bureaucratic expertise on the formulation and implementation of America's China policy, as the following chapter examines.

---

137 Zhou Enlai, interview with Edgar Snow (conducted on November 5, 1970), *Life*, July 30, 1971 p. 3. After the July 1971 secret talks, Zhou privately commented on Kissinger, "very intelligent – indeed a Dr." Chen, *Mao's China and the Cold War*, p. 266.

138 Memcon, February 26, 1972, p. 16, Box 87, POF, NSCF, NPMS, NA.

139 Lord, interview with the author, October 15, 2003.

140 Isaacson, *Kissinger*, p. 353. Holdridge recalls that: "I'm sure Nixon respected Kissinger for his intellectual capabilities, but the respect did not necessarily mean a warm and intimate friendship." John Holdridge, Oral History Interview, p. 108, July 20, 1995, FAOHC.

Chapter 2

Foreign Policy Decision-Making Machinery for the US Rapprochement with China

This chapter examines the revitalization of the National Security Council (NSC) as the principal decision-making body for the pursuit of strict secrecy by Nixon and Kissinger. It begins by investigating how Nixon and Kissinger reassessed the main structural and operational problems of previous NSCs and designed a White House centered decision-making machinery. Next, this chapter analyses the development of the systematic control of policy study papers by Kissinger and the NSC staff and the subsequent exclusion of the State Department from the direct decision-making process. Finally, it compares and contrasts the roles of the NSC staff and State Department officials for the US policy towards China in greater detail. Despite the pursuit of strict secrecy, Nixon and Kissinger still privately benefited from the expertise of the State Department to develop a broader set of policy options. Additionally, there were private interactions between the NSC staff and State Department officials. The existing diversity on policy options among foreign policy decision makers will be analyzed not as the mere extension of conflicting bureaucratic interests but as a more dynamic interplay among different geo-strategic perceptions, reflecting a broader debate within the foreign policy decision-making circle.

1. Organization and Procedure for a New NSC System

1.1 Problems of the previous NSCs

During the transition period from November 1968 to January 1969, President-elect Nixon and the Special Assistant to the President for National Security Affairs designate Kissinger sought to re-vitalize the function of the National Security Council to identify the US's capabilities, interests, and objectives.[1] In their meeting on November 25, 1968, President-elect Nixon talked with Kissinger about a "massive

---

[1] The functions and responsibilities of the National Security Council were set forth in the National Security Act of 1947, and amended by the National Security Act Amendments of 1949. Its membership included the President, Vice President, Secretary of State, Secretary of Defense, and other high officials, such as the Director of the Central Intelligence Agency as appropriate. See, for example, *History of the National Security Council* (http://www.whitehouse.gov/nsc/history.html); John Prados, *Keepers of the Keys: A History of the National Security Council from Truman to Bush* (New York: William Morrow and Company, Inc., 1991),

organizational problem."² Nixon did not trust the State Department bureaucracy because of his personal experiences: the Foreign Service had disdained him as Vice President during the 1950s and ignored him as a private citizen during the 1960s. Nixon also believed that the State Department would "leak secrets" and had some very conservative views in some areas that would "resist change."³ In response, Kissinger recommended that if the President-elect intended to operate foreign policy on a "wide-ranging basis," he would need to establish the best possible national security machinery within the White House that could plan, analyze, and review "policy options" systematically for him before making decisions.⁴

Nixon and Kissinger wanted to establish a system which would enable them to be presented with all sides of any issues in the presence of all concerned.⁵ The President needed to understand not only the substantive background of the issues but also their bureaucratic histories and political implications because he would inevitably be surrounded "by advocates with strong, often institutional, and nearly always conflicting views."⁶ The new administration thus needed a mechanism that would establish "clear, consistent, and feasible goals" in the national security field, which would translate these goals into "specific programs" and monitor the progress of these programs.⁷

Before entering office, Nixon and Kissinger had already shown their respective views towards a highly bureaucratized foreign policy decision-making process. During the 1968 campaign, Republican Presidential candidate Nixon promised to "restore the National Security Council to its pre-eminent role in national security planning."⁸ Kissinger criticized the combination of abstractness and rigidity resulting from traditional American idealism, insisting that foreign policy had to be based not on sentiment but on an assessment of strength. When policy became identified with the consensus of a committee, it was fragmented into a series of *ad hoc* decisions

---

pp. 29–32; and Charles W. Kegley, Jr. and Eugene R. Wittkopf, *American Foreign Policy: Pattern and Progress*, Sixth edition. (New York: St. Martin's Press, 2002), pp. 328–348.

2   Henry A. Kissinger, *White House Years* (Boston: Little Brown, 1979), p. 11. On December 2, 1968, Nixon officially announced the appointment of Kissinger as the Special Assistant for the President for National Security Affairs.

3   Richard Solomon, interview with the author, September 24, 2003.

4   Richard M. Nixon, *RN* (New York: Grosset & Dunlap, 1978), p. 341.

5   As for the development of the Nixon-Kissinger NSC system, see *NSC History: The Nixon Administration 1969–1974* (http://www.whitehouse.gov/nsc/history.html#nixonn); and Prados, *Keepers of the Keys*, pp. 265–267, pp. 277–283.

6   "The National Security Process, National Security Staffing in the White House," International Social Studies Division, November 6, 1968, p. 3, HAK Administrative and Staff Files (HAK-ASF), Box 1, Transition, November 1968–January 1969, Henry A. Kissinger's Office Files (HAKOF), The National Security Council Files (NSCF), Nixon Presidential Materials Staff (NPMS), National Archives (NA).

7   Lean Sloes to Kissinger, "Organizing the National Security Machinery," December 21, 1968, p.1, HAK-ASF, Box 3, General Transition Books, HAKOF, NSCF, NPMS, NA.

8   Richard M. Nixon, Radio Speech, October 24, 1968, cited in Kissinger, *White House Years*, p. 38.

which made it difficult to achieve a sense of overall direction.⁹ Thus, the National Security Council was "less concerned with developing measures" in terms of "a well-understood national purpose than with adjusting the varying approaches of semi-autonomous departments."¹⁰ In particular, Kissinger emphasized the importance of secrecy in the decision-making body:

> One reason for keeping the decisions to small groups is when an unpopular decision may be fought by brutal means, such as 'leaks' to the press or to congressional committees. The only way secrecy can be kept is to exclude from the making of the decision all those who are theoretically charged with carrying it out. In consequence, the relevance of the bureaucracy might continue to send out cables with great intensity, thereby distorting the effort with the best intensions in the world. You cannot stop them from doing this because you do not tell them what is going on.¹¹

Hence, the Nixon transition staff reassessed the main problems of the National Security Council during previous administrations.¹² President Truman was suspicious of congressional intent in establishing the NSC system, which might have restricted his flexibility of action. Thus, he initially restricted its policy role and began to pay substantive attention to its function only after the outbreak of the Korean War.¹³

President Eisenhower institutionalized the NSC into a large and highly structured body, with formal procedures, staff systems, and interdepartmental relationships.¹⁴ It appeared, however, that the Eisenhower administration's NSC mechanism became very formalized, especially during its second term, because the machinery spent a long time to reach an interdepartmental consensus, which resulted in delays in getting staff papers to the Council, and many staff papers without clearly defining policy alternatives. As Vice President, Nixon was frustrated by Eisenhower's practice of encouraging a consensus amon the NSC principals before an issue reached the President for the final decision. Nixon wanted a system that was "formal and orderly" but not as rigid as the Eisenhower system and which moved authority from the departments to the White House.¹⁵

---

9   Henry A. Kissinger, "Domestic Structure and Foreign Policy," in *American Foreign Policy: Three Essays* (New York: W.W. Norton & Company, Inc., 1969), pp. 29–34.

10 Henry A. Kissinger, *The Necessity for Choice; Prospects of American Foreign Policy* (New York: Harper & Brothers, Publishers, 1960), pp. 343–344.

11 Henry A. Kissinger, "Bureaucracy and Policymaking: The Effects of Insiders and Outsiders on the Policy Process," in Morton H. Halperin and Arnold Kanter (eds), *Readings in American Foreign Policy: A Bureaucratic Perspective* (Boston: Little Brown, 1973), p. 89, quotation marks in original.

12 Letter from Kissinger to Senator Henry M. Jackson, March 3, 1970, p. 1, Box H – 300, NSC System, NSC Organization [1 of 3], National Security Council Institutional Files (NSCIF), NPMS, NA.

13 Colonel J.M. Chambers to Bryce N. Harlow (Assistant to the President-Elect), "Suggested Revitalization for the National Security Council," November 12, 1968, p. 3, HAK-ASF, Box 1, Transition, November 1968–January 1969, HAKOF, NSCF, NPMS, NA.

14 Ibid. See Prados, *Keepers of the Keys*, pp. 57–95.

15 Morton H. Halperin, correspondence with the author, June 10, 2004.

The Kennedy and Johnson Administrations maintained the NSC system in "name only," downgrading its role as a continuing, objective entity and relying only on a few personal advisors.[16] The Kennedy NSC was relatively informal, more flexible, and, in many respects, action rather than policy-oriented. The Johnson NSC was based on informal and issue-oriented committees, and the so-called "Tuesday Lunches" at the White House, where current concerns were discussed in an unstructured and highly personalized manner. The Kennedy-Johnson national security policies thus relied too much on *ad hoc* planning which did not sufficiently engage the resources of the bureaucratic experts on the Council. In consequence, the Kennedy-Johnson national security decision-making suffered from the "absence of systematic policy planning," the "weakness of procedures for inter-agency coordination," and the "lack of continuous assessment of short and long range objectives."[17]

1.2 Goodpaster's memoranda

As for actual planning of a new NSC system, at Nixon's request, Kissinger consulted General Andrew Goodpaster, Eisenhower's NSC Staff Secretary, and asked him to produce option papers.[18] Goodpaster recommended strengthening the NSC as the President's "highest deliberative, advisory and policy-formulating body."[19] The system should formulate "broad and far-reaching conceptions of a long-range character" and provide the "main structure of the nation's approach to its international and security problems."[20] Its policy process should provide "coherence and reasoned dynamism, together with a sense of direction, to the whole complex of policy and action."[21] Goodpaster recommended that in order to decrease bureaucratic friction, the control of agenda creation should be managed by the White House, and the Special Assistant to the President for National Security Affairs should run the key committees.[22] It was crucial to impose some degree of order on the flow of

---

16   Chambers to Harlow, "Suggested Revitalization for the National Security Council," November 12, 1968, p. 5, HAK-ASF, Box 1, Transition, HAKOF, NSCF, NPMS, NA.

17   Sloes to Kissinger, "Organizing the National Security Machinery," December 21, 1968, p. 2, HAK-ASF, Box 3 General Transition Books, HAKOF, NSCF, NPMS, NA.

18   Halperin, correspondence with the author, June 10, 2004. See also Kissinger, *White House Years*, pp. 41–44; and Idem, *Years of Renewal* (New York: Simon & Schuster, 1999), pp. 72–76. As Staff Secretary of the NSC during the Eisenhower administration, Goodpaster was responsible for the flow of matters on security and international activities between the President and the departments and agencies. The roles of Staff Secretary and National Security Adviser were combined during the Kennedy-Johnson NSCs. Goodpaster to Kissinger, "Security Affairs Staff Responsibilities Under President Eisenhower," December 12, 1968, pp. 1–2, HAK-ASF, Box 1, Transition, HAKOF, NSCF, NPMS, NA.

19   Goodpaster to Kissinger, "Organization and Procedures for the Conduct of National Security Affairs," December 13, 1968, p. 1, HAK-ASF, Box 1, Transition, HAKOF, NSCF, NPMS, NA.

20   Ibid.

21   Ibid.

22   The idea of White House control of the NSC agenda was reinforced when Goodpaster and Kissinger consulted with former President Eisenhower at Walter Reed Army

information and action papers to and from the President and to have that supervised by the National Security Adviser who should be fully familiar with the President's views, priorities, and interests.

The new NSC structure appeared similar to the one Eisenhower used in terms of its structure for systematic analysis of policy options. Goodpaster recalls Eisenhower's statement: "Plans are nothing, but planning is everything" which emphasized the importance of preparatory work, giving all departments and agencies concerned a chance to present respective positions and bringing together all of the relevant facts.[23] Regarding Nixon's view, Goodpaster assesses that: "he put a real value on the way that had been done during the Eisenhower time." While Eisenhower "intended to maintain control through laying down the policies, main guiding policies, and then allowing that to evolve as the years went on," Nixon "personally intended to take an active part in major initiatives that could reshape the relationships – major relationships in the world – particularly the relationships among the great powers."[24] Goodpaster thus emphasizes that it was not just Presidential control of foreign policy, but that Nixon was going to "direct" it and "engage" himself in it.[25]

1.3 Halperin's memorandum

Kissinger also asked Morton Halperin, a former junior professor at Harvard and former Deputy Assistant Secretary of Defense for International Security Affairs, to produce a memorandum on how the analysis of bureaucratic politics could be applied to national security and foreign policy decision-making.[26] In theory, bureaucratic politics analysts focus on the politics of a government, where foreign policy decision-making is characterized as a resultant of a bargaining process among a multitude of bureaucracies with competing viewpoints and possessing different amounts of

---

Hospital in December 1968. Eisenhower insisted that the Senior Interdepartmental Group (SIG) structure (which was established in 1967 and chaired by the Under Secretary of State) should be abolished because the Defense Department would never like taking orders from the State Department. Kissinger, *White House Years*, p. 43; and Idem, *Years of Renewal*, p. 75.

23 Andrew J. Goodpaster, "The Nixon Administration National Security Council," p. 3, The National Security Council Project (NSCP), Oral History Roundtables (OHR), Center for International and Security Studies at Maryland and the Brookings Institution, December 8, 1998.

24 Ibid., pp. 4–5.

25 Ibid., p. 4. As for the study of the presidential leadership in foreign policy decision-making, see, for example, Alexander George, *Presidential Decision Making in Foreign Policy: The Effective Use of Information and Advice* (Boulder: Westview Press, 1980); and Richard E. Neustadt, *Presidential Power and the Modern Presidents: The Politics of Leadership from Roosevelt to Regan*, Fifth edition. (New York: Free Press, 1990); and Kegley and Wittkopf, *American Foreign Policy*, pp. 485–514.

26 Halperin, correspondence with the author, June 10, 2004. Kissinger consulted with Goodpaster and cleared Halperin's memo with him without saying that Halperin wrote it. Then Lawrence Eagleburger dealt with Goodpaster. Halperin was originally a junior professor and also Kissinger's former teaching assistant at Harvard. See also Walter Isaacson, *Kissinger: A Biography* (New York: McGraw-Hill, 1992), pp. 154–155.

power within the national governmental hierarchy.[27] Thus, policy-making is a matter of widening the base of support within the executive branch through the constant modification of the proposed policy. Concessions are made toward potential allies to satisfy their interests and overcome their objections to establishing a majority intradepartmental coalition. A major characteristic of policy-making is its time-consuming nature.

In practice, there were two fundamental issues to the new NSC system: who would control the agenda and the flow of policy papers; and who would chair the key NSC sub-committees. Halperin proposed two major changes. The first proposal, also reflecting General Goodpaster's view, was to eliminate the Senior Interdepartmental Group (SIG), which was chaired by the Undersecretary of State and was in charge of reviewing all options and proposals before they reached a formal NSC meeting. It would be replaced by a Review Group, chaired by the National Security Adviser, which would give Kissinger the power to approve any papers submitted to the President by departments and agencies; and the control of the agenda for NSC meeting. Halperin's other proposal was to give the National Security Adviser the power to direct National Security Study Memorandums (NSSMs, which were pronounced NIZ-ums) to departments and agencies. These directives would become a key tool for Kissinger to decide which policies should be reconsidered, when they would be placed on the agenda, and how they would be discussed. It would also allow him to use the bureaucracy without revealing his real purposes as well as to conduct negotiations secretly. In short, the new NSC system emphasized two principal objectives of the President: the retention of control over foreign policy decision-making at the top of the system; and the systematic development of clear policy analysis and alternative choices.

1.4 Objections from the Defense Department and the State Department

Kissinger sent his memorandum on the new NSC system to Nixon, which he privately approved. On December 28, 1968, Nixon summoned Secretary of State-designate William Rogers and Secretary of Defense-designate Melvin Laird to Key Biscayne, Florida, to discuss the Kissinger organizational plan. After the discussion, Nixon gave the final approval of the plan. On December 28, 1968, *The New York Times* reported that President-elect Nixon intended to "enlarge the role of National

---

27   For bureaucratic politics of foreign policy decision-making, see, for example, Morton H. Halperin and Arnold Kanter, "A Bureaucratic Perspective: A Preliminary Framework," in Morton H. Halperin and Arnold Kanter (eds), *Readings in American Foreign Policy: A Bureaucratic Perspective* (Boston: Little Brown, 1973), pp. 1–42; Morton H. Halperin, *Bureaucratic Politics and Foreign Policy* (Washington DC: The Brookings Institution, 1974); Morton H. Halperin and Priscilla Clapp with Arnold Kanter, *Bureaucratic Politics and Foreign Policy*, Second edition. (Washington DC: The Brookings Institution Press, 2007); John Spanier and Eric M. Uslaner, *American Foreign Policy Making and the Democratic Dilemmas*, Fifth edition. (Belmont, California: Wadsworth, Inc., 1989), pp. 61–71; Kegley and Wittkopf, *American Foreign Policy*, pp. 457–480; and Graham Allison and Philipe Zelikow, *Essence of Decision: Explaining the Cuban Missile Crisis*, Second edition. (New York: Longman, 1999), pp. 4–7.

Security Council."[28] In his memorandum to departments and agencies on January 16, 1969, Kissinger made clear the flow of policy papers under the control of NSC:

> All communication directed to the President originating in executive departments and agencies, including those from department and agency heads, should be delivered to the office of the Assistant for National Security Affairs. The NSC office under the direction of the Assistant to the President will establish secretariat control of all incoming papers prior to forwarding them to the office of the President. National security papers which the president asked upon or otherwise disposed of will be preceded out of the President Secretariat to the NSC office. Any subsequent actions required, such as the relay of Presidential decisions, return of signed correspondence or follow-up on Presidential comments will be accompanied under the direction of the Assistant to the President for National Security Affairs.[29]

In reality, however, the State Department and the Defense Department were not entirely convinced of the newly increased role of the National Security Adviser. Secretary of Defense-designate Laird objected to a "closed loop" in which "all intelligence inputs would be channeled through a single source" – the Assistant and his NSC staff.[30] Such an arrangement would isolate not only the President from direct access to intelligence community outputs, but also the Secretary of State, the Secretary of Defense, and other key members of the President's team. Laird also objected that the proposal would place in the hands of the Assistant and his NSC staff the primary right of initiating studies and directing where they would be performed as well as determining which policy issues should be placed on the agenda for NSC meetings. Laird thus suggested that there should be some "consultation" with the NSC principals to establish the priorities of these studies. The principals should be able to place policy issues on the agenda subject only to the veto of the President.

Secretary of State-designate Rogers had agreed to the general outline in Key Biscayne. However, "in light of the objections of his Foreign Service subordinates," Rogers wanted to reserve judgment, which Kissinger commented: "It would not be helpful to begin the Administration with a bureaucratic disagreement."[31] In their memorandum to the President-elect, State Department officials insisted that it should be the principal responsibility of the State Department to define and formulate the issues, and to bring them to the attention of the President. In foreign policy decision-making, the Secretary of State must have authority not only over the State Department, but also over other departments. In particular, State Department officials insisted that policy papers prepared by NSC Interdepartmental Groups for the NSC

---

28   *The New York Times*, December 28, 1968.
29   Memorandum for Executive Departments and Agencies, Attached to Memo from Kissinger to Haldeman, "Arrangements for Secretariat Control of National Security Papers," January 16, 1969, HAK-ASF, Box 1, Transition, HAKOF, NSCF, NPMS, NA.
30   Laird to Kissinger, "Your Memorandum dated on January 3, 1969 concerning a New NSC System," pp. 1–2, January 9, 1969, HAK-ASF, Box 1, Transition, HAKOF, NSCF, NPMS, NA.
31   Kissinger to Nixon, "NSC Procedures," January 7, 1969, p. 1, HAK-ASF, Box 1, Transition, HAKOF, NSCF, NPMS, NA.

should be transmitted through the Secretary of State to the NSC Review Group.[32] The Secretary of State, through the Under Secretaries Committee, must review papers on their way to the NSC to ensure all options were adequately examined, and the NSC should be seen primarily as an appeal board for when departments disagreed. In essence, the basic studies for NSSMs should be conducted at the assistant-secretary level of the State Department on an interagency basis, and then sent directly to the NSC Review Group.

Kissinger criticized the State Department for being unable to take the lead in managing interagency affairs because the Foreign Service, in training and background, was "inadequate" to the task of long-range planning and management, and that their forte was in "compromising differences," and "avoiding a confrontation of conflicting point of view."[33] In particular, Kissinger argued that the State proposal would restrict the Interdepartmental Groups in preparing policy papers to the scope and context of State Department functions, rather than fully and directly giving them the broader perspective of Presidential security concerns.[34] The only way the President could ensure that all options were examined, and all the arguments fairly presented, was to "have his own people" who were "responsive to him, and with a Presidential rather than departmental perspective" to oversee the preparation of the papers.[35]

Overall, the fundamental question was whether Nixon was going to have a State Department oriented system or an NSC oriented system. If the President wanted to control policy, he had to control the policy-making body. Kissinger thus recommended to Nixon that the State proposal should be "rejected."[36] Accordingly, Goodpaster had a meeting with Under Secretary of State-designate Elliot Richardson and the Under Secretary for Political Affairs-designate U. Alex Johnson. The fundamental confrontation with the State Department was "over control of the agenda and the exercise of chairmanship of the principal committees that would be established."[37] Finally, the conflict was resolved by enforcing Nixon's decision, "overruling" the position of the State Department.[38] Nixon urged that anyone who opposed his decision for the new NSC system "should submit his resignation."[39]

---

32   Ibid.
33   Ibid. As for State Department's organizational and operational problems, see, for example, Kissinger, "Bureaucracy and Policymaking," in Halperin and Kanter (eds), *Readings in American Foreign Policy*, p. 89, pp. 95–96; Spanier and Uslaner, *American Foreign Policy Making and the Democratic Dilemmas*, pp. 51–65; and Kegley and Wittkopf, *American Foreign Policy*, pp. 360–370.
34   Kissinger and Goodpaster to Nixon (n.d.), p. 1, HAK-ASF, Box 1, Transition, HAKOF, NSCF, NPMS, NA.
35   Ibid.
36   Ibid.
37   Goodpaster, "The Nixon Administration National Security Council," p. 3, NSCP-OHR.
38   Ibid., pp. 3–4.
39   Kissinger, *White House Years*, p. 46.

2. The Structure and Procedure of the New NSC System

The new National Security Council became the "principal forum" for consideration of policy issues requiring Presidential determination.[40] The issues ranged from current crises and immediate operational problems to middle and long-range planning.[41] At the Presidential direction and in consultation with the Secretaries of State and Defense, the Special Assistant to the President for National Security Affairs, as the chief supervisory officer, was responsible for "determining" the agenda and "ensuring" that the necessary papers were prepared.[42] There was a continual flow of memoranda to and from the President, and Presidential requests to Kissinger fell into two main categories: 1) directives and 2) requests for more information. The Nixon-Kissinger NSC system was structurally three-tiered with the Council at the top, the NSC Review and Operational Groups in the middle, and the Interdepartmental Groups at the base.[43]

Once the President, with recommendation from his National Security Adviser, determined that an issue involving interdepartmental considerations required analysis and Presidential decision, the NSC staff prepared a National Security Study Memorandum (NSSM) to "direct" a study of the issue to one of the Interdepartmental Groups (IGs) chaired by the Assistant Secretary of State.[44] The IGs drafted the basic paper for consideration by the NSC, defining the issue requiring Presidential decision, setting forth US objectives, and outlining the advantages and disadvantages of the alternative courses of action.[45] As a former NSC staff member, Winston Lord, recalls, at the beginning of the administration, there was a number of NSSMs being sent out asking for studies for two main reasons: one was a "genuine search for an intellectual path, analysis and preparation of options for policy by the various agencies," and the other reason was to "put so much work on the bureaucracy and

---

40 National Security Decision Memorandum 2 (NSDM2), "Reorganization of the National Security Council System," January 20, 1969, p. 1, National Security Decision Memorandums (NSDMs), Box 363, Subject Files (SF), NSCF, NPMS, NA.

41 The Council met regularly, and discussions were limited to agenda subjects except in unusual circumstances. At the first NSC meeting, President Nixon stated that the NSC would meet two times a week during January. After January, meetings would be once a week. Within approximately four months, meetings should be conducted on a bi-monthly basis. NSC Meeting, January 21, 1969, Box H-300, NSC Organization [2 of 3], NSCIF, NPMS, NA.

42 NSDM2, "Reorganization of the National Security Council System," January 20, 1969, p. 1, NSDMs, Box 363, SF, NSCF, NPMS, NA.

43 History of the NSC (n.d.), p. 1, NSC History Files (NSC-HF), Box H-314 [1 of 2], NSCIF, NPMS, NA.

44 National Security Decision Memorandum 1 (NSDM1), "Establishment of NSC Decision and Study Memoranda Series," January 20, 1969, p. 1, NSDMs, Box 363, SF, NSCF, NPMS, NA. There were six Interdepartmental Regional Groups, such as Africa, Latin America, East Asian and Pacific, Near and Middle East, Europe, Politico-Limitary – each chaired by the appropriate Assistant Secretary of State. History of the NSC (n.d.), p. 4, NSC-HF, Box H-314 [1 of 2], NSCIF, NPMS, NA.

45 NSDM2, "Reorganization of the National Security Council System," January 20, 1969, p. 4, NSDMs, Box 363, SF, NSCF, NPMS, NA.

keep them so busy" that enabled Nixon and Kissinger to establish their control over US foreign policy.[46]

After an IG meeting, the NSC staff prepared a Review Group meeting book which included the following items:

- Cover Memo, which briefly stated the subject of the meeting and pointed out any special problems of particular points;
- HAK Review Group Talking Points, in outline form, including all the issues Kissinger should raise at the meeting. (The views of the NSC staff on the answer and the likely responses of other Review Group members was also indicated);
- Review Group paper, which was the paper as it was distributed to the other members of the Review Group. A summary was prepared and placed on top;
- Background Papers;
- NSSM;
- Memo Requesting NSC Briefings, which was a draft of a memorandum to relevant agencies requesting briefing for the NSC discussion of this subject;
- Issues for Decision.[47]

After the papers were examined in Pre-Review Group meeting, the Review Group, chaired by the National Security Adviser, met as a "planning board" to examine policy study papers prior to their submission to the NSC.[48] The role of the Review Group was to "assure" that the issue under consideration was worthy of NSC attention; "all realistic alternatives" were presented; and the "facts" and "all department and agency views" were fairly and adequately presented.[49] In September 1970, the Review Group was re-named the Senior Review Group and raised from the Assistant to the Under-Secretary level.[50] The Washington Special Actions Group (WSAG), chaired by the

---

46   Winston Lord, "The Nixon Administration National Security Council," p. 7, NSCP-OHR.

47   Halperin to Kissinger, "NSC Procedures," June 23, 1969, p. 2, NSC, Vol. III, 6/1/69–12/31/69 [2of2], Box H-300, NSCIF, NPMS, NA.

48   Kissinger to Nixon, "Additional Provisions Concerning the Conduct of National Security Affairs," January 10, 1969, p. 1, HAK-ASF, Box 2, Transition, HAKOF, NSCF, NPMS, NA.

49   NSDM2, "Reorganization of the National Security Council System," January 20, 1969, p. 2, NSDMs, Box 363, SF, NSCF, NPMS, NA. The membership of the Review Group included: The Assistant to the President for National Security Affairs (Chairman); a representative of the Secretary of State; a representative of the Secretary of Defense; a representative of the Director of Central Intelligence; and a representative of the Chairman, Joint Chiefs of Staff.

50   National Security Decision Memorandum 85, "The National Security Council Senior Review Group," September 14, 1970, Box 363, SF, NSCF, NPMS, NA. The Senior Review Group comprised: the Under Secretary of State; the Deputy Secretary of Defense; the Director of Central Intelligence; the Chairman of the Joint Chiefs of Staff; and the Assistant to the President for National Security Affairs (Chairman). As for other interagency review groups in this category, the Verification Panel was formed to gather the essential facts relating to a

Assistant to the President, drafted contingency plans for possible crises, integrating the political and military requirements of crisis action on a daily basis.[51] Solomon emphasizes the importance of the "preparatory activity" that preceded a formal NSC meeting "where the issues of who really trusts whom, and who's really relying on whose judgment, and the pre-planning of positions gets worked out."[52]

Prior to the NSC meeting, the NSC staff prepared a briefing book for the President including:

- HAK Memo to the President – A brief memo summarizing what the issue was and calling any special problems to the attention of the President;
- Issues for Decision – An analytical paper summarizing the issues for decision from the Review Group paper, with recommendations on the issues;
- RN Talking Points – A brief memo including an introductory sentence, a list of the briefings, and an indication that Kissinger should be called on to discuss what the issues were;
- Review Group Paper, with a summary on the cover;
- Background Papers;
- HAK Talking Points – in outline form summarizing the main issues and pros and cons (included only in HAK's copy of book);
- NSSM (in HAK book only);
- Memo Requesting Briefings (in HAK book only).[53]

At the NSC meeting, with the President in the chair, the National Security Adviser outlined the issues and the alternative courses of action, and the President requested comments and recommendations from each NSC member. In addition to arguing for his own favored course of action, each NSC member had the opportunity to disprove the arguments of the other members with whom he did not agree.[54] Nixon encouraged a "free give and take discussion" at NSC meeting, because he wished to hear "all" points of view rather than a "consensus recommendation."[55]

A former NSC staff member, Helmut Sonnenfeldt, explains that the roles of the NSC meetings were mainly to "keep the President's options open" without allowing any officials to formulate a majority position, so that the President would not have

---

number of important issues of strategic arms limitation, such as Soviet strategic capabilities. The Vietnam Special Studies Group (VSSG) examined the factors which would determine the course of Vietnamization.

51   The WSAG consisted of the Review Group (later the Senior Review Group), enlarged by additional military and intelligence specialists.

52   Richard Solomon, "The Nixon Administration National Security Council," p. 34, NSCP-OHR.

53   Halperin to Kissinger, "NSC Procedures," June 23, 1969, pp. 3–4, NSC, Vol. III, 6/1/69–12/31/69 [2of2], Box H-300, NSCIF, NPMS, NA.

54   History of the NSC (n.d.), p. 5, NSC-HF, Box H – 314 [1 of 2], NSCIF, NPMS, NA.

55   NSC Meeting, January 21, 1969, Box H-300, NSC Organization [2 of 3], NSCIF, NPMS, NA.

to overrule other officials.⁵⁶ Nixon and Kissinger were also "very careful not to show their cards" in the meeting.⁵⁷ Thus, the President would "never decide at the meeting."⁵⁸ Moreover, Nixon and Kissinger were sensitive to the dangers of leakage. For example, during the first NSC meeting on January 21, 1969, President Nixon emphasized the importance of maintaining "the strictest security" with respect to the deliberation of the NSC and directed its members to inform their subordinates that "press leaks must be avoided."⁵⁹

After each NSC meeting, the NSC staff reviewed the records of it and presented their views and suggestions for a "follow-up" consideration by Nixon and Kissinger.⁶⁰ Kissinger summarized the main issues of the staff recommendations as well as his views in a memorandum to the President. After his private talks with Kissinger, the President made his final decision. At this stage, the NSC staff prepared a National Security Decision Memoranda (NSDM) to "report" the contents of the Presidential decision to the departments and agencies.⁶¹ In response to NSDMs, the Under Secretaries Committee (USC), chaired by the Deputy Secretary of State, with representation at the Deputy or Under Secretary level, developed operational plans and recommendations to implement policy decisions.⁶²

In essence, three levels of meetings in the new NSC system emerged: 1) State-chaired interdepartmental working group meetings at the Assistant Secretary level; 2) Kissinger-chaired meetings (where the basic decisions were essentially either made or prepared for the President); and 3) the NSC meetings. As Lord points out, the "crucial" factor in the Nixon-Kissinger NSC system was that many of the sub-committees were chaired by Kissinger or his staff, which Kissinger himself was "very conscious about."⁶³ Besides, reflecting Nixon's personal reluctance to settle disagreements directly with Cabinet members and heads of departments and agencies, the new NSC system came to rely heavily on "memoranda rather than face-to-face meetings."⁶⁴ In this new NSC system, the President became almost inaccessible or even isolated from the head of each department and agency. It was only Kissinger who had full access to the President, and thereby the influence of both Secretary of State Rogers and the State Department were decreased with regard to foreign policy decision-making.

---

56   Helmut Sonnenfeldt (senior NSC staff member on Soviet affairs, 1969–1974), "The Nixon Administration National Security Council," p. 33, NSCP-OHR.
57   Michael Guhin (NSC staff member, 1969–1974), "The Nixon Administration National Security Council," p. 33, NSCP-OHR.
58   Lord, "The Nixon Administration National Security Council," p. 33, NSCP-OHR.
59   NSC Meeting, January 21, 1969, Box H-300, NSC Organization [2 of 3], NSCIF, NPMS, NA.
60   Lord, "The Nixon Administration National Security Council," p. 33, NSCP-OHR.
61   NSDM1, "Establishment of NSC Decision and Study Memoranda Series," January 20, 1969, p. 1, NSDMs, Box 363, SF, NSCF, NPMS, NA.
62   History of the NSC (n.d.), p. 3, NSC-HF, Box H-314 [1 of 2], NSCIF, NPMS, NA.
63   Lord, "The Nixon Administration National Security Council," p. 7, p. 32, NSCP-OHR.
64   Kissinger, *Years of Renewal*, p. 68.

3. Other Key Players in the New China Policy

3.1 NSC staff

3.1.1 NSC staff procedures

Kissinger, as the executive secretary of the National Security Council staff, outlined the problems and options and managed the day-to-day policy process. In December 1968, General Goodpaster produced the outline of new NSC staff procedures, stressing the importance of its supporting role for the President's consideration of "broad, far-reaching conceptions of the central importance in guiding policy and operations."[65] The President would need a strong NSC staff that could present him with clear-cut alternatives, explain to him the implications of choosing between alternatives, and help him to articulate his chosen policies. Goodpaster suggested that the NSC staff should also prepare for, conduct, and take further action on the meetings, and to manage the NSC supporting structure.[66] Hence, during the transition period, Kissinger sought to recruit the best available young experts from the State Department, the Defense Department, the intelligence community, and academia.[67] The newly emerged National Security Council Staff was divided into three main groups, plus the military assistant:[68]

- Assistant for Program – three or four Assistants, such as Morton Halperin (1969), and Anthony Lake (1969–1970), integrating planning and operations by bringing a long-range (five-year) perspective to current operations.
- Operations Staff – approximately five senior staff members, each senior staff member responsible for certain geographic regions and functional activities (such as East Asia, Europe, Near East, South Asia, Latin America, Africa). Its main roles were to follow day-to-day matters, attend inter-agency meetings, and bring to the attention of the National Security Adviser matters requiring Presidential attention. Its senior members on East Asia included: John Holdridge (1969–1973), Richard Smyser (Vietnam expert, 1970–1971 and 1973–1975), Richard Sneider (Japan expert, 1969), Richard Solomon (China expert, 1971–1976). Holdridge explains that the "geographical line" of the NSC staff was organized more or less "corresponding to the same bureau that would be in the Department of State."[69] In particular, Kissinger highly

---

65   Goodpaster to Kissinger, "Organization and Procedures for the Conduct of National Security Affairs," December 13, 1968, p. 4, HAK-ASF, Box 1, Transition, HAKOF, NSCF, NPMS, NA.

66   Ibid., p. 1.

67   Peter Rodman, Oral History Interview, July 22, and August 22, 1994, p. 50, Foreign Affairs Oral History Collection (FAOHC), Association for Diplomatic Studies and Training, Lauinger Library, Georgetown University; and Kissinger, *White House Years*, pp. 23–24.

68   A New NSC System, pp. 4–5, NSC, Vol. II, 4/1/69–5/30/69 [2 of 2], Box H-299, Memo from William Watts to Kissinger (via Lake/Haig), "Revised NSC Staff Arrangements," September 12, 1969, NSC System, Staff and Committees [2 of 3], Box H-301, NSCIF, NPMS, NA.

69   John Holdridge, Oral History Interview, July 20, 1995, p. 81, FAOHC.

valued Solomon's expert insight regarding the implications on Chinese public statements and private messages, and on China's domestic political situation.[70] Solomon assesses that Kissinger worked by "departmentalizing different people in separate organizational 'boxes'."[71]
- Planning Staff – approximately three senior staff members, such as Richard V. Allen (1969) and Winston Lord (1969–1973; also special assistant to Kissinger for China policy, 1970–1973), and five junior staff members, such as Peter Rodman (1969–1977). Its roles included: preparing NSC agenda papers on planning matters, producing necessary follow-up papers, supporting Assistants for Programs, participating in inter-agency planning studies, and providing alternative thinking to the National Security Adviser. Lord explains that: "Our job was also to help manage the paper flow, working with the relevant regional honcho or functional honcho on the staff."[72]
- The Military Assistant – helped the National Security Adviser in developing staff papers on military matters, including judgments on military questions, and in monitoring and assembling intelligence material. Colonel Alexander M. Haig Jr. (1969–1970; promoted to Deputy Assistant to the President for National Security Affairs, 1970–1973), and Lawrence S. Eagleburger (1969) were in the Office of the Assistant to the President for National Security Affairs.

Rodman recalls that Kissinger "wanted to have all this sort of diversity of opinion," and contrary to the usual image of him, Kissinger "liked to have debates" and "respected people who stood up to him."[73] Overall, the NSC staff had "coherence and competence."[74] It was "bureaucratically very complex and very personalized."[75] Kissinger "kept everything very tightly controlled inside the White House" and the NSC staff practically operated as a "separate State Department."[76]

3.1.2 Drafting of policy papers

Kissinger valued and benefited from the individual contributions of the NSC staff members. Sonnenfeldt comments that: "the quality of a paper drafted by one individual with a couple of assistants is bound to be better than a State Department internally negotiated document, or a Defense Department internally negotiated document."[77] As for actual drafting of policy studies, Holdridge recalls that Kissinger "would have three different groups working on a problem in the National Security Council, which might even include China. Not one of the members of those groups knew

---

70 Peter Rodman, interview with the author, October 21, 2003.
71 Richard Solomon, interview with the author, September 24, 2003.
72 Lord, interview with the author, October 15, 2003.
73 Rodman, Oral History Interview, July 22, and August 22, 1994, p. 51, FAOHC. Rodman states further that Kissinger's NSC staff was "surprisingly liberal, moderate, and intellectual," especially for a Nixon administration. Ibid.
74 Lord, interview with the author, October 15, 2003.
75 Solomon, interview with the author, September 24, 2003.
76 Ibid.
77 Sonnenfeldt, "The Nixon Administration National Security Council," pp. 25–26, NSCP-OHR.

that the others were working on the same problem."[78] Kissinger's style of operation in a sensitive negotiation was to have both the "substantive experts" from the NSC staff and one of his "special assistants" to be his private secretaries.[79] For example, Winston Lord was Kissinger's principal special assistant, and thus was very much involved in the formulation and implementation of the China initiative. Lord also kept notes of Kissinger's talks with Chinese officials. Peter Rodman was a junior special assistant, and there was a division of labor between Lord and Rodman.[80] In his own operational role in particular, Lord explains that "I was working as part of a team for a variety of issues. I was always paired with a Vietnam expert on Vietnam, a China expert on China, and a Russia expert on Russia. I was the only one who was involved in all these in addition to Kissinger himself."[81] Overall, the NSC staff's role included "setting up meetings where various agencies submitted their views. And NSC papers usually summarized those views, trying to present them fairly but also often presenting Kissinger's views on top. These were usually drafted either by the regional experts concerned or by people like myself or some combination."[82]

Kissinger took speeches "very seriously, demanding many drafts" from his NSC staff.[83] In particular, during the transition period, Kissinger proposed to Nixon an idea to produce a document that would serve as a "conceptual outline of the President's foreign policy, as a status report, and as an agenda for action."[84] Kissinger expected that the report would also "guide our bureaucracy and inform foreign governments about our thinking."[85] Nixon approved the proposal on January 30, 1969. Richard Allen recalls the drafting of Nixon's Foreign Policy Report to Congress (February 1970, February 1971, February 1972 and May 1973) as one of the "great exercises" for the NSC staff, which was in a sense a "challenge to long-range planning."[86] Rodman agrees that the drafting of the report "educated" the NSC staff, because Kissinger "spent a lot of time on it with his staff in shaping ... what should be our approach, what is the philosophy of our policy in this area, what are our real goals and interests."[87] Holdridge emphasizes the drafting of the first report of February 1970 as the "turning point" because it was drafted "entirely inside" the Kissinger-NSC staff without any "clearances" or "input" from the State Department.[88] After the NSC staff issued the first report in late 1969, President Nixon called all of the

---

78 John Holdridge, Oral History Interview in *A China Reader*, Vol. II, p. 31, January 1995, FAOHC.
79 Rodman, Oral History Interview, July 22, and August 22, 1994, p. 9, FAOHC.
80 Rodman, interview with the author, October 21, 2003.
81 Lord, interview with the author, October 15, 2003.
82 Ibid.
83 Ibid.
84 Kissinger, *White House Years*, p. 158.
85 Ibid. However, Kissinger complains that although changes in US attitude toward China were "foreshadowed" in the reports, the media covered only the section on Vietnam. Ibid., p. 159.
86 Richard V. Allen, "The Roles of the National Security Adviser," p. 25, and p. 35, NSCP-OHR, October 25, 1999.
87 Rodman, Oral History Interview, July 22, and August 22, 1994, p. 47, FAOHC.
88 Holdridge, Oral History Interview, July 20, 1995, p. 79, FAOHC.

NSC staff members in the Cabinet Room, and expressed his personal distrust of Career Foreign Service officials that: "If the State Department has had a new idea in the last 25 years, it is not known to me."[89] Nixon thus made it very clear that his administration's foreign policy would be "run" by the NSC: "we were to keep our distance from State and not in fact do anything more than to ask for input, but certainly not for advice."[90]

3.1.3 The Kissinger-NSC staff relations

Within the White House, Kissinger himself was "an object of considerable suspicion throughout those early months," because he was originally a "Rockefeller man."[91] In addition, most of the newly recruited members of NSC staff Kissinger had appointed turned out to be Democrats, which greatly increased the suspicion of the White House political staff.[92] Thus, as Holdridge recalls, members of the NSC staff were 'always treated and sneered at as "the intellectuals" by the rest of the White House staff.'[93] On the other hand, Kissinger was "quite deliberately downgrading the staff in order to upgrade himself."[94] Moreover, in trying to avoid antagonizing other departments and also to prevent leaks, Kissinger ordered the NSC staff not to have contacts with outsiders, especially the press. In reality, however, Solomon reveals that he "developed a dialogue with some press people," particularly on the Asia issues, because what Kissinger was telling the NSC staff was usually very different from what he saw going on and he had to know the difference between Kissinger's "inside" game and his "outside" game in order to fulfill his roles.[95] Moreover, there were private communications that occurred outside of the official lines between the NSC and the CIA. Solomon emphasizes that Kissinger's excessive secrecy caused "compartmentalization of the policy process."[96] Kissinger could not even turn to the CIA for support in learning about senior Chinese leaders for his first trip to Beijing in July 1971. Thus, Solomon personally developed a covert "off-line" arrangement with CIA analysts to "draw on the intelligence community's expertise and grasp of history."[97]

---

89 Holdridge, Oral History Interview in *A China Reader*, Vol. II, p. 29, January 1995, FAOHC.
90 Holdridge, Oral History Interview, July 20, 1995, p. 79, FAOHC.
91 Richard Moose (Staff Secretary of the NSC, January–August 1969), "The Nixon Administration National Security Council," p. 12, NSCP-OHR. Kissinger was originally the chief foreign policy adviser to Nelson Rockefeller who competed with Nixon for the Republican presidential candidacy in 1968.
92 Lewis, "The Nixon Administration National Security Council," p. 11, NSCP-OHR.
93 Holdridge, Oral History Interview, July 20, 1995, p. 94, FAOHC.
94 Lewis, "The Nixon Administration National Security Council," p. 12, NSCP-OHR.
95 Solomon, "The Nixon Administration National Security Council," p. 47, NSCP-OHR.
96 Ibid. The US government had previously dealt with the Chinese Communist leaders during the 1940s in Chungking and Yenan, and therefore there were a number of documents on these contacts in the CIA files. However, as Solomon recalls, "no one was tasked to go look at this material, we never drew on our past experience." Ibid.
97 Ibid.

The NSC staff rarely saw the President because Kissinger gathered the information from his staff and did all the briefing of the President himself, even on subjects on which he was not necessarily an expert. Lord argues that Kissinger "did keep the staff from having access," and that NSC staff would attend meetings with foreign officials at times, however, no NSC staff members were allowed to be present "when he [Kissinger] was consulting with the President."[98] Lord also recalls that "When Nixon and Kissinger talked alone, he [Kissinger] would generally keep us informed."[99] Both foreign and US ambassadors tended to deal directly with the NSC, and Kissinger developed his own channels of communication with the ambassadors.[100] However, Kissinger "continued to mistreat and ignore most [US] ambassadors," although there were exceptions during the opening to China, especially Ambassador Walter Stoessel to Warsaw, Poland, and Ambassador Joseph Farland to Rawalpindi, Pakistan.[101] During the early months of the Nixon administration, diplomatic observers already began to speculate that Kissinger inevitably would be over-burdened in his new staff function. Kissinger himself was reported to have stated that "it may not be possible to handle both planning and coordination of operations in this job."[102]

At the beginning of the day, Kissinger did not necessarily give briefings to the President by himself, as Harry R. Haldeman (The White House Chief of Staff) or John Ehrlichman (Nixon's top domestic affairs adviser) was usually in the Oval Office. Kissinger had a "hard time" with their presence, because he was "not comfortable with it."[103] Very importantly, however, Rodman assesses that Haldeman did not "interfere in foreign policy," because he believed that Nixon was the "master" in foreign policy; Haldeman had "no claim" to know the foreign policy, and thus the most important substantive discussions were conducted between Nixon and Kissinger "just alone."[104] Haldeman also "backed up" Kissinger when there was a bureaucratic fight between the NSC and the State Department; Haldeman would sometimes ring up Secretary of State Rogers and say, "The President wants this."[105] Haldeman would

---

98   Lord, "The Nixon Administration National Security Council," p. 13, NSCP-OHR.
99   Lord, interview with the author, October 15, 2003.
100 Lord, "The Nixon Administration National Security Council," p. 59, NSCP-OHR.
101 Sonnenfeldt, "The Nixon Administration National Security Council," p. 56, NSCP-OHR.
102 *The Boston Globe*, January 30, 1969, in Box 95, Folder: Kissinger, Henry A., Elliot Richardson Papers, Manuscript Division, Library of Congress.
103 Moore and Sonnenfeldt, "The Nixon Administration National Security Council," p.14, NSCP-OHR. Philip Odeen (member of the NSC staff, 1971–1973) recalls that: 'when we'd be in a meeting and Haldeman would walk in, Henry would get "visibly nervous." ... It was different with Ehrlichman – Ehrlichman was less threatening. But Haldeman – everybody got nervous when Haldeman was around. He was, at least from my perspective, kind of a fierce guy. I would see Henry seemingly act differently when Haldeman was around.' Ibid., p. 13. Quotation marks in original. As for Haldeman's and Ehrlichman's involvement in the Watergate scandal, see, for example, Gerald S. Strober and Deborah Hart Strober, *Nixon: An Oral History of His Presidency* (New York: HarperCollins Publishers, 1994).
104 Rodman, Oral History Interview, July 22, and August 22, 1994, p. 16, FAOHC.
105 Ibid., p. 17. Kissinger recalls that: "Because Nixon's method of governing guaranteed incessant bureaucratic competition and disagreements, he was obliged to institute

play an intermediate role between Kissinger and Rogers on the China initiative after Kissinger's secret trip to Beijing in July 1971. Overall, Haldeman was a "totally loyal person who did things because of what the boss wanted." Haldeman was a "gate-keeper" of any access to the Oval Office because Nixon preferred interacting with a minimum number of people.[106]

There was "competition within Kissinger's sphere over who would be his deputy."[107] The White House staff, especially Haldeman and Ehrlichman did not want too many liberal academics on the NSC. The argument was that in order to "balance experience and perspective," a military person should be Kissinger's deputy.[108] Alexander M. Haig Jr. was thus appointed as the deputy, however in reality this was also to "keep an eye on Kissinger."[109] As the deputy to the National Security Adviser, Haig would advise Kissinger on questions involving military considerations and help to produce policy memoranda and other papers on foreign affairs to be placed before Nixon for his decision.[110] Haig was "very disciplined" in making the machinery work and dealing with the NSC staff, as Kissinger had less and less contact with them owing to his tight schedule. Haig was thus the "manager of the staff" and "master of the bureaucratic process" in the Nixon-Kissinger NSC system.[111]

Importantly, Haig knew "how to smooth the rough edges" between Kissinger and Secretary of Defense Melvin Laird.[112] Laird was a "more wily bureaucratic operator," in Kissinger's words, a "better guerrilla fighter" than senior officials in the State Department.[113] When it came to specific defense issues, Kissinger did not have the "competence to press hard" because he did not have the "depth of background or experience."[114] In particular, as for the pace of Vietnamization, which Laird himself defines as a program to "turn over the war in Vietnam to the South Vietnamese and give them the responsibility," there was a bureaucratic struggle between the NSC

---

ad hoc procedures for adjusting controversies. Sometimes he would ask Haldeman ... to settle the disputes he both fomented and resented." Kissinger, *Years of Renewal*, p. 69.

106   Ibid., pp. 17–18. As for the importance of a strong Chief of Staff, see Kegley and Wittkopf, *American Foreign Policy*, pp. 328–329.

107   Lord, interview with the author, October 15, 2003.

108   Solomon, Oral History Interview, September 13, 1996, p. 35, FAOHC. Goodpaster recalls that Kissinger asked him to call Alexander Haig, who was then serving at West Point, to serve as his military assistant in the new NSC staff. "The Nixon Administration National Security Council," p. 3, NSCP-OHR.

109   Ibid., p. 36.

110   Alexander M. Haig Jr. (with Maccarry Charles), *Inner Circles, How America Changed the World: A Memoir* (New York: Warner Books, 1992), pp. 190–191.

111   Rodman, Oral History Interview, July 22, and August 22, 1994, p. 23, FAOHC.

112   Ibid., p. 24.

113   Lord, "The Nixon Administration National Security Council," p. 8, NSCP-OHR. See also Isaacson, *Kissinger*, pp. 198–202. As for operational roles of the Defense Department, see Kegley and Wittkopf, *American Foreign Policy*, pp. 370–379.

114   Odeen, "The Nixon Administration National Security Council," p. 21, NSCP-OHR.

and the Defense Department.[115] Lord assesses that where Kissinger wanted on "the whole to go slower," Laird wanted to "speed it up."[116] To put it another way, while Laird, being a Congressman in the past, was familiar with the "congressional and domestic mood," Kissinger was more concerned with US capability to "maintain military balance" and "leverage" with the North Vietnamese.[117] Secretary of Defense Laird thus established direct "communications channels" between Kissinger's office and his own office regarding all official Department of Defense (DOD) elements which would be involved in NSC matters.[118] As a result, the Kissinger-Laird rivalry became a significant example where the new NSC system did not necessarily defeat bureaucratic politics.

Defense Department officials highly valued the intermediate role of Alexander Haig, Jr. between the DOD and the NSC. The "authoritative source" in the absence of Kissinger owing to his busy schedule was Colonel Haig who had "direct and continuing access" to Kissinger and the entire NSC staff. Haig was often able to "reflect the views of the President himself."[119]

Most importantly, Haig "had increasingly direct contact" with Nixon when Kissinger was away on trips, which made Kissinger "very sensitive."[120] Thus, there emerged a triangular dynamic between them: Kissinger sought to gain Haig's support and to co-opt him; Haig operated between Kissinger and Nixon, maintaining his good working relations with the President, and also working closely with Kissinger.[121] Overall, Haig presented himself as the President's man, an "enforcer," to make certain that the President's orders were followed.[122]

---

115   Melvin Laird, interview in CNN *Cold War, Episode 16: Détente*, Transcripts in National Security Archive (http://www.gwu.edu/~nsarchiv/coldwar/interviews/episode-16/laird1.html).

116   Lord, "The Nixon Administration National Security Council," p. 22, NSCP-OHR.

117   Ibid. Laird had his own information sources, such as the National Security Agency, learning that Kissinger often used the military's cable network. For example, to coordinate messages involving the secret opening to China, which was arranged with Pakistan as an intermediary, a secure channel was set up through the US Navy's attaché in Karachi. Secretary Laird and Navy Chief Admiral Elmo Zumwalt knew what was happening each step of the way, even if the CIA and the State Department did not. See Isaacson, *Kissinger*, p. 201; and Kissinger, *White House Years*, pp. 32–33.

118   Laird to Kissinger, "National Security Council, January 22, 1969, p. 1, and Kissinger to Laird, "National Security Council," January 25, 1969, Box H-300, NSC Organization [1 of 3], NSCIF, NPMS, NA.

119   Lemnitzer to Admiral Johnson, September 29, 1969, p. 1, Box H–300 NSC System, NSC Organization [1 of 3], NSCIF, NPMS, NA.

120   Lord, "The Nixon Administration National Security Council," p. 23, NSCP-OHR.

121   Solomon, Oral History Interview, September 13, 1996, p. 36, FAOHC.

122   Ibid.

3.2 The State Department

3.2.1 Secrecy in bureaucratic politics

As previously explained, one of the main reasons for the pursuit of strict secrecy by Nixon and Kissinger during the opening to China was their personal distrust of bureaucracy, especially the State Department.[123] For Secretary of State, Nixon appointed his long-term friend and colleague, former Attorney General of the Eisenhower administration, William P. Rogers.[124] By taking advantage of Rogers' unfamiliarity with foreign affairs, Nixon intended to assure his control of foreign policy decision-making from the White House.[125] Kissinger, on the other hand, had uneasy relations with Rogers. Sonnenfeldt argues: "Henry wasn't exactly sure where he was going to fit in this close friendship and long-time association. I think it became a total surprise to Henry that Nixon didn't want Rogers to play a major role, except publicly."[126] However, Secretary Rogers himself did not fight hard in the rivalry over the control of foreign policy, which resulted in the "demoralization of the State Department and its expertise."[127] Lord confirms that Kissinger "mistreated Rogers, although a lot of this was President Nixon's fault, not his. But he would admit he didn't resist the Nixon approach."[128] Whiting assesses that the State Department was "ready to serve," however, they had no access and were consequently "under-used."[129] Whiting emphasizes that it was "not a mobilization of expertise and knowledge" which one expects in a government.[130]

In reality, however, Nixon and Kissinger still needed help from the State Department. Levin points out that: "their work was the mortar and the bricks of what happened when the grand policy designs actually took form. They heavily influenced policymaking by the information and analysis they provided, through they had little opportunity for formal policy advocacy."[131] On China policy, Nixon and Kissinger "benefited from all the thinking in the administration."[132] In particular, Nixon and Kissinger "used the interagency process" to obtain what they thought was the "best

---

123 During his visit to China, Nixon stated to Zhou that: "our State Department leaks like a sieve. Also within our bureaucracy there is great opposition to some of the positions I have taken." Memcon, February 22, 1972, p. 3, CHINA – President's Talks with Mao and Chou En-lai February 1972, Country Files-Far East, NSCF, NPMS, NA.

124 Isaacson, *Kissinger*, p. 197; and Kissinger, *White House Years*, pp. 26–32.

125 Marshall Green (Assistant Secretary of State for East Asia and the Pacific, 1969–1973), Oral history interview, March 2 and 17, 1995, pp. 10–11, FAOHC.

126 Sonnenfeldt, "The Nixon Administration National Security Council," p. 25, NSCP-OHR.

127 Rodman, Oral History Interview, July 22, and August 22, 1994, p. 12, FAOHC. As for the general rivalry between the Secretary of State and the National Security Adviser, see Kegley and Wittkopf, *American Foreign Policy*, pp. 333–334.

128 Lord, "The Nixon Administration National Security Council," p. 44, NSCP-OHR.

129 Allen S. Whiting, interview with the author, October 19, 2003.

130 Ibid.

131 Herbert Levin (NSC staff member for East Asian affairs, 1970–1971), "China Policy and the National Security Council," p. 4, NSCP-OHR, November 4, 1999.

132 Rodman, interview with the author, October 21, 2003.

of the technical knowledge" of the bureaucracy, especially the State Department.[133] Thus, there was "a whole menu of steps" that was developed, namely a series of unilateral public signals, which the United States could send toward China, such as opening up trade and lifting travel restrictions.[134] Thereafter, Nixon and Kissinger would form the strategy themselves, deciding "how to play it" on their own initiative and schedule.[135] Nixon and Kissinger "did everything to minimize the risk of leak by dealing only with a very few officials," and therefore, most of the early cable communication abut engaging China went through CIA or Navy channels rather than the State Department's regular channels.[136]

3.2.2 Senior State Department officials

As Lord reassesses, despite their pursuit of secrecy, Nixon and Kissinger still could have brought in a few key State Department officials on the China policy and "sworn them to secrecy and used their expertise and had more bureaucratic support."[137] During the early months of the new administration, Kissinger still sought to smooth the relations between the NSC and the State Department and held regular meetings with Under Secretary of State Elliot Richardson (January 1969–June 1970), who chaired the Undersecretaries' Committee. Kissinger did not have intellectual uncertainties about "being overrun by the Foreign Service," as Rodman recalls, "[H]e knew that he could provide intellectual leadership; he found that they provided a lot of expertise."[138]

Under Secretary of State for Political Affairs U. Alex Johnson (February 1969–February 1973) developed a close working relationship with Under Secretary of State Richardson and also with Secretary of State Rogers.[139] Johnson also acted as an intermediary between the White House and the State Department. In particular, Johnson, a former US Ambassador to Japan, kept emphasizing the importance of coordination between the US and its major allies in Asia, especially Japan and the Republic of China (ROC) regarding the linkage between their respective sensitivities to possible US withdrawal from Asia in the post-Vietnam era and US moves toward the People's Republic of China (PRC).

Assistant Secretary of State for East Asian and Pacific Affairs Marshall Green (May 1969–May 1973) was a "very astute" career Foreign Service Officer who got along very well with both Secretary of State Rogers and Congress.[140] Green chaired

---

133 Rodman, Oral History Interview, July 22, and August 22, 1994, p. 13, FAOHC. Kissinger admits in his third memoirs that: "The interdepartmental process produced option papers from among which Nixon and I were able to select the course of action most compatible with our overall strategy without necessarily informing the authors of the decision until we had achieved a diplomatic breakthrough." Kissinger, *Years of Renewal*, p. 83.
134 Ibid.
135 Ibid.
136 Solomon, interview with the author, September 24, 2003.
137 Lord, "The Nixon Administration National Security Council," p. 44, NSCP-OHR.
138 Rodman, Oral History Interview, July 22, and August 22, 1994, p. 14, FAOHC.
139 U. Alexis Johnson, *The Right Hands of Power* (Englewood Cliffs, New Jersey: Prentice-Hall, 1984), pp. 516–517.
140 Arthur W. Hummel Jr., Oral History Interview, 1994, pp. 134–135, FAOHC.

an Interdepartmental Group: East Asian and Pacific Affairs (IG/EA&P/NSC-10), including the "China Working Group," which performed the following functions:

- discussion and decision on interdepartmental issues which could be settled at the Assistant Secretary level, including issues arising out of implementation of NSC decisions;
- preparation of policy papers for consideration by the NSC;
- preparation of contingency papers on potential crisis areas for review by the NSC.[141]

In reality, however, Green did not get along well with Kissinger, and remained very "bitter" about Kissinger's handling of East Asian issues and deliberate undermining of the roles of the State Department in the opening to China.[142] Green criticizes that: "Kissinger had lots of gaps in his knowledge of the world," and that "his failure to draw upon the expertise of people who had spent their lives working on East Asia was a great mistake on his part."[143] Green, who was the State Department's main counterpart toward Kissinger on East Asia, especially suffered from the secrecy surrounding the China initiative. Green recalls that:

When you are 'cut out' of things, you begin to lose confidence in yourself. ... Kissinger knew that you didn't have the complete picture, and therefore he tended to discredit your views accordingly. It ended up by nobody really knowing what the other person knew or didn't know. ... We had a wonderful opportunity but, of course, a lot of that was not properly used. We could have done much better.[144]

Despite his unpleasant experiences with Kissinger, Green continued to remain loyal to President Nixon, whom he greatly admired for his knowledge and understanding of foreign affairs. During the early months of the new administration in 1969, Green held some significant conversations with Nixon regarding possible options and steps of opening a new dialogue with China.[145] Overall, despite the exclusion from the direct decision making-process, the State Department's Bureau of East Asian and Pacific played a crucial role in the National Security Study Memorandum (NSSM) process.

3.2.3 Intelligence sources

The Bureau of Intelligence and Research (INR) is the State Department's representative in the US intelligence community.[146] The INR is the unit through which the State Department makes its input into various interagency committees that

---

141 Interdepartmental Group: East Asian and Pacific Affairs (IG/EA&P/NSC-10), Chartered by NSDM 2 (January 20, 1969), NSC Organization [2 of 3], Box H-300, NSCIF, NPMS, NA.
142 Nancy Bernkopf Tucker, interview with the author, October 1, 2003.
143 Green, Oral History Interview, March 2 and 17, 1995, p. 56, FAOHC.
144 Ibid. Quotation marks in original.
145 The main issues in their talks are examined in Chapters 3 and 4.
146 Bureau of Intelligence and Research, US Department of State (http://www.state.gov/s/inr//); United States Intelligence Community, Department of State: Bureau of

seek to guide intelligence operations. The INR draws on multiple intelligence source input from other agencies and also from overseas posts and provides value-added independent analysis of events to the Department's senior officials. In particular, its staff drafts very insightful intelligence analyses, such as the "Intelligence Note" and the "Research Study," which are among the most highly valued within the government.

In addition to US embassies abroad, the State Department had an intelligence base in the Consulate General in Hong Kong, which was a very vital place for China watchers.[147] A former State Department official and China watcher, Herbert Horowitz, recalls that: "people who came out of China as refugees or escapees would come to Hong Kong, and people who were going into China for business or trade would enter via Hong Kong and come out via Hong Kong."[148] Thus, Hong Kong was essentially a "gateway in and out of China" where China watchers obtained information from many different parts of Mainland China.[149] As for China's American policy, a former Deputy Chief of Station in the US Consulate General in Hong Kong, James Lilley, explains that: "we were dealing with the Chinese who were passing us messages from the Chinese Communists. They were telling us that they were reasonable and were coming out of this very bad experience during the Cultural Revolution. They said that they wanted to open up to the United States. ... We reported this in some detail to Washington."[150]

3.2.4 The State Department-NSC staff relations
There was a question of rivalry between the NSC staff and the State Department. As early as January 1969, there was already media coverage on Nixon's centralization of foreign policy decision-making within the White House. On January 29, President Nixon called upon the State Department to re-affirm his confidence in the nation's foreign policy establishment. Nixon denied the media's speculation that Kissinger and his NSC staff began to seize authority from Secretary Rogers.[151] Although Nixon's exact plans for the new NSC had not yet been made public (until the publication of Nixon's first Foreign Policy Report to Congress in February 1970), and Kissinger's

---

Intelligence and Research (http://www.intelligence.gov/1-members_state.shtml); and Kegley and Wittkopf, *American Foreign Policy*, p. 384.
    147   Kreisberg, Oral History Interview, p. 4, in *A China Reader*, Vol. III, January 1995, FAOHC.
    148   Herbert Horowitz (China watching, American Consulate General Hong Kong, 1965–1969), Oral History Interview, p. 1, in *A China Reader*, Vol. III, January 1995, FAOHC.
    149   Ibid.
    150   James R. Lilley, Oral History Interview, 1996, pp. 54–55, FAOHC. The following chapters examine cables and intelligence studies from the US Consulate General in Hong Kong.
    151   Crocker Snow Jr., "Nixon Denies Kissinger To Dictate Foreign Policy," *The Boston Globe*, January 30, 1969, in Box 95, Folder: Kissinger, Henry A., Elliot Richardson Papers, Manuscript Division, Library of Congress.

staff kept silent about its rules and procedures, it was widely speculated that the NSC had been "re-vitalized."[152]

Kissinger initially requested that the State Department conduct a number of policy studies, and thus State Department officials could express their views. However, after a while, the State Department officials became cynical because they felt that they were just doing a "make-work," and their views were not being taken seriously.[153] Without having a strong influence of its own, the State Department's bureaucracy "often would look for the NSC to take the lead on an issue in order to bring the other agencies into a workable sort of arena."[154]

In reality, as Solomon points out, most regional experts in the NSC staff were originally recruited from the State Department, and thus still kept "covert dealings" with their former colleagues "without telling Kissinger."[155] Holdridge emphasizes that: "Those of us who were on detail from the State Department had to be very cautious. We tried to be as open as we possibly could, to keep in good, personal contact with Marshall Green, [U.] Alexis Johnson."[156] Levin also confirms that Johnson and Green "never pressured me to do anything or tell them anything when I was on the NSC staff, but we did meet privately."[157]

3.2.5 The question of geopolitical perspective

There was a significant difference of geopolitical perspective between the White House and the State Department. In the first place, the State Department had a "weak organizational base," and that it was "very hard to get the State geopolitical view into a NSSM."[158] The State Department was also "much more anxious to try to keep some control of the regional issues," and it never fought nearly as hard on the "functional" issues.[159] Hence, there was a diversity of views on China within the State Department.

First, as Lord emphasizes, some officials in the State Department initially insisted that the United States would "alienate the Russians" if it "opened up with the Chinese."[160] The so-called "Slavophile" opinion group, especially Ambassadors Charles Bohlen and Lyewellyn Thompson, both specialists on the Soviet Union, claimed that Moscow was very suspicious of a Washington-Beijing "collusion," and therefore any effort to improve US relations with China would cause serious trouble

---

152   Ibid.
153   Solomon, interview with the author, September 24, 2003.
154   Samuel Lewis (career Foreign Service Officer, NSC staff aide for Latin America, 1968–1969), "The Nixon Administration National Security Council," p. 37, NSCP-OHR.
155   Solomon, interview with the author, September 24, 2003.
156   Holdridge, Oral History Interview in *A China Reader*, Vol. II, pp. 29–30, January 1995, FAOHC.
157   Herbert Levin (member of the NSC staff for East Asian affairs, 1970–1971), "China Policy and the National Security Council," p. 9, NSCP-OHR.
158   Lewis, "The Nixon Administration National Security Council," p. 20, NSCP-OHR.
159   Ibid., p. 32.
160   Lord, "The Nixon Administration National Security Council," p. 45, NSCP-OHR.

for the promotion of Soviet-American relations.[161] Sonnenfeldt recalls that: "until the Nixon administration, the State Department insisted on briefing the Soviets on every conversation that Alex Johnson and others had with the Chinese in Prague and Warsaw. ... Thompson religiously called Dobrynin [Anatoly Dobrynin, Soviet Ambassador to the United States] in and gave him a full briefing. The suggestion that we might have a relationship with the Chinese without reassuring or telling the Soviets would not have occurred to anybody in the State Department."[162]

Regarding a positive course for the new China policy, the so-called "Sinophile group" had long favored a "broad policy review."[163] Thomson stresses the importance of "a decade-old 'laundry list' of possible US initiatives towards China and a great deal of internal paper to support them."[164] For the public, the US government continued to express its support for the Republic of China on Taiwan. Rodman argues that China experts in the government insisted that: "Taiwan was such an overwhelming problem, and we could never have contact with China without sacrificing Taiwan."[165] Simultaneously, within the Bureau of East Asian and Pacific Affairs, there were a number of policy study papers that had been written on the recognition of Beijing. As a former Taiwan Desk officer, Thomas P. Shoesmith points out, there was increasing pressure to bring the People's Republic of China into the United Nations, and thus the State officials' main concern was to try to find a way to "retain the Republic of China in the General Assembly."[166] Thus, having assessed that the so-called "China Lobby" in Congress by the late 1960s was "no longer a significant factor," and that Taipei would be "increasingly isolated, diplomatically and internationally," State Department officials examined possibilities of pursuing "a two-China policy." In military-security terms, as Shoesmith stresses, the Republic of China was "very cooperative in allowing us to use their bases in support of our activities in Vietnam."[167] Nevertheless, even the US Embassy in Taipei came to share

---

161 Kissinger, *Diplomacy*, p. 720. After a meeting with Thompson and Bohlen in the summer of 1969, Nixon mocked "the incorrigible softheadedness" of the Foreign Service. The Soviet desk was not entirely unitary within the State Department. Finally, it was presidential authority that excluded the Sovietologists. Kissinger, *White House Years*, p. 182.

162 Sonnenfeldt, "The Nixon Administration National Security Council," p. 17, NSCP-OHR. Dobrynin recalls that Llewellyn Thompson told him confidentially in mid-June 1971 that there were two camps of views within the American leadership: one side leaned toward giving priority to agreements with the Soviet Union; and other view gave precedence to an opening to China, believing that China could help end the Vietnam war soon, partly by "bringing pressures to bear upon the Soviet Union." Anatoly Dobrynin, *In Confidence: Moscow's Ambassador to America's Six Cold War Presidents (1962–1986)* (New York: Times Books, A Division of Random House, Inc, 1995), p. 224.

163 A. Doak Barnett, *China and the Major Powers in East Asia* (Washington DC: The Brookings Institution, 1977), p. 381; Kissinger, *White House Years*, p. 165, p. 182; and Isaacson, *Kissinger*, p. 335.

164 James C. Thomson Jr. "On the Making of US China Policy, 1961–1969: A Study in Bureaucratic Politics," *China Quarterly* (April/June) 1972, p. 243.

165 Rodman, interview with the author, October 21, 2004.

166 Thomas P. Shoesmith (Taiwan Desk, Department of State, 1966–1971), Oral History Interview, p. 1, in *A China Reader*, Vol. III, January 1995, FAOHC.

167 Ibid., pp. 2–3.

a prevailing view within the State Department that "sooner or later relations [with China] should be normalized."[168]

From Kissinger's perspective, however, those within the State Department who supported the opening towards China appeared to be concentrated on "trade and cultural exchanges" with the Chinese, which was "secondary" compared to the "geopolitics and the Russian and Vietnamese dimensions."[169] As for the Soviet dimension, namely the US policy towards the Sino-Soviet rift, Paul Kreisberg, the former director of the Office of Asian Communist Affairs (ACA), recalls that one of the key differences between the State Department and the NSC was that while the State Department saw the normalization with China as being "beneficial to us in an Asian context," the NSC, especially Kissinger saw it in "Soviet terms" and regarded the Asian context as "minor."[170] Overall, Kreisberg reassesses: "We saw the Soviet Union as one factor, but not the driving one. He [Kissinger], obviously, saw it as the driving one."[171] In other words, while the State Department considered the restoration of Asian regional stability to be a priority in US policy toward China, Kissinger believed that the principal purpose of the US opening to China was to explore US leverage in Sino-Soviet rivalry.

As for the Vietnam dimension, the Kissinger NSC expected that the opening to China would influence North Vietnam to end the war. Lord explains that: "If we were dealing with both of Hanoi's patrons, Beijing and Moscow, it would help to isolate them and put pressure on them to be more reasonable at the negotiating table."[172] Kissinger interprets that Nixon regarded the opening toward China as "a somewhat great opportunity" in order to "squeeze" the Soviet Union "into short-term help on Vietnam."[173] Although the subject never came up in any official instructions, Nixon may also have thought that: "if we were able to improve relations with China, we would indirectly diminish the Chinese interest in supporting the Vietnamese."[174]

On the other hand, the State Department was principally concerned about reassuring the Chinese in the Warsaw ambassadorial talks that the US military operation in Indochina was "not designed to threaten China."[175] Thus, the State Department underestimated the degree of China's support for North Vietnam. Kreisberg explains that: "most of us were surprised as we found out to what degree the Chinese had engaged themselves. … we all saw the Vietnam-China issue as one

---

168 James Klemstine (Economic Officer, American Embassy, Taipei, Taiwan, 1970–1973), Oral History Interview, p. 2, in *A China Reader*, Vol. III, January 1995, FAOHC.

169 Lord, "The Nixon Administration National Security Council," p. 45, NSCP-OHR.

170 Paul Kreisberg (Director, Office of Asian Communist Affairs, Policy Planning, Department of State), 1965–81, Oral History Interview, p. 8, in *A China Reader*, Vol. III, January 1995, FAOHC.

171 Ibid.

172 Lord, interview with the author, October 15, 2003.

173 Kissinger, *White House Years*, p. 164.

174 Kreisberg, Oral History Interview, p. 11, in *A China Reader*, Vol. III, January 1995, FAOHC.

175 Ibid., p. 13.

that was, essentially, peripheral."[176] The State Department perceived the Beijing-Hanoi relations in regional security term. Kreisberg recalls that: "most of us at the EA Bureau level saw the Chinese, at most, as wanting to use the Vietnam War as a lever to weaken the United States, but not to expand the war and not to risk war with us. And when we talked about it in Warsaw, they never wanted to say very much about it other than to support the Vietnamese."[177]

In summary, the re-vitalization of the NSC system was much more systematic and complex than was previously estimated in the existing literature. The NSSMs and NSDMs were planned to provide a broad range of policy alternatives and perspectives. The fundamental source of Kissinger's power was his control of the flow of policy study papers by chairing the key subcommittees, such as the Review Group and the Washington Special Action Group.

On the other hand, the State Department lost its chairmanship of key committees for policy planning. However, it still remained the principal provider of ideas and recommendations in the NSSM process. The State Department obtained information from a number of sources, such as US embassies, foreign officials, and journalists and conducted a day-to-day analysis of change and development in Chinese foreign policy. Moreover, despite Kissinger's pursuit of strict secrecy, State Department officials and the NSC staff members maintained informal communication to exchange views and develop policy studies.

The NSC meeting became a formal occasion for departments and agencies to present their respective views and issues rather than acting as a decision-making body. Nixon's preference to avoid face-to-face meeting enhanced the development of communication by memoranda between the Oval Office and other senior officials in his administration. The President, accompanied by Kissinger, maintained the authority for making the final decision in a highly confidential way. Together, Nixon and Kissinger would pursue strict secrecy during the US opening to China. It was on the basis of this presidential initiative and highly centralized foreign policy decision-making machinery that the US rapprochement with China would evolve as demonstrated in the following chapters.

---

176   Ibid. The Chinese continued to provide aircraft gunners and logistics personnel in North Vietnam. See Foot, *The Practice of Power*, p. 286; and Chen Jian, "China's Involvement in the Vietnam War, 1964–1969," *China Quarterly*, 142 (June 1995), pp. 357–387.

177   Ibid.

PART II
The Evolution of the Rapproachement Policy

Chapter 3

The Development of Policy Options from January to July 1969

The first chapter of Part II explores the evolution of a new China policy during the first half of 1969. First, it examines President Nixon's initiatives from January to March, 1969. Nixon was quick to explore US policy toward China both as an NSC directive and as a central diplomatic issue in his talks with French President De Gaulle, while Kissinger remained skeptical of a possible new China initiative. Next, this chapter assesses the implications of the outbreak of the Sino-Soviet border clashes in March 1969. Despite his frequent emphasis on the importance of the event, at this earlier political stage, Kissinger still remained unconvinced of the seriousness of the Sino-Soviet differences. Finally, it conducts a detailed analysis of the policy option studies, including the State Department's recommendations and the inter-departmental studies, namely the National Security Study Memorandums (NSSMs). This book interprets the initial development of US policy toward China as a much more complex and dynamic political process than previously considered in the existing literature, on the basis of a number of policy option studies within the administration.[1]

1. First Development

1.1 Inaugural address

In his Inaugural address on January 20, 1969, President Nixon emphasized the entry of world politics into an "era of negotiation" after a long period of confrontation: "Let all nations know that during this Administration our lines of communication will be open. We seek an open world – open to ideas, open to the exchange of goods

---

1 "US-China Policy 1969–1972," Far East, Box 86, Countries Files (CF), HAK Office Files (HAKOF), National Security Council Files (NSCF), Nixon Presidential Materials Staff (NPMS), National Archives (NA). The date and issue of internal studies, policy statements, and public steps in the following analysis are based on a detailed chronological survey of this document. Media sources, such as *The New York Times* and *The Washington Post* are also used where appropriate. Finally, there remains the so-called "black-box," namely private exchanges between Nixon and Kissinger. Allen Whiting, interview with the author, October 19, 2003. This study thus examines the exchange of memoranda between Nixon and Kissinger as well as the records of their conversations.

and people, a world in which no people, great or small, will live in angry isolation."² The use of the phrase "angry isolation" was adopted from his message in the October 1967 *Foreign Affairs* article. In his memoirs, Nixon emphasized that he had intended to send a diplomatic signal toward Beijing.³

Nixon took the drafting of presidential addresses very seriously, reviewing the drafts prepared by the NSC staff and adding phrases reflecting his own thoughts. For his inaugural address, Nixon approved of the inclusion of some statements to the effect that the new administration believed in "open lines of communication," which Kissinger intended "toward Moscow."⁴ Kissinger recommended to Nixon that the overall implication in the inaugural address should be to present a new message of "sober, precise, methodical, and un-dramatic progress."⁵ On January 21, 1969, however, the New China News Agency strongly denounced Nixon as the "puppet" of the "monopoly bourgeois clique" attempting to implement the "vicious ambition of US imperialism to continue to carry out aggression and expansion in the world."⁶ *Renmin ribao* (People's Daily) and *Hongqi* (The Red Flag) also jointly published an editorial essay characterizing Nixon's address as nothing but "a confession in an impasse," which demonstrated that "the US imperialists ... are beset with profound crises both at home and abroad."⁷

---

2 For Immediate Release, Office of the White House Press Secretary, The White House, "Inaugural Address of President Richard M. Nixon" The Capitol, January 20, 1969, p. 5, HAK Administrative and Staff Files, Box 1, Transition, November 1968–January 1969, HAKOF, NSCF, NPMS, NA. Nixon reviewed his predecessors' inaugural addresses, especially that of Kennedy's.

3 Richard M. Nixon, *RN* (New York: Grosset & Dunlap, 1978), p. 545.

4 Kissinger to Nixon, January 8, 1969, Transition, November 1968–January 1969, HAK Administrative and Staff Files (HAK-ASF), Box 1, HAKOF, NSCF, NPMS, NA. Kissinger thus reminded Nixon that he would pass this implication to his "Soviet contact" on January 17. Ibid.

5 Kissinger to Nixon, "Proposed Foreign Policy Section of Your Inaugural Address, January 14, 1969, p. 2, HAK-ASF, Box 1, HAKOF, NSCF, NPMS, NA.

6 Chen Jian, *Mao's China and the Cold War* (Chapel Hill, NC: University of North Carolina Press, 2001), p. 238; Gong Li, "Chinese Decision Making and Thawing of US-China Relations," p. 333, in Robert Ross and Jiang Changbin (eds), *Re-examining the Cold War: US-China Diplomacy, 1954–1973* (Cambridge, Massachusetts, and London: Harvard University Press, 2001). Major newspapers all over China also reprinted Nixon's address, which was unprecedented in the history of the People's Republic. It was Mao Zedong who personally ordered the publication of Nixon's address. Ibid. In his memoirs, however, Nixon stated only that the Chinese "ignored the low-level signals" which the United States sent during 1969 and that it was not until 1970 that the US "began a serious approach" to open dialogue with China. Nixon, *RN*, p. 545. The Nixon memoirs thus failed to explore the administration's early efforts, including the NSC meetings on China policy as well as the State Department's attempt to resume the Warsaw ambassadorial talks, which this book examines in the present and following chapters.

7 Ibid.

1.2 Nixon's memorandum to Kissinger and the directive of NSSM 14

During early months, Nixon's public statements still included two contradictory elements. On January 27, 1969, in his first press conference at the White House, President Nixon stated that it was up to the Chinese representatives at the forthcoming Warsaw meeting on February 20 to clarify "whether any changes of attitude on their part on major substantive issued may have occurred."[8] In addition, Nixon also reiterated that the United States would "continue to oppose Communist China's admission to the United Nations."[9]

On February 1, 1969, Nixon sent a confidential memorandum to Kissinger, directing that: 'I think we should give every encouragement to the attitude that this administration is "exploring possibilities of raprochement [sic] with the Chinese." This, of course, should be done privately and should under no circumstances get into the public prints from this direction.'[10] In his memoirs, Kissinger explains that Nixon's memorandum did not ask him to do anything toward the Chinese; it only urged him to create the "impression" that the United States was *"exploring* a move toward China."[11]

In reality, however, Nixon's memorandum was much more important as the beginning of substantial policy studies on China during 1969. On February 5, Kissinger issued National Security Study Memorandum 14 (NSSC14) directing an inter-departmental study to examine:

- The current status of US relations with Communist China and the Republic of China;
- The nature of the Chinese Communist threat and intentions in Asia;
- The interaction between US policy and the policies of other major interested countries toward China;
- Alternative US approaches on China and their costs and risks.[12]

It was a general directive to review the US policy toward China. The directive requested that the paper should be forwarded to the NSC Review Group by March 10.

---

8   *The New York Times*, January 27, 1969.
9   Ibid.
10 Nixon to Kissinger, February 1, 1969, Quotation marks in original, White House Confidential Files (WHCF), White House Special Files (WHSF) Co (Countries), [Ex] Co 32 Chad, Republic of [1969–70] to [Gen] Co 34 China [1969–70], Box 17, NPMS, NA.
11 Henry A. Kissinger, *White House Years* (Boston: Little Brown, 1979), p. 169. Italic in original. On January 29, 1969, the National Security Study Memorandum 9 (NSSM9) entitled "Review of International Situation" already directed to examine the deepening strains in Sino-Soviet relations: "it is possible that each will become more active in seeking to prevent the other from aligning too closely with the US, and to use its own relations with the US as a means of checkmating the other's policies." National Security Memorandum 9 (NSSM 9) "Review of International Situation," January 23, 1969, and Department of Defense, Response to NSSM 9, Box 365, Subject Files (SF), NSCF, NPMS, NA.
12 National Security Study Memorandum 14 (NSSM14): United States China Policy, Box 365, SF, NSCF, NPMS, NA.

Because of the outbreak of Sino-Soviet border clashes in March, it would be submitted on April 30, 1969, and throughout 1969 there were crucial review meetings to discuss and improve the main issues and contents of NSSM 14, as the following sections and chapters examine. Winston Lord, a former NSC staff member and Kissinger's special assistant, emphasizes that Nixon was privately "very quick" to move to a new China initiative.[13] At this early stage, however, Kissinger still remained skeptical of both the necessity and possibility of opening toward China.[14]

On February 17, the first official meeting between President Nixon and the Soviet Ambassador to the US, Anatoly Dobrynin, was held. The pursuit of secrecy by Nixon and Kissinger was already emerging, and thus Secretary Rogers was not invited to attend. Nixon told Dobrynin that Kissinger would be his counterpart in a confidential communication channel. Calling for serious negotiations at various levels, Dobrynin delivered a letter from Moscow, which agreed to move forward on issues of the two superpowers' concern, such as Arms Control and Vietnam. Nixon in turn hinted that if US-Soviet relations did not develop well, he could explore opening to "others," which Dobrynin interpreted as China.[15]

1.3 The cancellation of the Warsaw Ambassadorial talks in February 1969

The immediate major issue between the United States and China was the resumption of the Warsaw Ambassadorial talks scheduled to take place on February 20, 1969. Although Kissinger's memoirs do not explain any particular issues, the preparation for the Warsaw talk provided an important opportunity for the new administration to re-examine the agenda for its China policy. As for possible Chinese motivations, both an airgram from the US Consulate General in Hong Kong and Kissinger's memorandum to President Nixon examined the following possibilities:

---

13 Winston Lord, interview with the author, October 15, 2003.

14 Alexander Haig recalls that Kissinger was very bewildered by Nixon's directive to reassess US China policy: "'Our Leader has taken leave of reality ... He thinks this is the moment to establish normal relations with Communist China. He has just ordered me to make this flight of fancy come true.' He grasped his head in his hands, 'China!'" Alexander Haig Jr. (with Charles McCarry), *Inner Circle: How America Changed the World, A Memoir* (New York: Warner Books, 1992), p. 257; Alexander M. Haig Jr., interview Transcript, *Nixon's China Game*, PBS American Experience (http://www.pbs.org/wgbh/amex/china/filmmore/reference/interview/haig01.html).

15 Memcon, Nixon, Kissinger, Dobrynin, and Toon, February 17, 1969, Subject Files (SF), Box 340, USSR, Memcons Dobrynin/President, NSCF, NPMS, NA. See also Richard Reeves, *President Nixon: Alone in the White House* (New York: Simon & Schuster, 2001), pp. 39–40; and Anatoly Dobrynin, *In Confidence: Moscow's Ambassador to America's Six Cold War Presidents (1962–1986)* (New York: Times Books, A Division of Random House, Inc, 1995), pp. 198–199. Neither Nixon nor Kissinger referred to this point in their respective memoirs. See Nixon, *RN*, pp. 369–370; and Kissinger, *White House Hears*, p. 143. On US-USSR SALT negotiations, see Walter Isaacson, *Kissinger: A Biography* (Simon & Schuster, 1992), pp. 316–332; and Raymond L. Garthoff, *Détente and Confrontation* (Washington DC: The Brookings Institution, 1985), pp. 146–226.

- Internal difficulties, caused by the Cultural Revolution, which might increase the desire for an easing of external relations;
- The continuing US-North Vietnamese Paris peace talks in accordance with the declining military outlook of the North Vietnam;
- A reaction to increased Sino-Soviet tensions, caused by the Soviet invasion of Czechoslovakia – the Chinese might believe in a US-USSR collusion and perceive the resumption of the Warsaw talks as a means to counter-pressure Moscow;
- An effort to explore the views of the new Administration of President Nixon;
- An effort to detect US positions, particularly in its relations with the Republic of China in Taiwan.[16]

Kissinger was still unfamiliar with China policy, and thus relied heavily on the recommendations of the NSC staff.[17] In his memorandum to Nixon, Kissinger argued that the Warsaw talks could offer an opportunity to shift the focus of US policy and to promote a dialogue with the Chinese which would provide "greater stability" for East Asia (a) "without abandoning our commitments to Taiwan or undermining its position" or (b) "damaging the interests of our Asian allies, principally Japan."[18] Kissinger's memorandum suggested three major approaches toward China. Option 1 was to indicate that the United States was "prepared to negotiate a normalization of relations" with Beijing. However, the memo suggested that this option would involve "considerable risk" because it could make the Chinese interpret "softness" on the part of the US, cause a "crisis of confidence" in Taiwan and "seriously upset" Japan.[19] Option 2 was to indicate that the US was "prepared to enter into serious discussions or negotiations with respect to our policies" except the US commitment to Taiwan.[20] However, this approach was likely to leave Japan and other Asian

---

16   Airgram, Consulate General Hong Kong, "Communist China: US Policy Assessment," January 24, 1969, pp. 2–3, POL Chicom-US. 1967–1969, Box 1973, Subject-Numeric Files (SNF), General Records of the Department of State, Record Group 59 (RG59), NA; and Kissinger to Nixon, "Warsaw Talks," February 11, 1969, pp. 1–2, Country File (CF)-Europe, Box 700 [1 of 2], NSCF, NPMS, NA.

17   Prior to Nixon's inauguration, NSC staff member-designate Richard Sneider wrote to Kissinger that the Warsaw ambassadorial talks scheduled for February 20 would provide the "first clear opportunity" for the new Administration to "signal its own policy." Sneider argued that: "At this stage I would be inclined to move very cautiously with the Chinese" and wait until they respond with "any specific proposals for peaceful co-existence but leaving the door open for reconsideration of our policies with the exception of our commitment to Taiwan." Finally, Sneider recommended that the China policy required a comprehensive NSC consideration in mid-term (four to five months) rather than short-term (within the next two months). Sneider to Kissinger, January 7, 1969, "Major Issues Anticipated During the Next Six Weeks in East Asia," pp. 1–2, HAK Administrative and Staff Files, Box 1, Transition, November 1968–January 1969, HAKOF, NSCF, NPMS, NA.

18   Kissinger to Nixon, "Warsaw Talks," February 11, 1969, p. 2, CF-Europe, Box 700 [1 of 2], NSCF, NPMS, NA.

19   Ibid., pp. 3–4.

20   Ibid., p. 4.

countries nervous if there was no immediate positive response from Beijing, and there would be a "quick and negative response" from Taipei. Option 3 suggested that the United States would pick up the Chinese reference to "peaceful coexistence" and "ask whether they have any specific proposals to make," without taking any initiatives.[21] Kissinger recommended the seemingly risk-free position of option 3.

In a memorandum to President Nixon, State Department officials recommended that the United States adopt a "firm posture" on its commitments to the Republic of China coupled with a "general expression of willingness to negotiate all other issues," as well as work toward peaceful coexistence with Beijing.[22] In particular, the "mutual hostility and suspicion" between Beijing and Moscow had led each side to regard any possibility of the other's rapprochement with the United States with the "greatest concern" and to do what they could to "prevent it."[23]

State Department officials declared: "Here is an opportunity for us to determine how far Peking may be prepared to move from its current positions."[24] The ultimate premise for any US move was that "it symbolizes the emphasis and direction in which the new Administration wishes to proceed."[25] The initial proposal represented a combination of the US proposal for (a) "renunciation of the use of force," and (b) "our desire not to prejudice our defense commitments on Taiwan." The key new element was an "explicit expression of willingness to negotiate normalization" with Beijing while "not changing" the US's "normal relations" with the Republic of China.[26] The State Department proposal was thus mainly concerned with the impact of the Warsaw ambassadorial talks on US relations with the Republic of China. Very importantly, moreover, State Department officials recommended that for the "first time," the United States offer to "send a special US representative" to Beijing.[27]

On February 18, however, the Chinese cancelled the planned 134th Warsaw meeting, because a Chinese diplomat in the Netherlands had defected and was given political asylum at the US Embassy in The Hague in late January 1969. On February 18, following President Nixon's instruction, Secretary of State Rogers expressed US regret at the Chinese cancellation of the Warsaw talks and declared that the United

---

21   Ibid.
22   Rogers to Nixon, "US Policy Toward Peking and Instructions for the February 20 Warsaw Meeting," February 12, 1969, p. 1, POL Chicom-US, 1967–1969, Box 1973, SNF, RG59, NA.
23   Ibid.
24   Ibid.
25   Ibid., p. 2.
26   Ibid., pp. 7–8.
27   Brown to Rogers (via Richardson), "US Policy Toward Peking and Instruction for the February 20 Warsaw Talks – Action Memorandum," February 5, 1969, p. 1, POL Chicom-US. 1967–69, Box 1973, SNF, RG59, NA. The notion of sending a special representative to Beijing was originally raised within the instructions for the Warsaw talks in November 1968. Memo from Paul H. Kreisberg to Ambassador Winthrop G. Brown, "Warsaw Talks Instructions," November 8, 1968, POL Chicom-US, 1967–1969, Box 1972, SNF, RG59, NA. The timing of sending a special representative re-emerged as one of the main issues of bureaucratic disagreement between the NSC and the State Department during the resumption of the Warsaw talks in January and February 1970, as Chapter 5 of this book examines.

States wanted to engage in a broad program of cultural and scientific exchange with China.[28] On March 4, however, Nixon himself stated at a news conference that: "Looking further down the road, we could only think in terms of a better understanding with Red China. But being very realistic, in view of Red China's breaking off the rather limited talks that were planned, I do not think that we should hold out any great optimism for any breakthroughs in that direction at this time."[29]

1.4 The Nixon-De Gaulle talks

It was during his first official European trip from February 23 to March 2, 1969 that Nixon held talks with French President Charles De Gaulle in Paris and discussed the need for a new China initiative.[30] Both the NSC staff's briefing paper and Nixon's Talking Points reveal that US officials paid particular attention to the appointment of a new French Ambassador to Beijing, Etienne M. Manach – their top Southeast Asian expert.[31] It was anticipated that De Gaulle would be likely to ask about US policy toward China, and the NSC staff suggested that the President inform the French leaders that the United States would "seek maximum contact" with mainland China.[32]

During their talk on February 28, 1969, it was Nixon who initially asked for De Gaulle's evaluation on China.[33] De Gaulle suggested that Nixon put himself in the position of the Soviet leaders to see China:

> This is an enormous country which has a common frontier thousands of miles long with Russia. The Chinese have always detested the Russians and will probably detest them tomorrow more than at any other time in the past. Chinese ambitions are directed mainly against Russia. ... The Russians know this and China is their main preoccupation. ... They are thinking in term of a possible clash with China tomorrow. They cannot face

---

28   "US China Policy 1969–1972," Box 86, HAKOF, NSCF, NPMS, NA.

29   President Richard M. Nixon, News Conference, March 4, 1969, Box 88, HAKOF, NSCF, NPMS, NA.

30   See Nixon, *RN*, pp. 371–374; and William Bundy, *A Tangled Web: The Making of Foreign Policy in the Nixon Presidency* (Hill and Wang, A Division of Farrar, Straus and Giroux: New York, 1998), pp. 100–103.

31   Talking Paper for European Trip, China, p.1, General Background Papers, President Nixon's Trip to Europe – February-March 1969, Box 442, President's Trip Files (PTF), NSCF, NPMS, NA.

32   Talking Paper on European Trip, France – General Talking Points, p. 9, General Background Papers, Box 442, PTF, NSCF, NPMS, NA.

33   Memcon, Nixon and De Gaulle, General De Gaulle's Office in the Elysee Palace, Paris, February 28, 1969, p. 1, Presidential/HAK MemCons (P/HAK Memcons), Box 1023, NSCF, NPMS, NA. Regarding secrecy, Nixon emphasized to De Gaulle that: "what would be said would not be put on the normal diplomatic circuit," and even Kissinger was not present. Ibid. A former NSC staff member, John Holdridge, recalls that Nixon "preferred one-on-one in his meetings with chiefs of state and heads of government." John Holdridge, Oral history interview in *A China Reader*, Vol. II, p. 10, January 1995, Foreign Affairs Oral History Collection (FAOHC), Association for Diplomatic Studies and Training, Lauinger Library, Georgetown University.

both China and the West (the US in particular) at the same time. ... they would like in the light of their growing quarrel with China to be sure that the West would not act against their back. They know that you and they are rivals. ... the Russians were willing to meet with the US to secure a détente, it was partly because of the fear of China.[34]

It was the growing Sino-Soviet mutual hostility within which the two Presidents came to share the idea of the Russian "primary fear" of China.[35] In their second talk on March 1, it was De Gaulle who raised the China issue by indicating that: "Some said that one should try and play the Chinese off against the Soviets and try to divide them. Others felt that it was worth trying to improve relations with both."[36] De Gaulle suggested:

> We should have exchanges at all levels and we might eventually see the beginnings of a détente. How this would affect the Soviets was difficult to know. ... The West should try to get to know China, to have contacts and to penetrate it. We should try to get them to sit at the table with us and offer them openings. ... If the US began to have relations with China this would mean that China would probably get into the UN.[37]

After the prolonged mutual hostility and the policy of isolation, the US should take an initial diplomatic step to recognize the increasing importance of China's presence in world politics. In his response, Nixon suggested a long-range policy toward China:

> [I]n looking down the road towards talks with the Soviet Union we might keep an anchor to windward with respect to China. This did not mean that we would do anything so crude as to suggest we play China off against the Soviet Union. The Soviets would resent this bitterly. In 10 years when China had made significant nuclear progress we would have to have more communications than we had today.[38]

De Gaulle agreed with Nixon by urging that: "it would be better for the US to recognize China before they were obliged to do it by the growth of China."[39]

In his memoirs, Kissinger assesses that Nixon did not ask for any specific assistance on March 1; it was De Gaulle who "initiated" the China issue by stressing its importance as a "huge entity with great resources," and Nixon appeared to be "skeptical" of it.[40] Kissinger thus argues that the new administration had "no clear-cut plan."[41] In reality, however, as a result of two decades of assessment, there was a solid basis for Nixon to realize that it would be better to resume a dialogue with China before it became too strong to deal with. Finally, it was during the Nixon-De Gaulle talk on March 2 in which Nixon proposed to establish a confidential direct

---

34   Ibid., pp. 1–2.
35   Ibid., p. 4.
36   Memcon, Nixon and De Gaulle, Grand Trianon, Versailles, March 1, 1969 [Morning session], p. 7, P/HAK Memcons Box 1023, NSCF, NPMS, NA.
37   Ibid., p. 8. See also Nixon, *RN*, pp. 373–374.
38   Ibid.
39   Ibid., p. 9.
40   Kissinger, *White House Years*, p. 170.
41   Ibid.

channel with De Gaulle: "if either of them wished to communicate directly with the other they could do so by private letters and such relations need not necessarily pass through the usual diplomatic channels."[42]

2. The Outbreak of the Sino-Soviet Border Clashes

2.1 The Sino-Soviet border clashes in March 1969

On March 2, 1969, the Sino-Soviet border dispute worsened when Chinese and Soviet patrolling troops exchanged fire at Chenpao (in Chinese)/Damansky (in Russian), an island on the Ussuri River.[43] *The New York Times* reported that: "Soviets and Chinese Clash on Border; Each Lists Deaths in Siberian Encounter."[44] The State Department's Bureau of Intelligence and Research (INR) analysts estimated that the clash was the result of "persistent efforts by both sides to establish control" over the islands in the Ussuri and was not likely to lead to "wider fighting in the near future," however, that similar incidents could be expected from time to time.[45] INR officials also monitored that Beijing had launched its "most extensive anti-Soviet denunciation campaign since January–February 1967."[46]

On March 4, 1969, during a briefing to the Congressional leaders on his trip to Europe, Nixon expressed that to side with the Soviets against the Chinese might be good short-range policy. However, it would be a suicidal long-range policy, for the Russians were "extremely sensitive" about this possibility. It was his experience that "fights between members of the same ideologies were more severe usually than fights between members of differing ideologies or religions."[47]

On March 15 and 17, the second and third Sino-Soviet border clash erupted at Chenpao/Damansky on a much larger scale. The State Department's INR analysts reported that Beijing responded to the March 15 and 17 border clashes with a "less

---

42   Memcon, Nixon and De Gaulle, General De Gaulle's Office – Elysee Palace, Paris, March 2, 1969, p. 1, P/HAK MemCons, Box 1023, NSCF, NPMS, NA.

43   See, for example, Yang Kuisong, "The Sino-Soviet Border Clash of 1969: From Zhenbao Island to Sino-American Rapprochement," *Cold War History*, Vol. 1, No. 1, August 2000; William Burr, "Sino-American Rapprochement, 1969: The Sino-Soviet Border War and Steps towards Rapprochement," *Cold War History*, Vol. 1, No. 3, April 2001; and Patrick E. Tyler, *A Great Wall: Six Presidents and China, An Investigative Story* (New York: Public Affairs, 1999), pp. 47–49.

44   *The New York Times*, March 3, 1969.

45   Intelligence Note, Bureau of Intelligence and Research (INR), Department of State, "USSR/China: Soviet and Chinese Forces Clash on the Ussuri River," March 4, 1969, p. 1, POL 32–1 Chicom-USSR, 1967–1969, Box 1975, SNF, RG59, NA.

46   Intelligence Note, INR, "Communist China: Millions Denounce Moscow," March 7, 1969, p. 1, POL Chicom-USSR, 1967–1969, Box 1975, SNF, RG59, NA.

47   Patrick Buchanan to Nixon (Buchanan's notes of the second bipartisan leadership meeting), March 4, 1969, pp. 18–19, Box 77, Memoranda for the President (MemforP), Records of Meetings, President's Office Files (POF), White House Central Files (WHCF), NPMS, NA.

threatening tone and far less internal propaganda exploitation."⁴⁸ It appeared that Beijing sensed a "greater danger of military escalation" than it did immediately after the March 2 clash and was assessing the problem in a "much more sober fashion."⁴⁹ Moreover, CIA intelligence officers concluded that it was the Chinese side that "triggered the initial clash" and thus the battle was the Chinese attempt to "contest" the Soviet presence.⁵⁰

Kissinger recalls that after the Ussuri River clashes, "ambiguity vanished, and we moved without further hesitation toward a momentous change in global diplomacy."⁵¹ Kissinger's memoirs thus create a misleading impression that the March border clashes were the decisive events for the Nixon administration, especially Kissinger himself, to comprehend the depth of Sino-Soviet mutual hostility. In reality, however, since January 1969, the State Department, the Defense Department, and the CIA had already engaged in a series of situational studies on the Sino-Soviet border dispute.⁵² In contrast, at this stage, Kissinger was still skeptical of a new China initiative.

---

48   Intelligence Note, INR, "Sino-Soviet Border: "Has Peking Bitten Off More Than It Can Chew?" March 18, 1969, p. 1, POL Chicom-USSR, 1967–1969, Box 1975, SNF, RG59, NA. Initially, the Chinese leadership, Mao and Zhou were "very poorly informed." The Chinese Foreign Ministry ceased its function during that period. There was only an element of the intelligence apparatus, which later became the China Institute of Contemporary International Relations (CICIR). At that time, CICIR was a part of the investigation department of the Central Committee of the Chinese Communist Party, and was the only institute that functioned. After the Sino-Soviet border clashes of March 1969, several members of that institution were brought back to Beijing to "brief Mao and the leadership specifically on world affairs, including the Soviet Union, the United States, and Japan." David Shambaugh, interview with the author, October 15, 2003. In late February, following Mao's instructions, Zhou told the four Marshals to meet "once in a week" to discuss "important international issues" and provide the Party Central Committee with their options. On March 18, they finished their first report, "An Analysis of War Situation in the World"; eleven days later they had completed their second report, "The Zhenbao Island as a Tree in the Forest of the Whole World." Chen, *Mao's China and the Cold War*, p. 246.

49   Ibid., pp. 2–3.

50   Central Intelligence Agency, Directorate of Intelligence, "Weekly Review," 21 March 1969, p.12, CIA Freedom of Information release to National Security Archive. On March 15, 1969, Mao gave instruction for the preparation for the outbreak of war: "The northeast, the north, and the northwest should be prepared... We will try to gain mastery by striking the enemy only after he has struck." "Mao Zedong's Talk at a Meeting of the Central Cultural Revolution Group," March 15, 1969, in Chen Jian and David L. Wilson (eds), "'All Under the Heaven is Great Chaos'–Beijing, the Sino–Soviet Border Clashes, and the Turn Toward Sino-American Rapprochement, 1968–1969," p. 162, Bulletin 11, Cold War International History Project (CWIHP), Woodrow Wilson International Center for Scholars.

51   Kissinger, *White House Years*, pp. 170–171.

52   For example, the State Department's Bureau of Intelligence and Research initiated an intelligence study series entitled "Sino-Soviet Affairs." *Sino-Soviet Affairs*, INR, POL Chicom-USSR, 1967–1969, SNF, RG59, NA.

On March 31, the day after Eisenhower's funeral in Washington DC, President Nixon held talks with French President De Gaulle.[53] Nixon asked De Gaulle to play the role of a go-between and inform the Chinese of the US decision for a withdrawal from the Vietnam War and of Washington's desire to improve its relations with Beijing.[54] Accordingly, on April 23, De Gaulle instructed the French Ambassador in Beijing, Etienne M. Manach, to deliver Nixon's private message to the Chinese leaders at the highest official level.[55]

Hereafter, Nixon and Kissinger would spend the next six months (until September 1969) to assess the nature of Sino-Soviet relations and their possible impact on US policy toward Asia. Therefore, the March border clashes should be regarded as the beginning of substantial White House assessment of Sino-Soviet mutual hostility.

2.2. The first official initiatives by the State Department

The first official diplomatic signal of the Nixon administration's policy toward China since Nixon's inaugural address and the cancellation of the Warsaw talks came from the State Department. On April 21, during an address in New York, Secretary Rogers made clear the US intention to promote a new dialogue with China:

> One cannot speak of a future of Pacific community without reference to China. The United State Government understands perfectly well that the Republic of China on the island of Taiwan and Communist China on the mainland are both facts of life. ... Not even a nation as large as mainland China can live forever in isolation from a world of inter-dependent states. Meanwhile, we shall take initiatives to re-establish more normal relations with Communist China and we shall remain responsive to any indication of less hostile attitudes from their side.[56]

---

53   Memcon, Nixon and De Gaulle, Yellow Oval Room, The White House, March 31, 1969, p. 2, P/HAK MemCons Box 1023, NSCF, NPMS, NA.

54   Ibid. Regarding Vietnam, De Gaulle stated that "the sooner it was clear the US was leaving, the greater would be the willingness of the Thieu regime and the NLF to get together and work out some sort of a solution." In other words, "the longer they believed the US would remain, the less likely they were to arrive at some solution." Ibid. On March 17, 1969, the United State secretly began to bomb the so-called Ho Chi Minh Trial through Laos and Cambodia – the North Vietnamese' supply road. The bombings, which became public knowledge on May 9, 1969, continued until May 1970. As for the Nixon administration's military operation of the Vietnam War, see Jeffrey Kimball, *Nixon's Vietnam War* (Lawrence, Kansas: University Press of Kansas, 1998); and Larry Berman, *No Peace, No Honor: Nixon, Kissinger, and Betrayal in Vietnam* (New York: The Free Press, 2001).

55   With De Gaulle's support, Nixon might have considered the "French backchannel" as a possible main means of communication with the Chinese. In reality, however, De Gaulle resigned the presidency on April 28, 1969 and died on November 9, 1970.

56   Address by Secretary of State William Rogers, before the Associated Press Annual Luncheon Waldorf-Astoria Hotel, New York, April 21, 1969, pp. 5–6, Extra Copies of Memo to President on Asia Trip [27 June–23 July 1969] [Part I], Box 465, PTF, NSCF, NPMS, NA. Nixon and Kissinger did not refer to Rogers' speech in their respective memoirs. From April 1 to 24, 1969, the Ninth Congress of the Chinese Communist Party was held, and Lin Biao was named Chairman Mao's heir-designate. Lin's speech reiterated that China would

In a broad sense, the State Department shared with the White House the general objective of improving relations with China. During the rest of 1969, senior officials in the State Department would give public statements on the China policy. However, the State Department was not entirely informed of the real intentions of Nixon and Kissinger. Therefore, the State Department operated independently in assessing a new China policy until the re-activation of the Warsaw channel in December 1969. The Bureau of East Asian and Pacific Affairs principally conducted interdepartmental studies on US policy toward China.

Particularly important, during his trip to Asia in March and April 1969, the Assistant Secretary of State for East Asian and Pacific Affairs-designate, Marshall Green, informed many of the Asian leaders that the United States "would make moves from time to time designed to prove that it is Peking, not Washington, that is isolating China."[57] Upon his return, Green produced a long report to the President. Green assessed that there was "less of a consensus" among Asian leaders on "whether Peking's growing nuclear capability would lead to adventurism."[58] In particular, Green emphasized that: "No one seemed to share the Soviets' concern that the US was contemplating normalization of relations with Peking." Green concluded that: "Moscow may not have any clear idea as to how to proceed in Asia. Moscow must have been left in a deep dilemma by the widening Sino-Soviet rift, the upheaval in Indochina, and the costs and risks of supporting Hanoi and Pyongyang in the years ahead."[59] Overall, the Green report thus demonstrated the widening anxiety among Asian leaders about Chinese nuclear threat, as well as Moscow's deepening concerns regarding the growth of Beijing's military capability and possible diplomatic prospects for Washington in the Sino-Soviet differences.

"This is Great," Nixon commented on the top page of Green's report, and Kissinger sent the copies of the report to Secretaries of State and Defense, the administrator of the Agency for International Development, and the director of the US Information Agency.[60] In reality, however, Kissinger was not pleased with Green's direct contact

---

not attack unless it was attacked and criticized US imperialism and Soviet revisionism as equal threats to China. "Mao Zedong's Addition to Lin Biao's Political Report at the Party's Ninth Congress," April 1969, p. 162, in Chen and Wilson (eds), "All Under the Heaven is Great Chaos," CWIHP. The State Department's intelligence officials analysed that while the party Congress promised "little change in the substance" of Beijing's foreign policy, it left "room for a normalization in the conduct of Chinese diplomacy." Intelligence Note, INR, "Communist China: Lin Piao's Report to Party Congress Published," April 28, 1969, p. 1; and Intelligence Note, INR, "Communist China: Lin Piao Charts China's Foreign Policy Course," April 30, 1969, p. 1, POL Chicom-US. 1967–1969, Box 1962, SNF, RG59, NA.

57   Marshall Green, Oral History Interview, March 2 and 17, 1995, pp. 52–53, and Idem, *Evolution of US-China Policy 1956–1973: Memoirs of An Insider*, p. 27, Oral History Interview in *A China Reader*, Vol. II, January 1995, FAOHCF. After his return from the Asia trip, Green became the Assistant Secretary by replacing William Bundy. Neither Nixon nor Kissinger refers to the Green memorandum in their respective memoirs.

58   Green to Nixon, "A View of East Asia," April 21, 1969, enclosed in Memo from Kissinger to Rogers, May 28, 1969, POL Asia, SNF, RG59, NA.

59   Ibid.

60   Ibid.

with Nixon, which had bypassed the National Security Adviser and his NSC staff. After this earlier contact, the relationship between Kissinger and Green began to deteriorate.

On April 16–17, April 25, and May 2, more clashes broke out along the Sino-Soviet border areas, about two thousand five hundred miles to the west of the frontier between Sinkiang and Kazakhstan. On April 26, Moscow publicly proposed to Beijing the resumption of the Sino-Soviet meetings of the Joint Commissions for Navigation on Boundary Rivers, which had been suspended since 1967. On May 11, Beijing accepted the Soviet proposal. The State Department's Bureau of Intelligence and Research experts interpreted Beijing's response in a May 24 government statement on the Soviet proposal as the affirmation of the Chinese desire to take the dispute off the battlefield to the conference table.[61]

However, more fighting erupted along the Amur River on May 12, 15, 25, and 28; and further clashes occurred on May 20 and June 10 in the Sinkiang border area. The INR analysts concluded that these Sino-Soviet border incidents suggested that the Chinese were the provocateurs.[62] In the short term, Beijing was trying to "agitate" the Soviets and "test" the reaction to these counter-pressures to determine "how far the Soviets may be prepared to go."[63] Beijing's tactics had been developed "out of fear to offset a position of weakness."[64] In his memoirs, Kissinger recalls that the Sinkiang clash convinced him that the Soviet Union was "the aggressor."[65] However, this statement is misleading, because Kissinger remained somewhat uncertain about the nature of the Sino-Soviet rivalry until late 1969, as this book demonstrates in the following sections and chapters.

2.3 NSC review group meeting on NSSM 14 in May 1969

On April 30, 1969, the East Asian and Pacific Interdepartmental Group completed the first comprehensive study entitled "United States China Policy" in response to NSSM 14 of February 5, 1969.[66] The paper explored the nature of the Chinese threat to US interests and the range of US objectives and options vis-à-vis the People's Republic of China (PRC). The paper also examined wide-ranging specific issues, such as the impact of US policy toward China on Communist states and Non-Communist states, US relations with the Republic of China (ROC) as a US military base, Sino-US normalization, the Chinese representation issue in the United Nations, and trade.

---

61   Intelligence Note, INR, "Peking Agrees to Soviet Border Talks," May 28, 1969, p. 1, POL Chicom-USSR, 1967–1969, Box 1975, SNF, RG59, NA.
62   Intelligence Note, INR, "Communist China: Peking Inflates Soviet War Threat," June 3, 1969, p. 1, POL Chicom-USSR, 1967–1969, Box 1975, SNF, RG59, NA.
63   Intelligence Note, INR, "Peking's Tactics and Intentions Along the Sino-Soviet Border," June 13, 1969, p. 1, POL Chicom-USSR, 1967–1969, Box 1975, SNF, RG59, NA.
64   Ibid., p. 3.
65   Kissinger, *White House Years*, p. 177.
66   Winthrop G. Brown (Acting Chairman, East Asian and Pacific Interdepartmental Group) to Kissinger, "United States China Policy (Response to NSSM 14), April 30, 1969, Senior Review Group Meetings, Box H-037, Review Group China NPG [Part 2], 5/15/69, National Security Council Institutional Files (NSCIF), NPMS, NA.

The paper assessed that the PRC wanted to extend its influence in Asia and to be treated as a major world power as well as the primary source of revolutionary ideological leadership.[67] In particular, the PRC would seek the removal of the US military presence from both the Taiwan Strait area and Taiwan, and simultaneously a US acceptance of its long-term claim that Taiwan was an internal matter.[68] As for China's security environment, the US-USSR bipolar situation that characterized Asia in the previous two decades was shifting toward a "four-sided relationship among the US, the Soviet Union, Japan and Communist China."[69] It was therefore likely, the paper judged, that China's leaders genuinely felt threatened by a US-USSR-Japan-India "encirclement." Their charges of US-Soviet "collusion" and Japan's alleged intention to re-establish the "greater East Asia co-prosperity sphere" were, in Chinese eyes, more than just propaganda.[70] The possible impact of the Sino-Soviet tensions on US policy toward the Soviet Union and China would be discussed in NSSM 63 in late 1969.

At the time, US strategy consisted of two elements: deterrence of any possible direct Chinese threat; and limited efforts to suggest to the Chinese the desirability of changing their policies. The paper suggested two alternative strategies: movement toward intensified deterrence and isolation; and movement toward reduction of points of conflict and international isolation.[71] To encourage the reduction of tension, while continuing necessary measures to deter any possible overt Chinese attack against US allies in Asia, the United States (a) could gradually de-emphasize the military aspect of its containment of the PRC; (b) could unilaterally reduce or eliminate economic and political measures designed to isolate Beijing; or (c) could acquiesce to the PRC's fuller participation in the international community.[72]

In their summary paper of NSSM 14, State Department officials recommended that decisions were required on three specific issues: the future use of Taiwan as a military base; US policy toward the Offshore Islands; and trade with Communist China.[73] In particular, the US military presence on Taiwan had increased in support of operations in Vietnam, and therefore a decision on the "over-all question of Taiwan as a military base" was required before these specific policy issues could be decided upon.[74] Thus, the principal interest of the State Department remained the Taiwan issue, namely the treatment of Taipei's status in the Washington-Beijing relations.

The NSC staff commented on NSSM 14 that there had not been a sufficient treatment of the "broader Asian context" and of possible effects upon relationships

---

67 NSSM14: United States China Policy, p. 2, Senior Review Group Meetings, Box H-037, Review Group China [Part 2], 5/15/69, NSCIF, NPMS, NA.
68 Ibid., p. 2.
69 Ibid., p. 5.
70 Ibid., Annex A-10.
71 Ibid., pp. 10–11.
72 Ibid., p. 5.
73 NSSM14: United States China Policy, Summary Paper on Major Issues for Decision Regarding US China Policy (Summary by State at May 2 RG Meeting), p. 1, Senior Review Group Meetings, Box H-037, Review Group China [Part 2], 5/15/69, NSCIF, NPMS, NA.
74 Ibid., p. 2.

with Japan and the Soviet Union.[75] The NSC staff recommended that that alternative strategy option of the "Gradual Reduction in Tension" represented the "most prudent course towards China at the moment."[76] In particular, immediate decisions could be made on both relaxing trade controls and lifting travel restrictions. Finally, the NSC staff recommended further studies on (a) steps and program for the gradual relaxation of trade controls, and (b) alternative UN scenarios. In essence, the NSC staff sought to reassess the China policy within a broader geopolitical context. These recommendations would be the basis of NSSMs 106 and 107 in late 1970.

On May 15, 1969, a Review Group meeting on China policy was held. Kissinger, who chaired the meeting, presented his fundamental questions: "[W]hat do we want from China over the longer term and what can we reasonably expect to do to influence that outcome?"[77] Kissinger believed that a "nation of 700 million people, surrounded by weaker states, could be a security threat no matter what type of policy it pursued."[78] The question was whether US policy toward China should be framed by security considerations, such as a balance of power approach, or by desire for a more conciliatory attitude. There was general agreement that US policy could have little impact on Chinese behavior over the short term. Kissinger asked: "whether we care if China maintains her policy of isolation so long as this is coupled with a relatively low level of aggression."[79] In response to Kissinger's questions, a NSC staff member, Morton Halperin, suggested that the basic choice was between maintaining the status quo and easing some of the tensions in US-China relations. CIA officer, Jack Smith, also argued that the essential issue was how to bring China into the world community in the long term, which might make her "more manageable."[80]

Suggesting Sino-Soviet difficulties as a "key issue," Kissinger asked: "What is our view of the evolution of Sino-Soviet relations, how much can we influence them, should we favor one or the other? [sic]" Kissinger noted that "the Soviets and Chinese each think we are playing with the other."[81] The so-called "Kremlinologists" in the bureaucracy believed that "any attempt to better our relations with China will ruin those with the Soviet Union." However, Kissinger counter-argued that history suggested to him that "it is better to align yourself with the weaker, not the stronger of two antagonistic partners," because it would function as a restraint on the stronger.[82] Kissinger thus criticized the NSSM 14 paper for not making clear what the desirable role of China in the world should be, nor fully exploring "the

---

75   Review Group Meeting, May 7, 1969, NSSM14: United States China Policy, HAK Talking Points, p. 2, Review Group China [Part 2], 5/15/69, Box H-037, Senior Review Group Meetings, NSCIF, NPMS, NA.

76   Ibid., pp. 2–3.

77   Lord to Kissinger (via Morton H. Halperin), "Review Group Meeting, 2:10–3:55pm, White House Situation Room, May 15, 1969," May 19, 1969, pp. 1–2, SRG Minutes Originals, Box H-111, Senior Review Group, Minutes of Meetings (1969–1974), NSCIF, NPMS, NA.

78   Ibid.

79   Ibid., p. 6

80   Ibid., pp. 6–7.

81   Ibid., p. 8.

82   Ibid., p. 9.

US-China-Soviet triangular relationship," to which a NSC staff member Richard L. Sneider added Japan.[83]

Kissinger appeared to remain skeptical of a new China initiative. Kissinger reiterated an alternative formulation that "it is not our interest – or at least our task – to bring China in. We need not strive to isolate her, but may not be worth great investment in US policy to move positively."[84] A State Department official Winthrop Brown disagreed, suggesting that the question remained how "we might be able to bring about better Chinese behavior as they emerge from present isolation."[85] Sneider also argued that "China policy is difficult because the short term threat is much less than the longer term threat; we have more flexibility in the short term because of the nature of the threat but we have less flexibility because of the Chinese attitude."[86] In other words, a more self-confident China armed with nuclear weapons would be much more difficult to accommodate in the long-term.

Overall, under the option of "reducing tensions," there was consensus on the three sets of issues: a) those that could be taken immediately if it were decided to change the China policy – trade and travel; b) those dependent on other decisions – use of Taiwan as a base; c) longer range problems – overall policy toward Taiwan, Offshore Islands, United Nations and possibly diplomatic recognition.[87]

2.4 The Sino-Soviet border clashes in June and July 1969

On June 8, 1969, Soviet General Secretary Leonid Brezhnev delivered an address to the International Conference of Communist parties in Moscow: "We are of the opinion that the course of events is also putting on the agenda the task of creating a system of collective security in Asia." On June 19, Beijing criticized that the USSR and the US were unifying their efforts to encircle China militarily and incite India against China's southwestern frontier, thereby "gravely threatening the security of China."[88] The State Department's intelligence analysis recognized the deepening mutual suspicions as a result of Sino-Soviet border tensions, namely Moscow's apprehension of Sino-US maneuverings as well as Beijing's fear of US-USSR collusion.

On June 22, 1969, the State Department's Bureau of East Asian and Pacific affairs estimated that the present Sino-Soviet border tension was "serious," and

---

83   Ibid., p. 10. However, it is likely that Kissinger read only the NSC staff's summary rather than the entire NSSM 14 papers, which explored the question of US-USSR-PRC-Japan relationship. China experts, such as Tucker and Whiting also argue that Kissinger did not carefully read policy study papers. Nancy Bernkopf Tucker, interview with the author, October 1, 2003; and Allen Whiting, interview with the author, October 19, 2003.

84   Ibid., p. 11.

85   Ibid.

86   Ibid., p. 12.

87   Ibid., p. 13. Owing to a number of recommendations for further studies at the interdepartmental level, the consideration of the China paper at the NSC meeting was postponed (materialized on August 14, 1969). See Chapter 4, Section 2.1 (pp. 101–103) of this study.

88   INR, "Concern Over China Pushes USSR Toward Collective Security Concept for Asia," p. 1, *Sino-Soviet Affairs*, No. 7, 1969, POL Chicom, 1967–69, Box 1963, SNF, RG59, NA.

there remained a possibility that the Soviets might launch a "surgical strike against the Chinese nuclear installations."[89] On June 26, Kissinger requested NSC staff to prepare a NSSM on "US Posture with respect to the Sino-Soviet Split and Our Role in the Triangle."[90]

On July 9, 1969, a Sino-Soviet border incident on an island in the Amur River had evoked the most direct Soviet threat to date towards China. A Soviet Foreign Ministry note of July 8 informed China that the USSR was "compelled to take additional measures against the actions of the Chinese authorities." The State Department's Bureau of Intelligence and Research assessed that the wording of this threat was deliberately ambiguous.[91] However, Moscow might then be persuaded that the credibility of its warning would be at stake if Beijing was allowed to continue to provoke border incidents.[92] On July 15, 1969, Premier Zhou Enlai portrayed to foreign officials the Soviet threat as a replacement of US efforts rather than "collusion" with the US.[93]

On July 14, in the National Security Study Memorandum 69 (NSSM 69) circulated to Secretary of State William Rogers, Secretary of Defense Melvin Laird, and CIA Director Richard Helm, Kissinger stated: "the President had decided on the preparation of a study" to examine "US strategic nuclear capability against China" and "a range of possible situations in which a US strategic nuclear capability against

---

89   US State Department, Bureau of East Asian and Pacific Affairs, Office of Asian Communist Affairs, "Implications of Sino-Soviet Developments: Meeting of June 21," Pol 32–1, Chicom-USSR, SNF, RG59, NA. Nixon showed continuing interest in achieving a breakthrough in the frozen US relationship with the PRC. On a return from his meeting with Vietnamese President Thieu at Midway Island in early June 1969, Nixon invited Green to his cabin on Air Force One where for nearly two hours they discussed China and other Asian issues. The President was "interested in the history of our efforts to achieve some thaw in US-China relations." Green, *Evolution of US-China Policy 1956–1973*, p. 27, Oral history interview in *A China Reader*, Vol. II, January 1995, FAOHC.

90   Haig to Halperin, "NSSMs to be Prepared," June 26, 1969, Box H-299, NSC Vol. II, 4/1/69–5/30/69 [2 of 2], NSCIF, NPMS, NA.

91   Intelligence Note, INR, "USSR-China: Renewed Border Fighting Evokes Soviet Threat," July 9, 1969, p. 1, POL Chicom-USSR, 1967–1969, Box 1975, SNF, RG59, NA.

92   Ibid., p. 2.

93   Intelligence Note, INR, "Communist China: Chou En-lai Hits Moscow's Asian Collective Security," July 15, 1969, p. 1, POL Chicom-US, 1967–1969, Box 1973, SNF, RG59, NA. In their July 1969 report, the four Chinese marshals warned of the danger of collusion and contention between the superpowers: "US imperialists and the Soviet revisionists collaborate with each other while at the same time fighting each other. The contradictions between superpowers, however, are not reduced because of collaboration between them; rather, their hostilities toward each other are more fierce than ever before." Report by Four Chinese Marshals – Chen Yi, Ye Jianying, Xu Xiangqian, and Nie Rongzhen – to the Central Committee, "A Preliminary Evaluation of the War Situation," July 11, 1969, in Chen and Wilson (eds), "All Under the Heaven," pp. 166–167; and Chen, *Mao's China and the Cold War*, p. 247.

China would be useful."[94] In other words, Kissinger asked Rogers, Laird, and Helm to consider how to prevent China from becoming a fully-developed nuclear power by targeting its nuclear facilities.

2.5 NSSM 35: Easing trade and travel restrictions

During June and July 1969, following the review of trade restrictions ordered by NSSM 35 on March 28, the US government publicly began to modify its two decade-old trade embargo against China.[95] On June 26, Kissinger signed a directive to the agencies: "The President has decided, on broad foreign policy grounds, to modify certain of our trade controls against China."[96] Accordingly, the NSC Under Secretaries Committee, chaired by Elliot Richardson, was asked to prepare detailed recommendations to implement the Presidential decision. In their respective memoranda to Nixon, Richardson and Kissinger pointed out the implications for the presidential decision at this particular time:

- The decision would "demonstrate the flexibility" that the President now had in administering trade controls.
- A delay might lead the United States into a period where "unforeseen circumstances," such as changes in Indochina and worsening of the Sino-Soviet border situation, could prevent the announcement and thus cause the President to lose the diplomatic benefits. Such a delay would also increase the likelihood of [a] press leak.
- If the President waited to announce this decision until his return from Bucharest [a friend of China], it would probably be tied in with speculation regarding a presumed anti-Soviet purpose in the Bucharest stopover. This would give his decision an "overly overt anti-Soviet significance." [97]

On July 21, 1969, two days before Nixon's departure for his official trip to Asia and Romania, the State Department announced a partial lifting of trade and travel

---

94 National Security Study Memorandum 69: US Nuclear Policy in Asia, July 14, 1969, SF, Box 365, NSCF, NPMS, NA. Tyler argues that there was an option for the United States to agree or cooperate with the Soviet Union to wipe out China's nuclear capability in return for Soviet help in Vietnam. Tyler, *A Great Wall*, p. 63. However neither Nixon nor Kissinger referred to this study in their respective memoirs.

95 National Security Study Memorandum 35: US Trade Policy Toward Communist Countries, March 28, 1969, Box 365, SF, NSCF, NPMS, NA. See also Kissinger, *White House Years*, p. 173.

96 National Security Decision Memorandum 17: China Trade, June 26, 1969, Box 363, SF, NSCF, NPMS, NA.

97 Richardson to Nixon, "NSDM 17: China Trade," July 10, 1969, pp. 1–2, Quotation marks in original; and Memo from Kissinger to Nixon, "Relaxation of Economic Controls Against China," July 11, 1969, p. 1, China, Box 839, Name Files (NF), NSCF, NPMS, NA. It was initially assumed that actual implementation had to await passage by Congress of the revised Export Control Act anticipated in September. Quotation marks in original.

sanctions on China.[98] *The New York Times* reported the announcement as "the first sliver of a break in the total embargo" against China since the outbreak of the Korean War in June 1950.[99] In his memoirs, regarding economic issues as secondary, Kissinger argues that the actual change itself was not important, however, the "symbolism" was vast.[100] Lord recalls: "These [The relaxation of trade and travel restrictions] were modest unilateral steps which did not require any response from the Chinese."[101] Overall, therefore, officials in the Nixon administration regarded unilateral actions as a diplomatic tool to send a low-key signal that the United States was willing to improve its relations with China.

In summary, it was Nixon's presidential leadership that launched the new China initiative during the first half of 1969. Fearing bureaucratic leak and US domestic conservative backlash, Nixon took the lead very secretly, directing Kissinger to conduct a series of NSSMs on the China policy. Nixon believed that a nuclear-armed China outside of the international community would be a great threat in the long run and thus that it would be important to initiate a new dialogue with Beijing before Washington would be forced to do so. In contrast, Kissinger did not have any particular interest in China at this earlier period and thus remained skeptical about a new China initiative.

The outbreak of the Sino-Soviet border clashes in March 1969 marked the beginning of the long process for US officials to assess the nature of Sino-Soviet relations throughout the remainder of 1969. It was the State Department, especially the Bureau of East Asian and Pacific Affairs and the Bureau of Intelligence and Research that conducted a number of studies. In particular, the first comprehensive inter-departmental policy study, NSSM 14, provided a broad range of policy alternatives for a new China initiative. During the latter half of 1969, while the interdepartmental studies on US policy toward China continued to develop at the bureaucratic level, Nixon and Kissinger sent a series of public and private signals to Chinese leaders, as the following chapter examines.

---

98   Department of State, July 21, 1969, A Matter of Record – No. 8, Public Statements on China by US officials, Box 86, US China Policy 1969–1972 [2of 2], Country Files (CF) – Far East, HAKOF, NSCF, NPMS, NA. The decision permitted tourists and residents abroad to purchase 100 dollars of Chinese goods and authorizing automatic validations of US passports for travel to China for certain categories of persons, such as members of Congress, journalists, scholars, scientists, medical doctors, and representatives of the American Red Cross. There was a brief delay for the announcement. On July 16, two American yacht men were captured by the Chinese when their lifeboat drifted into Chinese waters off Hong Kong. Chinese remained silent without playing the incident into any anti-American campaign. On July 24, the Chinese released the yachtsmen.

99   *The New York Times*, July 21, 1969.

100   Kissinger, *White House Years*, p. 179.

101   Lord, interview with the author, October 15, 2003.

Chapter 4

The Reassessment of the China Policy from July to November 1969

This chapter explores the bureaucratic reassessment of US policy toward China within the Nixon administration during the latter half of 1969. First, it examines President Nixon's initiative to send both public and private signals to Beijing for a new dialogue, such as the US redefinition of its policy toward Asia, symbolized by the Nixon Doctrine in July 1969, and the initial opening of the backchannels to the Chinese leaders via Pakistan and Romania. Through his presidential diplomacy, Nixon sought to create a more constructive political atmosphere to resume a dialogue with China. Second, this chapter analyzes the escalation of the Sino-Soviet border clashes from August to September, 1969 and the first full NSC meeting on the China policy. It was during this crucial period when Kissinger came to convince himself of the seriousness of Sino-Soviet mutual hostilities and more substantially considered the possibility of playing a pivotal role for the US within the US-Soviet-China strategic triangle. Finally, this study examines the further development of policy option studies by the NSC staff and the State Department in late 1969. These policy studies would materialize to further reduce trade restriction in US-China relations, as well as to resume the Warsaw ambassadorial talks in early 1970.

1. Nixon's Trip to Asia and Romania in July and August 1969

1.1 The Nixon Doctrine

By the late 1960s, realizing the limitation of power resources, the United States was reassessing its open-ended containment policy toward the monolithic threat from Communism.[1] A major opportunity arrived when President Nixon took an around-the-world trip from July 23 to August 3, 1969. On July 25, on his first stop in Guam, President Nixon announced major changes in US policy toward Asia, in what came to be known as the "Nixon Doctrine":

- The United States will keep its treaty commitments.
- We shall provide a shield if a nuclear power threatens the freedom of a nation allied with us, or of a nation whose survival we consider vital to our security and the security of the region as a whole.

---

[1] On this subject, see John Lewis Gaddis, *Strategies of Containment* (Oxford: Oxford University Press, 1982), chapters 9 and 10.

- In cases involving other types of aggression we shall furnish military and economic assistance when required and as appropriate, but we shall look to the nation directly threatened to assume the primary responsibility of providing the manpower for its defense.[2]

On July 26, *The New York Times* reported that: "Nixon Plans Cut in Military Roles for US in Asia."[3] In actuality, Nixon's announcement brought about anxiety among US allies that the United States would withdraw from Asia. Kissinger and the NSC staff members were not informed of Nixon's plan in advance. Winston Lord recalls that the pronouncement was "accidental."[4] John Holdridge also emphasizes it as a "complete and utter surprise."[5] In his memoirs, Kissinger admits that the Nixon speech was "quite to my surprise."[6] Kissinger insists further that: "To this day, I do not think that Nixon intended a major policy pronouncement in Guam."[7]

In reality, however, some evidence reveals how the fundamental themes of the Nixon Doctrine were outlined in advance. Marshall Green co-authored with Winthrop Brown and Robert Barnett the so-called "scope paper," which turned out to be the basis of the Nixon Doctrine.[8] In particular, the scope paper analyzed the growing ability of most East Asian countries to assume "greater burdens for their own defense." The paper thus urged that the US position in Asia should "not be one of trying to solve East Asia's problems but rather of helping East Asia's problem-solvers."[9] On July 22, 1969, during a meeting with Congressional leaders, Nixon emphasized the continuing US presence: "We must play a role in Asia if we are to avoid being dragged into the future war in Asia. ... Our role essentially should be to provide a nuclear shield for the Asian countries."[10] Nixon's handwritten-notes show his preparation for the main contents of the Guam announcement. Nixon was fully aware that many Asians wondered what the US's role would be in the post Vietnam

---

2   Richard M. Nixon, "US Foreign Policy for the 1970's: A Strategy for Peace," February 18, 1970 (Washington DC: Government Printing Office, 1970), pp. 40–41.
3   *The New York Times*, July 26, 1969.
4   Winston Lord, interview with the author, October 15, 2003.
5   John Holdridge, Oral History Interview, July 20, 1995, p. 90, FAOHC.
6   Henry Kissinger, *White House Years* (Boston: Little Brown, 1979), p. 223.
7   Ibid., p. 224.
8   Marshall Green, *Evolution of US-China Policy 1956–1973*, p. 27, Oral History Interview in *A China Reader*, Vol. II, January 1995, FAOHC; and Robert W. Barnett, Oral History Interview, March 2, 1990, p. 16, FAOHC. See also Marshall Green, John H. Holdridge, and William Stokes, *War and Peace with China: First-Hand Experiences in the Foreign Service of the United States* (Maryland: Dacor-bacon House, 1994), pp. 83–86.
9   Ibid. Since his first meeting with Nixon in April 1967, Green had been an advocate of a low-profile US policy in Asia. Lord objects to Green's suggestion: "It [the Nixon Doctrine] was not the introduction of low-profile policy in the Pacific. We wanted to preserve a high-profile in the Pacific." Lord, interview with the author, October 15, 2003.
10   Buchanan to Nixon, July 22, 1969, POF, Box 78, NPMS, NA.

era, and was thus determined to emphasize that: "we are [a] Pacific power."[11] Nixon wrote:

> Our Goal
> Encourage Asia responsibility (Japan e.g.)
> Keep commitments – but don't extend them
> Support their initiative.[12]

Hence, possibly reflecting the recommendations from other officials, it was the President himself who formulated the main premises of the Nixon Doctrine.

Solomon argues that the Nixon Doctrine was initially a "way of saying that the US would not get involved in international conflicts as deeply as it was in Vietnam"[13] Rodman also assesses that the Nixon Doctrine was "not a formula for withdrawal" from Asia but the means of ensuring that the United States "stay engaged" in a greater cooperation with its allies, but maintaining its non-involvement in the internal affairs of other states.[14] In essence, the Nixon administration sought to re-define the US role as "behind-the-scenes encouragement."[15] In other words, the Nixon Doctrine was designed to encourage US allies' further burden sharing as a substitute for US direct intervention to maintain regional stability. Importantly, State Department officials later learned that the Chinese followed the presidential statement closely.[16]

In particular, at almost every stop, Nixon sought to portray positive signals of US readiness to open communication with the Chinese.[17] On the day of his departure

---

11   Notes Guam Press Conference, Box 50, President's Speech Files, July–August 1969, Asia Trip [1 of 2] President's Personal Files (PPS), NPMS, NA. Kissinger recalls that while preparing for Nixon's trip in the summer of 1969, Nixon and he often discussed the problems of the US over-involvement in the world and the question of the US role in post-Vietnam Asia. Kissinger, *White House Years*, p. 223.

12   Ibid.

13   Richard Solomon, interview with the author, September 24, 2003.

14   Peter Rodman, interview with the author, October 24, 2004. See also Nixon, *RN*, p. 395.

15   Earl C. Ravenal, "Large Scale Foreign Policy Change: The Nixon Doctrine as History and Portent," Policy Papers in International Affairs, Number 35 (California, Berkley: Institute of International Studies, University of California, 1989), p. 2, p. 7, and p. 19. The Nixon administration reduced the level of force deployment from "a two-and-a-half strategy" to "a one-and-a-half-strategy." While the former strategy envisaged the possibility of fighting a war against China in Asia, with one against the Soviets in Europe, and a minor conflict elsewhere all simultaneously, the latter acknowledged the Sino-Soviet split and thus a conflict with the Soviets would not necessarily involve China. See Nixon, "US Foreign Policy for the 1970's: A Strategy for Peace," pp. 128–129.

16   The Chinese expressed privately to foreign diplomats that the US was going to "withdraw the bulk of its forces" from Vietnam. US officials interpreted that the Chinese appeared to have believed that the US posed a "significantly diminished threat" to Chinese security. Memo from Rogers to Nixon "Next Moves in China Policy and Bargaining Moves Toward the Soviet Union," October 21, 1969, pp. 1–2, Attached to Memo from Green and Martin J. Hillenbrand to Richardson, POL Chicom-US, 1967–1969, Box 1973, SNF, RG59, NA.

17   Richard M. Nixon, *RN* (New York: Grssett & Danlap, 1978), pp. 394–396; and Kissinger, pp. 180–181. Nixon's trip included stops in Guam, the Philippines, Indonesia, Thailand, South Vietnam, India, Pakistan, Romania, and Britain.

from Washington, Nixon said to Kissinger, "By the time we get through with this trip the Russians are going to be out of their minds that we are playing a Chinese game."[18] John Holdridge, a former INR staff member, who had recently joined the NSC staff after replacing Morton Halperin in July 1969, outlined an initial secret message to China. On, the presidential plane, Air Force One, flying between Jakarta and Bangkok, Kissinger asked Holdridge to "draft a cable to the Chinese," proposing that the United States and China get together to talk about an improvement in their relations.[19] Holdridge wrote in his draft, "[W]e should not look to the past, but look to the future. ... There were many issues that were of mutual value, and we should address them."[20] Holdridge recalls, "I gave the draft to Henry. He looked at it, gave his characteristic grunt, said nothing. ... That is the last I saw or heard of it."[21]

Nixon's handwritten-notes reveal his extensive preparation for meeting with leaders before and during the trip. Nixon wrote that US policy should not be "a Soviet-US Collusion against China" and that although there should be "no proposal of change now," the United States "[h]ope[s] to see [the] time when China changes."[22] On July 29, Nixon met with US Ambassadors to Asian countries in Bangkok. Regarding the US policy toward Sino-Soviet mutual hostility, Nixon stated that: "I don't think we should rush quickly into [an] embrace with [the] USSR to contain China."[23] The best US stance was to "play each – not publicly." US-USSR-Europe lined up against the rest of Asia was not a realistic prospect. Finally, a US-USSR security pact "would invite Soviet adventurism." What Nixon did not state explicitly at this stage was a possible US move toward China which would pressure the Soviets to improve relations with the US.

---

18   H.R. Haldeman, *The Haldeman Diaries* (Santa Monica, California: Sony Electronic Publishing, 1994), August 2, 1969. The Chief of Staff in the White House, H.R. Haldeman, kept diaries from January 1969 to June 1973. The written and recorded diaries reveal the development of Nixon's thinking on the China initiative. While the book version of the diaries is 700 pages, the CD-ROM version's vast capacity allows the full publication of 2,200 diary pages. This book uses the CD-ROM version of the diaries, which is more detailed and comprehensive than a book version. As for reference of the diaries, this work notes date rather than page. See also H.R. Haldeman, *The Haldeman Diaries: Inside The Nixon White House* (New York: G.P. Putnam's Sons, 1994).

19   Holdridge, Oral History Interview in *A China Reader*, Vol. II, pp. 25–26, January 1995, FAOHC.

20   Ibid.

21   Ibid. Holdridge estimated that the message was sent to the Chinese either through Pakistan or Romania. Ibid.

22   Notes Guam Press Conference, Box 50, President's Speech Files (PSF), July–August 1969, Asia Trip [1 of 2] President's Personal Files (PPF), NPMS, NA.

23   Memcon, Nixon and American ambassadors, US Embassy, Bangkok, Thailand, July 29, 1969, p. 5, P/HAK MemCons Box 1023, NSCF, NPMS, NA. The meeting was a gathering of regional Chief of Mission held during Nixon's trip to several Asian countries and Romania.

1.2 The Nixon-Yahya talks and the opening of the Pakistani channel

Toward the end of the trip, President Nixon made very significant private moves toward establishing back-channel communication with the Chinese through third parties, namely Pakistan and Romania. On August 1, 1969, Nixon visited Pakistan and held talks with Pakistani President Yahya Kahn.[24] Historically, owing to a prolonged rivalry with India, Pakistan valued military and economic aid from China and remained supportive of Beijing even during the chaotic period of the Cultural Revolution. US officials were aware of Pakistan's unique historical position vis-à-vis China. In the Cabinet meeting on June 3, 1969, reporting on his around-the-world trip [of May 1969], Secretary Rogers explained that Yahya Khan, who was taking over in Pakistan, "has had considerable contact" with Mao, Zhou and other leaders of China.[25] Nixon's handwritten-notes show that the President personally admired and respected the "strong vitality" and "friendship" of Pakistan.[26] In particular, Nixon was aware that what he would say to the Pakistani leader could possibly be said to the Chinese.

In his memoirs, without revealing any specific issues, Nixon states only briefly that he and Yahya discussed the idea of Yahya's help as an intermediary in "general terms."[27] In reality, however, the Nixon-Yahya talk was much more substantial than Nixon's brief account. During a strictly confidential talk on August 1, 1969 (even Kissinger was not present), Nixon stated that: "the US would welcome accommodation with Communist China and would appreciate it if President Yahya would let Chou Enlai know this."[28] Nixon did not consider passing this thought as "urgent," however he explained that President Yahya might convey this message "at some natural and appropriate time" in a "low key factual way."[29] The two Presidents also discussed China's view of the world. Yahya stated that China felt "surrounded by hostile forces – India, Soviet Union and the United States in Southeast Asia," and thus suggested a "dialogue with China to bring China back into the community

---

24   Nixon's visit on August 1, 1969 had been to Lahore rather than Rawalpindi as the official capital Islamabad had not yet been completed.

25   Memo from Jim Keogh, Cabinet Meeting, June 3, 1969, p. 5, Box 7, MemforP, Records of Meetings, POF, WHCF, NPMS, NA.

26   Nixon's handwritten notations, Box 50, July–August 1969, Asian Trip [2 of 2], PSF, PPF, NPMS, NA. In his memoirs, Nixon recalls his favorable impression of Pakistan during his previous visits as Vice President in 1953 and as a private citizen in 1964. See Nixon, *RN*, p. 133, and pp. 256–257.

27   Nixon, *RN*, p. 546. Former Pakistani President Ayub Khan had once unsuccessfully tried to mediate between the US and China in 1965. Department of State Telegram, STATE 154461(Extract), Attached to Memo from Holdridge to Kissinger, "Sino-American Contacts via Pakistan," September 16, 1969, Pakistan, Vol. 1, January 1–November 30, 1969, Box 623, Country Files (CF) – Middle East, NSCF, NPMS, NA.

28   Memcon, Ambassador Agha Hilaly and Harold M. Saunders, p. 1, in Cookies II, Chronology of Exchange with PRC, February 1969–April 1971, Box 1032, For the President's Files (FPF) – China Materials, NSCF, NPMS, NA.

29   Ibid.

of nations."[30] Nixon agreed that "Asia can not move forward if a nation as large as China remains isolated."[31] Nixon stated further that the US should "not" participate in "any arrangements designed to isolate China."[32] In the end, Yahya noted that: "it might take a little time to pass this message."[33]

Later in the same day, Yahya arranged a briefing meeting between Kissinger and Air Marshal Sher Ali Khan, who had visited China in July.[34] Kissinger asked if there was any perceptible change in the Chinese external behavior. The Marshal explained that Zhou insisted that the Soviets were "deliberately provoking" China by trying to extend their territory beyond recognized boundaries."[35] Thus, the Pakistani official confirmed that Beijing feared the Soviets might try a "preemptive attack on China."[36]

Overall, Nixon's trip to Pakistan was a huge success. The largest Pakistani daily newspaper, *JANG*, called on President Nixon to review US policy toward China in order to "reduce the threat to peace."[37] Haldeman recorded in his diaries that during the flight from Lahore, Pakistan to Bucharest, Romania, Nixon explained how impressed he was by the Pakistani leader who showed great insight into the relations between the Soviet Union, an Indian ally, and China, which was maintaining close relations with Pakistan.[38] Nixon said to Kissinger: "He could be a valuable channel to China – maybe Russia, too."[39]

On August 6, 1969, James S. Spain, American Chargé d'affaires in Rawalpindi, sent a letter of enquiry to Kissinger, after having discovered the substantial difference between the notes of the Nixon-Yahya talks provided by both the US side and the Pakistani side. Spain pointed out that President Nixon was supposed to have told President Yahya that the US wished to seek reconciliation with China, wanted Zhou to know this, and would appreciate the Pakistani passing the word and using their influence to promote it. President Yahya was supposed to have agreed

---

30   Ibid., p. 2.
31   Ibid.
32   Ibid.
33   Ibid. Nixon's handwritten-notes further show that Yahya personally informed Nixon of his two-hour talk with Mao regarding the Cultural Revolution and the Sino-Soviet rift. Mao and Zhou said to Yahya: "if Russia atomize [sic] us we will break out all over Asia – what are they going to do – atomize [sic] all over Asia?" Nixon's handwritten notations, Box 50, July–August 1969, Asian Trip [2 of 2], PSF, PPF, NPMS, NA.
34   Telegram, American Embassy Rawalpindi, Pakistan, August 1, 1969, Pakistan Vol. 1, 01 January–30 November, 1969, Box 623, CF-Middle East, NSCF, NPMS, NA. In his memoirs, without any reference to the Sino-Soviet differences, Kissinger briefly mentions the Marshal's description of the decline of China's dometistic upheaval caused by the Cultural Revolution. See Kissinger, *White House Years*, p. 181.
35   Ibid.
36   Ibid.
37   Special Memorandum, Foreign Radio and Press Reaction to President Nixon's Trip to Asia and Romania, 23 July–3 August, 1969, 6 August 1969, p. 6, East Asian Trip 1969 [Part 3], Box 464, PTF, NSCF, NPMS, NA.
38   Haldeman, *The Haldeman Diaries*, August 2, 1969.
39   Ibid.

on the desirability of this arrangement but stressed that Pakistan's relationship with Beijing "tended to be overrated in the West." He was reportedly debating whether to utilize the local Chinese Ambassador to convey the message or to wait for a still unscheduled visit to Pakistan by Zhou – which might be months in the further.[40]

On August 19, 1969, Kissinger sent a reply to Spain emphasizing that the Nixon-Yahya talks were conducted on a "strictly head-to-head basis" and the President contemplated that the contents of these discussions would go "no further than Yahya and himself."[41] Consequently, it was the President's personal desire that there be "no written record or further reference" to his private discussions with Yahya and that "no official communications refer to them."[42]

On September 16, 1969, Holdridge reported to Kissinger that President Nixon's interest in "using the Pakistanis as a line of communication" to the Chinese had become "known to a number of people in State."[43] In particular, Holdridge attached a State Department cable, which reported a conversation between Assistant Secretary for Near Eastern and South Asian Affairs, Joseph J. Sisco, and Pakistani Ambassador, Agha Hilaly. The cable showed that Hilaly referred to the Nixon-Yahya talks on "Pakistan's possible usefulness in communicating" with Beijing and reiterated Pakistan's willingness to "help" Washington's communication with Beijing.[44] At this stage, therefore, the pursuit of strict secrecy by Nixon and Kissinger was not as complete as they had expected.

On August 28, under Kissinger's instruction, NSC staff member, Harold Saunders, met Pakistani Ambassador, Agha Hilaly, and reiterated the US interest in improving relations via Pakistan. In particular, Saunders explained that the US wished to establish "a single channel" between Hilaly and Kissinger as "the two points of contact" for any further discussion of US-PRC relations.[45] Hilaly explained that Zhou accepted an invitation to Pakistan without specifying the timing. Hence, President Yahya might initially convey that the US had "no hostile intent" toward China. However, Yahya would wait until his meeting with Zhou to "convey President Nixon's specific views."[46] In November 1969, Yahya finally delivered Nixon's

---

40 Spain to Kissinger, August 6, 1969, Pakistan, Vol. 1, January 1–November 30, 1969, Box 623, CF–Middle East, NSCF, NPMS, NA.

41 Kissinger to Spain, August 19, 1969, Pakistan, Vol. 1, January 1–November 30, 1969, Box 623, CF-Middle East, NSCF, NPMS, NA. On his return to Washington, Nixon asked for information about the US Embassy staff in Pakistan. Letter from Assistant Secretary of Commerce to Nixon, August 11, 1969, Pakistan, Vol. 1, January 1–November 30, 1969, Box 623, CF-Middle East, NSCF, NPMS, NA.

42 Ibid.

43 Holdridge to Kissinger, "Sino-American Contacts via Pakistan," September 16, 1969, Pakistan, Vol. 1, January 1–November 30, 1969, Box 623, CF-Middle East, NSCF, NPMS, NA.

44 Ibid. Joseph J. Sisco was Assistant Secretary for Near Eastern and South Asian Affairs from 1969–1974.

45 Memcon, Ambassador Agha Hilaly and Harold M. Saunders, p. 1, in Cookies II, Chronology of Exchange with PRC, February 1969–April 1971, Box 1032, FPF–China Materials, NSCF, NPMS, NA.

46 Ibid., p. 2.

messages to Zhou. Thus was the origin of the so-called Pakistan backchannel, which would play the crucial role of "intermediary" in delivering secret messages between Washington and Beijing, especially from October 1970 to June 1971.[47]

1.3 The Nixon-Ceauşescu talks and the opening of the Romanian channel

On August 2 and 3, 1969, Nixon visited Bucharest and met with Romanian President Nicolae Ceauşescu, whom he personally respected for his strong presidency and the long-term preservation of his country's independence in Soviet dominated Eastern Europe. In 1967, Nixon, as a private citizen, had already met Ceauşescu and thus was aware that the Romania president was one of the few Eastern European leaders who had reached out to Beijing despite Moscow's displeasure.[48] Importantly, as the "first state visit by an American President" to the capital of a communist country in Eastern Europe since the end of the World War II, Nixon's visit to Romania caused media sensation.[49]

Nixon was fully aware of the long-term importance of this trip. For example, on July 22, Nixon explained his decision to Congressional leaders: "We do not go there to antagonize the Soviets. ... We go there to offer hope to the people of Eastern Europe."[50] In particular, Nixon's handwritten-notes before his arrival to Bucharest show that the President prepared his personal messages to Ceauşescu regarding the US attitude toward Sino-Soviet relations: 1) "We don't want Soviet v. China hostility" and 2) "We will not gang up with one against another."[51]

During his confidential talk with Ceauşescu on August 2, 1969, being aware that his statement would most likely be passed on to the Chinese, Nixon made clear, "We have no interest in creating a bloc or other arrangements in Asia which can be

---

47   Lord recalls that: "I don't know whose idea it [back-channel] was. But it clearly required tight control and secrecy which Nixon and Kissinger wanted for the secret opening to China." Lord, interview with the author, October 15, 2003. On Pakistan's interest in strengthening its security position against India by playing an intermediary role between Washington and Beijing, see G.W. Chroundhury, "Reflections on Sino-Pakistan Relations," *Pacific Community*, Vol. 7, January 1976, pp. 248–270; Dennis Kux, *The United States and Pakistan, 1947–2000: Disenchanted Allies* (Washington DC: Woodrow Wilson Center Press, 2001); and F.S. Aijazuddin (ed.) *The White House and Pakistan: Secret Declassified Documents, 1969–1974* (Oxford, New York: Oxford University Press, 2002).

48   Nixon, *RN*, pp. 281–282, pp. 395–396; and Kissinger, *White House Years*, pp. 155–158.

49   Nixon's handwritten-notes, Box 50, July–August 1969, Asian Trip [1 of 2], PSF, PPF, NPMS, NA. The Romania trip was Nixon's idea. In early June, Nixon wrote to Kissinger: "I believe we could needle our Moscow friends by arranging more visits to the Eastern Europe countries." On June 21, Kissinger met with Romanian Ambassador Corneliu Bodgan and conveyed the President's interest in visiting Romania. On June 28, 1969, the White House announced that the President had accepted an invitation from Romania, which surprised both the press and the public. See Kissinger, *White House Years*, p. 156.

50   Buchanan to Nixon, July 22, 1969, MemforP, Records of Meetings, Box 78, POF, WHCF, NPMS, NA.

51   Nixon's handwritten-notes, Box 50, July–August 1969, Asian Trip [2 of 2], PSF, PPF, NPMS, NA.

interpreted as fencing off Communist China."⁵² In the short term, Nixon explained, "We do not recognize Communist China and we oppose its entry into the UN, not because of China's internal policy but because of its policies toward its neighbors."⁵³ In the long term, however, Nixon expressed his hope that: "Our policy is to have good relations with the Soviet Union and eventually, when China changes its approach to other nations, we want to open communications channels with them to establish relations."⁵⁴ Nixon concluded that: "China is a reality and no real peace is possible without China's playing a role."⁵⁵

In response, Ceaușescu commented that "ideology was not crucial" in the Sino-Soviet dispute; the real issues were "national," because the Soviets were "reluctant to concede China its proper place in international affairs."⁵⁶ Ceaușescu insisted therefore that the US and the USSR eventually would have to recognize that China could "not occupy a second class position internationally." As for the growing tension in Sino-Soviet border areas, Ceaușescu did not think that the Beijing-Moscow antagonism would lead to war, but admitted that "the unexpected could always happen."⁵⁷

Finally, Nixon asked Ceaușescu to convey a confidential message to the Chinese regarding his willingness to restore US-China relations: "Frankly, if it serves your interest and the interest of your government, we would welcome your playing a mediating role between us and China."⁵⁸ Ceaușescu replied by affirming Romania's willingness to mediate between the US and China: "[W]e shall tell our opinion to the Chinese, and of your opinion of this problem. We shall act to establish relations on the basis of mutual understanding."⁵⁹

In his memoirs, Haldeman recalls his exchange with Kissinger before the departure from Romania: "You know, he [Nixon] actually seriously intends to visit China before the end of the second term."⁶⁰ "Fat chance," answered Kissinger.⁶¹ In particular, Nixon was considering the promotion of trade in order to open up communist countries. Aboard Air Force One (on his way from Pakistan to Romania), Nixon told Marshall Green that trade might be a good means to draw the Chinese out of their international isolation, since China's trade relations with the Soviets had already collapsed.⁶²

---

52   Memcon, Nixon and Ceausescu, Bucharest, Romania, August 2, 1969, p. 7, P/HAK MemCons Box 1023, NSCF, NPMS, NA. See also Nixon, *RN*, p. 546; and Kissinger, *White House Years*, p. 181.
53   Ibid., p. 7.
54   Ibid., p. 8.
55   Ibid., p. 9.
56   Ibid., p. 11.
57   Ibid.
58   Ibid.
59   Ibid.
60   H.R. Haldeman with Joseph Dimona, *The Ends of Power* (New York: Times Books, 1978), p. 91.
61   Ibid.
62   Green, Oral History Interview, March 2 and 17, 1995, FAOHC; and Memo from Green to Richardson, "Next Steps in China Policy," October 6, 1969, p. 1, POL Chicom-US. 1967–1969, Box 1973, SNF, RG59, NA.

Overall, the Romanian trip was very successful, illustrating the Nixon administration's policy to ease tensions with the Communist bloc and to promote a new dialogue. The Romanian media gave extensive news coverage to all phases of the President's Bucharest visit while seeking to limit comment in evident deference to Soviet sensitivities.[63] Thereafter, Nixon regarded Romania as one of the major back-channels in US-China relations. It turned out, however, that the Chinese did not prefer Romania as the main backchannel. Solomon explains that the Chinese distrusted Communist states, especially those in Eastern Europe and remained suspicious that Romanians were probably "penetrated by the Soviet intelligence agents."[64] In comparison, Lord argues that: "Pakistan was more attractive to China, because China always had a problem with India, and Pakistan had a close relationship with China. The Romanians, although they had independence from the Russians, were still in Eastern Europe, so it made the Chinese feel uncomfortable."[65]

1.4 Reactions to the Nixon trip

The White House and the State Department carefully monitored the local media in the countries in which the President visited, and noted that mostly favorable coverage with considerable comment was provided.[66]

The Soviet media "played down" the President's visit to Bucharest, "refraining from any direct comment."[67] However, it described the aim of the Asia trip as restoration of American influence in Asia in the wake of the damage caused by the Vietnam War. It pressed the Soviet's Asian Collective Security proposal as the proper alternative to US-sponsored "military blocs." There had been "only brief mention of US China policy" in Soviet comment on the tour. However, none of the Soviet comment was at an authoritative level.[68]

Beijing's comment at a low level sought to "undercut any tendency to credit" the Nixon Administration with a new approach to Asian affairs, denouncing both the United States and the Soviet Union for practicing "imperialism in Asia."[69] In particular, Beijing had "remained silent" on the State Department's June 21 announcement of a relaxation of trade and travel restrictions, and had also "avoided mentioning" the President's visits to Pakistan and Romania.[70] Importantly, Beijing's

---

63 Special Memorandum, Foreign Radio and Press Reaction to President Nixon's Trip to Asia and Romania, 23 July–3 August 1969, August 6, 1969, p. 17, East Asian Trip 1969 [Part 3], Box 464, PTF, NSCF, NPMS, NA.
64 Solomon, interview with the author, September 24, 2003.
65 Lord, interview with the author, October 15, 2003.
66 Special Memorandum, Foreign Radio and Press Reaction to President Nixon's Trip to Asia and Romania, 23 July–3 August 1969, August 6, 1969, p. i, East Asian Trip 1969 [Part 3], Box 464, PTF, NSCF, NPMS, NA.
67 Ibid.
68 Ibid., p. iii.
69 Ibid., p. iv; and Intelligence Note, INR, "Communist China: Peking's Reaction to the President's Trip," August 13, 1969, p. 1, Box 1973, SNF, RG59, NA.
70 Ibid.

comment on the President's trip did "not raise the question of Taiwan or other issues directly affecting Sino-American relations."[71]

On August 4, 1969, President Nixon gave a briefing on his recent trip to the legislative leaders of both parties, including Senate Majority Leader Mike Mansfield and the chairman of the Foreign Relations Committee, Senator J. William Fulbright. Nixon stated: "American policy in Asia is in a transition stage ... The US must move away from a monolithic approach to a country-by-country approach."[72] Nixon reiterated his strong belief in the continuation of the US presence in Asia, because the US withdrawal "would leave a vacuum of power in Asia which would be filled only by the Chinese or the Soviets."[73] Regarding the Soviet proposal of an Asian Collective Security System, Nixon emphasized that he sought to assure "every Asian leader" that the United States would not enter into an "anti-Chinese security pact with the Soviets in Asia," because it would "enormously enhance Soviet influence" in Asia.[74] Finally, Nixon concluded: "We should not go along with the Soviet-American condominium on Asia"; and that, "We have to find a way to communicate with the Chinese."[75]

In the meanwhile, the State Department took its initiative to clarify the new direction of US policy toward China. On July 31, 1969, Secretary Rogers stated in Tokyo that the Nixon administration had indicated "several times and in many ways" that "we would like to improve relations with Communist China."[76] On August 8, Secretary Rogers gave a speech at Canberra, Australia, expressing the administration's opinion that China had been "too isolated from world affairs," and indicated that the US was interested in a "useful dialogue and reduction of tensions" with China.[77] Thus, Washington had been seeking to open the channels of communication with Beijing. While the Rogers speech brought about favorable reactions from the media in the United States, it was a surprise for Nixon and Kissinger, both of whom seemed not to have been informed of the speech in advance, despite their attempt to minimize the role of the State Department in the US policy toward China.[78]

2. The Escalation of the Sino-Soviet Border Clashes in August and September 1969

2.1 NSC meeting on NSSM 14: US China policy in August 1969

During the summer of 1969, tension along the Sino-Soviet border areas continued to increase. After a particularly violent clash at the Xijiang province border on

---

71　Ibid., p. 27.
72　Buchanan to Nixon (Notes of Legislative Leadership Meeting August 4, 1969), August 5, 1969 p. 1, MemforP, Records of Meetings, Box 79, POF, WHCF, NPMS, NA.
73　Ibid., p. 3.
74　Ibid.
75　Ibid.
76　*The New York Times*, August 1, 1969.
77　*The New York Times*, August 8, 1969.
78　Raymond L. Garthoff, *Détente and Confrontation* (Washington DC: The Brookings Institution, 1985), pp. 247–248.

August 13, 1969 (the largest scale fighting since March of that year), the State Department's Bureau of Intelligence and Research reported that both the USSR and China were "determined to assert what they regard as their rights along the entire length of the frontier" and that, consequently, sharp border clashes were "likely to continue for some time."[79] Although the two sides probably intended to "contain these incidents and prevent them from getting out of hand," it was possible that "unintended escalation might take place."[80] The National Intelligence Estimate also reported that "for the first time" it was realistic to ask if a "major Sino-Soviet war" could take place in the near future.[81] The report estimated that Moscow might consider whether it could "launch a strike against China's nuclear and missile facilities" without getting involved into a "prolonged and large-scale conflict."[82]

On August 14, 1969, the first NSC meeting fully devoted to China policy was held in order to discuss the NSSM 14 paper. Given Nixon's recent Asian trip, it was a useful time to focus on US relations with China and to "develop a new policy toward Asia, and the Sino-Soviet dispute."[83] The unilateral steps which the US announced on July 23 with regard to travel and tourist purchases were designed to show Washington's "willingness to have a more constructive relationship" with Beijing while maintaining its commitments to Taipei. Nixon reiterated that he made these points clear throughout his recent trip.[84] There was a general agreement within the administration that US policy could have little impact on Chinese behavior in the short term.[85] In the long term, however, there was a concern that an isolated China would increase the danger of "miscalculation and irrational behavior."[86] Therefore, while a more moderate China was not necessarily less of a threat, it could be "more manageable and predictable."[87]

The revised NSSM 14 paper issued by the NSC staff (after the Review Group on May 15) included an updated reassessment of the deepening Sino-Soviet mutual

---

79   Intelligence Note, INR, "USSR-China: Ominous Rumbling From the Enigmatic East," August 13, 1969, p. 1, POL Chicom-USSR, 1967–1969, Box 1975, SNF, RG59, NA.
80   Ibid., p. 2.
81   National Intelligence Estimate, Number 11/13–69, "The USSR and China" August 12, 1969, p. 1, *Tracking the Dragon: Selected National Intelligence Estimates on China, 1948–1976*, National Intelligence Council, CD-ROM (Washington DC: US Government Printing Office, 2004).
82   Ibid.
83   NSC Meeting, August 14, 1969, Talking Points (The President): China, p. 1, Box H-023, NSC Meeting (San Clemente) Briefing Korea/China [2 of 3] 8/14/69, Minutes of Meetings (1969–1974), NSCIF, NPMS, NA. Nixon and Kissinger requested CIA director Richard Helms hold a briefing on "Assessment of Present Chinese Communist Situation, including development of their nuclear capability and political trends." Kissinger to Laird, "Briefing Requirements for NSC Meeting," August 9, 1969, p. 1, Box H-299, NSC Vol. II, 4/1/69–5/30/69 [2 of 2], NSCF, NPMS, NA.
84   Ibid.
85   NSC Meeting, August 14, 1969, HAK Talking Points: US China Policy, p. 4, Box H-023, NSC Meeting (San Clemente) Briefing Korea/China [2 of 3] 8/14/69, Minutes of Meetings (1969–1974), NSCIF, NPMS, NA.
86   Ibid.
87   Ibid., p. 5.

hostility. Both Beijing and Moscow were highly suspicious of US relations with the other. Thus, there were a few different angles within the administration about the US relations with each communist giant.[88] One view argued that the Soviets were so suspicious of US-Chinese "collusion" that any US efforts to improve relations with China would make better US-USSR relations impossible.[89] Those who held this view believed that Washington should give top priority to improving relations with Moscow and, for this reason, should avoid any effort to increase contact with Beijing. An opposing view argued that the Soviets were more likely to be conciliatory if they feared that the United States would otherwise pursue a rapprochement with China. Those who held this view (the so-called *Realpolitik* approach, in Kissinger's words) would urge that the United States expand its contacts with China as a "means of leverage against the Soviet Union."[90] A third view held that consideration of US relations with the Soviet Union should "not be a major factor" in shaping America's China policy.[91] Those who held this view believed that: a) the United States did not fully understand how its China policy would affect Soviet behavior; b) by talking to the Soviets, the US could decrease any fears they might have; and c) marginal actions to increase Soviet nervousness might be useful, however, fundamental changes in the US-China relationship should be guided by determining on its own merits what America's China policy should be.[92]

Nixon emphasized that he made clear to Asian leaders during his trip that the US did not intend to join the Soviets in any plan to "gang up" on China.[93] Particularly important, Nixon judged the Soviet Union as the more aggressive party in the Sino-Soviet conflict, stressing that it was against the US interest to let China be "smashed."[94] Overall, as Lord assesses, the Sino-Soviet border clashes in the summer of 1969 "made clear the potential for triangular diplomacy" of US-USSR-PRC relations.[95]

---

88   US China Policy, p. 4, NSC Meeting, August 14, 1969, Box H-023, NSC Meeting (San Clemente) Briefing Korea/China [2 of 3] 8/14/69, Minutes of Meetings (1969–1974), NSCIF, NPMS, NA. See also Kissinger, *White House Years*, p. 182.

89   Ibid.

90   Ibid.

91   Ibid.

92   Ibid., pp. 4–5.

93   NSC Meeting, August 14, 1969, Talking Points (The President): China, p. 1, Box H-023, NSC Meeting (San Clemente) Briefing Korea/China [2 of 3] 8/14/69, Minutes of Meetings (1969–1974), NSCIF, NPMS, NA. The NSC would meet again early in autumn to consider the Sino-Soviet conflict in greater detail, after Review Group consideration of NSSM 63 that was completed.

94   Rodman, interview with the author, October 21, 2003. See also Kissinger, *White House Years*, p. 182. On August 18, at San Clemente, Nixon reiterated his concern about the devastating impact of China being "smashed" in the Sino-Soviet border war. William Safire, *Before the Fall* (New York: Doubleday, 1975), p. 370.

95   Lord, interview with the author, October 15, 2003.

2.2 The Kissinger-Whiting consultation in August 1969

On August 16, 1969, Kissinger, accompanied by NSC staff member Holdridge, met with a distinguished academic expert on China, Allen Whiting.[96] Whiting stressed the arrival of an "historic opportunity" for the United States to explore the Chinese perception of a "common cause" with the US against the growing Soviet military threat. Whiting explained that the Chinese would have a "tendency to exaggerate the threat" and that "we could exploit and move forward to the Chinese but not on their terms but with our terms." The question was "not the literal threat" but it was a "perceived threat, as the Chinese perceived it."[97]

After the meeting, Whiting drafted a detailed memorandum in which he analyzed the massive Soviet military deployments along the Sino-Soviet border areas and warned of the danger of a Soviet military attack (including the use of nuclear weapons) on China possibly "aimed at destroying China's nuclear capability."[98] Perceiving the outbreak of a larger scale clash on the Sinkiang border on August 13 as a deliberate Soviet initiative, Whiting suggested that the US objectives should be: "(1) to deter a Soviet attack on China (2) to inhibit the use of nuclear weapons in a Sino-Soviet war, and (3) to maximize the possibility of China identifying Russia as its sole antagonist, in contrast with the rest of the world and particularly with the United States."[99] Finally, Whiting urged that by taking such concrete steps as to resume contacts with the Chinese in Warsaw and through third parties and to lift the trade embargo with China, the US should assure the Chinese of its opposition to a Soviet attack.[100]

Holdridge, however, was not convinced of Whiting's assessment of the possible Soviet air strike against China. The Soviets would be "appalled at the magnitude of the situation" which would develop if they entered a war with China, with its

---

96 Allen Whiting, interview with the author, October 19, 2003. Whiting had worked successively at the State Department's Bureau of Intelligence and Research and the US Consulate General in Hong Kong during the 1960s and then joined the faculty of the University of Michigan. He also worked as a consultant for the RAND Corporation in Santa Monica, California, where he was based during the summer of 1969. Whiting later became critical of the "strict limitations" of the participants in the planning of Kissinger's July 1971 secret trip. Whiting would meet with Kissinger for further consultations on August 12, October 14, and December 16, 1971. Whiting, Allen, Name Files (NF), Box 838, NSCF, NPMS, NA. Whiting criticizes that Kissinger neglected "the labors of John K. Fairbank and A. Doak Barnett, among others, who labored long and hard for public acceptance of normalization," and that Kissinger's disdainful accusation thus hindered a balanced judgment on the basis of "historical accuracy." Allen Whiting, "Sino-American Détente," *China Quarterly*, 82, June 1980, p. 336, p. 339.

97 Ibid.

98 Letter from Whiting to Kissinger, August 16, 1969, and an enclosed report, "Sino-Soviet Hostilities and Implications for US Policy," p. 1, China, Box 839, NF, NSCF, NPMS, NA.

99 Ibid., p. 8.

100 Ibid., p. 10.

vast territory and strong resistance from its large population.[101] Hence, Holdridge concluded that the Soviets were going to be "very careful about what kind of decision they make."[102] On the other hand, Whiting recalls that Kissinger and Holdridge had little understanding of the nature of Sino-Soviet mutual hostility and the Soviet military deployment along the Sino-Soviet border in August 1969.[103]

After that meeting, Whiting received no feedback from Kissinger and the NSC staff. In November 1971, Kissinger explained to Whiting, "You know, until you brought that memo [of August 1969], we had a laundry list of things we would do, individual kind of signals. But we didn't have it in a strategy. And your presentation put the whole thing into a strategic context."[104] Overall, despite Kissinger's omission in his memoirs, the consultation with Whiting in August 1969 provided a crucial opportunity for Kissinger to improve his understanding of the nature of Sino-Soviet relations.[105]

In the meantime, the Soviets remained highly suspicious of a possible Sino-US collusion against them. On August 18, 1969, during a meeting with State Department official William L. Stearman, Soviet Embassy official Boris N. Davydov raised the question of possible US reactions in the case of their direct air-strike against China's nuclear installations asking: "Wouldn't the US try to take advantage of this situation?"[106] Accordingly, on August 28, William Hyland, Soviet expert in the NSC staff, estimated that a limited Sino-Soviet war would involve Soviet strikes to destroy China's nuclear facilities, and consequently become a "solution" to China's nuclear problem.[107]

On August 29, a group of outside consultants to the State Department reviewed an on-going interdepartmental policy study, NSSM 63: "US Policy on Current Sino-Soviet Differences." Among them, the Asian experts, such as A. Doak Barnett, Ralph Clough, and Fred Greene, counter-argued that "any Soviet punitive strike at China or an effort to take out Chinese nuclear facilities would result in strengthening Chinese nationalism and unity, and would solidify Mao's position."[108] Finally, all

---

101 Holdridge, Oral History Interview, July 20, 1995, p. 105, FAOHC. See also Holdridge, *Crossing the Divide*, p. 34.

102 Ibid.

103 Whiting, interview with the author, October 19, 2003. Whiting regarded Holdridge as a generalist on Asia rather than a China expert.

104 Ibid.

105 There still remains ambiguity as to what extent Kissinger and the NSC staff came to realize the subtleness of Chinese diplomatic practice in 1969, because they occasionally failed to grasp the implications of China's diplomatic signals in 1970, as Chapter 6 of this book discusses later.

106 Memcon "US Reaction to Soviet Destruction of CPR Chinese People's Republic Nuclear Capability; Significance of latest Sino-Soviet Border Clash," August 18, 1969, p. 2, Def 12, Chicom, SNF, RG59, NA.

107 Hyland to Kissinger, "Sino-Soviet Contingencies," August 28, 1969, p. 2, CF–USSR Vol. IV, NSCF, NPMS, NA.

108 Miriam Camps (State Department Planning and Coordination Staff) to Richardson, "NSSM 63 – Meeting with Consultants," August 29, 1969, p. 2, Freedom of Information Act release to the National Security Archive.

the consultants agreed that the NSSC 63 paper "underestimated the danger in a Soviet preemptive strike" and that "even a non-nuclear Soviet strike would have a vast destabilizing effect in Japan, elsewhere in Asia, and in Western Europe." These experts urged that the US should make clear to the Chinese that the US was "not colluding" with the Soviets.[109] Overall, Rodman recalls that the Soviets "tested us and asked us if we would object to a Soviet attack on the Chinese nuclear facilities."[110] In consequence, the US government would privately send a "very important signal" toward Beijing that "we would not welcome a Soviet attack on China."[111]

2.3 The Zhou-Kosygin talks in September 1969

On September 3, 1969, Premier Zhou visited Hanoi to attend Ho Chi Minh's funeral. The event provided a crucial opportunity for US officials to assess the current situation in Beijing-Hanoi-Moscow triangular relations, and President Nixon ordered a large-scale intelligence operation. The State Department's Bureau of Intelligence and Research analysts estimated that Premier Zhou and Soviet Prime Minister Kosygin were "likely to cross paths for the first time since February 1965" at funeral ceremonies in Hanoi, yet their "separate consultations" with the North Vietnamese would highlight their different views on the Vietnam War.[112] Hanoi, in turn, would question the Soviets and the Chinese on their respective "intentions in the Sino-Soviet dispute."[113] INR officials anticipated that the Chinese might have calculated that it would provide an opportunity for conveying to the Soviets their growing concern about the "danger of war" by emphasizing the Chinese "determination to resist if attacked."[114]

In public, the State Department took a major step. On September 5, 1969, Under Secretary of State Elliot Richardson made a speech at a convention of the American Political Science Association in New York. Richardson stated that the "long-run improvement" of relations with China was "in our own national interest."[115] In particular, Richardson made it clear that the United States would "not seek to exploit" the hostility between the Soviet Union and "the People's Republic" and argued that ideological differences between the two Communist giants were "not our affair."[116]

The speech was crucial because it officially clarified the US attitude toward the Sino-Soviet border problem during the peak of its tension. Richardson's

---

109   Ibid., pp. 2–3.
110   Rodman, interview with the author, October 21, 2003.
111   Ibid.
112   Intelligence Note, INR, "Ho Chi Minh's Funeral – Chou Leads Parade to Hanoi, Soviet Leader to Follow, September 4, 1969, p. 1, POL Chicom-USSR, 1967–1969, Box 1975, SNF, RG59, NA.
113   Ibid.
114   Ibid., p. 4.
115   Address by Under Secretary of State Elliot L. Richardson, September 5, 1969, p. 15, Box 102, Folder speeches (1), Elliot Richardson Papers, Manuscript Division, Library of Congress.
116   Ibid.

handwritten notes show that he personally prepared the speech combining a set of recommendations from his staff. Particularly important, it was Richardson himself who changed the terms "Communist China" in the draft speech to "the People's Republic."[117] Media coverage was generally quite favorable to the Richardson speech. For example, *The New York Times* described the Richardson speech as "one of the most explicit public statements" on the Nixon Administration's position regarding the rift between Beijing and Moscow.[118] It also reported that diplomatic observers in Washington viewed the speech as the State Department's "opposition" to those who argued that it would be a good idea for the two Communist states to "engage into a full-scale war."[119] The State Department's INR experts assessed that, despite its public harshness toward the Nixon administration, since July Beijing had "privately exhibited increased curiosity about US Asian policy," which appeared to be influenced by a series of policy statements by Nixon as well as by other senior officials, such as Rogers and Richardson.[120]

On September 11, 1969, after their separate trips to Hanoi, Premier Zhou and Soviet Prime Minister Kosygin held a talk at the Beijing airport. Although rhetoric continued to remain harsh in public, especially from the Chinese side, the talk prevented rapid escalation of tension along the Sino-Soviet border areas.[121] On September 12, the State Department's INR analysts estimated that this first meeting between Zhou and Kosygin since February 1965 may have been suggested by the Soviets, and accepted belatedly by the Chinese, who were unwilling to appear as the obstacle to Communist unity and peaceful reduction in Sino-Soviet tensions. However, the Zhou-Kosygin meeting probably "produced no breakthrough in the dispute" between Beijing and Moscow.[122] On September 18, INR officials also reported that the recently published slogans for China's 20th anniversary celebrations on October 1 warned explicitly of "atomic war."[123]

On October 7, 1969, the New China News Agency announced that Beijing had agreed to resume border talks with Moscow at the Deputy Foreign Minister level in Beijing. The State Department's Bureau of Intelligence and Research judged that China had been motivated by the deepening "fear" of a possible Soviet preemptive

---

117   Richardson's notation in ibid.

118   *The New York Times*, September 6, 1969, in Box 108, Scrap books (1), Elliot Richardson Papers, Manuscript Division, Library of Congress.

119   Ibid. William Bundy emphasizes the Richardson speech as the most important public signal during 1969, for it sought to calm China's worries over a possible US move to the Soviet side. William Bundy, *A Tangled Web: The Making of Foreign Policy in the Nixon Presidency* (Hill and Wang, A Division of Farrar, Straus and Giroux: New York, 1998), p. 106.

120   Intelligence Note, INR, "Communist China: Increased Curiosity About US Asian Policy," September 8, 1969, p. 1, POL Chicom-US. 1967–1969, Box 1973, SNF, RG59, NA.

121   "Information About A.N. Kosygin's Conversation with Zhou Enlai on 11 September 1969," *The Cold War in Asia*, Cold War International History Project Bulletin.

122   Intelligence Note, INR, "Communist China/USSR: Kosygin Meets Chou at Peking Airport, September 12, 1969, p. 1, POL Chicom-USSR, 1967–1969, Box 1975, SNF, RG59, NA. See also Kissinger, *White House Years*, pp. 184–185.

123   Intelligence Note, INR, "Communist China: War Fears and Domestic Politics," September 18, 1969, p. 1, POL ChiCom, 1967–1969, Box 1962, SNF, RG59, NA.

attack on its nuclear installations which had surfaced in propaganda in the previous few months.[124] On October 8, the Chinese Foreign Ministry called for a mutual withdrawal from disputed border areas.[125]

The same day, Under Secretary of State Richardson sent a memorandum to President Nixon describing the decision for the resumption of Sino-Soviet border negotiations as a "new phase in Sino-Soviet and perhaps ultimately Sino-US relations" and as a "practical move demonstrating a flexible approach" in Beijing's external behavior.[126] State Department officials noted particularly that the Chinese statement of October 7 declared that "irreconcilable differences of principle" should not hinder the "maintenance of normal state relations" between China and the Soviet Union on the basis of the "five principles of peaceful coexistence." The Chinese further stated that even if no border agreement could be reached, the "status quo" should be maintained, and there should be "no resort to force."[127]

3. Two Lines of Policy Studies – the NSC and the State Department

3.1 Drafting of NSSM 63: Sino-Soviet differences

Meanwhile, the interdepartmental study on Sino-Soviet conflict was in progress, and the Review Group (September 25 and November 20, 1969) and the Washington Special Action Group (September 4, 17, 29, and October 20, 1969) met to review NSSM-63: "US Policy on Current Sino-Soviet Differences."[128] The paper examined the "triangular relationship" between the US, the USSR, and China, especially the "problems and opportunities" for US policy under two sets of circumstances: 1) the

---

124 Intelligence Note, INR, "Communist China/USSR: Peking Agrees to Resume Border Talks," October 7, 1969, p. 2, POL Chicom-USSR, 1967–1969, Box 1975, SNF, RG59, NA.

125 Intelligence Note, INR, "Communist China/USSR: Peking Publishes Position Paper on Border, October 10, 1969, pp. 1–2, POL Chicom-USSR, 1967–1969, Box 1975, SNF, RG59, NA.

126 Richardson to Nixon, "Significance of Peking's Agreement to Talk with the Soviets," October 8, 1969, p. 3, POL Chicom-USSR, 1967–1969, Box 1975, SNF, RG59, NA.

127 Ibid., p. 1. On October 20, Sino-Soviet border negotiations were finally resumed in Beijing between the Chinese and Soviet Deputy Foreign Ministers Ch'iao Kuan-hua and Vasily V. Kuznetsov.

128 The Chinese side was also conducting a series of policy option analyses. From July 29 to September 16, a committee of four Marshals met 10 times. On September 17, they submitted a report, suggesting that the Sino-US ambassadorial talks should be resumed when the timing was proper. Report by Four Chinese Marshals, "Our View about the Current Situation," September 17, 1969, in Chen Jian and David L. Wilson (eds), "'All Under the Heaven is Great Chaos'– Beijing, the Sino–Soviet Border Clashes, and the Turn Toward Sino-American Rapprochement, 1968–1969," p. 170, Bulletin 11, Cold War International History Project (CWIHP), Woodrow Wilson International Center for Scholars; and Chen Jian, *Mao's China and the Cold War* (Chapel Hill, NC: University of North Carolina Press, 2001), p. 249.

Sino-Soviet dispute continuing mainly in non-military ways, and 2) the outbreak of a major war.[129] The paper considered four broad strategies:

- To collaborate with China in its efforts to avoid Soviet-imposed political-economic isolation;
- To collaborate with the Soviets in isolating China;
- To adopt a "hands-off" attitude, refusing to have anything to do with either opponent that could be interpreted by the other as tilting the balance;
- To improve relations with both opponents, gaining "leverage" from the dispute where the US could in pursuit of its own interests.[130]

The "most important benefit" to Washington from the Sino-Soviet rivalry was that the growing dissidence between Beijing and Moscow had "limited both countries in the pursuit of policies basically antagonistic to US"[131] In other words, both sides genuinely feared the possibility of the US siding with the other. Importantly, however, the triangular relationship between the US, USSR, and China was "markedly unequal." It was therefore important "not to relieve Soviet concern about a possible improvement in Sino-American relations" in order to preserve the US leverage in the Sino-Soviet dispute.[132] Hence, the paper suggested that the US longer-term policy toward the USSR and China required a continuous effort to improve relations with both sides even-handedly, exerting pressure on the Soviets in the short-run, while "keeping the door open" to China in the long-run.[133]

However, Soviet specialists, such as former Ambassador to the Soviet Union Llewellyn Thompson and Charles Bohlen, still insisted that US overtures to China might introduce "irritants" into the US-Soviet relations, and thus the Soviets might adopt a "harder line both at home and in international affairs."[134] Hence, these experts argued for "caution in making moves toward better relations" with China.[135]

Overall, the NSSM-63 paper outlined the anticipated consequences which the dispute would have on Chinese and Soviet policy, and no official policy decisions were specifically made at this earlier political stage of the US opening to China.[136] Despite the Zhou-Kosygin talks, Kissinger still remained concerned about the Soviet posture toward China. In his memorandum to Nixon on September 29, 1969, Kissinger again raised the question of US reactions toward "a possible Soviet airstrike against China's nuclear/missile facilities or toward other Soviet military

---

129 NSSM-63: US Policy on Current Sino-Soviet Differences, Summary Statements, September 11, 1969, p. 1, NSC Review Group Meeting, Thursday, September 25, 1969, Sino-Soviet Differences (NSSM63), Box H-040, Senior Review Group Meetings, Minutes of Meetings (1969–1974), NSCIF, NPMS, NA.
130 Ibid. Quotation marks in original.
131 Ibid., p. 3.
132 Ibid., p. 4.
133 Ibid.
134 Ibid., p. 5.
135 Ibid.
136 Ibid., p. 2.

actions," including the use of nuclear weapons.[137] Kissinger estimated that the Soviets might be "using" the US to create an impression in China and the world that the US was "being consulted in secret and would look with equanimity on their military actions." Thus, the US should continue to "avoid the appearance of siding with the Soviets."[138] Finally, Kissinger anticipated that the Chinese were willing to put US-Chinese relations on "a more rational and less ideological basis."[139] In the middle-term, therefore, Nixon and Kissinger would privately seek to take an even-handed approach toward the two communist giants as the fourth strategic approach suggested in the NSSM63, which are later discussed in chapters 7 and 8 of this book.

3.2 State Department's policy studies in October 1969

On October 6, 1969, Assistant Secretary of State for East Asian and Pacific Affairs Marshall Green completed a detailed memorandum, reviewing US relations with China in the first 9 months of the new administration, and recommending the next public and private steps toward China.[140] The Nixon administration had indicated its "willingness to seek friendlier and more normal relations" through a series of public steps, such as modification of trade and travel restrictions on China and its repeatedly expressed "willingness to renew" its bilateral talks with the Chinese in Warsaw.[141] Despite public attacks against the administration in general and the President specifically, the Chinese privately had told a number of foreigners that they were "aware" that US policy toward China was "under review" and noted that the "trade and travel moves" were made within the context of this broad review.[142] However, the Chinese had stressed that these moves were "insufficient" and that "some move relating to Taiwan was necessary."[143] Green assessed that the Chinese had conveyed "mixed signals": while some reports suggested Beijing was seeking only some "symbolic" gestures, such as a minor troop withdrawal from Taiwan or

---

137 Kissinger to Nixon, "The US Role in Soviet Maneuvering Against China," September 29, 1969, p. 1, attached to Memo from Haig to Kissinger, October 11, 1969, Box 337, HAK/Richardson Meeting May 1969–December 1969, NSCF, NPMS, NA.

138 Ibid. The Soviet attitude toward Chinese representation in the UN was showing a sign of change. In his UN speech at the annual meeting of the General Assembly, Soviet Foreign Minister Andrei Gromyko for the first time did not refer to Beijing's admission. On September 22, 1969, Nixon sent a memorandum to Kissinger urging that: "I think that while Gromyko is in the country would be a very good time to have another move to China made." Confidential Files, 1969–1971, Box 6, CO 34, WHCF, NPMS, NA.

139 Ibid., p. 2.

140 Green to Richardson, "Next Steps in China Policy," October 6, 1969, POL Chicom-US. 1967–1969, Box 1973, SNF, RG59, NA. In their respective memoirs, however, neither Nixon nor Kissinger referred to Green's memoranda in late 1969.

141 Ibid., p. 1.

142 Ibid.

143 Ibid.

pull-back of the patrol ships in the Taiwan Strait, other reports focused on Beijing's long-term large objectives of complete US "withdrawal" from Taiwan.[144]

Importantly, Green emphasized that Beijing had privately expressed its understanding, through Premier Zhou to the French Ambassador to China, Etienne M. Manach, that the US had "not attempted to take advantage" of the Sino-Soviet dispute and that the US did not perceive a Sino-Soviet war as being in its interest.[145] Green indicated that there had been an internal Chinese "debate" over policy toward the US over the last year.

As for particular new steps, the United States had decided privately, for budgetary reasons, to withdraw the two US Navy destroyers which had regularly patrolled the Taiwan Strait.[146] Green recommended that the Administration attempt to use the opportunity presented by the withdrawal to "improve the atmosphere" for US-China talks in "Warsaw or elsewhere." In particular, Green recommended informing the Chinese of the US move through a CIA contact in Hong Kong, which Nixon approved as a diplomatic signal toward the Chinese.[147]

On October 10, 1969, during his trip to Washington, the Pakistani Minister of Information and National Affairs, Sher Ali Khan, told Kissinger that the Chinese had been informed that Yahya was ready to talk about US intentions in Asia when Premier Zhou would visit Pakistan, presumably early in the next year. In response, Kissinger informed Sher Ali and Hilaly that if Yahya was communicating with the Chinese Ambassador to Pakistan, he might say "confidentially" that US would remove two of its destroyers from Taiwan Strait.[148] Kissinger emphasized, however, that it did "not affect our basic position on Taiwan but it was an effort to remove an irritant."[149] After reviewing the report of the meeting, Nixon wrote his comment on the margin of the memorandum: "K, also open trade possibilities."[150]

On November 7, the State Department announced the US decision to terminate active routine patrolling by two destroyers of the Seventh Fleet in the Taiwan Straits. Their presence was a symbolic remainder of President Truman's decision to re-intervene in Chinese Communist-Nationalist relations at the outbreak of the Korean War in June 1950. Therefore, State Department officials anticipated that Beijing might

---

144 Ibid., pp. 2–3.
145 Ibid., p. 3.
146 Ibid., p. 2. Taipei had not been informed of this decision in advance.
147 Ibid., p. 4.
148 Kissinger to Nixon, "President Yahya and Communist China," October 16, 1969, p.1, "Exchange Leading Up to HAK Trip to China, December 1969–July 1971, 2 of 2," Box 1031, FPF-China/Vietnam Negotiations, NSCF, NPMS, NA.
149 Ibid.
150 Nixon's handwritten notations in ibid. On October 20, during a meeting with Nixon and Kissinger, Ambassador Dobrynin conveyed Soviet readiness to open SALT talks and also formally warned against any attempt to exploit Sino-Soviet tensions. Nixon made it clear that US policy toward China was "not directed against the Soviet Union." Anatoly Dobrynin, *In Confidence: Moscow's Ambassador to America's Six Cold War Presidents (1962–1986)* (New York: Times Books, A Division of Random House, Inc, 1995), p. 202. Dobrynin reassesses that the Soviet Union was making a mistake from the beginning by "displaying our anxiety over China" to the Nixon administration. Ibid.

interpret the decision as a "further indication of a diminished US threat" to Chinese security.[151] Washington also reiterated publicly that the US defense commitment to the Government of the Republic of China would "remain unaltered."[152]

The State Department's Bureau of Intelligence and Research analysts also assessed that since October, the Chinese media had "increased its abuse" directed at the US military presence in Asia in general and President Nixon in particular. Importantly, however, State Department officials also noticed that the difference between Beijing's public and private attitude towards the United States had widened during the past few weeks.[153]

Simultaneously, State Department officials continued to monitor developments in Sino-Soviet relations. On October 21, in his memorandum to Under Secretary of State Richardson, Green emphasized that the US interest was served by taking "parallel actions" and highlighting a general posture of "evenhandedness" regarding its relations with China and the Soviet Union.[154] On November 6, 1969, INR experts reported that the Sino-Soviet border talks were already "deadlocked" after only three weeks of negotiations in Beijing.[155] In short, while Beijing demanded disengagement along the border areas as a "prerequisite to further progress," Moscow insisted that disengagement could "only be part of the final settlement" and was seeking to "broaden the talks" to include political and economic issues.

3.3 NSC review group meeting on NSSM 63: Sino-Soviet differences in November 1969

On November 20, 1969, a Review Group meeting was held to examine Sino-Soviet differences. While there were no immediate operational decisions to be made, the NSC staff members, including Holdridge and Sonnenfeldt, carefully reviewed the NSSM 63 paper in advance to discuss any proposed restatements with the State Department's representatives. Kissinger commented that if the US actively supported the Chinese, the Soviets would be provoked, but he was still uncertain what the US could do operationally.[156] All-out support for the Soviets might also make Moscow

---

151   Green and Hillenbrand to Richardson, "Memorandum for the President: Next Moves in China Policy and Bargaining Moves Toward the Soviet Union," October 21, 1969, p. 3, POL Chicom-US, 1967–1969, Box 1973, SNF, RG59, NA.

152   Ibid. On November 26, this decision was conveyed to the Chinese through the CIA contact in Hong Kong.

153   Intelligence Note, INR, "Sino-Soviet Relations: Peking's Double Game, November 21, 1969, p. 1, POL Chicom-USSR, 1967–1969, Box 1975, SNF, RG59, NA.

154   Green and Hillenbrand to Richardson, "Memorandum for the President: Next Moves in China Policy and Bargaining Moves Toward the Soviet Union," October 21, 1969, p. 7, POL Chicom-US, 1967–1969, Box 1973, SNF, RG59, NA.

155   Intelligence Note, INR, "Sino-Soviet Border Talks Reach An Early Impasse," November 6, 1969, p. 1, POL Chicom-USSR, 1967–1969, Box 1975, SNF, RG59, NA.

156   Jeanne W. Davis to Kissinger, "Minutes of [November 20, 1969] Review Group Meeting on Sino-Soviet Differences," November 25, 1969, p. 2, Box H-111, NSSM 63: Sino-Soviet Differences 11/20/69, Washington Special Action Group Meetings, Minutes of Meetings (1969–1974), NSCIF, NPMS, NA.

consider this as a "signal" of a US support for them to make a preemptive move.[157] Hence, Kissinger asked what the US attitude would be in the event of a Soviet preemptive strike. A State Department official, William I. Cargo, suggested a minor injection of US support for China would only irritate the Soviets, and that massive US support of China, with the implication of military support, was not thinkable as a US policy.

Kissinger explained that the President thought "opening up certain exchange possibilities would not necessarily mean giving up neutrality." For example, the US could still take steps toward China by promoting "maximum trade with China without getting involved in the Sino-Soviet dispute."[158] Overall, there was consensus among the participants that the US should distinguish between neutrality on the dispute and neutrality in its relations with China and the USSR. In particular, Kissinger emphasized that neutrality on the dispute would not necessarily preclude the US leaning toward one or the other and that if there were such reciprocity, it would mean a "diplomatic revolution."[159]

In summary, the latter half of 1969 saw the development of a broad range of policy options within the Nixon administration for its opening to China. Nixon continued to lead the initiative, using his long-term personal relations with foreign leaders, such as Yahya and Ceausescu, to test and develop his ideas for a new China policy. In particular, Nixon established his private backchannels through these foreign leaders to begin sending secret signals to the Chinese leaders.

The escalation of the Sino-Soviet border clashes during the summer of 1969 provided crucial opportunities for US officials to reassess the seriousness of Sino-Soviet mutual hostility. By August, Nixon came to grasp the short-term importance of preventing China from being "smashed" in the border conflicts with the Soviets. On the other hand, Kissinger perceived the China policy as a part of the US policy toward the Soviet Union. Throughout 1969, Kissinger was preoccupied with the danger of a Soviet preemptive military attack on China. Thus, he depended on his NSC staff and academics for expertise on China. Kissinger's understanding of both the necessity and the possibility of a new China initiative was still limited in 1969.

During the latter half of 1969, the State Department's Bureau of Intelligence and Research and the Bureau of East Asian and Pacific Affairs continued to produce a number of intelligence analyses and policy recommendations. NSSM 63 provided a detailed assessment of the deepening difference in Sino-Soviet relations. Moreover, contrary to Kissinger's underestimation in his memoirs, the State Department was also in charge of the public presentation of a new China initiative, including easing trade and travel restrictions and ending the Seventh Fleet's regular patrol in the Taiwan Strait. Overall, during 1969, a wide range of policy options and issues were presented within the administration.

As the following chapter demonstrates, it was the resumption of the Warsaw Ambassadorial talks from December 1969 to January and February 1970 that provided concrete opportunities for both the White House and the State Department to have direct contact with the Chinese.

---

157 Ibid., p. 4.
158 Ibid., p. 6.
159 Ibid., p. 7.

Chapter 5

The Resumption of the Warsaw Ambassadorial Talks from December 1969 to May 1970

Chapter 5 examines the implications of the resumed Warsaw Ambassadorial talks. First, it analyzes the initial direct contact between the US and Chinese ambassadors in December 1969. Nixon and Kissinger bypassed Secretary Rogers and privately attempted to reactivate the Warsaw channel. Second, it examines the main issues during the Warsaw Ambassadorial talks in January and February 1970. While the State Department focused on the status of Taiwan, the White House sought to develop a broader strategic dialogue with the Chinese. Third, this chapter conducts a detailed analysis of the escalation of the bureaucratic rivalry between the Kissinger NSC and the State Department's Bureau of East Asian and Pacific Affairs during March and April. There was a major difference between the NSC and State Department proposals regarding the timing and speed of a new dialogue: Kissinger wanted to speed the process and send a special envoy to China for direct talks; however, State Department officials remained cautious and favored a slower approach via the regular diplomatic channel at Warsaw. Finally, this chapter explores the implications of the Cambodian military operation of May 1970. Kissinger regarded the outbreak of Cambodian conflicts as the detrimental force that ended the contacts in Warsaw. However, State Department officials continued to seek new opportunities to resume the Warsaw talks with Chinese counterparts.

It was Kissinger who had principally tended to downgrade the bureaucratic efforts which provided the groundwork for the development of a new dialogue with the Chinese. This book counter-argues Kissinger's underestimation and interprets that the resumption of the Warsaw Ambassadorial talks was a substantial diplomatic event during the US opening to China.

1. Initial Contact with the Chinese at Warsaw in December 1969

1.1 Nixon's instructions to Stoessel

From September to December 1969, the White House secretly sought to make direct contact with the Chinese. On September 9, 1969, President Nixon asked Walter Stoessel, US Ambassador to Poland who had returned to Washington for consultations, to "pass a message to the Chinese privately" suggesting that he attempted to talk directly with the Chinese Chargé d'affaires at a diplomatic reception at one of the neutral embassies in Warsaw.[1] Nixon requested for Stoessel to convey that the President was seriously interested in concrete discussions with China. Finally, Nixon emphasized that if the press noted Stoessel's conversation with the Chargé d'affaires, he should be "noncommittal" in his comments.

Without knowing the intentions of the White House, the State Department was also sending cable messages to Ambassador Stoessel in order to resume the Warsaw ambassadorial talks, which the Chinese had previously cancelled in February of 1969. On October 27, 1969, Ambassador Stoessel sent a cable to Paul H. Kreisberg, the Director of Asian Communist Affairs in the State Department, explaining that he had not yet managed to contact the Chinese because there had not yet been a social reception to convene diplomats at any locale or embassy which would foster relations between the US and China.[2] Stoessel also anticipated that an attempt to talk with the Chinese at a reception would be noticed by other diplomats present and would quickly be picked up by journalists.[3] Despite Nixon's warning in September, Stoessel had an impression that the President might prefer that his effort to talk with the Chinese should "become public."[4] Stoessel thus asked for more specific instructions from Washington regarding the handling of the press.

On November 21, 1969, the State Department's Bureau of Research and Intelligence reported that in late October or early November, a Chinese diplomat suggested to a Czech journalist that if Washington was to propose an agenda, Beijing might be "receptive to a resumption of the Warsaw talks" – the first specific hint since the cancellation of the meeting in February 1969.[5] In public, the Chinese still maintained a continuing ideological posture against the United States. INR officials interpreted that the Chinese wanted to worry the Soviets by reminding them of the possible policy option of closer Sino-American relations.[6]

---

1 Memcon, Nixon, Kissinger, and Stoessel, "Conversation with the President Concerning China and US-Chinese Contacts," September 9, 1969, 3:00pm, The White House, p. 1, POL Chicom-US, 1967–1969, Box 1973, Subject-Numeric Files (SNF), General Records of the Department of State, Record Group 59 (RG59), National Archives (NA). A former State Department official, Walter Jenkins recalls that: 'I think the first experience of how we worked together was a cable that came in from Henry Kissinger in early 1969 that said: "It's time to reopen our China talks. I want you to make contact with the Chinese ambassador to reopen these talks."' Walter Jenkins (Deputy Chief of Mission, United States Embassy, Warsaw, Poland, 1966–1970), Oral History Interview, p. 6, Poland, Country Collection, 1996, Foreign Affairs Oral History Collection (FAOHC), Association for Diplomatic Studies and Training, Special Collections Division, Lauinger Library, Georgetown University.

2 Stoessel to Kreisberg, October 27, 1969, p. 1, Country File (CF)-Europe, Box 700 [1 of 2], The National Security Council Files (NSCF), Nixon Presidential Materials Staff (NPMS), NA.

3 Ibid., p. 2.

4 Ibid.

5 Intelligence Note, Bureau of Intelligence and Research (INR), "Sino-US-Soviet Relations: Peking's Double Game," November 21, 1969, pp. 1–2, POL Chicom-US, 1967–69, Box 1973, SNF, RG59, NA.

6 Ibid., pp. 2–3.

Meanwhile, State Department officials were considering possible public moves. On December 2, 1969, Secretary Rogers sent a set of recommendations to President Nixon to proceed with the remaining measures to relax economic controls against China on the basis of NSDM-17 (which Nixon approved in June).[7] State Department analysts estimated that the Sino-Soviet negotiations in Beijing might lead to a "partial rapprochement," which might take the form of some restoration of normalcy in state-to-state relations. Simultaneously, Soviet agreement to negotiate both with China on border problems and with the US on SALT (Strategic Arms Limitation Talks), would enable the US to maintain its posture of "non-involvement in the Sino-Soviet dispute."[8]

1.2 The December 1969 contacts in Warsaw

On December 3, direct contact with China was finally made when US Ambassador Walter Stoessel spotted the Chinese Chargé d'affaires Lei Yang at a Yugoslav fashion show at Warsaw's Palace of Culture.[9] Stoessel conveyed a message to Lei's interpreter that: "I was recently in Washington and saw President Nixon. He told me he would like to have serious concrete talks with the Chinese."[10] Lei agreed to pass the message to Beijing. On December 7, 1969, without any public explanation, China released two Americans who had been held since February 16 when their yacht had strayed into Chinese waters off Kwangtung province.[11] On December 10, the Chinese suddenly proposed that Stoessel visit the Chinese embassy the next day. The State Department's instructions to Ambassador Stoessel directed that he should make a "generalized statement of US desire for improved relations" and suggest a

---

7   Rogers to Nixon, "Next Steps in China Policy," December 2, 1969, p. 1, Attached to Memo from Kissinger to Richardson, "Next Moves in China Policy," December 16, 1969, POL Chicom-US, 1967–1969, Box 1973, SNF, RG59, NA. The decision allowed unlimited tourist purchases and relaxed limits on trade in non-strategic goods by US-owned firms abroad.

8   Ibid., p. 1.

9   Richard Solomon, interview with the author, September 24, 2003; and Jenkins, Oral History Interview, p. 6, Poland, Country Collection, FAOHC. Jenkins recalls that Ambassador Walter Stoessel "kept things on an even keel, and [acted] very, very professionally. He developed very good relationships with other diplomats and Polish officials, because they really recognized him as a competent professional." As for initial Warsaw contact see also Henry Kissinger, *White House Years* (Boston: Little Brown, 1979), pp. 188–189; and Patrick E. Tyler, *A Great Wall: Six Presidents and China, An Investigative History* (New York: Public Affairs, 1999), pp. 74–75.

10   Stoessel to Rogers, "Contact with Communist Chinese," December 3, 1969, p. 1, POL Chicom-US, 1967–1969, Box 1973, SNF, RG59, NA.

11   Stoessel to Rogers, "Return of American Yachtsmen; Contact with Communist Chinese," December 7, 1969, p. 1, POL Chicom-US, 1967–69, Box 1973, SNF, RG59, NA. This was a different from the July incident, which is previously described in Chapter 4 (p. 89, Footnote No. 98).

date and arrangements for formal meetings but avoid any specific discussions on other issues.[12]

The State Department's Bureau of East Asian and Pacific Affairs interpreted the Chinese proposal within the context of the Sino-Soviet difficulties. Green wrote to Rogers, arguing that Beijing's motives reflected a change in its external behavior since November as a result of "deteriorating Sino-Soviet relations" and the beginning of US-USSR SALT talks.[13] On the other hand, Kissinger wrote to Nixon, suspecting that the Chinese may have called the meeting "primarily to get a feeling for your Administration's attitude toward them."[14] Hence, Kissinger remained cautious: "I do not believe that we should be under any illusions that a whole new era in Sino-US relations is opening."[15] Kissinger judged that Beijing might regard contact with the US as a "tactical step designed to put pressure on Moscow" by showing that the Chinese "have options open which are unpleasant to the Soviets."[16] Kissinger concluded that a "contact of even a limited nature could turn into something more significant if it can be maintained."[17]

On December 11, Ambassador Stoessel visited the Chinese Embassy in Warsaw and held talks with Lei Yang. Following the State Department's instructions, Stoessel formally proposed the resumption of ambassadorial talks at the US Embassy in mid-January, stressing, "We believe China has an important role in Asia, and that in the last analysis Asian decisions must be taken by Asian nations themselves, a process in which China should take part."[18] Lei agreed to deliver the message to Beijing. On December 12, a State Department spokesman, Robert McCloskey, gave a press statement, describing the contact as being held in a "cordial" atmosphere.[19] On December 14, 1969, *The Washington Post* ran the headline, "China Sees Leverage in US Talks." It also reported that although the details of the meeting had been "kept secret," Chinese suspicion that the United States was "colluding" with the Soviet Union was still speculated.[20]

The State Department sent its general account of the Stoessel-Lei meeting of December 11 to the US Embassies in Moscow, Tokyo, Taipei, and to the US Consulate General in Hong Kong.[21] The State Department also briefed the governments of Australia, Britain, Canada, France, Italy, and New Zealand before the announcement

---

12   Rogers to Stoessel, "Sino-US Meeting," December 11, 1969, p. 1, POL Chicom-US, 1967–1969, Box 1973, SNF, RG59, NA.

13   Green to Rogers, "Implications of PRC Agreement to Meet with US Ambassador – Information Memorandum," December 10, 1969, p. 1, Country File (CF)-Europe, Box 700 [1 of 2], NSCF, NPMS, NA.

14   Kissinger to Nixon, "Warsaw Talks, [December 10, 1969]," p. 1, CF-Europe, Box 700 [1 of 2], NSCF, NPMS, NA.

15   Ibid.

16   Ibid.

17   Ibid., p. 2.

18   Stoessel to Rogers, "Sino-US Meeting," December 11, 1969, POL Chicom-US. 1967–69, Box 1973, SNF, RG59, NA.

19   *The New York Times*, December 12, 1969.

20   *The Washington Post*, December 14, 1969.

21   Rogers to Nixon, "Warsaw Talks," December 18, 1969, pp. 1–2, POL Chicom-US. 1967–1969, Box 1973, SNF, RG59, NA.

of the Stoessel-Lei meeting.[22] In particular, the only governments which were "informed in advance" (a few hours before the December 11 meeting) were those of the Republic of China and Japan, and no leaks came from either capital.[23] However, Nixon and Kissinger became very concerned about "wide dissemination" and the danger of leaks which could undermine a new China initiative.[24] When Kissinger reported what had been done by the State Department, Nixon sighed: "We'll kill this child before it is born."[25]

Senior State Department specialists on US-Soviet relations, such as Llewellyn Thompson strongly insisted that the US government keep Soviet Ambassador Dobrynin informed of all contact with the Chinese. On December 12, Kissinger wrote to Secretary Rogers, who initially argued against advising Ambassador Dobrynin of the US talks with the Chinese, stating that the President had asked that "under no circumstance should we inform Dobrynin of the talks or their content."[26] Accordingly, the increasing concern about leaks would become a major reason for Nixon and Kissinger to almost completely cut off the State Department from involvement with the China policy from mid-1970.

Meanwhile, the US government continued to take unilateral public actions. On December 15, the State Department announced that the United States would remove all of its nuclear weapons from Okinawa, Japan, by the end of 1969.[27] The weapons were originally installed for the containment of China and were reportedly still aimed at the Chinese mainland. On December 16, 1969, Kissinger informed Under Secretary Richardson that President Nixon had approved the implementation of Secretary Rogers' December 2 memorandum in a "low-key manner" in order to "minimize public speculation."[28] On December 19, the State Department thus announced that it would remove financial restraints on foreign subsidiaries of United States firms engaged in "non-strategic" transactions with China; eliminate the present restrictions on US business participation in "third-country trade in presumptive Chinese goods"; and allow the purchase of non-commercial Chinese goods by Americans traveling or residing abroad.[29] Importantly, the State Department emphasized that: "It is with this same spirit that we have resumed discussions with Communist China in our talks

---

22   Ibid.
23   Ibid.
24   Kissinger to Nixon, "Memorandum from Secretary Rogers on Handling of Warsaw talks," December 20, 1969, p. 1, CF-Europe, Box 700 [1 of 2], NSCF, NPMS, NA.
25   Kissinger, *White House Years*, p. 190.
26   Kissinger to Rogers, "Ambassador Thompson's Recommendation that We Inform Dobrynin of Talks with the Chinese," December 12, 1969, p. 1, POL Chicom-US, 1967–1969, Box 1973, SNF, RG59, NA. In his memoirs, Kissinger argues that since the Soviets never informed the US of its contact with the Chinese or any other country, there was no point of giving the Russians an opportunity which might increase Beijing's suspicion from the beginning of the resumption of Warsaw meeting. Kissinger, *White House Years*, p. 190.
27   *The New York Times*, December 15, 1969.
28   Kissinger to Richardson, "Next Moves in China Policy," December 16, 1969, p. 1, POL Chicom-US, 1967–1969, Box 1973, SNF, RG59, NA.
29   "Changes in China Trade Restrictions," December 19, 1969, A Matter of Record – No. 18, Public Statements on China by US officials, Box 86, US China Policy 1969–1972 [2of 2], CF-Far East, HAKOF, NSCF, NPMS, NA.

at Warsaw."[30] In short, the State Department's approach to China policy was based on their long-term policy studies, namely the combination of sending unilateral public steps to lift trade and travel sanctions and simultaneously pursuing official diplomatic contacts to re-open the Warsaw channel.

1.3 The Kissinger-Hilaly backchannel exchanges

On December 18, 1969, in an end of the year briefing to the press, Kissinger outlined the US general approach toward China:

> We have always made it clear that we have no permanent enemies and that we will judge other countries, including Communist countries, and specifically countries like Communist China, on the basis of their actions and not on the basis of their domestic ideology. And we hope we have started a process towards Communist China, that over a period of years, will permit a more calibrated relationship to develop, and one in which such a large part of humanity will not be excluded from the international community.[31]

In public, Kissinger concluded the first year of the administration by reflecting the major premises of the Nixon inaugural address (and senior State Department officials' addresses), namely the US search for new opportunities to resume a diplomatic dialogue with a long-isolated China. In private, while trying to conceal information about US-China contact via the Warsaw channel from Soviet Ambassador Dobrynin, Kissinger also sought to bypass the State Department by actively utilizing the Pakistani backchannel to obtain information about the Chinese leadership.

On December 19, 1969, Kissinger had a meeting with Pakistani Ambassador Hilaly. Hilaly briefed Kissinger that shortly after November 5, President Yahya explained to the Chinese Ambassador in Rawalpindi that US interest in normalization with China and its withdrawal of the two destroyers from the Taiwan Straits (on November 7) should be seen "as a gesture."[32] Beijing appreciated Pakistan's role and explained that a recent Chinese decision to release two American yachtsmen (on December 7) was a direct response to the US initiative.[33] Kissinger asked Hilaly to convey a secret message to the Chinese that the US was "serious" in wishing to

---

30   Ibid.

31   HAK backgrounder, December 18, 1969, A Matter of Record – No. 8, Public Statements on China by US officials, Box 86, US China Policy 1969–1972 [2of 2], CF-Far East, HAKOF, NSCF, NPMS, NA. On December 22, 1969, Kissinger reiterated to Dobrynin that the United States would not accept permanent hostility in its relations with China, and that the US would "take no sides" in the Sino-Soviet dispute and its policy was "not against" the Soviet Union. See Kissinger, *White House Years*, pp. 192–193.

32   Saunders to Kissinger, "Your Meeting with Ambassador Hilaly," December 22, 1969, Box 624, CF-Middle East, Pakistan, Vol. II, December 1, 1969–September 1970, NSCF, NPMS, NA. On December 17, 1969, Romanian's First Deputy Foreign Minister Gheorghe Macovescu briefed Kissinger in general terms on the Chinese reaction to Nixon's talk with Ceauşescu. Kissinger interpreted this as a signal that the Chinese were ready to have contact with the US, however it did not necessarily through the Romanian channel. See Kissinger, *White House Years*, p. 191.

33   Ibid.

have conversations with them and if they wanted to have the talks "in a more secure manner than Warsaw or in channels that are less widely disseminated within the bureaucracy," President Nixon would be prepared to proceed.³⁴ In the end, Kissinger and Hilaly agreed that they would "keep the channel between them active."³⁵

On December 23, Kissinger met Hilaly and handed over President Nixon's letter to President Yahya (dated December 20) in which Nixon reiterated his "interest in trying to bring about a more meaningful dialogue with Chinese leaders."³⁶ Nixon's letter also noted that it was a "slow process at best," but he had "not abandoned it," and therefore the United States was still "exploring the possibilities of contact."³⁷ Kissinger re-emphasized to Hilaly that Nixon "wanted to stay in communication with the Pakistani President."³⁸ In response, Hilaly explained that soon after their previous meeting on December 19, he received a letter from Yahya (dated December 14). The letter explained that the Chinese appeared to be "willing for a resumption of talks at Warsaw at the Ambassador level without insisting on any preconditions"; they were still worried about the revival of Japanese militarism as a threat not only to China but also to the whole of Southeast Asia.³⁹ At this stage, therefore, the backchannel exchanges with Chinese leaders via Pakistan consequently prompted the resumption of regular diplomatic contacts via the Warsaw channel.

1.4 The State Department's instructions to Ambassador Stoessel

Without knowing about the secret messages passed from the White House to the Chinese through Pakistan and Romania, the State Department's Bureau of East Asian and Pacific Affairs had begun to prepare detailed instructions to Ambassador Stoessel.⁴⁰ On December 23, 1969, the Director of Asian Communist Affairs, Paul H. Kreisberg wrote to the Assistant Secretary for East Asian and Pacific Affairs,

---

34   Memcon, Kissinger and Hilaly, December 19, 1969, Exchange Leading Up to HAK Trip to China, December 1969–July 1971 (1 of 2), Box 1031, FPF-China/Vietnam Negotiations, NSCF, NPMS, NA. In his memoirs, however, Kissinger fails to refer to the US willingness to communicate with the Chinese in a more confidential channel.

35   Ibid., p. 3.

36   Nixon to Yahya, December 20, 1969, p. 1, in Exchange Leading Up to HAK Trip to China, December 1969–July 1971 (1 of 2), Box 1031, FPF-China/Vietnam Negotiations, NSCF, NPMS, NA.

37   Ibid.

38   Memcon, Kissinger and Hilaly, December 23, 1969, p. 1, in Exchange Leading Up to HAK Trip to China, December 1969–July 1971 (1 of 2), Box 1031, FPF-China/Vietnam Negotiations, NSCF, NPMS, NA.

39   Ibid; and "Direct and Indirect Specific Messages Between The US and PRC," p. 1, in Exchange Leading Up to HAK Trip to China, December 1969–July 1971 (2 of 2), FPF-China/Vietnam Negotiations, NSCF, NPMS, NA. In his memoirs, however, Kissinger fails to explain specific issues of the Yahya message.

40   In his memoirs, Kissinger misleadingly claims that the Stoessel-Lei contact of December 11, 1969 was the "first operational involvement of regular State Department machinery" in China policy since the beginning of the Nixon administration. See Kissinger, *White House Years*, p. 189. In reality, however, contrary to Kissinger's omission, the State Department already prepared a set of policy options and instructions to Ambassador Stoessel

Marshall Green, estimating that the main US objectives for the Warsaw talks were to "test the Chinese air [and] to keep the door open for subsequent meetings."[41] It was anticipated that the Chinese would be more interested in listening to the US position, especially regarding US military presence on Taiwan and Agreement on the Five Principles of Peaceful Coexistence (which was proposed on November 25, 1968). The Chinese might also raise the following issues: US-USSR collusion; Vietnam and the US presence in Southeast Asia; Trade and Travel; and Chinese representation at the United Nations.

More particularly, the Bureau of Intelligence and Research estimated that the Chinese were interested in how the US would apply the Nixon Doctrine to Taiwan. The report thus emphasized that the US would be "dangerously misunderstood," if it failed to make it clear that "we have no intention of weakening our commitment to defend the Republic of China against attack from the Mainland."[42] Finally, INR analysts suggested that the Chinese would take note if the US made it clear that the degree of US presence in Taiwan depended on the development of the Vietnam War and that "we will phase down our presence in Taiwan as the war in Vietnam subsides."[43] Therefore, it was the INR that first proposed the possible linkage between the US withdrawal from Taiwan and the progress of negotiated settlement in Indochina, which Nixon and Kissinger adopted for the joint communiqué of February 1972, as Chapters 7 and 8 discuss later.

Overall, the State Department's draft opening statement for Ambassador Stoessel was designed to "set a positive tone" for the resumption of ambassadorial talks as a "new beginning." The statement had avoided any concrete proposals, and instead had emphasized that "this is a new Administration with a sincere desire to improve Sino-US relations."[44]

Importantly, despite Kissinger's frequent criticisms on the lack of a geopolitical perspective, the State Department continued to analyze the implications of Sino-Soviet hostilities on the Warsaw talks. The Bureau of Intelligence and Research judged that while there might be "some gesture of interest in testing current US intentions," Sino-Soviet considerations had been the "predominating motive." The Chinese willingness to talk with the US was almost surely intended as a "reminder to the Soviets that the Chinese have other options" regarding the "potential interplay among the US, USSR, China, and even Japan."[45] In comparison, the Chinese might

---

for the Warsaw talk of February 1969, which was cancelled. See Chapter 3, Section 1.3 (pp. 74–77) of this book.

41   Kreisberg to Green, "Draft Opening Statement and Contingency Guidance for Possible Warsaw Meeting, December 23, 1969, p. 1, POL Chicom-US, 1967–1969, Box 1973, SNF, RG59, NA.

42   Intelligence Note, INR, "Communist China: Peking and Warsaw Talks," December 23, 1969, p. 3, POL ChiCom, 1967–1969, Box 1962, SNF, RG59, NA.

43   Ibid., p.4.

44   Harry E.T. Thayer to Barnett, "Draft Opening Statement and Possible Warsaw Meeting," December 30, 1969, p. 1, POL Chicom-US. 1967–1969, Box 1973, SNF, RG59, NA.

45   Intelligence Brief, INR, "Communist China: Peking Negotiates on Two Fronts," January 14, 1970, p. 1, POL Chicom-US, 1970–1973, Box 2187, SNF, RG59, NA.

"adopt enough flexibility to keep the talks going."[46] On the other hand, the Soviets might make a "minor concession in the border negotiations," but the basic Russian response would more likely to "continue the gradual build-up of military strength in [the] border area."[47]

2. The 135th Warsaw Ambassadorial Talks in January 1970

2.1 The development of the perception gap between the White House and the State Department

On January 8, 1970, there was an informal meeting between Walter Stoessel and Lei Yang at the American Embassy in Warsaw at which the date for the formal resumption of the Warsaw talks was set for January 20, 1970, to take place at the Chinese Embassy. The preparation for the 135th Warsaw talk, however, caused bureaucratic friction between the White House and the State Department. On the one hand, Nixon and Kissinger were willing to use the January meeting to reassure the Chinese directly that the US did "not propose to take sides in Sino-Soviet differences or to join any condominium against China" and that the US would "not participate in or encourage any Soviet sponsored security arrangement in Southeast Asia."[48] Moreover, Nixon and Kissinger wanted to propose sending a special envoy to Beijing. On the other hand, the State Department's Bureau of East Asian and Pacific affairs, especially Assistant Secretary Green emphasized a "new beginning in Sino-US relations and this Administration's new approach to Asian policy."[49] In particular, State Department officials insisted that the Taiwan issue was the "key to any improvement of relations with the PRC."[50]

In comparison, the White House was principally interested in assuring the Chinese of the US non-committal attitude toward the Sino-Soviet hostilities; State Department officials believed that it was important to emphasize that progress would depend on resolving long-standing issues, such as getting China to join in arms control talks and the renunciation of the use of forces to resolve the Taiwan issue.

---

46   Ibid., pp. 1–2.
47   Ibid., p. 3.
48   Haig to Theodore Eliot (Executive Secretary), "Rationale for Inclusion in Instructions to Ambassador Stoessel," January p. 1, CF-Europe, Box 700 [1 of 2], NSCF, NPMS, NA.
49   Rogers to Nixon, "Guidance for Sino-US Ambassadorial Meeting, January 20, 1970," January 14, 1970, p. 1, POL Chicom-US, 1970–1973, Box 2187, SNF, RG59, NA. Kissinger's underestimation of the State Department's role for the preparation of the Warsaw talks in January and February 1970 is very misleading. Kissinger, *White House Years*, p. 686. On the other hand, a bureaucratic friction emerged between the State Department and the Defense Department, and between Marshall Green and the Republic of China desk. Defense sought the renounce of the use of force in the Taiwan Strait. The ROC desk opposed Green, saying that the US would lose influence on Taiwan, and thus a sentence – "we intend to interfere in whatever the settlement may be reached" – was deleted from the original instructions to Stoessel.
50   Ibid.

While the White House wanted to move fast, the State Department wanted to take the East Asian reactions into consideration in a step-by-step manner. In the end, the White House and the State Department had made a bureaucratic compromise which combined the main interests of the respective sides.

2.2 The January talks

On January 20, 1970, during the 135th Warsaw Ambassadorial talk, Stoessel reiterated the US official position that "it did not seek to stand in isolation from China or to join in any condominium with the Soviet Union directed against China."[51] As the "single most complex problem," Stoessel also made clear that the US would continue to "honor its commitment" to the Republic of China by defending Taiwan from "military attack," and that its only concern was that this issue "not be resolved by force of arms." In this same spirit, the US would also "oppose any offensive military action from Taiwan against the mainland."[52] On the other hand, Stoessel assured that the limited US military presence on Taiwan was "not a threat to the security of your Government, and it is our hope that as peace and stability in Asia grew, we can reduce those facilities on Taiwan that we now have."[53] Importantly, this assurance was intended to reduce China's long-term concern of the US using of Taiwan as a stage from which to encircle and attack the mainland. Finally, Stoessel proposed that the United States "would be prepared to consider sending a representative to Peking for direct discussions with your officials or receiving a representative from your government in Washington for more through exploration of any of the subjects I have mentioned in my remarks today or other matters on which we might agree."[54]

In response, without calling for any specific US actions, Lei Yang reiterated that there had long existed "serious disputes" between the two sides on Taiwan which was an "inalienable part of China's territory" and a "province of the People's Republic of China."[55] Lei Yang also stressed that the discussion between the two sides should be promoted "in accordance with the five principles of peaceful coexistence" in order to "reduce tensions."[56] Finally, Lei Yang suggested that the bilateral talks might be continued "at the ambassadorial level" or "at a higher level or through other channels acceptable to both sides."[57] The January Warsaw talk thus played a crucial role in the breakthrough from the frozen Sino-American bilateral relations that had existed for over two decades. In particular, the January talk was the origin of the

---

51   Airgram, US Embassy, Warsaw, "Stoessel-Lei Talks: Report of 135th Meeting, January 20, 1970," January 24, 1970, p. 2, POL Chicom-US, 1970–1973, Box 2187, SNF, RG59, NA.
52   Ibid., p. 3.
53   Ibid., pp. 3–4. In his memoirs, however, Kissinger fails to refer to this crucial statement on the Taiwan issue. Kissinger, *White House Years*, p. 687.
54   Ibid., p. 4. The State Department's instructions to Ambassador Stoessel for the cancelled Warsaw meeting of February 1969 already included an explicit proposal of sending a presidential representative to Beijing. See Chapter 3, Section 1.3 (pp. 74–77) of this book.
55   Ibid., p. 5.
56   Ibid.
57   Ibid., p. 6.

US proposal to send a special representative to Beijing, an issue which the White House would keep raising in backchannels until the Chinese acceptance of this proposal on December 9, 1970.

On January 21 and 22, 1970, the State Department gave a briefing on the 135th Warsaw meeting in general terms to the governments of Japan, the Republic of China, Australia, Canada, and Britain, feeling it essential to do so promptly to maintain US "credibility" with them.[58] In particular, State Department officials considered that the briefing served to minimize Taipei's concern by reassuring that US defense commitments to the Republic of China would "remain unaltered."[59] On the other hand, the Soviets impatiently showed their anxiety. On January 21, Soviet Ambassador Dobrynin visited Kissinger, demanding a briefing on the Warsaw talks. Dobrynin emphasized his hope that the United States was not "using" China as a military threat against the Soviets.[60] However, Kissinger remained non-committal.

2.3 The game plan for the February talks

Meanwhile, the preparation for the 136th Warsaw meeting was proceeding. On February 3, 1970, Kissinger sent a presidential request to the State Department for a "game plan" to outline US objectives and the tactics in the following talks.[61] The Assistant Secretary Green wrote to Secretary Rogers the next day, anticipating that the Chinese might "put this issue [Taiwan] to one side" to proceed to discuss other bilateral Sino-US issues.[62] On February 7, Secretary Rogers sent the State Department's proposed guidance for the 136th Warsaw meeting to President Nixon. The memorandum outlined US objectives in the talks as being to reduce US-China tensions and to indicate the US interest in dealing even-handedly with Beijing as well as Moscow. In particular, the memorandum emphasized that during all previous negotiations, the Taiwan issue had "blocked any progress."[63] Hence, the key new elements in the State Department's instructions included:

- To state that the US was prepared to discuss with the Chinese a joint declaration incorporating the position on Taiwan in accordance with the Five Principles of Peaceful Coexistence;
- To indicate US intention to reduce those military facilities in Taiwan as tensions in the area diminished, but gave no indication of the timing of such moves or how far they would be taken.[64]

---

58   Eliot to Kissinger, "Discussing Warsaw Meeting with Other Governments," January 21, 1970, p. 1, CF-Europe, Box 700 [1 of 2], NSCF, NPMS, NA.
59   Ibid., p. 2.
60   Kissinger, *White House Years*, pp. 687–688.
61   Kissinger to Rogers, "Game Plan for Warsaw Talks," February 3, 1970, POL Chicom-US. 1970–73, Box 2188, SNF, RG59, NA.
62   Green to Rogers, "Sino-US Ambassadorial Talks on February 20, 1970 – Action Memorandum," February 4, 1970, p. 1, POL Chicom-US, 1970–1973, Box 2187, SNF, RG59, NA.
63   Rogers to Nixon, "Sino-US Negotiations in Warsaw," February 7, 1970, p. 1, CF-Europe, Box 700 [2 of 2], NSCF, NPMS, NA.
64   Ibid., p. 2.

The preparation of instructions for the 136th Warsaw meeting, however, caused more friction between the White House and the State Department regarding the US proposal of sending its emissary to Beijing or receiving a Chinese one in Washington. Kissinger strongly objected to Secretary Rogers' memorandum suggesting that "we pull slightly back from our proposal in January."[65] Thus, Kissinger wrote to Under Secretary Richardson, emphasizing that "the President believes that it would be preferable to take a more positive approach to a favorable Chinese response."[66]

In public, the US government continued its attempts to create a more cordial political atmosphere to bring China back into the international community. On February 18, 1970, in the first Foreign Policy Report to Congress, the Nixon Administration officially stated:

> The Chinese are a great people who should not remain isolated from the international community. In the long run, no stable and enduring international order is conceivable without the contribution of this nation of more than 700 million people.[67]

The above statement was designed to give a diplomatic signal to the Chinese and to enhance a positive political atmosphere for "improved practical relations" with Beijing.[68] The report also explicitly claimed that the US interest in improving relations with China was "not a tactical means of exploiting" the Sino-Soviet dispute: nor was the United States interested in "joining any condominium or hostile coalition of great powers" against either of the Communist giants.[69] Finally, the Kissinger NSC sought to take the lead in bureaucratic politics. As previously discussed, it was the NSC staff that drafted the entire report, and the State Department was completely excluded from its process.[70]

3. The 136th Warsaw Ambassadorial Talks in February 1970

On February 20, 1970, at the 136th Warsaw talks, the PRC Chargé d'affaires Lei Yang stressed that the "fundamental improvement" in Sino-US relations and the "settlement of other questions" could come about only when the Taiwan question was resolved.[71] He then added: "We are fully aware that the settlement of the Taiwan

---

65 Kissinger to Nixon, "Sino-US Negotiations in Warsaw," p. 2, CF-Europe, Box 700 [2 of 2], NSCF, NPMS, NA.
66 Kissinger to Richardson, February 18, 1970, Attached to Memo from Green to Richardson, "Guidance for 136th Warsaw Meeting – Action Memorandum," February 19, 1970, POL Chicom-US, 1970–1973, Box 2188, SNF, RG59, NA.
67 Richard M. Nixon, "United States Foreign Policy for the 1970's: A New Strategy for Peace," February 18, 1970 (Washington DC: Government Printing Office), p. 104.
68 Ibid.
69 Ibid., p. 106.
70 See Chapter 2, Section 3.1.2 of this book.
71 Airgram, US Embassy, Warsaw "Stoessel-Lei Talks: Report of 136th Meeting, February 20, 1970," February 21, 1970, p. 2, POL Chicom-US. 1970–73, Box 2188, SNF, RG59, NA.

question requires making every effort to create the conditions."⁷² After reiterating Chinese willingness to discuss the relaxation of tensions in the Far East, especially in the Taiwan area, Lei made it clear that: "... if the US Government wishes to send a representative of ministerial rank or a special envoy of the US President to Peking for further exploration of questions of fundamental principles between China and the United States, the Chinese Government will be willing to receive him."⁷³

In response, Ambassador Stoessel stated: "It is our Government's intention to reduce those military facilities which we now have on Taiwan as tensions in the area diminish."⁷⁴ Significantly, the US side altered the previous utilization of the term "hope," used in January, to "intention," used in February. Therefore, contrary to Kissinger's brief reference in his memoirs, the resumption of the Warsaw talks in January and February 1970 was the first major break-through in the US rapprochement with China. First, the State Department developed a new formula for the Taiwan issue and for the first time officially indicated the future possibility of US military withdrawal from Taiwan. Nixon and Kissinger would follow this formula in their direct talks with the Chinese leaders. Second, the timing and issues for a special representative mission became the major concern for the White House and the State Department during their respective attempts to communicate with Beijing until June 1971.

On February 22, 1970, Hilaly relayed to Kissinger the assessment by Yahya of Chinese thinking about US-PRC relations.⁷⁵ Yahya claimed that US initiatives had encouraged the Chinese, who no longer saw US-Soviet "collusion," and emphasized that the US should not regard Chinese readiness for meaningful dialogue as a sign of "weakness" or of "fear" of US-Soviet collaboration against China.⁷⁶ The possibility of the expansion of the Vietnam War was seen as having "lessened," and thus a China-US war was now seen as a "remote possibility."⁷⁷ Kissinger stated to Hilaly that Yahya should tell the Chinese that it was difficult to control press speculation, and thus the President would be prepared to "open a direct White House channel" to Beijing.⁷⁸ On the margin of Kissinger's memorandum reporting on the meeting, Nixon wrote "Good."⁷⁹

---

72   Ibid.
73   Ibid., p. 3.
74   Ibid., p. 5. In his memoirs, Kissinger fails to refer to the new formula for the Taiwan issue, and thus undermines the significance of the State Department's contribution. See Kissinger, *White House Years*, p. 689.
75   Kissinger to Nixon, "Message from President Yahya on China," February 23, 1970, "Direct and Indirect Specific Messages Between the US and PRC," Box 1031 (2 of 2), FPF-China/Vietnam Negotiations, NSCF, NPMS, NA.
76   Ibid., p. 2.
77   Ibid.
78   Ibid.
79   Nixon's handwritten notations in ibid.

4. Attempts for the Third Ambassadorial Talk

4.1 The March proposal

In the meantime, however, the perception gap between the White House and the State Department expanded further regarding the question of a higher-level meeting with the Chinese. While Kissinger wanted to proceed with sending a high-level representative to Beijing, the State Department's Bureau of East Asian and Pacific Affairs still remained cautious. Kissinger regarded the Chinese general acceptance of Washington's willingness to send a representative of "ministerial rank or a special Presidential envoy" to Beijing as the "most dramatic development" in terms of its effect on the outside world, such as its impact on Hanoi.[80] After months of assessment, Kissinger finally came to believe that the Chinese were serious, as a collapse of such a high-level contact might encourage the Soviets to believe that a Chinese rapprochement with the US had failed. Kissinger thus recommended to Nixon that the US would not need to "move immediately in naming a representative, however, it should not delay over this for too long, so as to "avoid creating a negative impression."[81]

Rogers and Green wanted to uncover the exact Chinese intentions for accepting the US proposal of sending or receiving a representative mission. As Kreisberg recalls, State Department officials were not sure "how far they were going to go."[82] State Department officials were generally more cautious in how far they wanted to go in their next step than the White House. In reality, Green was "shocked at the pace at which this was moving," considering incorrectly that the State Department was "pushing faster than the White House was pushing." He was also "very reluctant" to move one step further unless it was clear that the US government was going to "inform the Japanese, because he saw this as seriously damaging" the US's relationship with Japan.[83]

On March 10, 1970, Rogers sent a memorandum to Nixon, suggesting March 19 as the date for the next Warsaw meeting. The memo outlined that the US objectives were to "put the issue of Taiwan to one side" and to improve US-China relations in other areas, such as agreement on non-use of force, trade, and cultural exchanges.[84]

---

80   Kissinger to Nixon, "Chinese at Warsaw talks Suggest US Send High-Level Representative to Peking," February 20, 1970, p. 1, CF-Europe, Box 700 [2 of 2], NSCF, NPMS, NA.

81   Ibid., p. 2.

82   Paul Kreisberg, Oral History Interview, p. 6, in *A China Reader*, Vol. III, January 1995, FAOHC, ADST.

83   Ibid., p. 7. The Kissinger NSC insisted that: "We can't trust the Japanese, so we don't want them to know." Thus, State Department officials had a number of arguments on the possibility of leakage by Japan. However, as Kreisberg recalls, "None of us recall a single instance where we had ever told the Japanese anything really secret which they had then leaked." Ibid., pp. 7–8.

84   Green to Rogers, "How to Deal with the Question of a Higher-Level Meeting with the Chinese – Action Memorandum," March 5, 1970, p. 1, POL Chicom-US, 1970–1973, Box 2188, SNF, RG59, NA.

On the other hand, State Department officials suspected that Beijing might wish to give the "appearance of movement" in its discussion with the US in order to increase its pressure on the Soviets, and to damage US relations with the Republic of China without giving Washington anything in return. Therefore, a higher-level meeting in Beijing or Washington "should only come after progress at the ambassadorial-level talks in Warsaw." Moreover, the memo suggested that the US should "only reaffirm its willingness" to consider a higher-level meeting.[85] Finally, the memorandum recommended testing Beijing's positions on the peaceful resolution of the Taiwan issue between Beijing and Taipei.[86] On March 16, 1970, the State Department announced validation of US passports for travel to China for any legitimate purpose, which was aimed at sending a more positive diplomatic message to Beijing for the improvement of US-PRC relations.

4.2 The April proposal

In reality, however, the continuing friction between the White House (especially Kissinger) and the State Department (especially Green) delayed a formal US proposal for the date of the 137th Warsaw meeting. On March 20, 1970, Kissinger strongly urged the State Department to propose an immediate Warsaw meeting and to draft instructions to Ambassador Stoessel which would take a positive approach toward establishing a higher-level meeting. Accordingly, State Department officials revised instructions for the April meeting and proposed the explicit statement that the United States had no intention of imposing "Two Chinas" or "One China, One Taiwan."[87] The memorandum also suggested that the US emphasize its firm belief that "matters other than Taiwan can and should be discussed."[88]

On April 1, 1970, the US government finally proposed that the next Warsaw meeting take place on April 20 or any date thereafter. On April 28, the Chinese replied by suggesting May 20. State Department officials estimated that because of the military situation in Indochina, the Chinese might have been having "second thoughts" between late March and early April on the desirability of pursuing their

---

85   Ibid., p. 2.
86   Ibid., p. 3.
87   Theodore L. Eliot, Jr. (Executive Secretary, Department of State) to Kissinger, "Revised Warsaw Instructions, March 31, 1970, p. 6, POL Chicom-US, 1970–1973, Box 2188, SNF, RG59, NA.
88   Ibid. From April 22 to 29, 1970, the Vice Premier of the Republic of China, Chiang Ching-kuo visited the United States. Nixon privately reassured that: "The United States will always honor its treaty obligations and, to use a colloquial expression, I will never sell you down the river." James C.H. Shen, *The US and Free China: How the US Sold Out Its Ally* (Lakewood, Colorado: Acropolis Book, 1983), p. 51. The State Department's Bureau of East Asian and Pacific Affairs reported that Taipei strongly opposed to the Warsaw talks as the "disturbing trend," which "could seriously undermine the GRC's political position internationally." Memo from Thomas P. Shoesmith to Green, "An Appraisal of Vice Premier Chiang Ching-kuo's Visit, May 6, 1970, p. 1, POL Chicom, 1970–1973, Box 2202, SNF, RG59, NA.

"high-level meeting" with the US.[89] Overall, State Department officials considered that Beijing's interest in exploring the limits of US policy toward Taiwan would persuade the Chinese leaders to continue along the same track as the January and February meetings.[90] However, NSC staff member Holdridge wrote to Kissinger, suspecting that the "real motive" of the State Department could be to "soften him [Kissinger] up" for a new attempt to take a "more cautious line" in responding to the Chinese invitation to meet in Beijing.[91]

Meanwhile, intelligence analysts in various departments and agencies were closely continuing to monitor developments in Chinese foreign policy. On April 9, 1970, the State Department's Bureau of Intelligence and Research reported that the Chinese and the Soviets seemed to have made some progress in "lowering the tensions" between them, evinced by the fact that the Soviets had unilaterally withdrawn some troops from their disputed border areas.[92] The INR officials particularly noted that the Chinese and the Russians had agreed to exchange ambassadors "for the first time since 1967" and that there was enough confirmation from the Chinese side to suggest a limited break in the stalemate of the last six months.[93] On April 11, having grasped the "signs of life" in recent Chinese foreign policy, China watchers in the CIA estimated that a "new period" was underway and that anxiety about a "Soviet threat" encouraged China's "diplomatic offensive."[94] In particular, CIA analysts reported that Premier Zhou had signed a secret directive ordering a "limited flexible approach" toward the United States in order to put the Soviets off balance.[95]

5. The Cambodia Military Operation and the Collapse of the Warsaw Channel in May 1970

On April 30, 1970, believing in the need for a "bold move," President Nixon made public his decision to order military operations into Cambodia to destroy the supply

---

89   Elliot to Kissinger, "May 20 Sino-US Talk in Warsaw, April 28, 1970," p. 1, CF-Europe, Box 700 [2 of 2], NSCF, NPMS, NA.
90   Ibid., p. 3.
91   Holdridge to Kissinger, "Chinese Attitude on the Warsaw Talks, May 1, 1970," p. 1, CF-Europe, Box 700 [2 of 2], NSCF, NPMS, NA.
92   Intelligence Brief, INR, "Communists China/USSR: Sino-Soviet Stalemate Breaks," April 9, 1970, p. 1, POL Chicom-US. 1970–73, Box 2188, SNF, RG59, NA.
93   Ibid.
94   "Signs of Life in Chinese Foreign Policy," April 11, 1970, Secret, No Foreign Dissem, Directorate of Intelligence, Office of Current Intelligence, Central Intelligence Agency, Electric Reading Room.
95   Ibid. During his state trip to North Korea from April 5 to 7, 1970, Premier Zhou sought to ensure continued North Korean "neutrality" in the Sino-Soviet dispute and emphasized the revival of Japanese militarism as no longer just a "danger" but a "reality." Zhou's trip to North Korea was his first state visit outside China since June 1966 (except a brief trip to Hanoi to pay respects before Ho's funeral in September 1969). Intelligence Note, INR, "Communist China/North Korea: Chou Courts The North Koreans," April 14, 1970, p. 1, POL Chicom, 1970–1973, Box 2180, SNF, RG59, NA.

lines of the North Vietnamese.[96] As Holdridge recalls, the principal objective of the Cambodian operation was to "preserve the concept of Vietnamization," however, it "intensified the sentiment" against the war on the US domestic front.[97] On May 4 and 5, China strongly condemned the US for its "flagrant provocation" by quoting Mao's statement that the United States was a "paper tiger."[98] The White House sent a secret message to the Chinese via Major General Vernon Walters in Paris, informing that the US had "no aggressive intentions" concerning China.[99]

The State Department was still preparing instructions for the 137th Warsaw meeting. On May 12, following Green's recommendations, Secretary Rogers sent a memorandum to President Nixon with a set of alternative courses of action. The State Department recommended separating Southeast Asia and the Warsaw talks

---

96   Kissinger to Nixon, April 22, 1970, Box 2, Memoranda from the President, 1969–74, President's Personal Files (PPF), White House Special Files (WHSF), NPMS, NA. The presidential decision was made against opposition from Secretary of State Rogers and Secretary of Defense Laird. The so-called "Cambodia incursions" lasted from May 1 to June 29, 1970. NSC staff members, such as Anthony Lake, Roger Morris, William Watts and Larry Lynn resigned in protest. See Richard Reeves, *President Nixon: Alone in the White House* (New York: Touchstone, 2001), pp. 179–181, pp. 192–227, and pp. 232–234; Bundy, *A Tangled Web*, pp. 145–164; Isaacson, *Kissinger*, pp. 256–284; Nixon, *RN*, pp. 445–469; and Kissinger, *White House Years*, pp. 483–505. Former State Department official Michael Rives explains the Cambodian-Vietnamese historical rivalry: "I think the Cambodians have always hated the Vietnamese. They look down on them because, after all, Vietnam was part of the Cambodian Empire at one time. ... They rather admired the Chinese." Michael Rives (Charge d' Affairs, Phnom Penh, 1969–1970), Oral History Interview, p. 10, Cambodia, Country Collection, 1996, FAOHC.

97   Holdridge, Oral History Interview, July 20, 1995, p. 87, FAOHC. On May, 4, 1970, at Kent State University in Ohio, National Guardsmen shot unarmed student demonstrators protesting American invasion of Cambodia, and four students were killed and nine others wounded. The incident shocked and further divided the country regarding the prolonging US military involvement in Indochina. Congress placed unprecedented restriction on the executive branch, namely the Supplemental Foreign Aid Authoritalization Act of December 1970: "no funds were to be used to introduce ground combat troops into Cambodia or to provide US advisors to Cambodian military forces in Cambodia. Nor should the provision of military aid be considered as a US commitment to Cambodia for its defense." Emory C. Swank, Ambassador, Phnom Penh, 1970–1973, Oral History Interview, p. 6, A Cambodia Reader, Country Collection, 1996, FAOHC. From military point of view, the Cambodian operation ended the war in the southern half of South Vietnam. Peter Rodman, Oral History Interview, July 22, and August 22, 1994, p. 28, FAOHC.

98   Kissinger, *White House Years*, p. 694. "Paper Tiger" is an English translation of the Chinese phrase, *zhǐ lǎohǔ*, meaning something which seems as threatening as a tiger, however is harmless in actuality. During a meeting with North Vietnamese officials, Chairman Mao criticized the US for being "overextended" and affirmed the continual struggle against its interventionism. Importantly, however, Mao also hinted at the possibility of having a "shortened war." Mao Zedong and Le Duan; Beijing, the Great Hall of the People, May 11, 1970, CWIHP.

99   Message to be Passed to the Chinese, Box 333, Policy Planning Staff (Director's File – Winston Lord), RG59, NA.

by avoiding raising the question and continuing to focus on bilateral issues.[100] The guidance also suggested delaying detailed discussion of a higher-level meeting. Ambassador Stoessel was directed to limit his opening remarks to a request for confirmation on whether Beijing still felt that a higher-level meeting would be useful.[101] Finally, the memorandum recommended that the US government brief the governments of the Republic of China and Japan "at the higher level very candidly as soon as possible after the meeting."[102]

Kissinger wrote to Nixon criticizing the State Department for its continued preoccupation with the question as to "whether, and at what pace, we should press" for the higher-level meeting in Beijing.[103] In particular, Kissinger argued, "State believes that if we push forward, we might risk a total – and embarrassing – Chinese rebuff."[104] Finally, Kissinger suggested revising the State Department guidance in order to make sure that the US's "reference to reducing tensions in the Far East does not appear to be restricted to the Taiwan area and to avoid setting a time limit for the period during which we would engage in higher-level talks" in Beijing.[105]

On May 18, 1970, the New China News Agency issued a statement that in view of the "brazen" invasion of Cambodia, the Chinese government considered it "no longer suitable" for the 137th Warsaw Ambassadorial Talk to be held on May 20, and that the date for a future meeting would be decided "through consultation by the liaison personnel" of the two sides.[106] On May 19, Secretary Rogers sent a memorandum to President Nixon, comparing the previous day's cancellation with the Chinese handling of the cancellation of the meeting scheduled for February 20, 1969. The memorandum assessed that the Chinese: clearly implied a continuing interest in the Warsaw dialogue; attacked the US actions in Indochina in milder terms than circumstances might have permitted; and issued their public statement more routinely as an announcement by the New China News Agency rather than by the Foreign Ministry.[107] State Department officials thus argued that because of the "relatively moderate tone," the recent Chinese move should be seen as "tactical psychological warfare."[108] Overall, the memorandum estimated that with this cancellation, Beijing might be seeking to "warn" Washington that US military actions in Indochina would have a negative impact on developing the Warsaw talks and on the prospects for an

---

100 Rogers to Nixon, "Guidance for the May 20 Sino-US Ambassadorial Meeting," May 12, 1970, p. 2, CF-Europe, Box 700 [2 of 2], NSCF, NPMS, NA; and Green to Rogers, "Guidance for the May 20 Sino-US Ambassadorial Meeting – Action Memorandum," May 9, 1970, p. 1, POL Chicom-US, 1970–1973, Box 2188, SNF, RG59, NA.
101 Ibid., p. 3.
102 Ibid., p. 5.
103 Kissinger to Nixon, "State's Guidance for May 20 Sino-US Ambassadorial Meeting," p. 1, CF-Europe, Box 700 [2 of 2], NSCF, NPMS, NA.
104 Ibid., p. 2.
105 Ibid.
106 Chen, *Mao's China and the Cold War*, p. 252.
107 Rogers to Nixon, "Chinese Cancellation of May 20 Warsaw Meeting," May 19, 1970, p. 1, CF-Europe, Box 700 [2 of 2], NSCF, NPMS, NA.
108 Ibid.

early higher-level meeting in Beijing. In addition, Beijing welcomed this opportunity to subject the Nixon administration to US domestic criticism for their entry into Cambodia.[109]

On May 20, in the name of Chairman Mao Zedong, Beijing called for "People of the World, Unite and Defeat the US Aggressors and All Their Running Dogs."[110] The *New York Times* ran the headline, "Cambodia War Said to Cause Major Peking Shift."[111] In the meantime, China watchers in the US government carefully monitored Beijing's reactions to the Cambodian operation and noted signs of caution in their public statements. For example, the State Department's Bureau of Intelligence and Research analysts assessed that Mao's "rare pronouncement" was clearly intended to "convey Chinese concern at the highest level over the US military incursion into Cambodia and the bombing of North Vietnam."[112] On May 28, the Special National Intelligence Estimate reported that Beijing had been both "cautious and prudent," and its decision "not to intervene" overtly into the Vietnam War was "consistent" with its policy of not risking any major hostilities with either the US or the Soviets.[113] In his memorandum to Nixon, Kissinger commented that the "low-key nature" of the Chinese action had served to reduce the impact of this particular ploy.[114] As for the implications of Mao's statement, Kissinger interpreted that the announcement made no direct threat, offered no commitments, and was not personally abusive toward President Nixon himself.[115]

Thereafter, both the White House and the State Department respectively followed foreign governmental and media reactions to the Cambodian operation. US officials concluded that despite the harsh rhetorical attack in the Chinese press and their government statements surrounding the Cambodian incursions, the Chinese still showed restraint in Sino-US relations in order to avoid a complete break in dialogue with the Nixon administration.

In comparison, however, there was a widening gap between the White House and the State Department regarding both the pace and the agenda for the resumed dialogue with the Chinese. The White House was willing to move faster within a strategic context of formulating tacit cooperation with Beijing against Moscow. The

---

109   Ibid., p. 2.

110   Chen, *Mao's China and the Cold War*, p. 252. This statement enraged President Nixon. He thus ordered every element of the Seventh Fleet not needed for Vietnam into the Taiwan Strait: "I want them to know we are not playing this chicken game." Kissinger and other close associates quietly ignored it. See Kissinger, *White House Years*, pp. 695–696.

111   *The New York Times*, May 26, 1970.

112   Intelligence Brief, INR, "Communist China," May 20, 1970, p. 1, POL Chicom-US, 1970–1973, Box 2188, SNF, RG59, NA.

113   Special National Intelligence Estimate, Number 13-9-70, "Chinese Reactions to Possible Developments in Indochina," May 28, 1970, p. 3, *Tracking the Dragon: Selected National Intelligence Estimates on China, 1948–1976*, National Intelligence Council, CD-ROM (Washington DC: US Government Printing Office, 2004).

114   Kissinger to Nixon, "Secretary Rogers' Evaluations of the Chinese Cancellation of the May 20 Warsaw Meeting," May 28, 1970, p. 1, CF-Europe, Box 700 [2 of 2], NSCF, NPMS, NA.

115   Kissinger, *White House Years*, p. 695.

State Department, however, remained cautious, still regarding the Taiwan issue as the main problem to be discussed at ambassadorial-level talks before proceeding to higher-level meetings. Despite the increasing differences within the US government regarding the approach for the Warsaw talks, there was a general desirability for the continuation of sending conciliatory diplomatic signals to Beijing. During the middle of 1970, the White House thus sought to find ways to convey its intention of military withdrawal from Indochina and to reactivate a dialogue with Beijing through intermediaries, such as Pakistan and Romania. The following chapter examines how the White House and the State Department would seek to explore respective channels of communication with the Chinese in order to send a special envoy to China.

Chapter 6

The Development of Backchannel Communications from June 1970 to July 1971

The final chapter of Part II explores the development of secret diplomacy between the White House and the Chinese leaders. First, it examines the search for a channel of diplomatic communication with the Chinese, conducted by the Kissinger-NSC staff and the State Department. Moreover, it analyses President Nixon's secret initiative to re-activate the Pakistani and Romanian backchannels. Without knowing their respective intentions, the Kissinger NSC attempted to reach the Chinese in Paris, while the State Department continued to observe Chinese foreign policy and tried to resume the Warsaw talks. Nixon himself sought to create a more cordial political atmosphere by making positive public statements about the re-emergence of China in world politics, while searching to establish substantial private talks with Chinese leaders on major security issues of mutual concern. Next, this chapter analyzes the policy studies conducted by the Kissinger-NSC staff and the State Department. US officials in their respective organizations continued to assess Chinese attitude toward the Soviet Union and Taiwan, as well as their attitude regarding the issue of Chinese representation at the UN. Finally, chapter 6 assesses the progress of the US-China diplomatic correspondence which resulted in a final breakthrough via the Pakistan channel in the spring of 1971 that materialized the Chinese invitation of senior US officials to visit China. It was a result of the dramatic public developments by the so-called "ping-pong diplomacy" and a number of highly confidential exchanges between US and Chinese leaders.

1. The Exploration of the Channels of Communication with the Chinese in Late 1970

1.1 The State Department's attempt to preserve the Warsaw channel

During mid and late 1970, the State Department was still seeking to re-activate the Warsaw channel with the Chinese, preparing a list of new instructions for Ambassador Stoessel. On June 20, US officials in Warsaw had an informal liaison meeting with Chinese diplomats.[1] However, the Chinese postponed the Warsaw talks, stating that

---

1   US Embassy, Warsaw to Rogers, "Sino-US Talks: ChiCom Propose Liaison Officer Meeting," June 18, 1970, POL Chicom-US, 1970–1973, Box 2188, Subject-Numeric Files (SNF), General Records of the Department of State, Record Group 59 (RG59), NA.

their resumption would be "discussed later at the proper time." On July 10, Secretary Rogers stated publicly in Japan that China was the key to the future of Indochina and that a settlement in Vietnam could be achieved "very quickly" if Beijing was willing to make an effort.[2] On the same day, the Chinese suddenly released Bishop James Edward Walsh who had been imprisoned since 1958 on charges of spying and sabotage.[3] This was an important signal from Beijing which implied that China was seeking to ease tensions with the United States.

On July 21, 1970, the American Consulate General in Hong Kong sent Washington its assessment that China's approach to Sino-US relations had not fundamentally changed since the beginning of the year. On June 27, on the 20th anniversary of the outbreak of the Korean War, Beijing reiterated that Taiwan was the crucial issue in Sino-US relations, charging that the US had continuously refused to withdraw its armed forces from Taiwan.[4] However, China had not recently insisted on the abrogation of the ROC-US mutual security treaty. Hence, the China watchers in Hong Kong assessed that the definition of how the Taiwan question could be settled was "still open."[5] One complicating factor in Beijing's view was Japan's relations with Taiwan, particularly the link between Japanese security and the security of Taiwan and South Korea drawn in the Nixon-Sato Communiqué of November 1969.[6] Finally, the memo emphasized that it was the Soviet military threat that still motivated the Chinese to continue its renewed dialogue with the United States.

On July 23, 1970, the State Department's Bureau of Intelligence and Research completed its mid-year assessment of China's policy towards America. The memorandum argued that the Chinese attitude toward the Warsaw talks was designed to "play on Soviet fear of a Sino-American accommodation" in East Asia and to "undermine Soviet confidence in the US neutrality" in the event of a Soviet attack on China.[7] As for the Chinese view on the US threat, INR officials estimated that while the Nixon Doctrine provided the first real hope of reduction of US military presence in Asia since the end of the Korean War, Japan would replace the United States as the "principal obstacle to the recovery of Taiwan."[8] As for the conflicts in Cambodia, the US actions announced on April 30 probably caused "temporary uncertainty" in Beijing about the overall direction of US policy in Indochina.[9] To maintain their

---

2 *The New York Times*, July 10, 1970.

3 *The New York Times*, July 13, 1970. The State Department was also obtaining information from US embassies abroad. In early July, the Romanian Vice President privately informed the American Ambassador to Bucharest, Leonard Meeker that Mao was still interested in resuming a dialogue with the United States.

4 American Consulate General Hong Kong to Rogers, "Communist China: The Current State of Sino-US Relations," July 21, 1970, p. 7, POL Chicom-US, 1970–73, Box 2188, SNF, RG59, NA.

5 Ibid., p. 2.

6 Ibid., p. 5. This subject will be discussed further in Chapter 7, Section 2.3 (pp. 173–176) of this book.

7 Intelligence Brief, Bureau of Intelligence and Research (INR), "Communist China: A Mid-year Look at Peking's America Policy, July 23, 1970, p. 2, POL Chicom-US, 1970–1973, Box 2188, SNF, RG59, NA.

8 Ibid., p. 2.

9 Ibid., p. 3.

flexibility, the Chinese emphasized that they wanted "only a temporary postponement of the session, not a cancellation," and Zhou Enlai dropped hints to Eastern European diplomats that the talks "would soon be resumed."[10] Accordingly, on July 27, without knowing the real intentions of the White House, the State Department publicly expressed US willingness to resume the Warsaw talks. On December 23, Secretary of State Rogers still expressed the hope that the Warsaw talks would be resumed, indicating that the China policy was under review. In reality, however, from late 1970, the State Department was cut off from the White House's initiative to improve communication with Beijing.

1.2 The search for backchannels by Kissinger and the NSC staff

After the Chinese cancellation of the 136th Warsaw ambassadorial talks on May 20, 1970, the White House kept silence, waiting for emotions aroused by the Cambodian incursions to subside and making various secret plans to explore new and more restricted means of communication with the Chinese. On June 15, under Kissinger's instructions, Haig gave a message to Major General A. Vernon Walters to deliver to his Chinese contact in Paris (a defense attaché named Fang Wen). The message stated that the US government wished to continue exchanges through the Warsaw ambassadorial talks. However, owing to its formal nature (namely the number of officials having been involved in the Warsaw channel and the publicity surrounding the talks), it was difficult to maintain "complete secrecy."[11] The message thus suggested the establishment of an alternative channel "for matters of the most extreme sensitivity" with knowledge of the talks "confined to the President, his personal advisors and his personal representative unless otherwise agreed."[12] Finally, the message proposed the opening of a channel through General Walters and indicated the White House's readiness to send a "high-level personal representative of the President to Paris, or some other mutually convenient location for direct talks."[13]

Meanwhile, the White House continued its assessment of Sino-Soviet relations. For example, according to Haldeman's diaries, on August 15, 1970, Kissinger concluded that in their disputed border areas, the Soviets were moving forward and the Chinese were responding by building up their troops.[14] The Soviets intended to use nuclear weapons to destroy Chinese missile installations and were positioning

---

10   Ibid., p. 4.
11   Haig to Walters, June 15, 1970, enclosing a message to be delivered by Major General Vernon Walters to the Chinese Communist Government (approved by Nixon but unsigned), "Exchange Leading Up to HAK Trip" [1 of 2], Box 1031, FPF-China/Vietnam Negotiations, NPMS, NA.
12   Ibid.
13   Ibid.
14   *The Haldeman Diaries*, August 15, 1970. In his memoirs, Kissinger claims that the collusion against China was the "real Soviet price" for a US-USSR summit and that the US was being asked to give the Soviets a "free hand" against China. Kissinger, *White House Years*, p. 554. Former Soviet Ambassador to America Dobrynin argues in his memoirs that: "I do not remember any such demands about an alliance [by Moscow and Washington] against China." Anatoly Dobrynin, *In Confidence: Moscow's Ambassador to America's Six Cold War*

troops to defend against the possibility of the Chinese retaliatory land invasion. The idea seemed "absurd" to Nixon because of the possible massive impact such a conflict could have on East Asian as well as international security.[15] Even at this stage, there still remained a difference between Nixon and Kissinger regarding Sino-Soviet rivalry.

On September 12, 1970, Kissinger sent a memorandum to Nixon, explaining the current situation of US-China relations. There had been no response from the Chinese yet; it appeared that if there was to be any success, it would be "through Paris."[16] At that moment, Kissinger thus argued: "we have no choice but to wait and see if they are willing to respond."[17] Moreover, on September 27, Kissinger had a private meeting with French diplomat Jean Sainteny in Paris, asking him to play an intermediary role to "set up a channel" with the Chinese Ambassador in Paris, Hung Chen.[18] Hence, it was the Paris backchannel that Kissinger and the NSC staff took an initiative to activate for secret communication with the Chinese leaders.

1.3 Nixon's reactivation of the Pakistani and Romanian backchannels

On October 1, 1970 – China's National Day – as a symbolic diplomatic gesture, Chairman Mao invited American journalist Edgar Snow to stand next to him to watch the public parade in the Tiananmen Square.[19] As China experts, Chen and Shambaugh point out, Beijing intended to send a symbolic diplomatic signal to

---

Presidents (1962–1986) (New York: Times Books, A Division of Random House, Inc, 1995), p. 207.

15   Ibid.

16   Kissinger to Nixon, "Contact with the Chinese," September 12, 1970, p. 1 with an attached Memo to General Walters, "Sensitive Message to be delivered to Chinese Communist Government," June 15, 1970, in Cookies II, "Chronology of Exchange with PRC February 1969–April 1971," Box 1032, Files for the President – China Materials, NSCF, NPMS, NA.

17   Ibid. The secrecy for Kissinger's back-channel communication was not entirely preserved. In mid August 1970, the Joint Chiefs of Staff placed a spy on Kissinger's staff, a Navy yeoman, Charles Radford, officially a stenographer. He was assigned to copy and forward every piece of paper he saw to the Joint Chiefs of Staff. In mid January 1974, *The Chicago Tribune* reported the story. See Richard Reeves, *President Nixon: Alone in the White House* (New York: Simon & Schuster, 2001), p. 244.

18   Memcon, Kissinger and Sainteny, at Sainteny's apartment in Paris September 27, 1970, p. 3, Box 1031, Exchange Leading Up to HAK Trip (1 of 2), FPF-China/Vietnam Negotiations, NSCF, NPMS, NA. Sainteny had previously served in Hanoi, and his wife was a student of Kissinger at Harvard.

19   Edgar Snow, *The Long Revolution* (London: Hutchinson & Co. Publishers LTD., 1973), pp. 10–12. From August 23 to September 6, 1970, the Second Plenum of the Ninth Congress of the Party Central Committee had been held at Lushan. Mao revealed his readiness to accept a US proposal for a representative to visit China. Accordingly, Mao's support for the opening to the US temporarily postponed the deepening rivalry between the moderate faction led by Zhou Enlai and the military faction led by Lin Biao (supported by Mao's wife Jiang Qing). Philipe Short, *Mao: A Life* (New York: Henry Holt & Company, 1999), pp. 592–594; and Chen Jian, *Mao's China and the Cold War* (Chapel Hill, NC: University of North Carolina Press, 2001), pp. 253–254.

improve its relations with Washington.[20] However, as Kissinger defensively admits in his memoirs, US officials were slow to comprehend the implication of the Chinese gesture: "we have missed the point when it mattered. Excessive subtlety had produced a failure of communication."[21]

Coincidently, President Nixon was looking for public and private opportunities to reiterate his continuing interest in China. In a *Time* magazine interview published on October 5, 1970, Nixon stated that: "If there is anything I want to do before I die, it is to go to China. If I don't, I want my children to."[22] Nixon also sought to renew secret communications with the Chinese through the Pakistani and Romanian channels. On October 25, 1970, after the twenty-fifth anniversary celebrations of the establishment of the United Nations, the US President held a private meeting with Pakistani President Yahya Khan in the Oval Office (at which even Kissinger was not present). Having read Kissinger's memorandum in advance, Nixon was aware that Yahya was scheduled to visit Beijing in the following month (which took place from November 10 to 15).[23] Nixon briefed Yahya that the US had been disappointed at the lack of response from the Chinese as well as the failure to resume the Warsaw talks; however it was gratified at the release of Bishop Walsh.[24] In particular, Nixon asked Yahya to convey a message to the Chinese that it was "essential" for the United States to "open negotiations with China" and that the US would make "no condominium" with the Soviets against China.[25] Finally, Nixon made it clear that the US was willing to send a high-level personal representative, such as retired diplomat Robert Murphy, or the senior Republican leader Thomas E. Dewey to Beijing to "establish links secretly."[26]

On October 26, Nixon held talks with Romanian President Nicolae Ceaușescu and explained his willingness to improve relations with both China and the Soviet Union.[27] In particular, Nixon asked Ceaușescu's assistance in informing Beijing that the US would bear them "no hostility" and would "welcome a more normal

---

20 Chen, *Mao's China and the Cold War*, p. 255; and David Shambaugh, interview with the author, October 8, 2003.
21 Kissinger, *White House Years*, p. 699.
22 Rodman to Kissinger, "Who Invited Whom?" October 13, 1971, Box 13 China, HAKOF, NPMS, NA.
23 Kissinger to Nixon, "Your Talk with President Yahya – October 25, 1970," p. 1, Memoranda for the President, Records of Meetings, Box 82, President's Office Files (POF), White House Central Files WHCF), NPMS, NA.
24 Ibid., p. 2.
25 Memcon "Meeting Between the President and Pakistan President Yahya," October 25, 1970, p. 2, Box 1032, Cookies II "Chronology of Exchange with PRC February 1969 – April 1971," NSCF, NPMS, NA.
26 Ibid.
27 Rodman to Kissinger, "Who Invited Whom?" October 13, 1971, p. 2, Box 13 China, HAKOF, NSCF, NPMS, NA; and Kissinger to Nixon, "My Conversation with President Ceausescu, October 27, 1970," with Memcon attached, October 31, 1970, Box 1032, Cookies II "Chronology of Exchange with PRC February 1969–April 1971," NSCF, NPMS, NA.

relationship."[28] Ceauşescu replied that he believed China wanted to improve relations with the United States. Finally, Nixon declared US readiness for talks with China and for the exchange of high-level special representatives. During the state dinner, Nixon used his toast for a public expression of US interest in improved relations with the "People's Republic of China," which was, very importantly, the first use of China's official name by a US President.[29]

On October 27, at Nixon's instruction, Kissinger held a private talk with Ceauşescu and reiterated the US interest in establishing diplomatic communications with the People's Republic of China. Kissinger explained that such communications could be "free from any outside pressures or questions of prestige" and stressed that such communications would be restricted to the White House.[30] Ceauşescu reconfirmed that he would inform the Chinese leaders of their conversation and would pass on any communication from them as he had done in the past. Accordingly, in early November, Romanian Deputy Premier Gheorghe Radulescu visited Beijing and delivered Nixon's message to the Chinese.

2. Progress in Backchannel Communications

2.1 NSSMs 106 and 107: The Chinese representation issue in the UN in November 1970

On November 7, 1970, Kissinger received a letter from Jean Sainteny regarding his contact with the Chinese Ambassador in Paris, Huang Chen. Huang passed Kissinger's message (which he conveyed to Sainteny in September) to his leaders, which indicated the White House's desire to set up a secret channel.[31] Sainteny reported that Hung had been a member of the Central Committee and thus his view must be listened to in Beijing. NSC staff member Richard Smyser assessed that Sainteny's information was still basic; however, he added that the Chinese were recently expressing their interest in "being admitted to the UN."[32] Kissinger interpreted the Sainteny-Huang contact as Beijing's confirmation on the use of other backchannels.[33]

---

28   Kissinger to Nixon, "Your Meeting with Romanian President Ceausescu, October 26, 1970," p. 6, Memoranda for the President (MemforP), Records of Meetings (ROM), Box 82, POF, WHCF, NPMS, NA.

29   In his memoirs, Nixon recalled that he intended to send a "significant diplomatic signal" to Beijing. Nixon, *RN*, p. 546.

30   Kissinger to Nixon, "My Conversation with President Ceausescu, Tuesday, October 27," October 31, 1970, pp. 1–2, Box 1024, Memcons – The President/HAK and President Ceausescu October 26 and 27, 1970, Presidential/HAK MemCons, NSCF, NPMS, NA.

31   Smyser to Kissinger, "Letter from Your Friend in Paris, and Other Chinese Miscellania," November 7, 1970, p. 1, Cookies II, Chronology of Exchanges with PRC February 1969–April 1971, Box 1032, FPF-China/Vietnam Negotiations, NSCF, NPMS, NA.

32   Ibid., p. 2.

33   Kissinger, *White House Years*, p. 703.

The Development of Backchannel Communications

Regarding the major issues in Washington's relations with Beijing, Kissinger and his NSC staff were now paying more attention to the Chinese representation issue in the United Nations. On November 19, 1970, the day before the UN vote, Kissinger initiated two inter-departmental studies, NSSM 106: "China Policy" and NSSM 107: "Study of Entire UN Membership Question: US-China Policy."[34] Coincidently, on November 22, President Nixon sent a memorandum to Kissinger to launch a study of the Chinese representation issue in the UN:

> On a very confidential level, I would like for you to have prepared by your staff – without any notice to people who might leak – a study of where we are to go with regard to the admission of Red China into the UN. It seems to me that the time is approaching sooner than we might think when we will not have the votes to block admission.
>
> The question we really need an answer to is how we can develop a position in which we can keep our commitments to Taiwan and yet will not be rolled by those who favor admission of Red China.
>
> There is no hurry on this study but within two or three months I would like to see what you come up with.[35]

As former CIA official James Lilley recalls, in the following four months, the NSC staff, State Department, and the CIA would conduct a wide range of policy studies.[36] It was the State Department officials who took the principal initiative to develop concrete issues for the technically complicated UN representation question. While continuing to support the Republic of China in Taiwan to remain in the UN General Assembly, the State Department was also formulating a new policy toward the admission of the People's Republic of China into the UN.

2.2 Initial invitation through the Pakistani channel

Meanwhile, the Pakistan backchannel began to function actively. On December 9, Nixon and Kissinger received Zhou's reply (approved by Mao and Lin) through Yahya. The letter stated that in order to discuss the subject of "the vacation of

---

34 National Security Study Memorandum 106 (NSSM106): "China Policy," and National Security Study Memorandum 107 (NSSM 107): "Study of Entire UN Membership Question: US-China Policy," November 19, 1970, Subject Files (SF), Box 365, NSCF, NPMS, NA. In October 1970, a China expert in academia, Richard Moorsteen, wrote to the Kissinger-NSC that China-related questions usually came up the policy making level as "part of another problem," and China did not come into focus as a "national entity." Moorsteen thus suggested the establishment of a "high-level China Study Group." Letter from Moorsteen to Kissinger, October 8, 1970, and Memo from Lord to Holdridge and Kennedy, "Establishing a China Policy Group," October 30, 1970, Box 334, Policy Planning Staff (Director's Files – Winston Lord), RG59, NA.

35 Nixon to Kissinger, November 22, 1970, Memoranda from the President, 1969–1974, Box 2, President's Personal Files (PPF), White House Special Files (WHSF), NPMS, NA.

36 James R. Lilley (CIA Station, Hong Kong, 1969–1970, China Operations Division, CIA, 1971–1973), Oral History Interview, p. 67, 1996, FAOHC.

Chinese territories called Taiwan [sic]," a "special envoy" of President Nixon would be "most welcome" in Beijing.[37] Zhou also noted that it was "the first time the proposal had come from a Head, through a Head, to a Head" and that China attached special importance to this message because the US knew that Pakistan was "a great friend of China."[38] Yahya commented that it was important that Zhou had consulted Mao and Lin before he replied and that during his recent contact with the Chinese, there was no direct rhetorical criticism of the United States. Thus, these were some additional signs of the "modification" in the Chinese approach to their relations with the United States.[39]

In his memoirs, Kissinger downgrades the Chinese continuing reference to Taiwan as a "standard formula," insisting that the Chinese were "driven by some deeper imperative," namely the security of China itself rather than the future of one province.[40] However, this interpretation is misleading, given China's persistence on Taiwan throughout the Warsaw ambassadorial talks in the 1950s and 1960s. While over-emphasizing the Soviet military threat toward China, Kissinger underestimated Chinese long-term sensitivity to the Taiwan question as the symbol of US intervention into the Chinese civil war.

At a press conference on December 10, 1970, President Nixon stated that no change in the Chinese representative issue at the UN would be made at this time. However, Nixon reiterated explicitly, "[W]e are going to continue the initiative that I have begun, an initiative of relaxing trade restrictions and travel restrictions, an attempting to open channels of communication with Communist China, having in mind the fact that looking long toward the future we must have some communication and eventually relations with Communist China."[41]

On December 16, 1970, Kissinger handed to Hilaly an unsigned memorandum for delivery to Yahya, which stated that the US government would be prepared to proceed to a higher-level meeting in Beijing in order to discuss not only the Taiwan question, but also "other steps designed to improve relations and reduce tensions."[42] Very importantly, the message made clear that the US policy was to "reduce its military presence in the region of East Asia and the Pacific as tensions in this region diminish."[43] In his memoirs, Kissinger explains that the last sentence, a product of

---

37 Kissinger to Nixon, "Chinese Communist Initiative," December 10, 1970, enclosed draft note of verbal message and message from Zhou, as conveyed by Hilaly, and with comments by Yahya. Exchange Leading Up to HAK Trip (1 of 2), Box 1031, FPF-China/Vietnam Negotiations, NSCF, NPMS, NA.

38 Ibid.

39 Ibid., p. 4

40 Kissinger, *White House Years*, p. 701.

41 President Nixon, Press Conference, December 10, 1970, "US China Policy 1969–1972," CF, Far East, Box 86, HAKOF, NSCF, NPMS, NA.

42 Memorandum of Record by Col. Richard T. Kennedy, December 16, 1970, enclosing the response to the PRC (via Hilaly and Yahya, delivered in Beijing on January 5 1971), p. 1; and Memorandum by Pakistani Ambassador Agha Hilaly, "Record of a Discussion with Mr. Henry Kissinger On [sic] the White House on 16th December 1970," pp. 1–2, Exchange Leading Up to HAK Trip, Box 1031, FPF-China/Vietnam Negotiations, NSCF, NPMS, NA.

43 Ibid., pp. 1–2.

many interagency studies, was designed to induce Chinese interest in a negotiated settlement in the Vietnam War by "tying" the US military withdrawal from Taiwan to the ending of conflicts in Indochina.[44]

On December 18, 1970, Mao Zedong received American journalist Edgar Snow for a five-hour interview. Mao explained that the Chinese Foreign Ministry was considering the matter of admitting Americans, including the President, into China. Mao made clear his preference that "at present the problems between China and the U.S.A. would have to be solved with Nixon."[45] Therefore, Mao would be "happy to talk with him either as a tourist or as President."[46] As Bundy interprets, the Chinese grasped two major aspects of the US Presidential initiative: Nixon's personal willingness for a "large and visible" role in the rapprochement, and the "political timing" in his desire to present the new China initiative in public.[47] In his memoirs, Nixon recorded that: "We learned Mao's statement within a few days after he made it."[48] On the contrary, in his memoirs, Kissinger states that neither Nixon nor he knew of Mao's comments until Snow's report of the interview was published in *Life* magazine on April 30, 1971.[49]

On December 24, 1970, in his end-of-the-year briefing to the press, Kissinger stated that: "We are in the process now of reviewing the still existing restrictions. We remain prepared, at Warsaw, or elsewhere, to talk to the Communist Chinese about differences that divide us."[50] Kissinger concluded that despite the interruption of the Warsaw talks, the US principles would remain the same as to "seek, on the basis of equality, to remove the causes that have produced the tensions" with China.[51] In the latter half of 1970, the Nixon-Kissinger White House operated China policy almost single-handedly, sending more positive and explicit public signals to resume diplomatic contacts with Beijing and simultaneously privately seeking to convey via the third parties their intentions in holding direct talks with the Chinese leaders.

---

44   Kissinger, *White House Years*, p. 702.

45   Edgar Snow, "A Conversation with Mao Tse-Tung," *Life*, April 30, 1971, p. 3, in Book V-a, The President, Briefing Papers for the China Trip, For the President's Files (Winston Lord) (FPF/Lord)– China Trip/Vietnam, Box 847, NSCF, NPMS, NA. Mao made it clear to Snow that he would not object to the publication of his comments without the use of direct quotations several months later. Snow received the notes of the talk taken by Chinese interpreter Nancy T'ang. For a detailed account of the entire talk, see Snow, *Long Revolution*, pp. 160–163, pp. 172–176; and Tyler, *A Great Wall*, pp. 83–86. In May 1971, Mao ordered the complete transcript of his interview with Snow be relayed to the entire party and the whole country. Chen, *Mao's China and the Cold War*, p. 262.

46   Ibid.

47   William Bundy, *A Tangled Web: The Making of Foreign Policy in the Nixon Presidency* (New York: Hill and Wang, A Division of Farrar, Staus and Giroux, 1998), p. 166.

48   Nixon, *RN*, p. 547.

49   Kissinger, *White House Years*, pp. 702–703.

50   Kissinger, Press Backgrounder, December 24, 1970, "US China Policy 1969–1972," Countries Files, Far East, Box 86, HAKOF, NSCF, NPMS, NA.

51   Ibid.

2.3 Another invitation through the Romanian channel

From the beginning of 1971, the Romanian backchannel also became active. On January 11, 1971, Romanian Ambassador Corneliu Bogdan brought an oral message to Kissinger, which was passed from Vice Premier Gheorghe Radulescu, who had visited Beijing in late November 1970. It was a message from Premier Zhou, "reviewed by Chairman Mao and Lin Biao," expressing that if the US had a desire to settle "one outstanding issue" – "the US occupation of Taiwan" – the PRC would be prepared to receive a US special envoy in Beijing.[52] Zhou also suggested that since President Nixon had already visited Bucharest and Belgrade, he would also be welcome in Beijing.[53] The message had two particularly important implications. First, the Chinese emphasized the fact that because of their independence from Moscow, Nixon had already visited these two communist capitals. Second, apart from an informal comment by Nixon in an October 1970 *Time* interview, the first reference to a Presidential visit to China came from the Chinese side.[54] Kissinger interpreted that importantly, Zhou's message did not refer to Indochina and that the Chinese interest was the Soviet military threat regardless of their public statement on the Taiwan issue.[55] On January 29, Kissinger gave an oral message to Bogdan, which stated that the United States was prepared to discuss the whole range of international issues, including Taiwan.[56] The message was given orally in an attempt to indicate preference for the Pakistani channel, the White House being wary of possible Russian eavesdropping in Romania. Moreover, on January 18, 1971, Kissinger received a message from Sainteny.[57] Sainteny explained that acting upon Kissinger's letter of November 9, he held a talk with his Chinese counterpart and asked to transmit the message to Beijing on December 23.

2.4 The State Department's reassessments of China policy

Meanwhile, without knowing of the White House's reactivation of back-channel communications, the State Department was conducting its own assessment of the present nature of US-PRC relations. The Bureau of Intelligence and Research assessed Edgar Snow's interview with Premier Zhou of December 1970, seeking

---

52 Kissinger to Nixon, "Conversation with Ambassador Bogdan, January 11, 1971," FPF-China Materials, Box 1032, NSCF, NPMS, NA.
53 Ibid.
54 The Chinese would reiterate this issue on April 21, 1971 after Nixon's public remark about his daughter's honeymoon, possibly to China.
55 Kissinger, *White House Years*, p. 704.
56 Memcon, Corneliu Bogdan and Kissinger, January 29, 1971, Cookies II – Chronology of Exchange with PRC, February 1969–April 1971, FPF-China/Vietnam Negotiations, Box 1032, NSCF, NPMS, NA.
57 Smyser to Kissinger, "Message from Sainteny," January 18, 1971, with Kissinger's handwritten comments, Cookies II – Chronology of Exchange with PRC, February 1969–April 1971, Box 1032, FPF-China/Vietnam Negotiations, NSCF, NPMS, NA.

to detect any change regarding Beijing's position on the Taiwan issue.[58] Snow reported Zhou's remarks on the importance of "respect for territorial integrity."[59] Thus, Zhou demanded US recognition of Taiwan as an inalienable part of the PRC; US withdrawal of its forces from the island and from the Strait of Formosa; and US recognition of the five principles of peaceful coexistence.[60] It appeared that while the Taiwan issue remained crucial in Sino-US relations, Beijing was prepared to seek diplomatic co-existence with Washington. The INR concluded therefore that: "The door is open."[61]

On January 20, 1971, the American Embassy in Taipei reported to Secretary Rogers that the Republic of China's evaluation of the Beijing-Moscow relations had been "largely shaped by propaganda considerations and wishful thinking rather than by dispassionate objectivity."[62] The airgram stated that Taipei dismissed the increasing signs of the Sino-Soviet rift as a "Communist trick to deceive the Free World." For State Department officials, however, Taipei's sensitivity to the Beijing-Moscow relations remained the main concern in the promotion of US diplomatic contacts with China.

On January 25, 1971, the American Consulate General in Hong Kong also sent an airgram to Washington, assessing a "continuing fluidity" in Beijing's triangular relationship with Washington and Moscow. China watchers argued that although the capacity of the US for influencing the course of this relationship with the PRC might be "limited," Beijing would still need to promote Sino-US rapprochement as a "counter to Soviet military pressure."[63] In other words, the Soviet Union still constituted a "far greater military threat" to the PRC than the US did.[64]

2.5 The Laos military operation in February 1971

Meanwhile, the situation in Indochina was showing developments. In early February 1971, the US supported the South Vietnamese strike against the North Vietnamese main land-supply line along the Ho Chi Minh Trail in Laos. On February 4, without criticizing President Nixon directly, China's *People's Daily* denounced the US military operation in Laos. On February 9, 1971, *The New York Times* ran the

---

58   Intelligence Note, INR, "Communist China/US: Did Chou Tell Snow Anything New About Taiwan?" January 4, 1971, p. 1, POL Chicom-US, 1970–1973, Box 2189, SNF, RG59, NA. This record suggests that some evidence of Edgar Snow's interview with the Chinese leaders in December 1970 existed within the US government before the publication of *Life* magazine in April 1971. Kissinger might have overlooked the INR record.
59   Ibid., p. 2.
60   Ibid., Annex, p. 1.
61   Ibid.
62   American Embassy, Taipei, "GRC Views of the Peking-Moscow Relationship," January 20, 1971, p. 1, POL Chicom-USSR, 1970–73, Box 2192, SNF, RG59, NA.
63   American Consulate General Hong Kong, "Peking's Triangular Relationship with the US and USSR," January 25, 1971, p. 1, POL Chicom-US, 1970–73, Box 2192, SNF, RG59, NA.
64   Ibid., p. 2.

headline: "Red China Warns on Move in Laos."⁶⁵ The Special National Intelligence Estimate judged that Beijing probably saw the US and its allies "still bogged down" in a war that offered "no graceful exit."⁶⁶ CIA officials estimated that Beijing would thus continue to "publicly and privately encourage Hanoi to persist in its protracted people's war."

On February 17, President Nixon clarified in a press conference: "this action is not directed against Communist China. It is directed against the North Vietnamese who are pointed toward South Vietnam and toward Cambodia. Consequently I do not believe that the Communist Chinese have any reason to interpret this as a threat against them or any reason therefore to react to it."⁶⁷ Nixon also sought to re-assure Beijing via the Pakistan backchannel regarding Washington's continuing commitment to promoting a new bilateral dialogue and that the military operation in Laos would last only six weeks.⁶⁸ Finally, with regard to domestic criticism of the conflicts in Indochina, the President assured Congressional leaders that: "we must not lose sight of the main objective – to continue US withdrawals on schedule and develop a self defense capability of our South Vietnamese friends."⁶⁹ Overall, as Holdridge argues, Laos was a "side show" until the US discovered that the Ho Chi Minh Trail ran into its very significant areas.⁷⁰

The time was ripe for another public gesture. On February 25, 1971, the Nixon administration published its second Foreign Policy Report to Congress, encouraging China's participation in the international community:

> It is a truism that an international order cannot be secure if one of the major powers remains largely outside of it and hostile toward it. In this decade, therefore, there will be no more important challenge than that of drawing the People's Republic of China into a constructive relationship with the world community, and particularly with the rest of Asia.⁷¹

---

65   *The New York Times*, February 9, 1971. In private, however, Chinese Deputy Foreign Minister Chiao Kuan-hua told the Norwegian Ambassador in Beijing, Ole Aalgard, that China was aware of a new trend in US foreign policy and that sooner or later, direct Sino-US meeting would resume. Chiao implied that he was interested in meeting with Kissinger. Kissinger, *White House Years*, p. 706.

66   Special National Intelligence Estimate, Number 13-10-71, "Communist China's Reactions to Developments in Laos," February 18, 1971, *Tracking the Dragon: Selected National Intelligence Estimates on China, 1948–1976*, National Intelligence Council, CD-ROM (Washington DC: US Government Printing Office, 2004).

67   *The New York Times*, February 17, 1971. See also Nixon, *RN*, p. 548; Kissinger, *White House Years*, pp.706–707; and Reeves, *President Nixon*, p. 300. From March 5 to 8, 1971, Premier Zhou visited Hanoi and expressed moral support to North Vietnam. Importantly, however, Zhou avoided criticizing Nixon directly.

68   The Laos operation lasted from February 8 to March 25, 1971.

69   Notes from the GOP Congressional Leadership Meeting with the President, Tuesday, February 23, 1971, p. 4, MemforP, ROM, Box 84, POF, WHCF, NPMS, NA.

70   Holdridge, Oral History Interview, July 20, 1995, p. 85, FAOHC.

71   Richard M. Nixon, "US Foreign Policy for the 1970's: Building the Peace," February 25, 1971 (Washington DC: Government Printing Office, 1971), pp. 105–109.

Very importantly, the United States used China's official name for the first time in an official document, intending to send a diplomatic signal to the Chinese. Compared with the first report, the February 1971 report more explicitly emphasized the importance of the restoration of diplomatic relations with China for the promotion of stability and peace in Asia and the world. *The New York Times* reported that: "Mr. Nixon prepared to establish dialogue with Peking."[72]

The foreign policy report, however, also caused apprehension in Taipei regarding the possibility of a two-China policy. On March 3, 1971, the American Embassy in Taipei reported that the Republic of China's Ministry of Foreign Affairs had instructed "a strong representation" with the US government, opposing the President's use of the term "People's Republic of China."[73] On March 4, during the press conference, President Nixon thus reiterated, "… under no circumstances will we proceed with a policy of normalizing relations with Communist China if the cost of that policy is to expel Taiwan from the family of nations."[74]

On March 15, as a diplomatic signal to Beijing, the State Department announced the termination of all restrictions on the use of American passports for travel to the People's Republic of China. Equally important, the State Department also announced that the US was seeking private channels to resume the Warsaw talks. On March 16, 1971, *The New York Times* reported the decision: "US Lifts Ban on China Travel."[75] The State Department's purposes, based on the long-term bureaucratic policy studies, were to gradually resume the comings-and-goings between the peoples of the two states, and simultaneously trying to improve diplomatic relations between the two governments through Warsaw ambassadorial talks.

2.6 NSC meeting on NSSMs 106 and 107: The Chinese representation issue in the UN in March 1971

From November 1970 to February 1971, interdepartmental studies on the US China policy (NSSM 106) and the Chinese representation question in the UN (NSSM 107) had been proceeding. On March 12, 1971, a Senior Review Group meeting was held on NSSMs 106 and 107.[76] The prevailing estimation, especially among China experts

---

72 February 26, 1971, *The New York Times*.

73 American Embassy, Taipei to Rogers, "GRC To Protest Use of Term "PRC" by President Nixon, March 3, 1971, p. 1, POL ChiNat-US, 1970–1973, Box 2205, SNF, RG59, NA.

74 President's news conference, March 4, 1971, Public Statements on China by US officials, Box 86, US China Policy 1969–1972 [2of 2], CounF-Far East, HAKOF, NSCF, NPMS, NA.

75 *The New York Times*, March 16, 1971.

76 Senior Review Group, March 12, 1971, National Security Council Institutional Files (NSCIF), NPMS, NA. In short, from 1961, the US had pursued a resolution making any proposal to change the representation of China an "Important Question," which required a two-thirds majority of the General Assembly for approval. In November 1970, although having failed for two-thirds, the majority had voted for the first time for in favor of the so-called "Albanian Resolution" to seat Beijing and to expel Taipei (51 votes for, 49 against, and 25 abstentions). See Foot, *The Practice of Power*, pp. 45–48; and Kissinger, *White House Years*, pp. 770–774.

in the State Department was that before improving US-PRC relations, Washington would have to recognize Beijing as the sole government of China or at least allow it into the United Nations. The State Department thus pursued the so-called dual-representation formula, namely, while preserving Taipei's seat in General Assembly, Washington would also admit Beijing's entry into the UN. In reality, however, both Beijing and Taipei had made it clear that they would not tolerate any kind of a "two-Chinas" resolution.

On March 25, 1971, the NSC met to discuss NSSMs 106 and 107.[77] The purposes of the meeting were to examine policy options to deal with a "growing sentiment" in the General Assembly for admission of Beijing, and to "protect" the US relationship with Taiwan.[78] In the NSSM 107 paper, the central argument was whether to maintain the present US policy on Chinese representation, or to work for a dual representation formula, seating both Chinese entities. On the one hand, the Republic of China's expulsion from the UN would erode international support for Taipei and would make Washington vulnerable to the charge that its defense treaty with the Republic of China constituted interference in Chinese internal affairs.[79] On the other hand, Beijing's entry into the UN would enable Washington to maintain regular and high-level contacts.[80] In the end, Nixon and Kissinger still favored continuing the existing policy of keeping Taipei in and Beijing out.[81] However, Nixon was reluctant to overrule Rogers, and thus delayed his decision by allowing the State Department to handle the UN issue.

Another crucial point was the US-Republic of China defense relationship. The fundamental question in the NSSM 106 paper was to determine "how far" Washington should go in improving its relationship with Beijing and making it possible for Beijing to "play a constructive role in the family of nations."[82] Particularly important, the reduction of the US military presence in Taiwan would be a "useful test" of Beijing's

---

77   National Security Council Meeting, "UN Membership and China (NSSMs 106 and 107)," March 25, 1971, Box H-031, UN Representation and China [Part I], Minutes of Meetings (1969–1974), NSCIF, NPMS, NA.

78   President's Talking Points, NSC Meeting – Chirep – March 25, 1971, p. 1. National Security Council Meeting, UN Membership and China (NSSMs 106 and 107), March 25, 1971, Box H-031 UN Representation and China [Part I], Minutes of Meetings (1969–1974), NSCIF, NPMS, NA.

79   Issues Paper – NSSM 107, p. 2, National Security Council Meeting, "UN Membership and China (NSSMs 106 and 107)," March 25, 1971, Box H-031 UN Representation and China [Part I], Minutes of Meetings (1969–1974), NSCIF, NPMS, NA.

80   Ibid.

81   Mr. Kissinger's Talking Points, NSC Meeting, China-UN Representation and China Policy, March 25, 1971, National Security Council Meeting, UN Membership and China (NSSMs 106 and 107), March 25, 1971, Box H-031 UN Representation and China [Part I], Minutes of Meetings (1969–1974), NSCIF, NPMS, NA. See also Kissinger, *White House Years*, p. 723.

82   Issues Paper – Department of State, NSSM 106 – United States China Policy, p. 1, National Security Council Meeting, UN Membership and China (NSSMs 106 and 107), Thursday, March 25, 1971, Box H-031 UN Representation and China [Part I], Minutes of Meetings (1969–1974), NSCIF, NPMS, NA.

willingness to improve relations with the US[83] One view was that Taiwan was so strategically located that US facilities there were "essential" to fulfilling its regional defense commitments in the Western Pacific.[84] Another view was that a reduction in the US military presence in Taiwan would be "consistent with the Nixon Doctrine" without seriously damaging the morale of America's Asian allies or its ability to meet its defense commitments to them.[85]

On April 9, 1971, Kissinger sent a memorandum to Nixon regarding the Chinese Representation at the UN.[86] Nixon's main concern was to prevent Taipei's exclusion from the United Nations. However, Kissinger was very pessimistic that the US would not be able to prevent Taipei's "expulsion" – "probably this year, certainly next."[87] Thus, Kissinger recommended to Nixon that he should be prepared to lessen his problems with Chiang Kai-shek, the President of the Republic of China, by: reaffirmation of the US-ROC Defense Treaty; assurance on the maintenance of US force levels in Taiwan; and sympathetic consideration of his military assistance needs.[88]

3. Breakthrough from April to June 1971

3.1 Ping pong diplomacy

After the Chinese denouncement of the Laos operation in early February 1971, back-channel communications between Washington and Beijing became quiet for approximately eight weeks. Meanwhile, the State Department assessed that

---

83   Ibid.
84   Ibid.
85   Ibid., p. 3. The Defense Department insisted that the removal of the US military presence should be linked to the renunciation of the force agreement with Beijing. The US withdrawal from Taiwan would also impact on other areas in East Asia where the US was phasing down its military presence in accordance with the Nixon Doctrine. Jeanne W. Davies (Staff Secretary) to Agnew, Rogers, and Laird, "DOD Papers for NSC Meeting on China," March 24, 1971, pp. 2–3, Box H-031, NSCIF, NPMS, NA. As the following chapters demonstrate, the handling of the US-ROK defense relations would remain highly complex in the Washington-Beijing talks.
86   Kissinger to Nixon, "Chinese Representation at the United Nations, April 9, 1971, p.1, Memcons-President/HAK January–April, 1971, Box 1025, President/HAK MemCons, NSCF, NPMS, NA.
87   Ibid., p. 2.
88   Ibid., p. 3. On June 1, at the news conference, Nixon announced that: "a significant change has taken place among the members of the United Nations on the issue of admission of mainland China. ... After we have completed our analysis, which I would imagine would take approximately six weeks, we will then decide what position we, the Government of the United States, should take at the next session of the United Nations this fall, and we will have an announcement to make at that time with regard to that participation problem." The President's News Conference, June 1, 1971, Public Statements on China by US officials, US China Policy 1969–1972 [2of 2], Country Files – Far East, Box 86, HAKOF, NSCF, NPMS, NA. Chapter 7, Section 2.1 (pp. 169–170) of this book further examines the Chinese representative issue in UN.

Beijing's diplomatic offensive was "gaining momentum" through "increased flexibility" regarding the possible improvement of its relations with Washington. State Department officials estimated, however, that Beijing still appeared to be "in no hurry" to resume the Warsaw talks.[89]

On April 7, 1971, to the surprise of US officials, China took a major public initiative to indicate the changes in its policy toward America. During the World Table Tennis Championship game in Nagoya, Japan, the Chinese team invited the American team to Beijing.[90] Accordingly, the so-called "Ping Pong Diplomacy" produced a media sensation. On April 10, *The New York Times* reported that: "15-Man US Table Tennis Team Crosses Into China From Hong Kong."[91] On April 14, Premier Zhou welcomed the American team (which stayed in China from April 10 to 17), describing their visit as an opening for a "new page" in Sino-American relations.[92]

Both the White House and the State Department were carefully monitoring the developments. The State Department's Bureau of Intelligence and Research analyzed that this move toward "people's diplomacy" altered Beijing's longstanding refusal to accept American visitors and revived the more flexible policy toward the US which initially developed in late 1969.[93] On April 14, President Nixon announced additional travel and trade initiatives.[94] On April 16, during a statement to the American Society of Newspaper Editors in Washington, President Nixon reiterated his administration's interest in achieving a normalization of relations with the government of the People's Republic of China. In particular, Nixon also introduced a conversation with his daughters on the possibility of their going to China some day: "I hope they do. As a matter of fact, I hope sometime I do."[95]

---

89   Eliot to Kissinger, "Peking's Increasingly Activist Diplomacy," April 1, 1971, p. 1, POL Chicom-US, 1970–1973, Box 2188, SNF, RG59, NA.

90   The ping-pong diplomacy was Chairman Mao's initiative. See Chen, *Mao's China and the Cold War*, pp. 259–261.

91   *The New York Times*, April 10, 1971.

92   Chen, *Mao's China and the Cold War*, p. 261; and Kissinger, *White House Years*, p. 710.

93   Intelligence Brief, INR, 'Communist China/US: Peking's People's Diplomacy: A "New Page" in Sino-American Relations,' April 14, 1971, p. 1, POL Chicom-US, 1970–1973, Box 2188, SNF, RG59, NA. The Soviets criticized that China's policy had not really changed at all, and that Beijing remained a disruptive factor in world affairs. Intelligence Brief, INR, "Ping-Pong Diplomacy Triggers Soviet Attack on Peking's Global Policies," April 23, 1971, p. 1, POL Chicom-US, 1970–1973, Box 2188, SNF, RG59, NA.

94   Statement by the President, April 14, 1971, pp. 1–2, Box 1031, Exchange Leading Up to HAK Trip to China December 1969–July 1971 (1 of 2), and "US China Policy, 1969–1972," p. 3, HAKOF, CF-Far East, Box 86, NSCF, NPMS, NA. Thereafter, the Chinese could get visas to visit America, the US dollar could be used to purchase Chinese goods, US oil companies could sell fuel to ships and planes en route to China, and US-owned ships under foreign flags could visit China.

95   Statement by President Nixon to American Society of Newspaper Editors, April 16, 1971, China – Public and private moves toward a Presidential visit 1970–1971, p. 2, Box 1031, FPF-China/Vietnam Negotiations, NSCF, NPMS, NA. During Kissinger's secret trip to Beijing in July 1971, Zhou stated that Nixon's remark about his daughter's honeymoon

Despite the strict secrecy, there were some unexpected interruptions in the Nixon-Kissinger back-channel communication with Beijing from other cabinet officials. On April 19, 1971 US Vice-President Spiro Agnew publicly expressed his disagreement with any opening to China, which, in the eyes of Nixon and Kissinger, almost undermined the secret preparation of direct talks with the Chinese. According to Haldeman's diaries, Nixon argued that Agnew did not understand the "big picture," explaining further that: "the whole China initiative was about the Russian game – using the thaw with China to shake up the Russians."[96] Most senior cabinet officials of the Nixon administration had not yet comprehended the emergence of triangular diplomacy between the US, the Soviets, and China. On April 27, 1971, *The New York Times* reported that administration officials disclosed that Romania was acting as an "intermediary" in communications between Washington and Beijing.[97] The *Times* also disclosed that the Romanian Deputy Premier informed Premier Zhou of the American desire to improve relations with China during meetings in November 1970 and in March 1971.[98] Solomon recalls that despite Kissinger's worries, the public did not pay much attention to the media disclosers, because secret diplomacy toward China was "unbelievable, outside the regular range of diplomacy" during that period.[99] The United States was still militarily in Indochina – China's periphery, and Beijing also kept criticizing Washington for having occupied the Chinese province of Taiwan.

3.2 Breakthrough via the Pakistani channel

Behind the dramatic public scene of the ping pong diplomacy, there was a development in US secret contacts with China through backchannels. On April 27, Hilaly delivered Zhou's message (dated on April 21, responding to Nixon's message of December 16, 1970) to Kissinger. The message reaffirmed the Chinese willingness to publicly receive in Beijing "a special envoy of the President of the US (for instance, Mr. Kissinger) the US Secretary of State or even the President of the US himself for direct meeting and discussions [sic]."[100] On April 28, Kissinger asked Hilaly to deliver an oral message. The message showed Nixon's appreciation

---

"prompted the invitation." Rodman to Kissinger, October 13, 1971, "Who Invited Whom?" HAK-ASF, Box 13, China, HAKOF, NSCF, NPMS, NA. In his private talks with Kissinger, Nixon argued that the American public opinion was "still against Communist China." In terms of the US relations with Taiwan, however, "the story change" was going to take place. Kissinger replied that: "we have to be cold about it." Nixon and Kissinger, April 16, 1971, p. 2, Box 29, Henry A. Kissinger Telephone Conversation Transcripts (Telcons), NPMS, NA, in William Burr (ed.), "History Declassified: Nixon in China," NSA.

96 Haldeman, *The Haldeman Diaries*, April 20, 1971.
97 *The New York Times*, April 27, 1971.
98 *Times*, April 27, 1971.
99 Solomon, interview with the author, September 24, 2003.
100 Message from Zhou to Nixon, April 21, 1971 (delivered on April 27, 1971), Exchange Leading Up to HAK Trip (1 of 2), Box 1031, NSCF, NPMS, NA. Hilaly called at 3:45pm and delivered message to Kissinger at 6:12pm. See Kissinger, *White House Years*, p. 713.

to Zhou for his "positive, constructive and forthcoming" message of April 21 and promised an early response.¹⁰¹ Kissinger asked Hilaly to convey a separate message to Zhou reflecting Yahya's personal view that: "President Nixon is very anxious to handle these negotiations entirely by himself and not let any politicians come into a picture until a government-to-government channel is established."¹⁰²

On April 27 and 28, Nixon and Kissinger discussed the selection of a special envoy to Beijing, and Nixon finally decided to send Kissinger.¹⁰³ Very importantly, during the spring of 1971, Nixon and Kissinger increased their confidence in the Chinese seriousness of direct talks. Lord recalls that: "Once the Chinese agreed to broaden the agenda for the secret trip, they [Nixon and Kissinger] became more confident that they were really interested in a serious opening of relations. And, we didn't think they would humiliate us. Therefore, I don't think Nixon and Kissinger were overly nervous about the trip."¹⁰⁴

Meanwhile, without knowing of the secret exchanges between the White House and the Chinese, State Department officials made contradictory public statements. On April 28, 1971, in a recorded interview with the BBC, Secretary Rogers stated that President Nixon's visit to China might be possible if relations continued to improve. Rogers said that he was "very much in favor of an exchange of journalists, students, and non-professional people with mainland China in the near future."¹⁰⁵ On April 28, a State Department spokesman, Charles W. Bray, stated that it might be possible to resolve the status of Taiwan through negotiations between Nationalist China and Communist China. "Mainland China," Bray stated, "has been controlled and administered by the People's Republic of China for 21 years and for some time we have been dealing with that government on matters affecting our interests."¹⁰⁶ This incident reveals that some State Department officials still considered that the opening to China would be unrealistic in the short-term.

---

101 Haig, "Extract of Memcon dated May 5, 1971," and Memo from Haig to Nixon, "China," May 5, 1971, Exchange Leading Up to HAK Trip (1 of 2), Box 1031, FPF-China/Vietnam Negotiations, NSCF, NPMS, NA.

102 Ibid. On May 7, 1971, Kissinger held a meeting with US Ambassador to Pakistan Joseph Farland, informing that he would set up a Navy backchannel via the US navy attaché in Karachi, assisted by Admiral Elmo R. Zumwalt. Kissinger to Nixon, "Meeting with Ambassador Farland, May 7, 1971," May 15, 1971, Exchanges Leading Up to HAK Trip [1 of 2], Box 1031, FPF-China/Vietnam Negotiations, NSCF, NPMS, NA. Kissinger also discussed with Farland the itinerary of his trip to China via Pakistan. Kissinger, *White House Years*, pp. 721–723.

103 Record of Nixon-Kissinger Telephone Conversation, Discussing Zhou's message and Possible Envoy to China, April 27, 1971, Exchange Leading Up to HAK Trip to China December 1969–July 1971 (1 of 2), Box 1031, FPF-China/Vietnam Negotiations, NSCF, NPMS, NA; and Conversation 2–52, The Nixon White House Tapes, 8:18pm, April 27, 1971, NPMS, NA. See also Nixon, *RN*, pp. 549–550; Kissinger, *White House Years*, p. 717; and Isaacson, *Kissinger*, pp. 339–340.

104 Lord, interview with the author, October 15, 2003. From the spring of 1971, the NSC staff began to prepare briefing papers for the upcoming meeting with the Chinese. An analysis of the briefing papers is conducted in the following chapter.

105 "US China Policy, 1969–1972," p. 3, CF, Box 86, Far East, HAKOF, NSCF, NPMS, NA.

106 Ibid.

On April 29, Nixon urged Haldeman to warn Secretary Rogers regarding the administration's current relations with the media on the China policy. Haldeman's handwritten notes record the messages to Rogers: he should be "very careful" that "we'll not indicate any further decision"; and, if pressed, he should state "we are not in any way trying to irritate [the] Soviet[s] by our own China policy."[107] On the same day, in a news conference, President Nixon called the "two-Chinas" idea "unrealistic" and emphasized that some recent speculation about the State Department officials' statements was "not useful."[108] Instead, Nixon expressed that: "I hope, and, as a matter of fact, I expect to visit Mainland China sometime in some capacity – I don't know what capacity. But that indicates what I hope for the long term."[109] On May 4, the official Chinese newspaper *Jenmin Jih Pao* denounced Bray's statement of April 28 as "brazen interference in China's internal affairs." The article spoke of the continuing friendship between the Chinese and American people, but added that Nixon's expressed desire for better relations with China had proven "fraudulent" in light of Bray's remarks.[110]

On May 10, 1971, Kissinger sent Nixon's unsigned message to Zhou via Hilaly (a reply to Zhou's message of April 21).[111] Nixon made clear that he was "prepared to accept" the Premier's suggestion that he visit Beijing for direct conversations with the leaders of the People's Republic of China. Nixon proposed a preliminary "secret" meeting between Kissinger and Zhou or another appropriate high-level official to exchange views on "all" issues of mutual concern and to prepare for a presidential visit. In addition, the message suggested that the technical arrangements be done through Pakistani President Yahya Kahn. Finally, the message emphasized strongly that: "*For secrecy, it is essential that no other channel be used. It is also understood that this first meeting between Dr Kissinger and high officials of the People's Republic of China be strictly secret*"(The message was received by the Chinese on May 17).[112] It was a symbolic remark reflecting the increasing sensitivity by Nixon and Kissinger to the preservation of secrecy.

---

107 Meeting with President at the Executive Office Building, 10:24–10:50am, April 29, 1971, File 5-48-05, Papers of the Nixon White House, Part 5. H.R. Haldeman: Notes of White House Meetings, 1969–1973, Manuscript Division, Library of Congress.

108 Ibid.

109 Rodman to Kissinger, "Who Invited Whom?" October 13, 1971, p. 3, HAK-ASF, Box 13, China, HAKOF, NSCF, NPMS, NA.

110 "US China Policy 1969–1972," p. 3, Box 86, CF-Far East, HAKOF, NSCF, NPMS, NA.

111 Message from Nixon to Zhou via Hilaly, May 10, 1971, Exchanges Leading Up to HAK Trip to China – December 1969–July 1971 [1 of 2], Box 1031, FPF-China/Vietnam Negotiations, NSCF, NPMS, NA.

112 Ibid. Italic in original. The Chinese initially resisted the idea of secrecy because they suspected the Americans were ashamed to be seen with them. In his memoirs, Kissinger notes that "We later learned that the Chinese were extremely suspicious of our desire for secrecy: perhaps they saw it as a device to allow us to reverse course quickly." Kissinger, *White House Years*, p. 724. Kissinger focused on the Chinese sensitivity to the development of US-USSR relations. On May 20, 1971, Kissinger handed a note to Farland (to be delivered to the Chinese via Pakistani President Yahya), informing the Chinese of the May 20 SALT

3.3 Final invitation

On May 31, 1971, Nixon received a message from Pakistani President Yahya Khan via Ambassador Hilaly. Yahya added his latest assessment of Sino-US relations:

- There is a very encouraging and positive response to the last message.
- Please convey to Mr. Kissinger that the meeting will take place on Chinese soil for which travel arrangements will be made by us.
- Level of meeting will be as proposed by you.
- Full message will be transmitted by safe means.[113]

On June 2, 1971, Hilaly met with Kissinger and delivered a message from Zhou to Nixon (dated May 29).[114] It was a comprehensive reply to Nixon's previous messages on April 29, May 17, and May 22. Zhou's letter clarified that Chairman Mao "welcomes President Nixon's visit." Particularly important, the Chinese treated the idea of a Presidential visit for direct conversations with Chinese leaders as Mao's "suggestion" which Nixon was prepared to "accept." In other words, the Chinese sought to create the impression that it was Chairman Mao who took the principal initiative to have generously invited President Nixon to China. The Chinese agreed that during Nixon's visit, the two sides could raise "the principal issues of concern." However, Zhou re-emphasized that "the first question to be settled" was "the withdrawal of all US armed forces from Taiwan and the Taiwan Strait Area."[115] Finally, Zhou welcomed Kissinger's visit to China as the US representative for a preliminary secret meeting with high-level Chinese officials to prepare and make necessary arrangements for Nixon's presidential visit. On June 4, Kissinger met with Hilaly and delivered Nixon's reply to Zhou. Nixon's message approved that Kissinger would be authorized to meet with Zhou Enlai in China from July 9 to 11.[116] Nixon finally stated that he looked forward to "the opportunity of a personal exchange" with the leaders of the People's Republic of China.[117]

---

announcement, assuring that the US would make "no agreement which would be directed against" China. Memo from Kissinger to Farland, enclosing message to the People's Republic of China on SALT announcement, May 20, 1971, Exchanges Leading Up to HAK Trip [1 of 2], Box 1031, FPF-China/Vietnam Negotiations, NSCF, NPMS, NA.

113 Assessment of Zhou message by Yahya Khan, conveyed by Hilaly to Nixon on May 31, 1971, Exchanges Leading Up to HAK Trip [1 of 2], Box 1031, FPF-China/Vietnam Negotiations, NSCF, NPMS, NA.

114 Message from Zhou to Nixon, May 29, 1971, with commentary, conveyed by Hilaly to White House, Exchanges Leading Up to HAK Trip [1 of 2], Box 1031, FPF-China/Vietnam Negotiations, NSCF, NPMS, NA.

115 Ibid.

116 The Chinese initially preferred the date from June 15 to 20. On June 21, Hilaly transmitted a short message from Zhou (dated June 11) which accepted the July 9 date. Letter from Hilaly to Kissinger, June 19, 1971, with message from Yahya on Kissinger's travel arrangement, Exchanges Leading Up to HAK Trip [1 of 2], Box 1031, FPF-China/Vietnam Negotiations, NSCF, NPMS, NA.

117 Message for the Government of the People's Republic of China (From Nixon to Zhou handed to Hilaly on June 4), Exchanges Leading Up to HAK Trip [1 of 2], Box 1031, FPF-China/Vietnam Negotiations, NSCF, NPMS, NA.

On June 10, 1971, President Nixon authorized the export of a wide range of non-strategic items to China and lifted all controls on imports from China, ending the "21-Year Embargo" on trade with the People's Republic of China since the outbreak of the Korean War.[118] The US's unilateral restrictions on China were thus dismantled, which completed a series of public signals, based on the interdepartmental studies, which the Nixon administration had sent to the Chinese leaders for the previous two and half years.

In summary, during the final stage of the opening process from June 1970 to June 1971, it was Nixon's even stronger conviction for the importance of the historic breakthrough with Beijing that drove the White House's secret diplomacy. Nixon and Kissinger sought to completely cut off the State Department from their highly personalized attempt to send a special envoy to China. Only a very restricted number of officials within the White House, such as Haig, Haldeman, Holdridge, and Lord, were involved in this final stage. The power balance between the White House and the State Department's Bureau of East Asian and Pacific Affairs shifted toward the Kissinger NSC for the planning and implementation of the new China initiative. Without knowing of the exchange of back-channel messages between the White House and the Chinese leaders, the State Department operated in its own initiative to continue to assess change and development in Chinese foreign policy, still seeking to resume the Warsaw Ambassadorial talks.

In comparison, while the Kissinger NSC mainly focused on the deepening Sino-Soviet hostilities, State Department officials considered Taiwan as the central issue in US relations with China. Moreover, while the White House sought to establish direct new talks with the Chinese and discuss major security issues within the broader international context, the Taiwan issue dominated the main contents of the Chinese backchannel messages. Finally, the White House repeatedly stressed the importance of strict secrecy for higher-level meetings with the Chinese leaders. It was the above-examined signal exchange process that resulted in Kissinger's trips to Beijing in July and October 1971, the PRC's admission to the United Nations in October 1971, and finally, Nixon's trip to China in February 1972.

---

118 *The New York Times*, June 11, 1971.

PART III
Direct Talks

Chapter 7

Kissinger's Trips to Beijing in July and October 1971

Chapter seven investigates the major issues between the United States and China during Kissinger's trips to Beijing in July and October of 1971.[1] First, it examines the preparation for the direct talks with the Chinese, including the interdepartmental study NSSM 124, the NSC staff's briefing books, and the Nixon-Kissinger private conversations. The preparation for the July trip was conducted in a highly confidential manner, and only a strictly limited number of officials were involved, namely Nixon, Kissinger, Haig, and a few NSC staff members. The preparation process shows how US officials developed their perceptions on what the US and Chinese sides respectively sought to achieve by resuming a diplomatic dialogue. In the main analysis of the Kissinger-Zhou talks, this chapter conducts five case studies: 1) the Taiwan issue; 2) the conflicts in Indochina; 3) Japan's future role; 4) the India-Pakistan rivalry; and 5) the growth of the Soviet military threat. The overall framework of the talks was the restoration of stability in the Asia-Pacific region. Finally, this chapter assesses foreign reactions to the US opening to China as well as Nixon's briefings on the domestic front. Nixon and Kissinger sought to maximize the impact of a dramatic beginning of rapprochement between the two long-term enemies.

1. The Preparations for the Secret Meeting with the Chinese

1.1 NSSM 124

On April 19, 1971, soon after Premier Zhou's dramatic invitation of the American table tennis team to Beijing, Kissinger directed an inter-departmental study, the National Security Study Memorandum 124 (NSSM 124): "Next Steps Towards the People's Republic of China."[2] In short, NSSM 124 attempted to explore the major

---

1   For Kissinger's July and October trips to Beijing, see Henry A. Kissinger, *White House Years* (Boston: Little Brown, 1979), pp. 736–763, and pp. 774–784; John Holdridge, *Crossing the Divide: An Insider's Account of the Normalization of US-China Relations* (Lanham, Boulder, New York, Oxford: Rowman & Littlefield Publishers, INC., 1997), pp. 55–63, and pp. 67–75; and Patrick E. Tyler, *A Great Wall: Six Presidents and China, An Investigative History* (New York: Public Affairs, 1999), pp. 94–103, and pp. 114–117.

2   National Security Study Memorandum 124 (NSSM124): "Next Steps Toward the People's Republic of China," April 19, 1971, p. 1, National Security Study Memoranda, Subject Files (SF), Box 365, National Security Council Files (NSCF), Nixon Presidential

objectives of furthering the improvement in relations with China in terms of the following aspects:

- anticipated reaction or response by the PRC;
- the advantages and disadvantages of the initiative;
- an assessment of the possible effects on our relations with and the anticipated reactions of the Government of the Republic of China, the USSR, Japan and other nations as appropriate;
- an illustrative scenario by which the initiative could be pursued.[3]

Accordingly, the NSC Interdepartmental Group for East Asian and Pacific Affairs produced a policy study paper. The NSSM 124 paper proposed three groups of alternative actions. Group 1 suggested a collection of relatively modest steps, such as permission for an American flag ship to port at China's coasts and the reduction of close-in intelligence and reconnaissance flights. Group 2 suggested "greater inducements" for the Chinese, including (1) "an offer to establish a Washington-Peking hotline"; and (2) "the reduction of US forces on Taiwan consonant with the withdrawal of US forces from Viet-Nam."[4] More detailed Group 3 suggested important changes in the US policy on the Taiwan question, such as: "(a) some form of US presence in Peking; (b) an indication of US willingness to regard Taiwan as part of China; [and] (c) removal of US forces from the Taiwan area" on the basis of an assurance that the PRC government would not cause a crisis in the Taiwan Strait area.[5]

The first issue to address was whether and how soon the United States should take further steps after announcing the easing of trade with the PRC. Accordingly, the question was whether the US should "limit" its policy to the modest steps of Group 1 in order to "test" the Chinese willingness to move ahead without substantial change in US policy toward Taiwan.[6] The study further questioned whether the US should "directly proceed" toward a more active initiative from Group 2, and possibly Group 3, in order to "persuade" the Chinese leaders to begin to resolve the major problems before formulating any "basic and lasting accord" between the two sides.[7]

Importantly, the Taiwan issue remained fundamental. The memo expressed doubt over whether or not Beijing would make a major move towards governmental contacts without US "flexibility" on 1) the question of Taiwan's legal status, 2) the

---

Materials Staff (NPMS), National Archives (NA). NSSM 124 directed that this study be submitted to the Assistant to the President for National Security Affairs by May 15, 1971, for consideration by the Senior Review Group. At the same time, the Chinese were also preparing for direct talks with the US, which was summarized in the official document: "The Central Committee Politburo's Report on the Sino-American Meeting," on May 26, 1971. Chen Jian, *Mao's China and the Cold War* (Chapel Hill, NC: The University of North Carolina Press, 2001), pp. 264–265.

3   Ibid.
4   Memorandum for the Chairman, NSC Senior Review Group, "NSSM124: Next Steps Toward the People's Republic of China," p. 1, SF, Box 365, NSCF, NPMS, NA.
5   Ibid., p. 2.
6   Ibid.
7   Ibid.

US's "political involvement" with the Taipei government, and 3) the US "military presence" in Taiwan.[8] The memo also estimated that China might "renew and progressively broaden contacts" with the US at the governmental level in order to increase pressure on the Soviets.[9]

The memorandum suggested that the US long-term objective should be "to draw the PRC into a serious discussion of the problems" not only in the bilateral relations but also in a broader "relaxation of tensions in East Asia."[10] The memo also estimated that because of the continuing difficulties with the Soviets and the fear of Japan's re-emergence, Beijing might see its interests improved by a dialogue with Washington. Hence, the memorandum suggested that the US-PRC contacts should move forward "as rapidly as possible" at an official level.[11]

1.2 The "Books"

Parallel with the interdepartmental study, there was another analysis at a more restricted level. In the early spring of 1971, soon after the decision to hold direct talks with the Chinese at a higher official level was confirmed, Kissinger ordered to the NSC staff: "I want you to start working on a book ... Start working up position papers on all the issues that would be discussed with the Chinese."[12] The NSC staff thus began to produce the so-called "Books" – "a detailed set of briefing papers in loose-leaf binders" for an eventual trip to China.[13]

On May 12, 1971, NSC staff member Winston Lord sent a memorandum to Kissinger regarding the on-going drafting of the "Books."[14] The "Books" included the estimation of the situation in China at that period, the major objectives of the trip, the opening statement to be made by Kissinger, and a number of position papers covering every possible major issue which might be raised. Each position paper consisted of an explanation of specific issues, a brief description of the conceivable Chinese position and response, and the US's likely response. Kissinger prepared the Soviet papers with Winston Lord and the Vietnam papers with Richard Smyser, while John Holdridge prepared papers regarding other East Asian issues, including Japan, Korea, and Southeast Asia.[15]

---

8   Ibid., p. 4.
9   Ibid.
10 Ibid.
11 Ibid., p. 3.
12 John Holdridge, Oral History Interview in *A China Reader*, Vol. II, pp. 33–34, January 1995, Foreign Affairs Oral History Collection (FAOHC), Association for Diplomatic Studies and Training, Lauinger Library, Georgetown University.
13 Holdridge, *Crossing the Divide*, p. 45.
14 Lord to Kissinger, "Exchanges with China," May 12, 1971, China – Communiqué & memorabilia July 1971 HAK visit, For the President Files (FPF) – China/Vietnam Negotiations, Box 1033, NSCF, NPMS, NA.
15 Winston Lord, interview with the author, October 15, 2003; and Holdridge, Oral History Interview in *A China Reader*, Vol. II, p. 34, January 1995, FAOHC. In addition, Kissinger read widely on Chinese history, culture, and philosophy. Details of the "Books" are examined in the following sections.

1.3 The Nixon-Kissinger private talks

Behind the preparation of the policy studies at bureaucratic levels, Nixon and Kissinger held their own talks prior to the July 1971 secret meeting with the Chinese. About a week before his departure to Beijing, Kissinger showed Nixon the completed briefing book, code named "POLO." Nixon studied the book, underlining significant points and writing comments on its cover page.[16] In his "Scope Paper" to Nixon, Kissinger proposed that a major task of his trip was to concentrate on the fundamentals of the international situation. Within that broader framework, Kissinger argued, the Chinese would anticipate that the PRC's prestige would increase enormously in becoming unequivocally one of the "big five"; the ROC's international position would erode very considerably; the PRC's chances of getting into the UN that year on its terms (especially the expulsion of the ROC) would rise; and the Soviets would be faced with a "new complexity in their confrontation with the Chinese."[17] Overall, the Chinese might be hoping that the US would end its defense treaties with its allies and "get out of Asia."[18]

Regarding the question of Chinese seriousness toward the direct talks, Kissinger estimated that they were acting partly in response to the Soviet military threat along their borders, stating "it would not help them to humiliate us if they want to use us in some way as a counterweight to the Soviets."[19] Hence, years of Chinese propaganda calling for a total US withdrawal from Asia might not benefit China's interests, since it would inevitably "leave areas of vacuum" into which the Soviets could "move quickly."[20] Kissinger argued further that there was a possibility to explore the value of the US presence in Asia to "exercise restraints" on Japan, which was increasingly seen to China as a "rival and potential threat."[21]

The Chinese would almost certainly focus upon Taiwan as the first order of any substantive talks. Kissinger would therefore seek to develop Washington-Beijing relations while the US at the same time would "retain" its diplomatic ties and mutual defense treaty with the ROC.[22] Regarding Indochina, Kissinger was determined to seek indications firm enough to be taken as "assurances" that the Chinese would "use their influence on the North Vietnamese to move them toward a peaceful and acceptable settlement of the Vietnam War."[23] Finally, Kissinger would seek to assure

---

16   Kissinger recalls that he is not sure how carefully Nixon reviewed "POLO," because Nixon's usual procedure was to concentrate on the cover memorandum and ignore the backup paper. Kissinger, *White House Years*, p. 735.

17   Scope Paper, p. 1, Briefing book for HAK's July 1971 trip, POLO I, For the President's Files (Winston Lord) (FPF/Lord) – China Trip/Vietnam, Box 850, NSCF, NPMS, NA. In his memoirs, Kissinger only briefly reconstructs the contents of the "Book." Kissinger, *White House Years*, pp. 734–736. Regarding the issue of Chinese representation at the UN, see Section 2.1 (pp. 169–170) of this chapter.

18   Ibid.
19   Ibid., p. 2.
20   Ibid.
21   Ibid.
22   Ibid.
23   Ibid., p. 6.

the Chinese that the US would accept China as a "great power with a legitimate role to play in international and particularly Asia affairs."[24]

On July 1, 1971, Nixon and Kissinger (accompanied by Haig) reviewed Nixon's comments on "POLO." Concerning the question of US credibility, Nixon wrote: "Put [the Chinese] in fear."[25] In particular, Nixon wanted Kissinger to stress that, if pushed, he would "turn hard" on Vietnam.[26] Nixon also suggested that Kissinger play up a US "possible move" toward the Soviet Union.[27] Thus, Nixon wanted a somewhat "heavier emphasis" on the Soviet threat and directed Kissinger to state to the Chinese that there were more Soviet divisions on the Chinese border than those arrayed against all of the NATO pact countries. Overall, Nixon instructed that Kissinger should build on three fears: 1) the fear of what the President might do in the event of continued stalemate in the Vietnam War; 2) the fear of a resurgent and militaristic Japan in the case of US withdrawal; and 3) the fear of the Soviet Union on their flank.[28]

Nixon also emphasized that US-PRC dialogue could not appear to be a "sellout" of Taiwan.[29] On the basis of the Nixon Doctrine, Nixon believed, it would "not be essential" for the US military presence to "remain in some areas forever." However, the current US presence in Taiwan was "directly related" to the US military conduct in South Vietnam. Essentially, therefore, Nixon wanted to make the US overall willingness on the Taiwan issue to be somewhat "mysterious." Finally, as it had already conveyed through the Pakistani channel, Nixon told Kissinger to make it very clear to the Chinese that he expected them to institute a "severe limit on political visitors" prior to any presidential trip itself.[30] It was quite crucial for Nixon to maximize the political impact of his trip both on the domestic and international fronts in order to obtain sole credit for the historical opening to China.

1.4 The emergence of multipolarity in the world

The US government publicly continued to illustrate the re-emergence of China's great power dynamism in the world. In his speech in Kansas City on July 6, 1971, just three days prior to Kissinger's secret arrival in Beijing, President Nixon outlined the emergence of the multipolar image of the world, referring to the five great economic powers, such as the United States, Western Europe, the Soviet Union, China, and Japan: "these are the five that will determine the economic future and, because economic power will be the key to other kinds of power [sic]."[31]

---

24   Ibid., p. 8.
25   Nixon's notations on the cover page, Briefing book for HAK's July 1971 trip, POLO I, FPF/Lord – China Trip/Vietnam, Box 850, NSCF, NPMS, NA.
26   Ibid.
27   Ibid.
28   "Meeting between President, Dr. Kissinger, and General Haig, Thursday, July 1, 1971, Oval Office," p. 2, China – general – July–October 1971, FPF, Box 1036, NSCF, NPMS, NA.
29   Ibid., p. 3.
30   Ibid., p. 2.
31   *The New York Times*, July 6, 1971. Critics argued that Western Europe and Japan were not yet able to defend themselves without US help and that China still lacked substantial

Nixon's handwritten notes show that he drafted the main theme of the Kansas City speech.[32] Nixon questioned: "After Vietnam – What kind of a world?" He saw that the US position in world politics had changed over the past two decades: "We live in world which is totally different from [the] world of 25 years ago – even 5 years ago – US was pre-eminent – in 1946 ... US was superior militarily and economically." As a result of US relative economic decline; "Today we see: 5 great powers playing a major role." As for China, Nixon reiterated the long-term theme from his *Foreign Affairs* article of October 1967: "We must end isolation – or risk danger." In other words, China outside of international communication was a great source of instability. Thus, the US moved to develop dialogue with China: 1) "We have taken steps [on] trade and travel"; and 2) "Normalization – essential." Overall, Nixon sought co-existence with China, moving beyond the previous two decades of mutual hostility: "We enter competition. We shall welcome challenge."

The Nixon speech, however, was a surprise for other officials in the administration. For example, during the first meeting on July 9, 1971, Premier Zhou expressed his general agreement with the concept which Nixon outlined in his speech, especially "China as a country with potential strength."[33] However, as Solomon argues, the speech was made while Kissinger was secretly traveling to China. Thus, Kissinger did not even know about it and was "embarrassed" when he held talks with Premier Zhou Enlai.[34] Kissinger admits in his memoirs that: "This put me at some disadvantage since I was unaware of either the fact or the content of the speech."[35] Lord argues that the multipolar world itself was "already there before the Kansas speech," and the main concept of the speech was "a reflection of the basic worldview" of Nixon and Kissinger.[36] While realizing the re-distribution of power resources in military, political, and economic terms in the late 1960s and early 1970s, Nixon and Kissinger still viewed the United States as the most powerful state.

2. Kissinger's trips to Beijing in July and October 1971

From July 6 to 12, 1971, Kissinger took what was announced as a fact-finding trip to Asia during which he secretly traveled to Beijing (July 9 to 11) and held extensive

---

military and economic power resources. See Stanley Hoffmann, "Weighing the Balance of Power," *Foreign Affairs*, July 1972; and Zbigniew Brzezinski, "The Balance of Power Delusion," *Foreign Policy*, No. 7, Summer 1972.

32   Kansas City, July 6, 1971, Speech Files, Box 67, President's Personal Files (PPF), White House Special Files (WHSF), NSCF, NPMS, NA. The quotations in this paragraph are all from Nixon's handwritten notations in preparation for his Kansas City speech.

33   Kissinger and Zhou, Memorandum of conversation (Memcon), July 9, 1971, Afternoon and Evening (4:35pm–11:20pm), p. 38, China-HAK memcons July 1971, FPF, Box 1033, NSCF, NPMS, NA.

34   Richard Solomon, interview with the author, September 24, 2003.

35   Kissinger, *White House Years*, pp. 748–749.

36   Lord, interview with the author, October 15, 2003.

talks with Premier Zhou.[37] At the beginning of the talks, Kissinger emphasized the importance of secrecy: "The President asked that this mission be secret until after we meet, so we can meet unencumbered by the bureaucracy."[38]

After two decades of mutual hostility, one of the most fundamental issues between Washington and Beijing was the reduction of tension and the restoration of stability in Asia. Kissinger encouraged the People's Republic of China to "participate" in all matters affecting "the peace in Asia and peace in the world" and play an "appropriate role in shaping international arrangements."[39] In response, Premier Zhou argued that: "the world outlook and stands of our two sides are different," however, the two sides should formulate "a channel for co-existence, equality, and friendship."[40] Finally, Kissinger and Zhou discussed the language and content of a joint announcement for the respective domestic audiences and the rest of the world. These talks became a substantial mutual learning process regarding decreasing the degree of direct threat between the two sides.

From October 20 to 26, 1971, Kissinger took an interim visit to Beijing to make arrangements for the Presidential trip.[41] Compared with the July secret trip, the October trip was widely covered in the media. The NSC staff composed another set of "Books," code named "POLO II," on not only "grand political-military strategy" but also what was to be included in the joint communiqué for the Nixon's trip.[42] In addition to the NSC staff members, State Department officials, such as Alfred L. Jenkins, office director of the Office of Mainland China and Mongolian Affairs, and his associates were brought into the preparation. Marshall Green, the Assistant Secretary of State for East Asian and Pacific Affairs, was the chief liaison between the NSC staff and the State Department.

President Nixon principally sought to enhance his presidential leadership. During Kissinger's official trip to Beijing in October 1971, Nixon (via Haldeman) asked

---

37 As for Kissinger's cover-up trip, see, Walter Isaacson, *Kissinger: Biography* (New York: McGraw-Hill, 1992), pp. 343–344. Foreign Minister Zhang Wenjin [1971–1972] "flew from Beijing to pick up Kissinger and take him back." From 1969 to 1971, there were some America specialists working in Beijing. In the spring of 1971, the Foreign Ministry had brought back some officials from the countryside, one being Zhang Wenjin, the other being Ji Chauzhu to help Zhou and Mao to prepare for Kissinger's visit. Ji Chaozhu was the interpreter for that visit, Nixon's visit, and subsequent visits. David Shambaugh, interview with the author, October 15, 2003.

38 Memcon, July 9, 1971, Afternoon and Evening (4:35pm–11:20pm), p. 3, China memcons and memos – originals July 1971, FPF, Box 1033, NSCF, NPMS, NA. In the following sections, unless otherwise noted, only the date of the memcons of the July 1971 and October talks is indicated.

39 Ibid., p. 4.

40 Ibid., p. 7.

41 On August 16, Kissinger discussed with Chinese Ambassador Huang Chen his plan to pay a four-day "interim" visit to China in late October. Kissinger also proposed to Huang a possible date for the presidential visit, suggesting two ideas, February 21 and March 16, 1972. The Chinese accepted February 21, 1972. Memcon, Huang Chen and Kissinger, August 16, 1971, pp. 8–9, China exchanges – July–October 20, 1971, FPF/Lord, Box 849, NSCF, NPMS, NA.

42 Holdridge, *Crossing the Divide*, pp. 67–68.

Haig to transmit a message by wire to Kissinger on an urgent basis. The message explained that the President wished Kissinger to ensure that a "specific time" was arranged for "two private head-to-head meetings" between the President and Mao with no one in attendance other than interpreters; and in the second instance, with Zhou "under identical circumstances."[43] As the next chapter demonstrates, Nixon's talks with the key Chinese leaders would be the highlight of his trip to China in February 1972.

2.1 The Taiwan issue

The question of Taiwan remained the most sensitive issue between Washington and Beijing. The briefing book "POLO" listed the Taiwan issue on the top of its agenda, involving political considerations, and identified that it could "not be lightly set aside."[44] Kissinger anticipated that apart from Taiwan, there was basically no great conflict between PRC and US national interests.[45]

It was on the Taiwan issue that Kissinger and his NSC staff particularly depended on the State Department's past efforts and expertise, but without revealing their specific intentions. The most difficult task was finding appropriate acceptable language to express the US's official position on Taiwan. In short, since the period of the Warsaw ambassadorial talks in the 1950s and 1960s, Beijing maintained that the Taiwan issue was part of China's internal affairs, which allowed the use of force for its resolution, if necessary. However, Washington insisted on "peaceful means" to resolve the differences.[46] Throughout the back-channel exchanges, Beijing still attempted to create the impression that it was Washington that desired a direct Sino-American meeting in order to discuss the Taiwan question. On the other hand, after the Warsaw talks in January and February 1970, the White House reiterated that the agenda for direct talks between the two sides consisted of the broad range of issues of mutual concern, "including, but not limited to" the Taiwan question.[47]

In his memoirs, Kissinger states very misleadingly that: "Taiwan was mentioned only briefly during the first session."[48] A participant in the July 1971 meeting, John Holdridge argues that: "the sole declared reason that Zhou Enlai had agreed to talks was to discuss the Taiwan question, even though pressing strategic considerations

---

43   Haig to Kissinger, October 20, 1971, p. 1, China-HAK October 1971 visit, FPF, Box 1035, NSCF, NPMS, NA.

44   Taiwan, p.1, Briefing book for HAK's July 1971 trip, POLO I (hereafter referred to as Taiwan, POLO I), FPF/Lord, Box 850, NSCF, NPMS, NA.

45   Ibid.

46   Ibid., p. 4. See also Richard Nixon, "United States Foreign Policy in the 1970s: Building for Peace," President Nixon's Report to Congress, Vol. 2, February 25, 1971 (Washington DC: Government Printing Office, 1971), p. 277. As for the strategic importance of the Republic of China in US policy toward Asia, see John W. Garver, *The Sino-American Alliance: Nationalist China and American Cold War Strategy* (New York: An East Gate Book M.E. Sharpe, Inc., 1997), pp. 283–284.

47   Summit, p. 3, Briefing book for HAK's July 1971 trip, POLO I, FPF/Lord, Box 850, NSCF, NPMS, NA.

48   Kissinger, *White House Years*, p. 749.

growing out of the Sino-Soviet dispute would surely be involved as well."[49] Holdridge recalls further that the Taiwan question was presented "to diminish, if not entirely eliminate, for the time being its role as an item of contention in Sino-US relations."[50] In reality, however, the record of the talks between Kissinger and Zhou show that the two sides held extensive exchanges on Taiwan.

Although the two sides agreed not to mention Taiwan in a joint announcement that followed the talks, Zhou repeatedly stressed that Taiwan was the "first" and "crucial" issue, and had to be regarded as "a part of China."[51] In response, as "POLO" suggested, Kissinger made a crucial statement, "[W]e are not advocating a 'two Chinas' solution or a 'one-China, one-Taiwan' solutions."[52] The statement immediately brought about Zhou's positive response: "[T]he prospect for a solution and the establishment of diplomatic relations between our two countries is hopeful."[53]

Kissinger brought a major concession on the "eventual removal" of all US armed forces from Taiwan and the Taiwan Strait.[54] Within "a specified brief period of time after the ending of war in Indochina," Kissinger explained, the US was prepared to remove two-thirds of its armed force.[55] In reality, one-third of the military presence was related to the defense of Taiwan itself, however, Kissinger argued, its reduction depended on the general state of the Sino-American relations in the following years. Kissinger made it clear to Zhou that the US was prepared to materialize diplomatic normalization during "the first two years" of Nixon's second term.[56]

Equally important, regarding the so-called "Taiwan Independence Movement," Kissinger clarified that the US would not try to "encourage, support, finance, or give any other encouragement."[57] Zhou expressed concern that after Washington's opening to Beijing, Chiang Kai-shek might collude with leaders in Tokyo or Moscow. Zhou was also preoccupied with Japan's possible re-entry into Taiwan before and after the US withdrawal. Hence, Kissinger repeatedly assured that the US would "strongly oppose" any Japanese military presence in Taiwan.[58]

Finally, as the briefing book emphasized, Kissinger reiterated: "We hope very much that the Taiwan issue will be solved peacefully."[59] In essence, Kissinger was trying to link the US withdrawal from Taiwan to Chinese assurance of renouncing the use of force in its relations with Taiwan. However, Zhou reiterated China's long-

---

49   Holdridge, *Crossing the Divide*, p. 58.
50   Ibid.
51   Memcon, July 9, 1971, p. 13.
52   Ibid; and Taiwan, p. 2, POLO I.
53   Ibid. On the afternoon of July 10, 1971, Zhou proposed Kissinger to tape-record their discussions. The Chinese wanted all the promises on tape, especially Kissinger's assurances concerning Taiwan. The two sides later agreed that there was no need for a tape recording. James H. Mann, *About Face: A History of America's Curious Relationship with China, from Nixon to Clinton* (New York: Alfred Knopf, 1999), p. 32.
54   Taiwan, p. 2, POLO I.
55   Memcon, July 9, 1971, p. 12.
56   Memcon, July 10, 1971 (12:10pm–6:00pm), p. 16, and p. 19.
57   Memcon, July 11, 1971 (10:35am–11:55am), p. 11.
58   Ibid.
59   Ibid., p. 10; and Taiwan, p. 4, POLO I.

term principle – the use of force as the ultimate means to deal with its internal issue. Hence, Kissinger reported to Nixon, regarding Taiwan, "we can hope for little more than damage limitation by reaffirming our diplomatic relations and mutual defense treaty."[60]

In "POLO II," the briefing book for Kissinger's trip to Beijing in October 1971, the NSC staff argued that during the July 1971 talks, the Chinese had "not set any specific time-frame" for the withdrawal of US forces from Taiwan, and therefore that the question remained open-ended.[61] Accordingly, the NSC staff suggested that Kissinger "avoid committing the President to any kind of a formal stand on normalization and troop withdrawals." Nixon himself wished to "avoid the appearance of selling out an ally."[62] Therefore, the NSC staff recommended that what should be stressed to the Chinese was US "intention, not the formality."[63] During the talks with Zhou, Kissinger thus reiterated, "We recognize that the People's Republic of China considers the subject of Taiwan an internal issue, and we will not challenge that."[64]

Importantly, Kissinger and Zhou held intensive negotiations on the language of Taiwan's status to be included in the joint communiqué for the upcoming summit. Lord explains that the NSC staff prepared a draft of what was to be known as the Shanghai Communiqué. It was originally a typical diplomatic draft with two sides agreeing on issues. After consulting with Mao, Zhou rejected it and criticized, "We haven't talked to each other for 25 years. It's dishonest. It will make our allies suspicious, and it won't make any sense to our publics. So let each side state its own positions, and then we can state where our views converge."[65] Accordingly, Kissinger and Lord re-drafted the entire communiqué overnight, producing the revised version in which the US and Chinese sides independently stated their respective positions on ideology and on specific issues. Moreover, Lord admits that: "we did draw on [the] State's ideas for the Taiwan portion."[66] In reality, however, Lord's statement is only a limited explanation. More particularly, it was during the preparations for the January and February 1970 Warsaw talks that State Department officials, especially the Director of Asian Communist Affairs, Paul Kreisberg, and a China Desk official, Donald Anderson, developed the whole "conceptual approach." These officials drafted "the new formulations" to describe US "acceptance of the idea of the unity

---

60   Kissinger to Nixon, "My Talks with Chou En-lai," July 14, 1971, p. 27, miscellaneous memoranda relating to HAK's trip to PRC, July 1971, FPF, Box 1033, NSCF, NPMS, NA.

61   Taiwan, p. 5, Briefing book for HAK's October 1971 trip POLO II [Part I], For the President's Files (Winston Lord) – China Trip/Vietnam, Box 850, NSCF, NPMS, NA.

62   Ibid., p. 7.

63   Ibid., p. 9.

64   Memcon, October 21, 1971, 10:30am–1:45pm, p. 20, HAK visit to PRC October 1971 Memcons – originals, FPF, Box 1035, NSCF, NPMS, NA.

65   Lord, "The Nixon Administration National Security Council," p. 27, The National Security Council Project (NSCP), Oral History Roundtables (OHR), Center for International and Security Studies at Maryland and the Brookings Institution, December 8, 1998.

66   Ibid. In his memoirs, Kissinger admits only in general terms that he adapted the Taiwan language from a State Department's planning document. Kissinger, *White House Years*, p. 783.

of China" as well as the removal of US forces.⁶⁷ On the basis of these bureaucratic inputs, the US draft statement of October 25, 1971 read as follows:

> The United States acknowledges that all Chinese on either side of the Taiwan Straits maintain there is but one China and that Taiwan is a province of China. The United States Government does not challenge that position…
>
> The United States accepts the ultimate objective of the withdrawal of its armed forces from the Taiwan Straits, and pending that will progressively reduce them as tensions diminish [sic].⁶⁸

Throughout the talks, Zhou stressed that the Chinese side was "exerting great restraint" on the Taiwan issue and that it would not demand "an immediate solution" but that it would be resolved gradually.⁶⁹ However, Zhou still sought private reassurance that the US would withdraw not only from Taiwan Strait but also from Taiwan as a whole.⁷⁰

Kissinger reported to Nixon that Taiwan remained the "single most difficult issue."⁷¹ On the other hand, Kissinger interpreted that the PRC was "in no a hurry" to have all US armed forces removed from Taiwan but wanted the "principle of the final withdrawal" established; China was most interested in "global acknowledgement that Taiwan is part of China."⁷²

In late 1971, the Nixon administration had faced one delicate problem, namely the Chinese representation issue in the United Nations which showed a perception gap between the White House and the State Department. In short, as previously discussed, the Nixon administration adopted the so-called "dual position": while supporting Beijing's new entry into the Security Council and General Assembly, it continued to support the representative of the Chinese Nationalists of Taiwan in the General Assembly.⁷³ Since Kissinger's October trip coincided with the UN General Assembly's annual debate on Beijing's representation issue, UN Ambassador George H.W. Bush requested that President Nixon delay Kissinger's schedule, because it would "not be helpful at all."⁷⁴ Nixon considered that Taiwan still received

---

67 Paul Kreisberg (Director, Office of Asian Communist Affairs, Policy Planning, Department of State, 1965–1981), Oral History Interview, p. 9, and p. 14, in *A China Reader*, Vol. III, January 1995, FAOHC; and Donald Anderson (China Desk/Warsaw talks, Department of State, 1966–1970), Oral History Interview, pp. 17–18, in *A China Reader*, Vol. III, January 1995, FAOHC.
68 Memcon, October 26, 1971, 5:30am–8:10am, p. 2.
69 Memcon, October 24, 1971, 10:28am–1:55pm, p. 25.
70 Memcon, October 26, 1971, p. 2.
71 Kissinger to Nixon, "My October China Visit: Discussions of the Issue," November 11, 1971, p. 14, China – HAK October 1971 visit, FPF, Box 1035, NSCF, NPMS, NA.
72 Ibid., p. 4.
73 See Rosemary Foot, *The Practice of Power: US Relations with China since 1949* (Oxford, New York: Clarendon Press, 1995), chapter 2.
74 The Nixon White House Tapes, Conversation 581–1 and 582–2, NA; and Transcript of "Conversation between President Nixon and National Security Adviser Kissinger, followed by Conversation among Nixon, Kissinger, and UN Ambassador George Bush," September 30,

important support in America, however the rapprochement with Beijing had priority over Taipei's status in the UN. Nixon thus advised Bush to "fight hard" and did not alter Kissinger's schedule.[75] On October 25, 1971, as a consequence of a vote of substantial majority, the General Assembly admitted the People's Republic of China to the UN and expelled the Republic of China. On October 26, *The New York Times* reported that: "US Seats Peking And Expels Taipei; Nationalists Walk Out Before Vote."[76] In the end, Nixon and Kissinger privately regarded Beijing's entry into the UN as a matter of inevitability.

2.2 Conflicts in Indochina

It has been pointed out that by opening to China, the US sought to induce a cooperative attitude from the Chinese to promote a negotiated settlement in the Vietnam War.[77] In his memoirs, however, Kissinger describes only that: "I would seek some moderating influence on Indochina, bearing in mind that the mere fact of the meeting and the substantial summit was bound massively to demoralize Hanoi."[78] Kissinger therefore fails to show what he precisely sought to obtain from Zhou. In fact, it is Kissinger himself who has repeatedly denied the US specific interest in inducing Chinese to put pressure on Hanoi.[79] Moreover, Holdridge states only that the Vietnam issue was "sidestepped."[80] In reality, however, the Indochina issue required a number of intensive exchanges between the two sides.

In the briefing book "POLO," the NSC staff made it clear that the US wanted to end the war in Vietnam through negotiations, however they also stated, "[W]e will not purchase its ending at the price of our humiliation."[81] Kissinger was therefore mainly concerned about the question of US credibility. The longer the war continued, the less influence the US would have in Saigon, and the less impact the US would have on a political settlement.[82]

1971, p. 2, in William Burr (ed.) *Negotiating US-Chinese Rapprochement: New American and Chinese Documentation Leading Up to Nixon's 1972 Trip*, National Security Archive (NSA).

75   Ibid., p. 4.

76   *The New York Times*, October 26, 1971.

77   See, for example, Seymour Hersh, *The Price of Power* (New York: Summit Books, 1983), p. 375; and Robert Ross, *Negotiating Cooperation: The United States and China 1969–1989* (Stanford, California: Stanford University Press, 1995), p. 34.

78   Kissinger, *White House Years*, p.735. Kissinger brought in a Vietnam expert, Richard Smyser, for the preparation of the briefing book and the secret trip to Beijing. Holdridge, Oral History Interview in *A China Reader*, Vol. II, p. 34, January 1995, FAOHC.

79   During an interview with CNN, Kissinger states that: "We did not expect that China would bring pressure on Vietnam to settle ... We never expected China to do anything active to help us." CNN, *The Cold War*, Episode 15, *China*, Interview transcript collected at NSA (http://www.gwu.edu/~nsarchiv/coldwar/interviews/episode-15/kissinger1.html).

80   Holdridge, *Crossing the Divide*, p. 60.

81   Indochina, p. 1, Briefing book for HAK's July 1971 trip, POLO I, FPF/Lord, Box 850, NSCF, NPMS, NA.

82   Ibid., p. 4.

During the talks with Zhou, Kissinger explained that the US was willing to end the Vietnam War through negotiations, and would be interested in setting a "date" for the withdrawal.[83] On the other hand, Kissinger insisted that it would be crucial for the US to make a settlement consistent with its "honor" and "self-respect."[84] Thus, Kissinger argued that the US and China should take a "great" country point of view rather than seeing the issue in terms of a "local" problem.[85] Kissinger sought to point out the significance of a broader geopolitical framework of a new US-Soviet-China relationship instead of focusing on regional conflicts in Indochina, which deepened the long-term mutual hostilities between the US and China.

Zhou was not convinced, insisting that "all" foreign troops, including the US military installations, should be withdrawn from Indochina, and the three countries (Vietnam, Cambodia, and Laos) should be "left alone" to determine their own political path.[86] Kissinger claimed that the US would eventually withdraw unilaterally.[87] He also admitted that there should be a ceasefire, but North Vietnam should not demand for the US military withdrawal and its complete departure from South Vietnam simultaneously. Zhou thus criticized the US policy for being a conditional withdrawal, questioning that if the US took a "broad" perspective, why it still wanted to leave a "tail" (implying Thieu in South Vietnam and Lon Nol-Sirik Matak in Cambodia).[88]

Importantly, the US pursued a political settlement in Indochina. As the NSC briefing book advised, Kissinger thus emphasized that the US required a "transition" period between the "military withdrawal" and the "political evolution."[89] During this interim period, Kissinger argued, Washington would be prepared to accept "restrictions" on the types of assistance that could be provided to the states in Indochina.[90] Zhou replied that as long as the war did not stop, Beijing would "continue" its own support for the peoples in Indochina. However, Zhou made it clear that China would not "intervene" or negotiate on their behalf. Hence, Kissinger claimed that the US was not asking China to "stop" giving aid to its friends.[91]

In his report to Nixon, Kissinger stated that the current peace talks in Paris were blocked by the remaining differences between Washington's proposal for a "ceasefire" and Hanoi's insistence on the "overthrow" of Thieu.[92] Kissinger claimed

---

83 The Nixon administration regarded Vietnamization as "not a substitute for negotiations, but a spur to negotiations." See Richard M. Nixon, "United States Foreign Policy for the 1970s: A New Strategy for Peace, A Report by President Richard Nixon to the Congress," February 18, 1970 (Washington DC: Government Printing Office, 1970), p. 51.
84 Memcon July 9, 1971, p. 17.
85 Ibid., p. 26.
86 Ibid., pp. 24–25.
87 Ibid., pp. 32–33.
88 Ibid.
89 Memcon, July 10, 1971, p. 22; and Indochina, p. 5, Briefing book for HAK's July 1971 trip, POLO I, FPF/Lord, Box 850, NSCF, NPMS, NA. Nixon's handwritten comments on the briefing book read: "We want a decent interval. You have our assurance." Ibid.
90 Ibid.
91 Ibid., p. 26.
92 Kissinger to Nixon, "My Talks with Chou En-lai," July 14, 1971, p. 14.

that Zhou's attitude reflected the "ambivalence" of Beijing's position on the possible escalation of the war.[93] Henceforth, Kissinger concluded that the mere fact that the US and China were holding talks would bring about an "impact" in North Vietnam, anticipating that Beijing might "exert some influence" on Hanoi.[94]

In "POLO II," the NSC staff estimated that the China initiative was a positive factor for negotiations in Indochina "because of the ricochet effect on Moscow, giving it more incentive to get into the act; and the greater likelihood that Hanoi would substantively honor the terms of a settlement (at least in the short run) given her allies' stake in it."[95]

During the October 1971 talks, Kissinger prepared to give specific assurance that the President was prepared: (1) to withdraw completely from Indochina and give a fixed date, and (2) leave the political solution to the Vietnamese people alone.[96] More particularly, Kissinger explained to Zhou, "We have offered new elections six months after a peace is signed. We have offered that all American troops withdraw one month before the election. We have offered that the President and Vice President of Vietnam resign one month before the election so that they do not run the election."[97]

As for the Soviet threat in Indochina, the NSC staff estimated that the Soviets might favor North Vietnamese dominance of Indochina as a counterweight to the United States. Because of both Hanoi's consistent streak of independence and the small percentage of Beijing's military aid, the Chinese influence in Hanoi might "not be very substantial."[98] The NSC staff thus pointed out the Chinese fear of "enlarged Soviet prestige generally and influence in Southeast Asia in particular."[99] On the other hand, the Chinese had made it clear that they did not want to play an intermediary role in Indochina.[100] In conclusion, the NSC staff recommended that: "we should downplay any potential Soviet role."[101]

In reality, however, Kissinger exaggerated that the continuation of war in Indochina would only help "outside forces," implying the Soviets.[102] As for the question of Beijing's influence on Hanoi, Kissinger stated only that Washington would "appreciate" Beijing's "telling its friends its estimates of the degree of our

---

93   Ibid.
94   Ibid., p. 16. Three days after Kissinger's departure from Beijing in July 1971, Zhou flew to Hanoi and attempted to emphasize China's continual support. However, the North Vietnamese believed that the Chinese used the Vietnam issue to settle the Taiwan question. See Qiang Zhai, *China and the Vietnam Wars, 1950–1975* (Chapel Hill, NC: The University of North Carolina Press, 2000), pp. 196–197.
95   Indochina, pp. 9–10, Briefing book for HAK's October 1971 trip POLO II [Part I], FPF, Box 850, NSCF, NPMS, NA.
96   Ibid., p. 2.
97   Memcon, October 21, 1971, 4:42–7:17pm, p. 13.
98   Indochina, p. 11, Briefing book for HAK's October 1971 trip POLO II [Part I], FPF, Box 850, NSCF, NPMS, NA.
99   Ibid.
100   Ibid., p. 12.
101   Ibid., p. 13.
102   Memcon, October 21, 1971, 4:42–7:17pm, p. 24.

sincerity in making a just peace."[103] Kissinger thus reported to Nixon that the Chinese could be "helpful, within limits" on Indochina.[104]

2.3 Japan's future role

Nixon and Kissinger sought to justify the continuation of the US-Japan Security Treaty by deliberately using Japan's feared military resurgent in their talks with the Chinese leaders. Until the publication of books in the late 1990s, the question of how Kissinger and Zhou discussed the Japan issue during the July and October 1971 talks was either overlooked or given relatively minor attention.[105] In his memoirs, without revealing any details of his talks with Zhou, Kissinger points out Zhou's concern about a "militaristic Japan" and states only that during the July 1971 talks in Beijing, Zhou "accused us of tempting Japan into traditional nationalist paths." He went on to recall, "It took me some time to convince him that the US-Japan alliance was not directed against China."[106] Zhou's criticism reflected China's long-term opposition to the US-Japan security ties.

In reality, however, the NSC staff recognized that Kissinger was neither familiar with nor interested in Japan.[107] Thus, as the former Assistant Secretary of State for East Asian and Pacific Affairs, Marshall Green, recalls, it was State Department officials who took the initiative to develop the US policy toward Japan from early 1969 to mid 1971.[108] In essence, as the National Security Decision Memorandum 13 (NSDM 13) stated on May 28, 1969, the vital US interests were to encourage "moderate increases and qualitative improvement" in Japan's defense efforts, "while avoiding any pressure on her to develop substantially large forces or to play a larger regional

---

103 Kissinger to Nixon, "My October China Visit," November 11, 1971, pp. 17–18, China – HAK October 1971 visit, FPF, Box 1035, NSCF, NPMS, NA.

104 Ibid., p. 4.

105 See, for example, William Bundy, *A Tangled Web: The Making of Foreign Policy in the Nixon Presidency* (New York: Hill and Wang A Division of Farrar, Straus and Giroux, 1998), p. 236; Mann, *About Face*, p. 43; and Michael Schaller, 'Détente and Strategic Triangle Or, "Drinking your Mao Tai and Having Your Vodka, Too"' in Robert Ross and Jiang Changbin (eds), *Re-examining the Cold War: US-China Diplomacy, 1954–1973* (Cambridge, Massachusetts: Harvard University Press, 2001), p. 366. Bundy emphasized the importance of the July 1971 talks in which Kissinger sought to ease China's antagonism towards the US-Japan Mutual Security Treaty, at least in the short run. Mann explains that Zhou was still preoccupied with the danger of Japanese militarism, the "wild horse," during his talks with Nixon in February 1972. Schaller argues that Nixon explained to the Chinese leaders that the US-Japan Security Treaty not only "protected" Japan, but also served to "police Japan against turning to communist [sic] or returning to militarism."

106 Kissinger, *White House Years*, p. 334.

107 Solomon, interview with the author, September 24, 2003. Kissinger defensively admits that he did not possess a "very subtle grasp of Japanese culture and psychology." Kissinger, *White House Years*, p. 324.

108 Marshall Green (Assistant Secretary for East Asian and the Pacific, 1969–1973), Oral History Interview, March 2 and 17, 1995, pp. 60–61, FAOHC. Green recalls that there had been a tendency for officials in the Foreign Service, which went back for "at least 100 years," to be "either pro-Chinese or pro-Japanese." Ibid.

security role."[109] During the US-Japan summit in November 1969, President Nixon and Japanese Prime Minister Sato agreed to preserve the US-Japan Mutual Security Treaty, affirming that the two governments "should maintain close contact."[110] In particular, Sato expressed Japan's interest in the security of the Republic of Korea as "essential" and that of the Taiwan area as "important."[111] These statements reflected the Nixon Doctrine which encouraged US allies, especially Japan, to make more active contributions to the maintenance of stability in East Asia in the post-Vietnam era.

Regarding US China policy, State Department officials, such as U. Alexis Johnson and Marshal Green, were principally concerned with calming Tokyo's growing anxiety over Washington's opening to Beijing. In April 1971, the NSSM 124 paper had already emphasized: "we should concert our moves with Japan through close and frequent consultations."[112] However, without utilizing the State Department's expertise, Kissinger and the NSC staff used a geopolitical framework to assess the conceptual possibilities of Japan's future role.[113] As former NSC staff member Peter Rodman recalls, the Kissinger-NSC believed: "Japan is a very nationalist country that may some day be asserting itself again." It would "move in a very nationalist direction if ever it loses confidence in the US."[114]

As "POLO" shows, there was an urgent need to respond to a consistent PRC propaganda that a "revival of Japanese militarism" was taking place "at the instigation of the American imperialists."[115] This long-term theme represented Chinese sensitivity to the rapid growth of Japan's economic power and political influence, and even without the ingredient of military power, the Chinese regarded Japan as a "serious rival" in Asia.[116] The NSC staff also anticipated that the Chinese would bring up the Japan issue by specifically referring to the US-Japan Mutual Defense Treaty as being "directed against China."[117] The principal issue for direct

---

109 National Security Decision Memorandum 13 "Policy Toward Japan," May 28, 1969, National Security Decision Memoranda, SF, Box 363, NSCF, NPMS, NA.

110 *The New York Times*, November 22, 1969.

111 Ibid. On July 5, 1971, during an interview with Ross Terrill, Premier Zhou became very "agitated," accusing the Americans of joining the Japanese reactionaries to revive "militarism." Zhou was especially resentful of Japan's inclusion of its security interests in Korea and Taiwan in the US-Japan joint communiqué of November 1969. See Seymour Hersh, *The Price of Power* (New York: Summit Books, 1983), p. 382.

112 NSSM124: Next Steps Toward the People's Republic of China, p. 3, NSSMs, SF, Box 365, NSCF, NPMS, NA.

113 In the NSC staff, Richard Sneider was the only official who had expertise on Japan. However, Sneider did not get along with Kissinger and was assigned to Japan in late 1969. Solomon, interview with the author, September 24, 2003.

114 Peter Rodman, Oral History Interview, July 22, and August 22, 1994, pp. 52–54, FAOHC.

115 Review of US and PRC Views on Other Great Powers, Japan, p. 1, Briefing book for HAK's July 1971 trip, POLO I (hereafter referred to as Japan, POLO I), FPF/Lord, Box 850, NSCF, NPMS, NA.

116 Ibid.

117 Ibid., pp. 1–2.

talks therefore was to justify the US's continuous presence in Asia by persuading the Chinese that the US-security relationship with Japan had the particular effect of "containing" Japan rather than the reverse.[118] Being unfamiliar with the historical complexity of Sino-Japanese relations, Kissinger would follow Nixon's private instructions of July 1 along with the briefing book's recommendations.

During the July 1971 secret meeting, it was Premier Zhou who raised the Japan issue and accused the US of rearming the Japanese militarists, for "economic" expansion would lead to "military" expansion.[119] Following Nixon's instructions, Kissinger explained: "our defense relationship with Japan keeps Japan from pursuing aggressive policies."[120] In other words, Kissinger warned Zhou that if Japan felt "forsaken" by the US, and if it built its own "nuclear weapons," the emergence of a strong Japan would raise the question of "expansionism."[121] Thus, Kissinger clarified: "Neither of us wants to see Japan heavily re-armed."[122] Finally, adopting an expression from the briefing book, Kissinger sought to assure Zhou that the US was not "using" Japan against China, as that would be "too dangerous."[123]

Nevertheless, Zhou was still preoccupied with the revival of Japanese militarism, warning of its expansive ambitions not only in "Korea, Taiwan and Vietnam," but also in "Northeast China, Indochina and the Philippines and areas up to the Straits of Malacca."[124] Kissinger replied that the US would not "encourage any military expansion by the Japanese" and that if it took place, the US would oppose it.[125] Kissinger reported to Nixon that Zhou understood the "restraining role" which the US played on Japan.[126] In essence, although the development of Japan's independent defense policy was a conceptual possibility in the long-term rather than a realistic possibility in the short-term, Nixon and Kissinger sought to justify the US-Japan alliance as a political device to restrain Japan's role in East Asia.

In the briefing book for Kissinger's October trip, the NSC staff assessed that China was still attempting to "drive a wedge" between the US and Japan.[127] The *People's Daily* editorial of September 18 stated, "US imperialism has no wish to see an independent, prosperous and strong Japan in Asia. While glibly calling Japan its 'close partner,' it is actually ready to betray her at any time."[128] The Chinese paper then called on Japan to "take another road, the road of independence…and neutrality."[129]

---

118   Ibid., p. 3.
119   Memcon July 9, 1971, p. 29.
120   Ibid., p. 42.
121   Ibid.
122   Ibid.
123   Ibid; and Japan, p. 3, POLO I.
124   Memcon July 10, 1971, p. 7.
125   Ibid., p. 27; and Japan, p.4, POLO I.
126   Kissinger to Nixon, "My talks with Chou En-lai," July 14, 1971, p. 17.
127   Japan, p. 6, Briefing book for HAK's October 1971 trip POLO II [Part II], FPF/Lord, Box 851, NSCF, NPMS, NA. Section 3.1.2 of this chapter (pp. 187–188) examines the so-called "Nixon shock."
128   Ibid., p. 7. Inverted commas in original.
129   Ibid.

During the October 1971 talks, Premier Zhou emphasized that at the present economic level, it would be difficult to "put brakes" on Japan.[130] Zhou warned further that once Japan took "the road of military expansion," it would be difficult to measure "to what degree" it would develop.[131] In response, Kissinger stated that Moscow was seeking influence over Tokyo, and it would be "dangerous for others to use Japan against the United States."[132] Kissinger reiterated that the present relationship with the US was a "restraint" on Japan.[133] However, Zhou was still unconvinced of whether or not the US was capable of limiting Japan's "self-defense strength."[134] Hence, Kissinger explained that the US would oppose a nuclear re-armed Japan and that, with its nuclear umbrella [the US's protection of Japan by the deployment of its nuclear weapons in East Asia], the US would do its best to "limit" Japanese armament and expansion.[135] In his report to Nixon, Kissinger estimated that the Washington-Beijing-Tokyo triangular relationship could be "one of our most difficult problems."[136]

2.4 The India-Pakistan rivalry

Nixon and Kissinger regarded the India-Pakistan conflict in 1971 as a crucial opportunity for the US to develop a cooperative relationship with China and Pakistan against the Soviet Union and India.[137] This book examines the India-Pakistan rivalry in South Asia as one of the major security issues between Kissinger and Zhou during the July and October 1971 talks.[138] Equally important, the following account focuses on the interpretation of the nature of India-Pakistan rivalry in South Asia, which showed the widening geopolitical perceptional gap between the White House and the State Department from March to December 1971.

On March 25, 1971, President Yahya Khan of Pakistan ordered his military to crush the separatist movement in East Pakistan, which was calling for an independent

---

130   Memcon, October 22, 1971, 4:15–8:28pm, p. 19.
131   Ibid., p. 21.
132   Ibid., p. 24.
133   Ibid.
134   Ibid., p. 26.
135   Ibid.
136   Kissinger to Nixon, "My October China Visit," November 11, 1971, p. 4.
137   Previous accounts have mainly focused on the development of the India-Pakistan war of December 1971. See, for example, Raymond L. Garthoff, *Détente and Confrontation* (Washington DC: The Brookings Institution, 1985), pp. 295–322; Walter Isaacson, *Kissinger: A Biography* (New York: McGraw-Hill, 1992), pp. 371–379; Hersh, *The Price of Power*, pp. 444–464; and Tyler, *A Great Wall*, pp. 117–125. As for recent work on the India-Pakistan crisis of 1971 based on new documentary sources, see, for example, F.D. Aijazuddin (ed.), *The White House & Pakistan: Secret Declassified Documents, 1969–1974* (Oxford: Oxford University Press, 2002), pp. 423–489; and Jussi Hanhimaki, *The Flawed Architect: Henry Kissinger and American Foreign Policy* (New York: Oxford University Press, 2004), pp. 154–184.
138   Garthoff misinterprets that there was no substantial exchange on the India-Pakistan relations between Kissinger and Zhou in the July 1971 talks. Ibid., p. 315.

Bangladesh. Nixon and Kissinger perceived the situation in South Asia through the prism of US policy toward the Sino-Soviet rivalry and were mainly concerned about the emergence of India's regional dominance in South Asia, backed by the Soviet Union.[139] Nixon and Kissinger were also privately concerned with the protection of Pakistan's role as an intermediary in US-China secret communication.[140] On the other hand, in an unusual unanimity, the State Department denounced the brutality of the Pakistani troops' suppression of citizens in East Pakistan as a "reign of terror," and supported India politically and diplomatically.[141]

During April and May 1971, Nixon and Kissinger urged President Yahya Khan to take a more moderate and conciliatory policy toward East Pakistan. On April 28, 1971, Nixon approved an effort to help Yahya achieve a negotiated settlement and wrote: "Too all hands, Don't squeeze Yahya at this time. RN."[142] Kissinger and the NSC staff recognized that Nixon personally held Pakistani President Yahya Khan in "high regard."[143] On May 10, 1971, during a talk with Pakistani officials, Nixon himself made it clear that Yahya was a "good friend" and that the US would "not do anything to complicate the situation for President Yahya or to embarrass him."[144]

On May 26, 1971, State Department officials judged that President Yahya was "not likely" to take steps to bring about a "political accommodation" until he realized himself how essential it was.[145] For the State Department, it was Pakistan that took an aggressive policy toward India and increased tensions in South Asia. The State Department had also "confidentially briefed" India on the positions the US was taking privately with Pakistan.[146] Nixon and Kissinger were seriously concerned about the State Department's approach toward India. On June 3, 1971, during a talk

---

139 Nixon, *RN*, p. 525; and Kissinger, *White House Years*, p. 767.

140 Kissinger, *White House Years*, p. 854. As for a recent controversial work which criticizes Kissinger's quiet approval of Yahya's suppression of civilians in East Pakistan, see Christopher Hitchens, *The Trial of Henry Kissinger* (London, New York: Verso, 2001), pp. 44–50.

141 Telegram, US Consulate, Dacca, "Selective Genocide," March 28, 1971, Pol and Def, Box 2530, Subject-Numeric Files (SNF) 1970–73, General Records of the Department of State, Record Group 59 (RG59), NA. See also, Christopher Van Hollen, "The Tilt Policy Revisited: Nixon-Kissinger Geopolitics and South Asia," *Asian Survey*, Vol. 20, April 1980, pp. 339–361. Van Hollen, former Deputy Assistant Secretary of State for Near Eastern and South Asian Affairs (1969–1972), argues critically that Kissinger unnecessarily elevated the local crisis in the subcontinent into a US-USSR competition. The White House-centered system was not suitable for a "multifaceted regional crisis" which required a number of operational decisions over several months. Ibid., p. 357.

142 Nixon's handwritten notation, Underline by Nixon in original, in Kissinger to Nixon, "Policy Options Toward Pakistan," April 28, 1971, p. 6, Country Files (CF)-Middle East, Box 625, NSCF, NPMS, NA.

143 Memcon, M.M. Ashmad, Agha Hilaly, Henry Kissinger, and Harold H. Saunders, 3:05–3:30pm, May 19, 1971, p. 3, CF-Indo-Pak War, Box 578, NSCF, NPMS, NA.

144 Memcon, Nixon, M.M. Ashmad, Agha Hilaly, and Harold H. Saunders, 4:45–5:20pm, May 19, 1971, p. 1, p. 3, CF-Indo-Pak War, Box 578, NSCF, NPMS, NA.

145 Rogers to Nixon, "Possible India-Pakistan War, May 26, 1971, p. 1, CF-Indo-Pak War, Box 578, NSCF, NPMS, NA.

146 Ibid., p. 2.

with US Ambassador to India, Kenneth Keating, and a South Asia expert of the NSC staff, Harold Saunders, Kissinger thus made clear that President Nixon's main concern was to discourage India from military action.[147] Kissinger explained more explicitly that: "We want to buy time … We have no illusion that West Pakistan can hold East Pakistan and we have no interest in their doing so."[148] It was essential for Nixon and Kissinger to protect Pakistan as a secret intermediary in US-Chinese diplomatic communication.

In "POLO" for Kissinger's July 1971 trip to Beijing, the NSC staff analyzed that South Asia was an area where the US was pursuing "no special geopolitical interests of its own," which was unlike both the Soviets and the Chinese whose positions in South Asia were basically each developed against the other.[149] The NSC staff also estimated that the Chinese would be pleased to see radical elements in East Pakistan come to surface and India "weakened."[150] Hence, Kissinger was prepared to assure Zhou that the US would not want to "play anyone off against anyone else," or to "stir up anti-Chinese sentiment in India."[151]

During the July 1971 talks, it was Premier Zhou who raised the question of South Asia, insisting that India was "committing aggression against Pakistan," and that South Asia was becoming a region in "turmoil."[152] Zhou thus suggested that the US "advise India not to provoke such a disturbance."[153] Zhou's concern regarding Indian aspirations pushed Kissinger to clarify the US policy toward India-Pakistan rivalry. In his reply, therefore, Kissinger sought to give an assurance to Zhou: "we would under no circumstances encourage Indian military adventures against the People's Republic of China."[154] Beijing remained suspicious of Indian aspirations, and therefore Zhou made it clear: "if India commits aggressions, we will support

---

147 Memcon, Kissinger, Keating, and Saunders, June 3, 1971, p. 1, CF-Middle East, Box 596, NSCF, NPMS, NA.

148 Ibid., p. 3. During his trip to Asia, which would lead to the secret visit to Beijing, Kissinger made a brief visit to India. Kissinger assured Indian officials that under any conceivable circumstances, the US would "back India against any Chinese pressures" and that in any dialogue with China, "we would not encourage her against India." Memcon, Sarabhai and Kissinger, July 7, 1971, p. 3, Presidential/HAK MemCons, Box 1025, NSCF, NPMS, NA.

149 South Asia, p.1, Briefing book for HAK's July 1971 trip, POLO I, FPF/Lord, Box 850, NSCF, NPMS, NA. In his memoirs, Kissinger notes the India-Pakistan relations as a topic in the briefing book without describing any specific contents. Kissinger, *White House Years*, p. 731. A South Asia expert in the NSC staff, Saunders, stayed in Pakistan. "I joined the party and accompanied him [Kissinger] to New Delhi and Pakistan. On the plane ride from Bangkok to New Delhi, he told me that he was going to Beijing from Pakistan. That was the first time I had ever heard of the plan. The only reason Kissinger told me was because he asked me to write talking points." Harold H. Saunders (South Asia Specialist for the National Security Council, 1971; Near East Affairs Department of State, 1974–1976), Oral History Interview, p. 1, Pakistan, Country Collection, 1996, FAOHC.

150 Ibid.

151 India and Pakistan, pp. 1–2, Briefing book for HAK's July 1971 trip, POLO I, FPF/Lord, Box 850, NSCF, NPMS, NA.

152 Memcon July 10, 1971, p. 6.

153 Ibid., p. 11.

154 Ibid., p. 29.

Pakistan."[155] Kissinger misinterpreted what Zhou meant by "support Pakistan." It was not yet clear at that time whether China would support Pakistan not only politically but also militarily. Thus, Kissinger agreed to oppose Indian aggression, although the US could not take "military measures."[156] Zhou emphasized that the US still had the "strength to persuade India."[157]

By the summer of 1971, as a Soviet expert of the NSC staff, Helmut Sonnenfeldt assessed, the Soviets might see the Indian subcontinent as offering the "most tempting opportunities" for exploiting US-Chinese difficulties and for achieving "unilateral advantages."[158] On August 9, 1971, India signed a twenty-year "Treaty of Peace, Friendship, and Cooperation" with the Soviet Union. In his memoirs, Kissinger stresses that the Soviets discovered an opportunity to "humiliate" China and also "punish" Pakistan for its role as "intermediary" between Washington and Beijing.[159] On August 11, 1971, during a meeting with the principal members of the Senior Review Group, Nixon expressed his conviction with a "great deal of emphasis" that the US "must not – cannot – allow" India to use the East Pakistani refugees as a "pretext for breaking up Pakistan."[160] Moreover, Nixon made it clear that the US still had to "use its influence to keep the war from happening."[161]

On August 16, during a secret talk with the Chinese Ambassador in Paris, Huang Chen, Kissinger gave private assurance that the US would "do nothing to embarrass the government of Pakistan by any public statements."[162] In his report to Nixon, Kissinger explained that they were "building a solid record of keeping the Chinese informed," especially assuring that the US was "not colluding against their ally."[163]

In "POLO II," the NSC staff estimated that the Soviet-Indian Treaty was aimed at China as well as Pakistan.[164] The NSC staff assessed, however, that the Chinese were "not militarily prepared" to sustain major operations against India and that

---

155   Memcon July 11, 1971, p. 17.

156   Ibid.

157   Ibid.

158   Sonnenfeldt to Kissinger, "US-Soviet Relations in Light of the President's Visit to China," July 20, 1971, p. 3, Box 500, China Trip – July–November 1971 [Part 1], PTF, NSCF, NPMS, NA.

159   Kissinger, *White House Years*, p. 767. Since Nixon's presidential visit in August 1969, Pakistan was an "enthusiastic" cooperator for the promotion of Washington-Beijing relations. The Pakistani leaders sought to have the US "weight" as a corner of national security. See Bundy, *A Tangled Web*, p. 245, and pp. 269–284.

160   Memorandum for the Record, August 11, 1971, p. 3, CF-Indo-Pak War, Box 578, NSCF, NPMS, NA.

161   Ibid., p. 4.

162   Memcon, Huang Chen and Kissinger, August 16, 1971, p. 8, China exchanges – July–October 20, 1971, FPF/Lord, Box 849, NSCF, NPMS, NA. In his memoirs, however, Kissinger fails to provide any specific details of his briefing to the Chinese. Kissinger, *White House Years*, p. 768.

163   Kissinger to Nixon, "My August 16 Meeting with the Chinese Ambassador in Paris," August 16, 1971, p. 4, China exchanges – July–October 20, 1971, FPF/Lord, Box 849, NSCF, NPMS, NA.

164   The Soviet Union, pp. 11–12, Briefing book for HAK's October 1971 trip POLO II [Part I], FPF/Lord, Box 850, NSCF, NPMS, NA.

a clear-cut Indian victory would seriously weaken Pakistan and enhance India's prestige to China's detriment.[165] Hence, China would judge that a "short war," which the international community would stop, would enable it to join in an effort to give Pakistan a "face-saving way to pull back" from East Pakistan.[166]

During the October 1971 talks, as anticipated, Zhou criticized the Soviet Union for "threatening" Pakistan.[167] Kissinger reiterated that the US would "totally oppose" India's military action against Pakistan.[168] However, Zhou was not convinced, insisting that India was seeking to "get two big powers to contend for it in the Indian Ocean."[169] In his report to Nixon, Kissinger assessed that China would stand clearly "behind Pakistan" but it did "not want hostilities to break out" and was afraid of giving the Soviets a "pretext for attack."[170]

2.5 The Soviet military threat

Nixon and Kissinger sought to develop a common perception with Beijing to counteract against Soviet military power.[171] In his memoirs, Kissinger interprets that "China needed us precisely because it did not have the strength to balance the Soviet Union by itself."[172] Hence, Kissinger clarifies that while keeping the Chinese informed of the US-USSR negotiations "in considerable detail," Washington would not give Beijing a "veto" over its actions.[173] In essence, Kissinger was seeking to develop an even-handed approach towards both Beijing and Moscow.[174] Realizing Beijing's growing sensitivity toward the superpowers' détente – the easing of tensions, the NSC staff emphasized in "POLO" that: "Our approaches to the USSR are not directed against China and should not be regarded as US-USSR collusion at China's expense."[175]

---

165 South Asia, p. 3, Briefing book for HAK's October 1971 trip POLO II [Part II], FPF/Lord, Box 851, NSCF, NPMS, NA.
166 Ibid.
167 Memcon, October 22, 1971, p. 30.
168 Ibid., p. 31.
169 Memcon, October 24, 1971, p. 17.
170 Kissinger to Nixon, "My October China Visit: Discussions of the Issues," November 11, 1971, p. 27.
171 The Soviet military threat had been a major issue of analysis in previous works on the US rapprochement with China. See, for example, Garthoff, *Détente and Confrontation*, pp. 261–262. Garthoff argues that Kissinger provided to Zhou "high-resolution satellite photographs" of Soviet military activities.
172 Kissinger, *White House Years*, p. 749.
173 Ibid., p. 837. On the other hand, Bundy argues that Kissinger developed a "double standard" of triangular diplomacy within which US relations with China essentially came to possess a similarly close basis as with that of the allies. Bundy, *A Tangled Web*, p. 238.
174 Goh argues that the United States shifted its emphasis from an even-handed approach toward the two communist giants (1971–1972) to a "tacit" tilt toward China (1973–1974). Evelyn Goh, *Constructing the Rapprochement with China, 1961–1974: From 'Red Menace' to 'Tacit' Ally* (Cambridge: Cambridge University Press, 2005).
175 Review of US and PRC Views on Other Great Powers, the Soviet Union, pp. 4–5, Briefing book for HAK's July 1971 trip, POLO I, FPF/Lord, Box 850, NSCF, NPMS, NA.

In his memoirs, Holdridge states only that during Kissinger's secret visit to Beijing in July 1971, the US-PRC problem with the Soviets was "mentioned but not stressed."[176] In reality, however, Zhou emphasized: "we would absolutely not become a superpower."[177] Moreover, Zhou warned that the Soviet Union was following America's path "in stretching its hands all over the world."[178] In response, Kissinger explained that the US would not exclude "the possibility of Soviet military adventurism" (possibly implying the Soviet policy toward Sino-Soviet border situation and the Soviet involvement in regional conflicts, such as Indochina and South Asia)[179] Importantly, Kissinger took steps beyond the NSC briefing book's recommendations and gave a crucial assurance to Zhou: "I am prepared to give you any information you may wish to know regarding any bilateral negotiation we are having with the Soviet Union on such issues as SALT."[180] In his report to Nixon, Kissinger evaluated that the Chinese appreciated "the balancing role" the US was playing in Asia and that the US must be "exceptionally careful not to drive them away."[181] It was crucial to assure the Chinese that the US would "never collude with other powers against China."[182]

In "POLO II," the NSC staff estimated that the US had skillfully managed the delicate US-Soviet-Chinese triangle better than the US-Japanese-Chinese one. With the Soviets, the US had stressed its "priority in dealing with them" in the near future, having moved ahead on negotiations and having agreed on a summit. The Soviets, at least publicly, had to say that they favored the normalization of Washington-Beijing relations with emphasis on this "not being directed against Moscow."[183]

The NSC staff judged that Zhou was thinking in "balance of power terms" and did not want any sudden shifts in this balance in Asia, demonstrated by the "absence of a time-limit for US withdrawals."[184] In reality, Zhou could hardly admit that the US was doing China a favor by maintaining a balance vis-à-vis the USSR.[185] The NSC staff thus recommended to Kissinger to stress that US forces in Asia did "not constitute a threat to the PRC" and that a US withdrawal from Asia could create a vacuum that other major powers might be tempted to fill.[186]

During the October 1971 talks, Premier Zhou insisted that despite the existence of profound differences regarding world outlook, the two sides came to share a common

---

176   Holdridge, *Crossing the Divide*, p. 60.
177   Memcon July 9, 1971, p. 36.
178   Memcon July 10, 1971, Afternoon (12:10pm–6:00pm), p. 9.
179   Ibid., p. 27.
180   Ibid., pp. 28–29.
181   Kissinger to Nixon, "My Talks with Chou En-lai," July 14, 1971, p. 10.
182   Ibid., p. 22.
183   Ibid., p. 12. It was originally the Soviet Union that had, since 1949, insisted on the recognition of the People's Republic. Therefore, by the late 1960s, Moscow could hardly justify its private opposition to Washington's move toward Beijing.
184   The US Role in Asia, p. 4, Briefing book for HAK's October 1971 trip POLO II [Part II], FPF/Lord, Box 851, NSCF, NPMS, NA.
185   Ibid., p. 5.
186   Ibid., pp. 5–6.

interest in easing tensions in East Asia.[187] Hence, Zhou emphasized: "no country should make efforts to establish hegemony and no major power should collude with any country."[188] Moreover, Zhou suggested that the two sides, through their respective actions and influences, "affect" allies "not to go to certain extremes."[189] Finally, Zhou claimed that both sides should "not allow another greater power far away feel easy in coming into the Far East for hegemony."[190]

Kissinger and Zhou thus agreed to include in the communiqué the so-called "anti-hegemony clause," a joint opposition to the emergence of any major threat seeking hegemony in the Asia-Pacific region. In his memoirs, Kissinger recalls that although the term, hegemony, later became "a hallowed Chinese word, it actually was introduced first by us."[191] Holdridge interprets that China removed the "American hegemonists" from the lists of "offenders" of this principle and it was the Soviet Union that remained.[192]

After the October trip, Kissinger reported and emphasized to Nixon that "a deep and abiding Chinese hatred of the Russians" repeatedly came through during his conversations with Zhou.[193] Kissinger assessed that for the US, a rapprochement was a "matter of tactics," but for the Chinese, it involved a "profound moral adjustment."[194] However, the July 15 presidential announcement had "not changed the direction of

---

187 Memcon, October 24, 1971, pp. 7–8. On October 23, 1971, after having read the draft communiqué, Chairman Mao showed dissatisfaction, for it had "no voice." Zhou carefully followed Mao's instructions to revise the draft in order to clarify both agreements and disagreements between China and the US. "Kissinger's Second Visit to China in October 1971," pp. 7–8, Diplomatic History Institute of the Chinese Ministry of Foreign Affairs, *Xin zhaogguo wenjiao fengyun [New China's Diplomatic Experience]* (Beijing: Shijie shishi, 1991), Vol. 3, pp. 59–70, in Burr (ed.), *Negotiating US-Chinese Rapprochement*, NSA.
188 Ibid., p. 15.
189 Ibid., p. 16.
190 Ibid.
191 Kissinger, *White House Years*, p. 783. The term, "hegemony," originally came from a Greek word for "leader." Isaacson, *Kissinger*, p. 403n. Viotti and Kauppi define "hegemony" as the relations between states when a major power exercises "dominance" over other states within its sphere of influence. They also explain "leadership" as a "pre-eminent" position for a major state in international relations. Paul R. Viotti and Mark V. Kauppi, *International Relations Theory: Realism, Pluralism, Globalism*, Second edition. (New York: Macmillan Publishing Company, 1993), p. 582.
192 Holdridge, Oral History Interview in *A China Reader*, Vol. II, p. 37, January 1995, FAOHC. The Chinese sense of the world is that "international affair is fluid, constantly changing, constantly dynamic, nothing is fixed." One needs "mobility and flexibility and feeling of potential adversaries." Thus, the Chinese leaders remain suspicious of the US, viewing its behavior as to create an "American world" at maximum and to pursue "American leadership" at minimum. David Shambaugh, Interview with the author, October 15, 2003; and Idem, *Beautiful Imperialist: China Perceives America, 1972–1990* (Princeton, New Jersey: Princeton University Press, 1991), p. 79, and p. 253.
193 Kissinger to Nixon, "My October China Visit: The Atmosphere," October 29, 1971, p. 7, Book III, China Trip, Record of Previous Visits, FPF/Lord, Box 847, NSCF, NPMS, NA.
194 Ibid., p. 8.

Soviet policy but had improved Russian manners."[195] Finally, therefore, Kissinger emphasized that the Chinese should be "under no illusions that we fully intend to pursue our interests with Moscow while we try to improve our dialogue with Peking."[196]

2.6 Kissinger's report to Nixon after the July and October 1971 trips

In his report to Nixon, Kissinger described the secret trip as the "most searching, sweeping and significant discussions."[197] Premier Zhou spoke "with an almost matter of fact clarity and eloquence. He was equally at home in philosophic sweeps, historical analysis, tactical probing, light repartees. His command of facts, and in particular his knowledge of American events, was remarkable."[198] Former NSC staff Lord also re-assesses: "Zhou Enlai was a survivor. You don't survive the Cultural Revolution without being brutal, although he was more pragmatic than Mao. He certainly was the most impressive foreign leader I have ever met."[199]

More specifically, Kissinger emphasized the remaining profound perception gap with the Chinese:

> The Chinese clearly like to picture themselves as free from the vice of great power ambitions ... Their attitude toward great powers now is a mix of hostility, suspicions, and fear ... they may be making a virtue out of a necessity. And their very interest in a US-Chinese summit has them playing a great power game.[200]

Finally, Kissinger defined the US role in world politics:

> For Asia and for the world we need to demonstrate that we are enlarging the scope of our diplomacy in a way that, far from harming the interest of other countries, should instead prove helpful to them. Our dealings, both with the Chinese and others, will require reliability, precision, finesse.[201]

---

195 Ibid., p. 22.
196 Kissinger to Nixon, "My October Visit: Discussions of the Issues," November 11, 1971, p. 29.
197 Kissinger to Nixon, "My Talks with Chou En-lai," July 14, 1971, p. 1, Miscellaneous Memoranda Relating to HAK Trip to PRC, July 1971, FPF, Box 1033, NSCF, NPMS, NA.
198 Ibid., p. 7. As for the Chinese negotiation style, see Richard H. Solomon, *Chinese Negotiating Behavior: Pursuing Interests Through 'Old Friends'* (Washington DC: United States Institute of Peace, 1999). Solomon's work is based on top-secret documents, which he produced for the CIA while he was at the Rand Cooperation. See Richard H. Solomon, *Chinese Political Negotiating Behavior, 1967–1984*, December 1985, Electronic Reading Room, The Central Intelligence Agency.
199 Lord, interview with the author, October 15, 2003.
200 Kissinger to Nixon, "My Talks with Chou En-lai," July 14, 1971, pp. 22–23, Miscellaneous Memoranda Relating to HAK Trip to PRC, July 1971, FPF, Box 1033, NSCF, NPMS, NA.
201 Ibid., p. 27.

As his handwritten comments on "POLO II" show, President Nixon strongly believed that the Chinese continuing demand for US total withdrawal from Asia was "out of [the] question."[202] Therefore, during the "very intensive substantive discussions for some twenty-five hours" in October 1971, while Zhou continued to pressure "the prospect of a lower American military profile in Asia," Kissinger sought a "built-in restraint on Chinese activities in Asia" by repeatedly emphasizing the significance of the continuing US presence in East Asia.[203] Together, Kissinger and Zhou attempted to ensure "less danger of miscalculation" and develop a "counterweight to the Soviet Union."[204] In consequence, the two sides established the "basic technical and substantive framework" for the upcoming summit.[205] Kissinger particularly explained to Nixon that: "they are clearly gambling on your re-election."[206] Finally, Kissinger estimated "if we can navigate the Taiwan issue successfully, we should have a communiqué that is realistic, clear, dignified, reassuring to our friends and positive for the further development of US-Chinese relations."[207]

3. Reactions to the China Breakthrough

3.1 The Nixon presidential announcement of July 15, 1971

On July 13, the day of Kissinger's return from his secret trip to Beijing, Nixon and Haldeman discussed how to "set something up" for Secretary Rogers and agreed that Rogers should not state "anything about China."[208] Nixon urged Haldeman to ask Kissinger to inform the press that it was the President who "did the whole thing."[209] Nixon and his advisers decided to remind the press that the recent China

---

202 Nixon's handwritten note on the cover page of Briefing book for HAK's October 1971 trip POLO II [Part I], FPF/Lord, Box 850, NSCF, NPMS, NA.
203 Kissinger to Nixon, "My October China Visit: Discussions of the Issue," November 11, 1971, pp. 1–2, China – HAK October 1971 visit, FPF, Box 1035, NSCF, NPMS, NA.
204 Ibid., p. 2.
205 Ibid., p. 3.
206 Kissinger to Nixon, "My October China Visit: Drafting the Communiqué (n.d.), p. 1, China – HAK October 1971 visit, FPF, Box 1035, NSCF, NPMS, NA.
207 Ibid., p. 8. However, as the following chapter demonstrates, Kissinger still underestimated the Chinese persistence on Taiwan as their domestic issue.
208 Meeting of the President with H.R. Haldeman, Henry Kissinger, Alexander Haig, and William Rogers at San Clemente, July 13, 1971, p. 1, File 5-53-92, Papers of the Nixon White House, Part 5. H.R. Haldeman: Notes of White House Meetings, 1969–1973, Manuscript Division, Library of Congress. Haldeman took notes during Nixon's meetings with his advisors and Congressional leaders. The handwritten meeting notes began on January 12, 1969, and they were kept for Haldeman's use only. Haldeman was at almost every major meeting in the Oval Office. The notes show the President's directives as well as describe the atmosphere of the meetings. The collection helps the examination of the Nixon White House Tapes, where it is often difficult to understand what is being discussed.
209 Ibid. Nixon sent instructions to Kissinger for press briefings, to describe how the President and Zhou had similar characteristics: "(1) Strong convictions; (2) Came up through adversity; (3) At his best in a crisis; (4) Tough, bold, willing to take chances; (5) A man who

initiative did not happen "accidentally" and that it was a "culmination of a long process."[210] Accordingly, it became Haldeman's task to enhance Nixon's "world leader image."[211] Secretary Rogers agreed later that there was no need to "say anything beyond announcement."[212] On the morning of July 15, 1971, Haldeman, Rogers, and Kissinger discussed the upcoming presidential announcement. The United States would need to "reassure Pacific allies" that "no secret deal" was made during Kissinger's trip to Beijing.[213] The main issues of US messages to allies were: 1) "we are not changing our policy"; and 2) "we don't deal with our friends behind their back."[214]

On July 15, 1971, at 8pm local time in California, President Nixon appeared on a major TV network broadcast and read the joint announcement, prepared by Kissinger and Zhou and issued simultaneously in the United States and in China. Nixon accepted Zhou's invitation to visit China before May 1972 "to seek the normalization between the two countries and also to exchange views on questions of concerns to the two sides."[215] Anticipating a wide sensation which would be likely to follow the announcement, Nixon read an additional explanation that the US opening to China "will not be at the expense of our old friends. It is not directed against any other nation."[216] Finally, Nixon expressed his profound conviction that "all nations will gain from a reduction of tensions and a better relationship" between the United States and China.[217]

The seven-minute presidential announcement brought about wide-ranging reactions not only within the American public but also abroad. The *New York Times* reported in its headline that: "Nixon Is Expected To Visit China Around End of Year; To See Both Mao and Chou."[218] The US Information Agency reported that the overwhelming majority of media commentators in non-Communist countries

---

takes the long view; (6) A philosophical turn of mind; (7) A man who works without notes; (8) A man who knows Asia; (9) Steely but who is subtle and appears almost gently." Nixon to Kissinger, July 19, 1971, POF, Box 85, WHCF, NPMS, NA. Nixon worried that Kissinger might overshadow him. See Isaacson, *Kissinger*, pp. 340–341.

210 Ibid., p. 8.
211 Ibid.
212 Ibid.
213 Meetings of H.R. Haldeman with William Rogers and Henry Kissinger at San Clemente, 12pm, July 15, 1971, File 5-54-18, Papers of the Nixon White House, Part 5. H.R. Haldeman: Notes of White House Meetings, 1969–1973, Manuscript Division, Library of Congress.
214 Ibid.
215 Announcement of Trip to China, July 15, 1971, Speech Files, Box 67, PPF, WHCF, NSCF, NPMS, NA.
216 Ibid. Regarding the US relations with its allies, Nixon revised a draft statement by the NSC staff from "Our action in seeking a new relationship with the People's Republic of China does not mean that the United States will abandon its old friends." to "will not be at the expense of our old friends." Underline by Nixon in original. Ibid.
217 Ibid.
218 *The New York Times*, July 17, 1971. Foot explains that the US opening to China stimulated the American ambition that the nation was still capable of taking a bold action to embrace a long-term enemy. Foot, *The Practice of Power*, pp. 263–264.

enthusiastically greeted the news as a "momentous event." The announcement was also described as a "diplomatic triumph" for President Nixon that dramatically confirmed his pledge to seek to transform an era of "confrontation" into one of "negotiation."[219] However, several observers held that the development enhanced Beijing's prestige and posed some serious risks for the United States. A few right-of-center commentators also presented a note of caution, warning against "expecting too much too soon."[220] Finally, the "unusual secrecy" for the conduct of American foreign policy was perceived by some as "very disturbing and very unhealthy."[221]

3.1.1 The Republic of China's reactions
Less than two hours after the President's statement, the US Ambassador to Taipei, Walter P. McConaughy was given an official government of the Republic of China statement which protested "in the strongest terms possible" the President's statement and termed it "a most unfriendly act" which "will have gravest consequences."[222] The US Information Agency reported that Taipei media replayed the Taiwan government's "serious protest." It also reported that President Chiang Kai-shek received a personal letter from President Nixon reassuring him that the US would "continue to honor its defense treaty commitment" to the Republic of China and maintain the continuing friendship with her.

On August 9, 1971, Secretary Rogers sent a memorandum to Nixon, re-assessing the ROC's "feelings of shock and betrayal" over the announced intention to visit the mainland, which might generate further "emotionalism." On the other hand, the ROC government had a "realistic appreciation of its vital interests," the primary one being its "continued existence as a viable entity on Taiwan."[223] State Department officials thus concluded that the ROC would go through the motions of "bitter protest for the sake of face," but might privately feel "some sense of reassurance" concerning its existence over the mid-term future.[224]

---

219 Barbara M. White (Acting Director, US Information Agency) to Haig, July 23, 1971, "President's Acceptance of Invitation to Peking: An Assessment of Foreign Media Reaction, July 22, 1971," p. 1, Box 500, China Trip – July–November 1971 [Part 1], President's Trip Files (PTF), NSCF, NPMS, NA.

220 Ibid., p. 2.

221 "China Trip Secrecy Muddies The Waters," July 27, 1971, *Philadelphia Bulletin*.

222 Elliot to Kissinger, "Reactions to the President's Announcement on July 15, 1971," July 16, 1971, p. 1, POL Chicom-US, 1970–1973, Box 2191, SNF, RG59, NA. On July 15, the new ROC ambassador to the United States, James C.H. Shen was informed of Kissinger's trip through a phone call by Secretary Rogers just twenty minutes before Nixon's announcement. Shen met Assistant Secretary Green to stress how "shocked" and "bewildered" everyone in Taipei was, asking: "Where is all this going to end?" James C.H. Shen, *The US and Free China: How the US Sold Out Its Ally* (Washington DC: Acropolis Books, 1983), p. 72.

223 Rogers to Nixon, "Probable GRC Reaction to Your Announced Visit to Mainland," p.1, Attached to Memo from Kissinger to Nixon, "Estimates of Future Reaction to China Initiative," August 9, 1971, Box 499, Reaction to China Initiative (July 1971) Memos, Letters, etc., PTF, NSCF, NPMS, NA.

224 Ibid., p. 2.

3.1.2 The Japanese reactions

In public, the Japanese Acting Foreign Minister Takeo Kimura termed the President's announcement a "very good thing," commenting that, although such a development was "anticipated," events had taken a "sudden turn."[225] The State Department reported that the Sato government was "taken by surprise and embarrassed by the announcement."[226] The US Information Agency also noted the Japanese media's coverage of "an air of uneasiness" in Tokyo.[227]

Soon after the secret trip, Kissinger reported to Nixon: "With Japan our task will be to make clear that we are not shifting our allegiance in Asia from her to China."[228] However, Nixon and Kissinger were seriously concerned about the danger of leaks from Tokyo as they personally did not trust the Japanese government.[229] In reality, the day before the July 15 announcement, following the recommendations from the Bureau of East Asian and Pacific Affairs, Secretary Rogers had planned to send Under Secretary of State for Political Affairs U. Alexis Johnson to Tokyo to inform Japanese officials privately in advance. However, Kissinger vetoed the idea, telling Johnson that the President was too worried about the possible danger of a leak, and thus the trip was never materialized.[230] Lord recalls that alternatively, soon after leaving China, Kissinger could have sent Holdridge or himself to Tokyo. Although the Japanese would still have been upset, at least they "would not have been humiliated publicly."[231] Moreover, Secretary of State Rogers also attempted to reach Japanese Ambassador to the US Nobuhiko Ushiba, however was restricted

---

225 Elliot to Kissinger, "Reactions to the President's Announcement on July 15, 1971," July 16, 1971, p. 3, POL Chicom-US, 1970–1973, Box 2191, SNF, STATE-RG59, NA.

226 Eliot to Kissinger, "Reactions to the President's Announcement on July 15, 1971," July 22, 1971, p. 2, Box 499, Reaction to China Initiative (July 1971) Memos, Letters, etc., PTF, NSCF, NPMS, NA.

227 White to Haig, "President's Acceptance of Invitation to Peking: An Assessment of Foreign Media Reaction, July 22, 1971," p. 3, July 23, 1971, Box 500, China Trip – July–November 1971 [Part 1], PTF, NSCF, NPMS, NA.

228 Kissinger to Nixon, "My Talks with Chou En-lai," July 14, 1971, p. 27.

229 Solomon, interview with the author, September 24, 2003. Solomon further recalls that a former NSC staff member and a Japan specialist, Richard Sneider was "furious" after hearing about the Kissinger secret trip on the radio, considering that it would "foul up" the US relationship with Japan "very badly." Ibid. Nixon later stated to British Prime Minister Edward Heath that the Japanese had "the leakiest government in the world, so we couldn't afford to give them advance word." Memcon, Nixon and Heath, December 20, 1971, p. 5, Memoranda for the President (MemforP), Records of Meetings (ROM), Box 87, POF, WHCF, NPMS, NA.

230 Johnson found out about the cancellation from Lord on the airplane on the way to California. Lord, "The Nixon Administration National Security Council," p. 45, NSCP-OHR.

231 Lord, Interview with the author, October 15, 2003. In reality, Secretary of Defense Laird, who was in Tokyo, knew exactly what was happening, through his own sources, such as naval communication channels, Yeoman Radford's secret reports, National Security Agency communications intercepts, and the special mission plane that Kissinger used. Laird privately told his Japanese counterpart about the Kissinger trip and the forthcoming summit six hours before it was announced. See Isaacson, *Kissinger*, p. 348.

by Nixon's insistence on only an hour's prior-notice.[232] Consequently, the Japanese officials were "astonished" and "outraged" that there had "not been any advance consultation, much less warning. ... Privately, the Japanese felt that Kissinger had betrayed them."[233] Johnson assesses that: "The damage had been done. After this 'Nixon shokku' as the Japanese called it, there has never again been the same trust and confidence between our two governments."[234] Thereafter, Tokyo would begin to initiate its own diplomatic move toward Beijing.[235]

3.1.3 The Soviet reactions
The Soviet media reported President Nixon's acceptance of Premier Zhou's invitation. However, it did not mention the President's statement that his trip to the PRC was "not directed against any other nation."[236] The unofficial Soviet reaction to the President's Beijing visit remained a "low key approval."[237] The State Department reported that there had been no comment from official Soviet sources in Moscow.

On July 20, 1971, a Soviet expert in the NSC staff, Sonnenfeldt sent a memorandum to Kissinger, analyzing the implications of the presidential announcement on US-Soviet relations. In the Soviets' view, immediate US goals had been to "bring the USSR under pressure" in various negotiations and to limit the Soviet role in the

---

232 State Department officials Richard Erickson and Marshall Green drafted a message of explanation from President Nixon to Prime Minister Sato. Green recalls that there had been a tendency in the Foreign Service for officials to be either pro-Chinese or pro-Japanese. This went back for at least 100 years and the US Government had fallen into "that syndrome, with the President favoring China over Japan." Green, Oral History Interview, March 2 and 17, 1995, p. 58, pp. 60–61, FAOHC.

233 William Sherman (Consul General, Osaka-Kobe, 1968–1970, Political Counselor, 1970–1972), Oral History Interview, p. 14, Japan, Vol. II, Country Collection, FAOHC. Kissinger had been quoted on more than one occasion: "Who cares if some civil servant is embarrassed? He could care less." Robert, Duemling (Head of Political-External Section, United States Embassy, Tokyo, 1970–1974), Oral History Interview, p. 2, Japan, Vol. II, Country Collection, 1996, FAOHC.

234 U. Alexis Johnson, *The Right Hand of Power* (Enlgewood Cliffs, New Jersey: Prentice-Hall, 1984), pp. 552–554. Inverted commas in original. In August 1971, Japan was surprised by another "Nixon shock" – the announcement of the end of gold currency to impose an import surcharge and suspend the dollar's convertibility into gold.

235 This subject is discussed in Michael Schaller, 'Détente and the Strategic Triangle: Or, "Drinking Your Mao Tai and Having Your Vodka, Too," in Robert Ross and Jiang Changbin (eds), *Re-Examining the Cold War: US-China Diplomacy, 1954–1973* (New York: Harvard University Press, 2001); and Ogata Sadako, *Normalization with China: A Comparative Study of US and Japanese Process* (Berkley: Institute of East Asian Studies, University of California, 1988).

236 Elliot to Kissinger, "Reactions to the President's Announcement on July 15, 1971," July 16, 1971, p. 4, POL Chicom-US, 1970–1973, Box 2191, SNF, RG59, NA.

237 Elliot to Kissinger, "Reactions to the President's Announcement on July 15, 1971, July 22, 1971, p. 6, Box 499, Reaction to China Initiative (July 1971) Memos, Letters, etc., PTF, NSCF, NPMS, NA.

Asia-Pacific.[238] These suspicions, reinforced by deep-seated "antagonism toward the Chinese," would have been raised further by the presidential announcement. Finally, regarding a possible US-USSR summit, Sonnenfeldt estimated that the materialization of the Beijing trip would make Soviet interest in a summit greater than it was before, but the Soviets, and Brezhnev personally, would still be reluctant to disclose this interest.[239] In other words, the Soviet leaders were unwilling to appear overly eager to hold a summit with the US leaders after the dramatic development in US-China relations.

On July 22, Kissinger sent an analysis of the China initiative to Nixon. The following point drew Nixon's attention: "Moscow simply cannot help gaining the conviction that our new China policy is but a symptom of our overwhelming desire to see reconciliation and disengagement anyway and everywhere."[240] At the end of the memo, Nixon wrote: "K[issinger] – Our task is to play a hard game with the Soviet[s] and to see that wherever possible – including non Communist Asia – our friends are reassured."[241]

In reality, Nixon's announcement of his presidential trip to China brought about a more cooperative attitude from the Soviets, at least in the short-term. On July 19 and August 17, 1971, Kissinger gave a briefing on his trip to the Soviet ambassador to the US, Anatoly Dobrynin. Kissinger mainly sought to re-assure Dobrynin that the U.S opening to China was not against the Soviet interests. However, Moscow was anxious that Washington's quick opening might push Tokyo to move close to Beijing, leading to the real danger of a "combination of China and Japan."[242] The Soviets were thus worried that a Sino-Japanese rapprochement would lead to the worst strategic situation, namely encirclement by the United States, China, and Japan. Despite Kissinger's denial, Dobrynin was still concerned about a US attempt to engage in "an anti-Soviet maneuver."[243] On September 29, 1971, Soviet Foreign Minister Andre Gromyko formally invited President Nixon to meet Secretary Leonid Brezhnev in Moscow in May 1972.[244]

The US and Chinese officials carefully monitored the Soviet reactions to the Nixon announcement. After the July trip, Kissinger established the Paris channel with the Chinese, namely General V.A. Walters' contact with the Chinese Ambassador

---

238 Sonnenfeldt to Kissinger, "US-Soviet Relations in Light of the President's Visit to China," July 20, 1971, p. 1, Box 500, China Trip – July–November 1971 [Part 1], PTF, NSCF, NPMS, NA.

239 Ibid., pp. 7–8.

240 Kissinger to Nixon, "Analysis of the China Initiative," July 22, 1971, underline by Nixon in original, Reaction to China Initiative (July 1971) Memos, Letters, etc., PTF, Box 499, NSCF, NPMS, NA.

241 Nixon's handwritten notations, in ibid.

242 Memcon, Kissinger and Dobrynin, August 17, 1971, p. 1, Box 340, Policy Planning Staff (Director's Files – Winston Lord), RG59, NA. See also Anatoly Dobrynin, *In Confidence: Moscow's Ambassador to America's Six Cold War Presidents (1962–1986)* (New York: Times Books, A Division of Random House, Inc, 1995), pp. 227–228.

243 Ibid., p. 2.

244 On October 12, 1971, Nixon officially announced his decision to visit Moscow in late May of 1972.

in Paris, Huang Chen. On August 16, Kissinger affirmed to Huang that he would carefully be "keeping the PRC informed" on any developments with Moscow.[245] On September 13, Kissinger informed Huang in advance that Gromyko would be likely to convey a formal invitation for the President to visit Moscow.[246] Accordingly, on October 9, General Walters gave Huang a text of the October 12 announcement of the US-USSR summit set for May 1972, stressing the importance that China being the "first country to be informed."[247]

3.1.4 Briefings of the new China initiative

After the July 15 presidential announcement, Nixon and Kissinger conducted domestic briefings on the background of the China initiative. On July 19, 1971, Nixon explained to the White House Staff the need to bring "one-fourth of the world's population" into the community of nations:

> They're [the Chinese] not a military power now but 25 years from now they will be decisive. For us not to do now what we can do to end this isolation would leave things very dangerous ... it means a dialogue, that's all. Looking to the future, the world will not be worth living in if we can't get the great potential explosive forces under control.[248]

Regarding the secrecy of the new initiative, Nixon emphasized strongly that: "Without secrecy, there would have been no invitation or acceptance to visit China.

---

245 The Soviet Union, pp. 8–9, Briefing book for HAK's October 1971 trip POLO II [Part I], FPF/Lord, Box 850, NSCF, NPMS, NA. See also Vernon A Walters, *Silent Missions* (New York: Doubleday, A Division of Random House, Inc, 1978), pp. 535–539.

246 Ibid., p. 10.

247 Ibid., p. 11. The major political incident in China between Kissinger's secret trip in July and his official trip in October was the so-called "Lin Biao Incident" of September 1971. On September 24, 1971, the State Department's Bureau of Intelligence and Research assessed that just before September 12, "some event of the highest importance" took place, including Mao's "incapacity and uncertain recovery, or his death," giving rise to "political uncertainty and concern for internal security." Intelligence Note, Bureau of Intelligence and Research (INR), Department of State, "People's Republic of China: Succession Crisis?" September 24, 1971, pp. 1–2, POL Chicom, 1970–1973, Box 2177, SNF, RG59, NA. On the other hand, despite rumors of the "mysterious recent happenings," namely the disappearance of Defense Minister Lin Biao and the clash of a Chinese Trident jetliner deep inside Mongolia on September 13, the NSC staff had "no hard facts." The Soviet Union, pp. 11–12, Briefing book for HAK's October 1971 trip POLO II [Part I], FPF/Lord, Box 850, NSCF, NPMS, NA. On February 21, 1972, Mao explained to Nixon that: "In our country also there is a reactionary group which is opposed to our contact with you. The result was that they got on an airplane and fled abroad." Memcon, February 21, 1972, 2:50–3:55pm, p. 5, CHINA – President's Talks with Mao and Chou En-lai February 1972, Box 91, CF-Far East, HAKOF, NSCF, NPMS, NA. For the recent works, based on Chinese archival materials, see, for example, Qiu Jin and Elizabeth Perry, *The Lin Biao Incident and the Cultural Revolution* (Stanford, California: Stanford University Press, 1999); and Chen, *Mao's China and the Cold War*, pp. 269–271.

248 "Briefing the White House Staff on the July 15 Announcement of the President's Trip to Peking," July 19, 1971, 11:40am, The Roosevelt Room, The White House, pp. 3–4, MemoforP, ROM, Box 85, POF, WHCF, NPMS, NA.

Without secrecy, there is no chance of success in it."[249] Nixon explained further that in the "critical early stages" of the initiative, "No one else on his staff knew," except Kissinger.[250] Finally, Nixon demanded the continuation of strict secrecy for his staff: "What can we say? Stick to the President's announcement and say you know no more."[251] Kissinger warned the staff further: "The most impressive thing we can do as far as the Chinese are concerned is to shut up. Don't even quote what the President said here."[252] Kissinger, who was particularly sensitive to leakage from his staff, explained the importance of reliability in that: "Our problem is to keep discipline ... The Chinese wanted to keep it secret, as we did, but they wondered about us."[253]

On July 20, 1971, Nixon and Kissinger briefed the Republican Congressional leaders. Kissinger stressed that there were "no secret agreements or understandings" during his trip and it was improbable that the Chinese would cancel the presidential visit.[254] Similar to their way of briefings toward the ambassadors from the Soviet Union, Japan and the Republic of China, Nixon and Kissinger used a double-standard, namely the continuing denial of secret deals with the Chinese leaders, in their briefings on the domestic front. Nixon also made it clear that "each of us agreed to this visit for our own reasons," and therefore there would still be a "basic disagreement in policy" between the two sides.[255] It was his way of pre-deterring possible over-expectation in US domestic politics for his upcoming trip to China.

On July 22, 1971, during the Bipartisan Senate Briefing, President Nixon reiterated the world outlook from his Kansas City speech that "the world was evolving into one of five economic giants" and that "as we move into the post-Vietnam world, military confrontation will be replaced by economic competition."[256] Finally, Nixon emphasized the fact that China was "a reality" and it was best to attempt to "bring her into the family of nations."[257]

3.2 The India-Pakistan War in December 1971

The most severe event related to the US breakthrough with China in 1971 took place in South Asia. On November 4, Nixon met with Prime Minister Indira Gandhi and

---

249 Ibid., p. 1.
250 Ibid.
251 Ibid., p. 2.
252 Ibid., p. 3.
253 Ibid., p. 4.
254 "Notes on Republican Leadership Meeting on Tuesday, July 20, 1971, at 8:00am," p. 1, MemforP, ROM, Box 85, POF, WHCF, NPMS, NA.
255 Ibid. Nixon took notes extensively, reviewing his thoughts behind the July 15 announcement. While anticipating wide speculation in the headlines of major newspapers regarding secrecy, Nixon wrote: "Without secrecy – we could not agree on meeting. Without secrecy – meeting will not succeed ... speculation would jeopardize the results we want." Nixon's handwritten notations, Leadership Meetings – China, Monday, July 19, 1971, Speech Files, Box 67, PPF, WHCF, NSCF, NPMS, NA.
256 "Bipartisan Senate Briefing – July 22, 1971 in the Cabinet Room," p. 1, MemforP, ROM, Box 85, POF, WHCF, NPMS, NA.
257 Ibid.

discussed the latest developments in South Asia. Gandhi made it clear that: "India has never wished to the destruction of Pakistan or its permanent crippling. Above all, India seeks the restoration of stability. We want to eliminate chaos at all costs."[258] Privately, however, Nixon was not convinced, suspecting that India was motivated by anti-Pakistan attitude.[259]

On November 22, 1971, India conducted a cross-border operation to support the rebellion within East Pakistan against West Pakistan. Kissinger interpreted this incident as the "beginning" of an India-Pakistan war that India had started.[260] On December 3, 1971, the day of the outbreak of a full-scale India-Pakistan war, Kissinger told representatives from State, Defense, CIA, and the NSC staff in the Washington Special Action Group meeting that President Nixon was criticizing that "we are not being tough enough on India ... He wants to tilt in favor of Pakistan."[261] The President believed that India was "the attacker."[262] As Harold Saunders assesses, Kissinger thought that the Chinese would "measure our steadfastness by our willingness to support our Pakistani allies" in the context of Soviet expansionism.[263] "If the Chinese were permitted to doubt America's reliance, then they might have questioned the utility of closer relationships. ... When the war broke out, our main objective was to make sure that the Pakistanis would not [be] seriously damaged."[264]

State Department officials believed that India was limiting its aims in East Pakistan and had no designs for West Pakistan, and therefore assessed that the danger of Soviet or Chinese intervention was small. Assistant Secretary for Near Eastern and South Asian Affairs, Joseph J. Sisco, strongly disagreed with an intelligence report that stated "the Indians intended to go beyond separating Bangladesh from Pakistan, but also to pursue military operations in order to destroy effectively the

---

258 Memcon, Nixon and Indira Gandhi, November 5, 1971, POF, Box 86, MemforP, WHCF, NPMS, NA.

259 In his memoirs, Nixon criticizes that Gandhi had "purposely deceived" him, because during the November meeting, she already knew in private that her generals and advisers were planning to intervene in East Pakistan and were also considering contingency plans to attack West Pakistan. Nixon, *RN*, pp. 525–526.

260 Kissinger, *White House Years*, p. 885; and Van Hollen, "Tilt Policy in South Asia," p. 350. Garthoff criticizes that Kissinger misinterpreted that the Soviets wanted to destroy West Pakistan. Garthoff, *Détente and Confrontation*, pp. 301–302.

261 Kennedy and Saunders to Commander Howe, The Anderson Papers, January 6, 1972, p. 2, CF-Middle East, Box 643, NSCF, NPMS, NA. The main reasons for Pakistan's move were not entirely clear. President Yahya Khan told US Ambassador Joseph Farland that India conducted an air and land invasion into West Pakistan in Kashmir and east of Lahore, and Pakistan responded defensively. Richard Reeves, *President Nixon: Alone in the White House* (New York: Simon & Schuster, 2001), p. 396. Pakistani Foreign Secretary Sultan Khan recalls that Yahya was "counting on the United States to save Pakistan." Sultan M. Khan, *Memories and Reflections of a Pakistani Diplomat* (London: London Centre for Pakistani Studies, 1997), pp. 268–269.

262 Ibid., p. 3.

263 Harold Saunders (South Asia Specialist for the National Security Council, 1971; Near East Affairs Department of State, 1974–1976), Oral History Interview, p. 1, Pakistan, Country Collection, 1996, FAOHC.

264 Ibid., p. 2.

overall military capacity of Pakistan for an indefinite period."[265] Donald Anderson explains that the Indians were "very furious" when the US, particularly Kissinger, was tilting very heavily toward Pakistan. In the eyes of State Department officials, "there's no question Pakistan started the war."[266]

On December 10, 1971, Kissinger held a secret talk with the Chinese Ambassador to the United Nations, Huang Hua, at a CIA "safe house" in New York.[267] Kissinger handed Huang Hua a top-secret folder of US intelligence as well as photos of how the US was "moving a number of naval ships in the West Pacific toward the Indian Ocean."[268] Kissinger sought to induce China's move against India by indicating that: "if the People's Republic were to consider the situation on the Indian subcontinent a threat to its security, and if it took a measure to protect its security, the US would oppose efforts of other to interfere with the People's Republic."[269] In response, Huang emphasized that: "The Soviet Union and India now are progressing along on an extremely dangerous track in the subcontinent. And as we have already pointed out this is a step to encircle China."[270] Realizing China's sensitivity, Kissinger emphasized that "both of us must continue to bring pressure on India and the Soviet Union."[271]

In reality, however, China remained very cautious throughout the war. Although Chinese troops were positioned on the Indian border, they did not take the risk of aiding Pakistan by attacking India. As Huang Hua informed Haig on December 12, China would be willing to support the UN General Assembly's call on India and Pakistan to "institute an immediate cease fire and to withdraw troops from each other's territory."[272] On December 14, Nixon and Kissinger received a formal note

---

265 Joseph J. Sisco (Assistant Secretary for Near Eastern and South Asian Affairs, 1969–1974), Oral History Interview, p. 1, Pakistan, Country Collection, 1996, FAOHC. Tyler interprets that Kissinger tried to induce China to consider attack on India's frontier, while the crisis still remained only a regional scale. See Tyler, *A Great Wall*, pp. 119–120.

266 Donald Anderson (Political Officer, New Delhi, 1970–1972), Oral History Interview, pp. 4–5, India, Country Collection, 1996, FAOHC. Anderson argues further that the Indians viewed China with a "mixture of awe, envy, and contempt." Thus, there was a sense of competition that "China gets treated better than India. That the West, and in particular the United States, doesn't recognize the importance of India and accept India's logical hegemonic position in South Asia." Ibid.

267 Memcon, December 10, 1971, China exchanges – October 20, 1971–December, 31, 1971, FPF/Lord, Box 849, NSCF, NPMS, NA. After the October trip, Kissinger opened the New York channel through CIA officer Jonathan Howe to Chinese Ambassador to the UN Huang Hua. This channel enhanced the preparation for Haig's advance trip to China in January 1972 and Nixon's presidential trip to China in February 1972.

268 Ibid., p. 5. On December 10, Nixon authorized the creation of a task force of eight ships centered around the nuclear aircraft carrier *Enterprise*, which would head from waters off Vietnam to the Bay of Bengal.

269 Ibid., p. 6.

270 Ibid., p. 11.

271 Ibid., p. 14.

272 Memcon, Haig and Huang Hua, December 12, 1971, pp. 1–2, China exchanges – October 20, 1971–December 31, 1971, FPF/Lord, Box 849, NSCF, NPMS, NA. Nixon assessed that the Chinese played a "very cautious role" because they understandably "feared"

from Moscow which informed them of "firm assurances by the Indian leadership that India has no plans of seizing West Pakistani territory."²⁷³ On December 16, 1971, India offered a cease-fire, and Pakistan surrendered unconditionally.

Nixon and Kissinger believed that if India and the Soviet Union succeeded in "destroying Pakistan as a military and political entity," it could have a "devastating effect in encouraging the USSR to use the same tactics elsewhere."²⁷⁴ "A victory of India over Pakistan was the same as a victory of the Soviet Union over China."²⁷⁵ The best solution would therefore be an arrangement in which "neither the USSR nor China are in a position of having won or lost."²⁷⁶ However, because of the highly secretive decision-making style and the lack of effective communication with the State Department from the summer to the winter of 1971 (namely the exclusion of State Department officials from decision-making process), Nixon and Kissinger became somewhat isolated within the administration. Finally, as the US rapprochement with China came to be materialized from July 1971 to February 1972, Pakistan's role as the intermediary between Washington and Beijing ended.

In summary, the US breakthrough with China in 1971 took place as US officials came to realize the reduction of the direct threat from China. In the short term, it was China's weakness in the Sino-Soviet border clashes and the conflicts in Indochina that provided a crucial opportunity for US officials to reassess US policy toward China. As for the Chinese strategic perception, Nixon estimated that "the Chinese view the US as no longer its major enemy. The Soviets are their greatest fear; Japan is second [because of the likelihood of its rearmament] and very probably India in the light of recent events [the India-Pakistan conflicts]."²⁷⁷ For his upcoming trip, Nixon was thus determined to exploit China's growing sense of fear of being surrounded by its major neighboring states.

In the long term, it was China's potential strength that persuaded US officials to pursue a new dialogue with her. Nixon assessed that "China is a reality."²⁷⁸ Nixon illustrated the China initiative as "the culmination of a long period of careful preparation," which originated in his *Foreign Affairs* article of October 1967. Despite

---

that the Soviets might use Chinese aid of Pakistan as an "excuse for attacking China." Nixon, *RN*, p. 530. Moreover, after the Lin Biao incident of September 1971, the Chinese leadership was still seeking to resolve internal division, and it was too risky to use its army abroad. See Garthoff, *Détente and Confrontation*, p. 316.

273   Kissinger, *White House Years*, p. 911. On December 12, in a public statement, Indian Prime Minister Gandhi already denied any territorial ambitions in West Pakistan. Van Hollen, "Tilt Policy in South Asia," p. 352. Dobrynin recalls that Kissinger privately acknowledged the importance of Soviet "assurance about India's intensions" as the "breakthrough" in ending the war. Dobrynin, *In Confidence*, p. 238.

274   Memcon, Nixon and Pompidou, December 13, 1971, 4:00pm, p. 4, MemforP, ROM, Box 87, POF, WHCF, NPMS, NA.

275   Ibid.

276   Ibid.

277   Memcon, Nixon and Brandt, December 29, 1971, p. 2, MemforP, ROM, Box 87, POF, WHCF, NPMS, NA.

278   Memcon, Nixon and Brandt, December 28, 1971, p. 7, MemforP, ROM, Box 87, POF, WHCF, NPMS, NA.

the difficulties posed by the US treaty commitment to Taiwan, China's continued isolation "could no longer be tolerated. In ten years, China will be a great nuclear power and an incalculable danger to peace should it continue to be isolated from the world community."[279] Finally, Nixon believed that his visit to Beijing would be "the opening of a channel of communication" with the PRC Government which had been "isolated" from the US for a quarter of a century.[280] It was on the basis of the above conviction that Nixon would take his trip to China in February 1972, as the following chapter examines.

---

279 Ibid., p. 1.
280 Memcon, Nixon and Brandt, December 29, 1971, p. 2, MemforP, ROM, Box 87, POF, WHCF, NPMS, NA.

Chapter 8

Nixon's Trip to China in February 1972

The final chapter investigates the major issues in Nixon's trip to China in February 1972. First, it examines the final preparations for the summit, including Haig's advance trip to China in January 1972, the NSC staff's briefing books for the President, Kissinger's briefing to the President, and Nixon's review of the briefing papers. US officials conducted extensive policy studies in order to identify both the newly emerging common ground and the remaining disagreements with the Chinese leaders. The main body of the chapter is devoted to the analysis of the Nixon-Mao talks and the Nixon-Zhou talks. The US and Chinese leaders agreed on the reduction of direct threat from their respective sides and discussed major security issues from the Kissinger-Zhou talks in both July and October 1971, in order to restore stability in the Asia-Pacific region. Finally, this chapter assesses the reactions of foreign governments toward Nixon's trip to China. Upon their return from China, Nixon and Kissinger briefed Cabinet members and Congressional leaders. The main issues of these briefings are also analyzed. By emphasizing the long-term importance of pulling China back into the international community, Nixon and Kissinger sought to characterize the February 1972 summit as an historical week that had changed the world – the ending of two decades of mutual hostilities and the easing of tensions between the US and China.

1. Haig's Advance Trip to China in January 1972

From January 3 to 10, 1972, General Alexander Haig Jr., the Deputy Assistant to the President for National Security Affairs, headed a delegation to China to make final technical arrangements for President Nixon's visit to China.[1] His main role was to play the role of Nixon's "stand-in."[2] Although Haig's two memoirs do not reveal

---

[1] The trip was arranged through the New York channel between NSC staff member Jonathan Howe and Chinese Ambassador to the UN, Huang Hua. The White House wanted to "ensure" that this major foreign policy initiative would be "given full world-wide coverage." Janka to Haig, "Official Media on China Trip," December 23, 1971, China – HAK October 1971 visit, Box 1035, For the President's Files (FPF)-China/Vietnam Negotiations, National Security Council Files (NSCF), Nixon Presidential Materials Staff (NPMS), National Archives (NA).

[2] For Haig's accounts of the trip, see Alexander M. Haig, Jr., *Caveat; Realism, Regan, and Foreign Policy* (London: Weidenfeld and Nicolson, 1982), pp. 201–202; Alexander M. Haig, Jr. with Charles McCarry, *Inner Circles: How America Changed The World* (New York: Warner Books, 1992), pp. 258–266; and Alexander M. Haig, Jr., interview Transcript, *Nixon's China Game*, American Experience, PBS Online (http://www.pbs.org/wgbh/amex/

substantial details, nor does he refer to any particular documents, Haig held intensive and substantive talks with Premier Zhou Enlai on such major issues as the Indochina conflicts, the India-Pakistan conflict, and the question of Taiwan's status.

On January 3, during his first talk with Zhou, Haig explained the US assessment of the Soviet military threat. Referring to the India-Pakistan war of December 1971, Haig warned that the Soviet policy toward South Asia was "to keep the subcontinent divided."[3] Drawing from the record of Kissinger's previous talks with Zhou, Haig also exaggerated that the Soviets were seeking to "encircle the PRC with unfriendly states."[4] Haig thus sought to make it clear that "the future viability of the PRC" was of the greatest interest to the United States.[5] In his cable to Kissinger, Haig suggested that the Chinese were still "sensitive" to Soviet criticism of US-PRC "collusion."[6]

Haig also warned that the continuation of war in Indochina would "only give Moscow an opportunity to increase its influence in Hanoi."[7] As for Nixon's visit, Haig claimed that it had to be successful "in fact and in appearance."[8] Finally, regarding the future of Taiwan, Haig re-affirmed Kissinger's assurance for the "One China" principle, the prevention of Japanese entry into Taiwan, and the reduction of US armed forces in Taiwan.[9] Haig interpreted Zhou's silence as approval.

After the talk, Haig sent a cable to Kissinger, reporting his impression in rather optimistic terms. It was likely that the US could achieve "some PRC movement on more positive expressions," especially "some better language" on the Taiwan issue in the joint communiqué.[10] Haig decided to refrain from discussing these issues further during his visit. He would only seek to assure the Chinese that the US was prepared to make "positive suggestions" in February.[11]

---

china/filmmore/reference/interview/haig06.html) See also Kissinger, *White House Years*, pp. 1049–1051.

3   Memcon, Haig and Zhou, January 3, 1972, Midnight, p. 2, Alexander M. Haig Special File (Haig-File), Haig China Trip File [Haig Advance Party, December 29, 1971–January 10, 1972], Box 1015, NSCF, NPMS, NA.

4   Ibid., p. 3.

5   Ibid.

6   Haig to Kissinger, January 6, 1972, p. 1, Haig China Trip December 29, 1971–January 10, 1971, p. 5. Haig-File, Box 1015, NSCF, NPMS, NA.

7   Ibid., p. 4; and Cable from Haig to Kissinger, January 6, 1972, p. 1. Haig originally anticipated that the Chinese would not push hard on Vietnam. For example, Haig reviewed the New China News Agency's non-authoritative article of December 30, 1971, which denounced the US Government for its "insolence and adventurism" in the twelve day bombing campaign against North Vietnam. The article, however, did not directly criticize the US action, nor attack the President by name. By Wire, Richard T. Kennedy to Haig, December 31, 1971, and Richard Solomon, "Peking Media on the US Bombing of North Vietnam," December 31, 1971, China-HAK October 1971 visit, Box 1035, FPF, NSCF, NPMS, NA.

8   Ibid., p. 7.

9   Ibid., p. 8.

10   Haig to Kissinger, January 4, 1971, p. 1, Haig China Trip December 29, 1971–January 10, 1971, Haig-File, Box 1015, NSCF, NPMS, NA.

11   Ibid.

On January 7, Zhou presented the Chinese reply, formally approved by Chairman Mao, to Haig's previous statements.[12] Zhou reiterated that the Chinese perceived the Soviet conclusion of a treaty of peace with India as, "friendship and cooperation in name," but "a military alliance in substance."[13] Hence, by supporting the Indian armed aggression against Pakistan, the Soviets were continuously "contending for hegemony."[14] As for the US policy in Indochina, Zhou criticized that the US bombing of North Vietnam in December 1971 consequently increased the Soviet influence in Southeast Asia. Zhou insisted that it was Washington that was "insulting Hanoi" rather than the other way around.[15] In his memoirs, however, Haig admits his own over-estimation that Chinese leaders would help the US end the war in Vietnam on terms favorable to the United States and South Vietnam.[16]

Zhou argued further that China was "a big country" but not yet "a very strong one."[17] However, disagreeing with Haig's description of China's "future viability," Zhou insisted that: "no country should ever rely on external forces to maintain its independence and viability."[18] As for Haig's reference to the importance of the "appearance" of Nixon's visit, Zhou claimed that one's image depended on his own "deeds" and expressed serious doubt about "self styled" attitude in public.[19]

Haig explained somewhat defensively that "the simple language of a soldier" might have been "misinterpreted."[20] In particular, Haig argued that the US would not unilaterally assume the role of "protector" or the "guarantor" of China's viability, but China's "viability and future health" were in the US's national interest.[21] Finally, Haig sought to defend that "popularity" was not the "criteria" for President Nixon's

---

12   On January 6, Zhou reported the issues in his first talk to Mao. In Chinese eyes, Haig appeared to be "excited and nervous." Mao was unconvinced by Haig's assessment of the Soviet threat. Mao viewed that not only the Soviets, but also South Asia, Indochina, Taiwan, the Philippines, and South Korea were all "surrounding" China. Regarding Nixon's political standpoint, Mao claimed that the worst case would be that the visit itself was to be "cancelled." "Haig's Preparatory Mission for Nixon's Visit to China in January 1972," p. 3, Diplomatic History Institute of the Chinese Ministry of Foreign Affairs, *Xin zhaogguo wenjiao fengyun [New China's Diplomatic Experience]* (Beijing: Shijie shishi, 1991), Vol. 3, pp. 71–82, in William Burr (ed.), *Negotiating US-Chinese Rapprochement: New American and Chinese Documentation Leading Up to Nixon's 1972 Trip*, Electronic Briefing Book No. 70, The National Security Archive.

13   Memcon, Haig and Zhou, January 7, 1972, 11:45pm, p. 2, Haig-File, Haig China Trip File [Haig Advance Party, December 29, 1971–January 10, 1972], Box 1015, NSCF, NPMS, NA.

14   Ibid.

15   Ibid., p. 3.

16   Haig, *Inner Circles*, p. 266.

17   Memcon, Haig and Zhou, January 7, 1972, 11:45pm, p. 3, Haig-File, Haig China Trip File [Haig Advance Party, December 29, 1971–January 10, 1972], Box 1015, NSCF, NPMS, NA.

18   Ibid., p. 4.

19   Ibid.

20   Ibid., p. 6.

21   Ibid., p. 7.

decisions.²² In reality, the President was determined to discuss major security issues of mutual concern with the Chinese leaders. Thus, the Haig statement was not entirely clear. The political necessity for presenting the Nixon trip as a journey for peace on the US side was perceived suspiciously as being untrustworthy by the Chinese leaders.

In his report to Kissinger, Haig characterized the Chinese reply as "tough and polemic in tone" on Indochina and South Asia. Haig also noted that Zhou criticized the US assessment of Soviet expansion as being "[in] error."²³ Most importantly, Haig reported Zhou's assurance that the Chinese would "do nothing to embarrass the President during his trip."²⁴ Overall, Haig made logistical arrangements for Nixon's trip to China. Haig's talks with Zhou played a crucial role in clarifying the respective sides' view on the latest development of global and regional security issues. Haig clarified the US commitment to "One China" principle and also explained the newly emerging common interest between the US and China in counter-balancing the Soviet Union in Indochina and South Asia. Finally, the two sides determined to leave the remaining differences to be discussed at the later February summit.

2. Final Preparations for the China Summit

2.1 The "Books"

From early January to mid February 1972, the NSC staff and the State Department prepared their respective briefing papers for Nixon's presidential trip to China. Kissinger and his NSC Staff prepared the "Books" – six black-ring notebooks including the main briefing papers on major security issues between the US and China, such as Taiwan, Indochina, Japan, South Asia, and the Soviet Union. Since it was anticipated that the President's conversations with the Chinese leaders would be very "lengthy and intensive," these papers were "more detailed than usual," arranged as follows:

- Chinese broad perceptions of the problem (including relevant background and what they would want);
- Issues and Talking Points (including the <u>Chinese Position</u> in specific terms, along the lines Zhou used with Kissinger; and <u>Your Position</u>, consistent with the line Kissinger used with Zhou); and
- The draft language of the joint communiqué.²⁵

---

22   Ibid., p. 8.
23   Haig to Kissinger, January 8, 1972, p. 2, Haig China Trip December 29, 1971–January 10, 1971, Haig-File, Box 1015, NSCF, NPMS, NA.
24   Ibid p. 3, Solomon explains further that Haig "warned the Chinese that they should make Nixon 'look good' – if the Chinese 'embarrassed or humiliated' the President, it would 'undermine domestic support for the China opening and make it more difficult for the President to deal with the Soviet Union.'" Richard Solomon, interview with author, September 24, 2003.
25   Kissinger to Nixon, "Briefing Papers for the China Trip," February 8, 1972, underline in original, Book V, The President, Briefing Papers for the China Trip, For the

The State Department's "Books" contained issues papers, which were considerably briefer but substantively consistent with the NSC briefing papers on subsidiary questions and background information.[26] Kissinger also requested for the CIA to prepare background studies on the following subjects: 1) the philosophies and the political roles of Mao Zedong and Zhou Enlai; 2) the internal political situation in the PRC; 3) the PRC's approach to international affairs; and 4) the situation of Sino-Soviet relations.[27] The CIA papers were used as the basis of the NSC staff's briefing papers to the President.

2.2 Kissinger's briefings to Nixon

In his detailed memos to Nixon, Kissinger stressed that the conversations with the Chinese leaders would be at a "far greater intensity and length" than any previous talks the President had conducted.[28] In essence, the Chinese leaders would take a "very principled approach," but within that framework they would be "realistic."[29] Thus, it was important for the President to demonstrate his grasp of the strategic outlines:

> [T]heir main attention will be on the perspectives you paint. They will be primarily interested in your judgment of the future and the principles and reliability of your policy. Accordingly, one basic task is to get across to them that we can make certain moves they want in the future because it is in our own self-interest, and that we will make such moves in the future because we are reliable.[30]

Kissinger also presented a detailed briefing on the Chinese leaders. Premier Zhou was "the tactician, the administrator, the negotiator, the master of details and the thrust and party."[31] Zhou would talk in "philosophic and historical" terms, but his

---

President's Files (Winston Lord)-China Trip/Vietnam (FPF/Lord), Box 847, NSCF, NPMS, NA. The NSC staff considered that Nixon knew little about most international issues apart from the US relations with the Soviets and with Vietnam. They thus sought to produce the main book as more of a "tutorial" for the President. John H. Holdridge, *Crossing the Divide: An Insider's Account of the Normalization of US-China Relations* (Lanham, Boulder, New York, Oxford: Rowman & Littlefield Publishers, 1997), p. 77.

26   Kissinger to Rogers, "Briefing Books for the President's Visit to the People's Republic of China," January 20, 1972, p. 1, Box 501, China Trip – January 1972 [Part I], PTF, NSCF, NPMS, NA.

27   Kissinger to Helms, "Studies to be Prepared for the President's Visit to the People's Republic of China," January 20, 1972, p. 1, Box 501, China Trip – January 1972 [Part I], PTF, NSCF, NPMS, NA.

28   Kissinger to Nixon, "Your Encounter with the Chinese, February 5, 1972, p. 1, Box, 13, China, HAK-ASF, HAKOF, NSCF, NPMS, NA. As for Chinese leaders' diplomatic practice see Richard Solomon, *Chinese Negotiating Behavior: Pursuing Interests Through 'Old Friends'* (Washington DC: United States Institute of Peace, 1999).

29   Ibid.

30   Ibid., p. 3. Underline in original.

31   Ibid., p. 7. As for Zhou's diplomatic career, see, for example, Shu Guang Zhang, "In the Shadow of Mao: Zhou Enlai and New China's Diplomacy," in Gordon Craig A., and

main concern would be on "the concrete substantive issues." He could also be "extremely – and suddenly – tough," possibly directed by Mao.[32] Overall, one could "have a dialogue" with Zhou who was clearly "running China."[33]

Relying on the NSC staff's briefing information and the CIA background studies, Kissinger wrote that Chairman Mao was "the philosopher, the poet, the grand strategist, the inspirer, the romantic." Mao would set the "direction and the framework" and leave the negotiations to Zhou. He would want to talk about the "long view, the basic tides running in the world, where China and the US are heading, with each other and with others."[34]

Mao and Zhou had believed that "the US has learned the hard way that it cannot manipulate political affairs in Asia to its own advantage."[35] They would thus try to persuade that "China constitutes no threat to the US"[36] Mao felt that "the other barbarians, the Russians and Japanese," had become "far more dangerous." Thus, he would "let the American barbarians come in briefly, just enough to offset the other dangers."[37] Mao would "study our President's mind" and test the "degree of determination and shrewdness."[38] Overall, Nixon had brought many of his experiences for the trip to make assumptions about how Mao thought about politics.

2.3 Nixon's handwritten notations

President Nixon reviewed the briefing material, memorizing his basic positions and taking extensive notes. The notes essentially show the development of Nixon's thoughts on the vital interests in US-PRC relations.[39] Former NSC staff member Winston Lord recalls that: "Nixon read every page, almost all of the briefing books for his China trip. You can see him marking up almost every page. Even during the trip over in the plane [to China in February 1972], he sent them pages back, asking

---

Francis L. Loewenheim. (eds), *The Diplomats 1939–1979* (Princeton, New Jersey: Princeton University Press, 1994); Suyin Han, *Eldest Son: Zhou Enlai and the Making of Modern China* (London: Pimlico An Imprint of Random House, 1994); Ronald Keith, *The Diplomacy of Zhou Enlai* (New York: St. Martin's Press, 1989); and Dick Wilson, *Zhou Enlai: A Biography* (New York: Viking, 1984).

32   Ibid., p. 6.
33   Kissinger to Nixon, "Mao, Chou and the Chinese Litmus Test," February 19, 1972, p. 4, Box, 13, China, HAK-ASF, HAKOF, NSCF, NPMS, NA.
34   Kissinger to Nixon, "Your Encounter with the Chinese," February 5, 1972, p. 7. As for the biographical accounts of Mao, see, for example, Philipe Short, *Mao: A Life* (New York: Henry Holt & Company, 1999); Jonathan D. Spence, *Mao Zedong* (New York: Viking, Penguin, 1999); and Shaun Breslin, *Mao* (London and New York: Longman, 1998).
35   Kissinger to Nixon, "Your Meetings with Mao," February 15, 1972, p. 3, underline by Nixon in original, Book IV, The President, China Visit, Readings on Mao Tse-Tung and Chou En-lai, FPF/Lord, Box 847, NSCF, NPMS, NA.
36   Ibid., p. 4. Underline by Nixon in original.
37   Ibid., p. 8. Underline by Nixon in original.
38   Ibid., p. 9. Underline by Nixon in original.
39   Nixon preferred to talk without notes whenever possible in order to impress people. See James H. Mann, *About Face: A History of America's Curious Relationship with China, from Nixon to Clinton* (New York: Alfred Knopf, 1999), pp. 13–15, and pp. 40–49.

for additional information."[40] Nixon's handwritten notes on the cover page of the main "Books" show his broad aim of the China trip:

> We will play a role in Pacific.
> We do not threaten anyone's freedom – or peace.
>
> China and America have unique opportunity to change the world –
> Let us not miss it.
>
> We were to write a new page in history
> The world is watching.
>
> We like you believe in honesty
> We have had differences
> We will continue to have –
> Let's talk about what brings us together[41]

Nixon perceived his trip as a "major turning point" in US-PRC relations hoping that "our discussions this week will lay the foundation for a new and enduring relationship."[42] He also recognized the depth of the remaining perception gap between the two sides regarding their respective world outlooks. Thus, while reviewing the briefing books on February 15, Nixon wrote:

> Understanding of difference is worth achieving –
>
> We must be honorable – (to our friends) or our friendship is worthless to new friends –
> We don't ask them to give up their ideology or their friends
> They must not ask us to do so.[43]

During a stopover in Hawaii on February 18, Nixon wrote his positions for negotiating with Chairman Mao:

> Trust him (as emperor)
>
> 1. Don't quarrell [sic]
> 2. Don't praise him (too much)
> 3. Praise the people – art, ancient
> 4. Praise poems.
> 5. Love of country –[44]

---

40 Winston Lord, interview with the author, October 15, 2003.
41 Nixon's handwritten notations on the cover page, Book V, The President, Briefing Papers for the China Trip, FPF/Lord, Box 847, NSCF, NPMS, NA.
42 Plenary Opening Statement, p. 1, underline by Nixon in original, Book V, The President, Briefing Papers for the China Trip, FPF/Lord, Box 847, NSCF, NPMS, NA.
43 Nixon's handwritten notations, February 15, 1972, p. 3, China Notes, Alpha/Subject File, Box 7, PPF, WHSF, NPMS, NA.
44 Nixon's handwritten notations, February 18, 1972, p. 11, China Notes, Alpha/Subject File, Box 7, PPF, WHSF, NPMS, NA.

We <u>will</u> make moves in our self interest
<u>can</u> because we are reliable –
We'll tell you nothing if I can't
Prudence, Will do more than say[45]
Be strong so that they respect you –[46]

Nixon also wrote his thoughts on the vital issues in US-PRC rapprochement as follows:

What they want:

1. Build up their world credentials –
2. Taiwan
3. Get US out of Asia –

What we want:

1. Indo China (?)
2. Communication – To restrain Chinese expansion in Asia –
3. In Future – Reduce threat of confrontation by Chinese Super Power

What we both want

1. Reduce danger of confrontation + conflict
2. A more stable Asia –
3. A restraint on USSR.[47]

On February 21, prior to his arrival on the Chinese mainland, Nixon again wrote on Chinese interests:

What do you want?

You must think of your security
1. Soviet – present threat
2. Japan – future
3. India – an irritation (except of built by Soviet)
4. Peace – but a need to retain your principle –

How can we work together?

Your opponents are ours –
Taiwan – V.nam [Vietnam] are irritants –[48]

With these respective vital national interests in mind, Nixon prepared his negotiating positions with the Chinese leaders.

---

45   Ibid., p. 12.
46   Ibid., p. 14.
47   Ibid.
48   Nixon's handwritten notations, February 21, 1972, p. 15, China Notes, Alpha/Subject File, Box 7, PPF, WHSF, NPMS, NA.

3. Nixon's Presidential Trip to China in February 1972

3.1 The Nixon-Mao talks

On February 21, 1972, President Nixon arrived at the Beijing airport where the Chinese Premier Zhou Enlai welcomed the historic arrival. The handshake between the two leaders sparked the public spectacle of the summit to "mark the end of a generation of hostility" and to "begin a new but still undefined" relationship between the most powerful and most populous nations in the world.[49]

After the arrival ceremony, Zhou visited the US guesthouse and informed Kissinger that Mao was "inviting" Nixon to hold a meeting "fairly soon."[50] Until that time, Nixon and Kissinger were not entirely sure whether the Chairman would meet with the President.[51] Lord recalls that Mao and Zhou were "extremely charismatic figures" who had a "broad worldview which concerned strategic and long-term interests."[52] The Chinese understanding of the nature of the international situation from the late 1960s to the early 1970s "was remarkably sophisticated." Lord also assesses that Mao and Zhou had a "very good grasp of geopolitics and they understood what they needed." On the other hand, as Solomon recalls, Zhou Enlai remarked to the President "how young they all were. This perception may have made them feel uneasy, made them feel like old guys, dealing with these young Americans."[53]

---

49   "Nixon Arrives in Peking to Begin an 8-Day Visit; Met By Chou at Airport," *The New York Times*, February 21, 1972. The trip was heavily televised, creating tremendous impact in America, leading to instant euphoria.

50   Memcon, Kissinger and Zhou, February 21, 1972, 2:30–2:40pm, p. 1, Dr. Kissinger's Meetings in the People's Republic During the Presidential Visit February 1972, Box 92, Country Files (CF)-Far East, HAKOF, NSCF, NPMS, NA. From the US side, only the President, Kissinger, and a NSC staff member Winston Lord attended the meeting with Mao. Kissinger told Zhou: "We won't tell him [Secretary of State William Rogers]. We can announce it a little later." Ibid. On February 29, 1972, President stated to the Congressional leaders that there was some "nonsense" that Kissinger's attendance "downgraded the Secretary of State." Nixon explained that in the Chinese system, the Foreign Minister was fifth ranking in protocol, and if the President had brought in the Secretary of State, they would have had to bring in five additional Chinese. "Meeting with Bipartisan Leadership, February 29, 1972, 10:00am The Cabinet Room," p. 2, Memoranda for the President (MemforP), Records of Meetings (ROM), Box 88, POF, WHCF, NPMS, NA.

51   Soon after the Nixon-Mao talk, Kissinger admitted to Zhou that: "I did not know we were going to see the Chairman today. I was going to raise this problem with you. It is not right for the President to wait until he is summoned to see the Chairman." Memcon, Kissinger and Zhou, February 21, 1972, 4:15–5:30pm, p. 9, Dr. Kissinger's Meetings in the People's Republic During the Presidential Visit February 1972, CF-Far East, HAKOF, NSCF, NPMS, NA. On the other hand, State Department officials worked out a plan to minimize damage if Mao decided not to grant an audience. See Walter Isaacson, *Kissinger: A Biography* (New York: McGraw-Hill, 1992), pp. 400–401.

52   Lord, interview with the author, October 15, 2003.

53   Solomon, interview with the author, September 24, 2003.

The Mao-Nixon meeting, originally planned for fifteen minutes, turned out to be more than an hour-long talk which set the fundamental direction of the following negotiations that took place between the two sides at various official levels.[54] Nixon emphasized the importance of strict secrecy in the confidential talk at the highest official level, assuring that "nothing goes beyond this room."[55] Nixon then sought to illustrate the great forces in Asia:

> We, for example, must ask ourselves ... why the Soviets have more forces on the border facing you than on the border facing Western Europe. We must ask ourselves, what is the future of Japan? ... [I]s it better for Japan to be neutral, totally defenseless, or is it better for a time for Japan to have some relations with the United States? The point being – I am talking now in the realm of philosophy – in international relations there are no good choices. One thing is sure – we can leave no vacuums, because they can be filled. ... The question is which danger the People's Republic faces, whether it is danger of American aggression or Soviet aggression.[56]

In essence, Nixon was justifying the US presence in Asia by urging the Chinese leaders to re-assess the degree of threat from each superpower.[57] In response, Mao

---

54   Memcon, February 21, 1972, 2:50–3:55pm (hereafter referred to as Memcon 21 February 1972), CHINA – President's Talks with Mao and Chou En-lai February 1972, Box 91, CF-Far East, HAKOF, NSCF, NPMS, NA. See also Richard Nixon, *RN* (New York: Grssett & Danlap, 1978), pp. 560–564; and Henry Kissinger, *White House Years* (Boston: Little Brown, 1979), pp. 1057–1066. As for Mao's weakened health condition prior to Nixon's arrival, see Li Zhisui, *The Private Life of Chairman Mao: The Memoirs of Mao's Personal Physician* (London: Arrow Books, 1994), pp. 544–568. There was a plan for a second Mao-Nixon meeting which never materialized.

55   Memcon 21 February 1972, p. 5. The Nixon-Mao talk was interpreted by Chinese interpreter T'ang Wen-sheng (also known as Nancy Tang, born in Brooklyn, New York, and emigrated to China in 1955), and NSC staff member Winston Lord attended as a note-taker.

56   Ibid, p. 6. In his description of the Nixon-Mao talk, Kissinger misleadingly quotes Mao's statements that supported postponing the resolution of the Taiwan issue. Kissinger, *White House Years*, p. 1062. Mao's statements were made in February and November 1973 and October 1975, not in February 1972.

57   In reality, before his trip to China, Nixon tested his notion of justifying the continuing US presence in the Asia-Pacific. On February 14, 1972, President Nixon invited the French writer and philosopher, Andre Malraux, to the White House to discuss his China trip. Nixon outlined his view on the fundamental security issues in the Asia-Pacific region and the world: "[T]he relations over the next 25 years between the US and Japan and between the US and China would determine the fate of the Pacific. The relations between the US and the USSR and between the USSR and China could determine the fate of the world." With regard to the US policy in the Pacific, Nixon emphasized that if Japan, soon to be the second most economically productive nation in the world, were to be "left without the US nuclear umbrella to protect it," it would "consider building up its defense and becoming a nuclear power." The President did "not see how a militarily independent Japan could be more peaceful than a Japan protected by the US nuclear umbrella." Malraux agreed by suggesting a hypothesis, Japan's possible move toward the Soviets, arguing: "if Japan stopped believing in the US nuclear protection and found itself faced with a China having a nuclear arms and the USSR, it would seek guarantees of the USSR." Hence, Nixon stressed that US would not

outlined the fundamental change between the two sides that materialized in the rapprochement:

> At the present time, the question of aggression from the United States or aggression from China is relatively small; that is, it could be said that this is not a major issue, because the present situation is one in which a state of war does not exist between our two countries. You want to withdraw some of your troops back on your soil; ours do not go abroad.58

It was the mutual realization of the reduction of direct threat that motivated both sides to initiate direct talks in this particular period.

> President Nixon: ... I think you know the United States had no territorial designs on China. We know China doesn't want to dominate the United States. We believe you too realize the United States doesn't want to dominate the world. ... Therefore, we can find common ground, despite our differences, to build a world structure in which both can be safe to develop in our own ways on our own roads. That cannot be said about some other nations in the world.
>
> Chairman Mao: Neither do we threaten Japan or South Korea.
>
> President Nixon: Nor any country. Nor do we.[59]

In essence, the above exchanges established the broad framework for the Nixon-Zhou talks that followed. The United States and China would not impose direct threats or territorial ambition against each other. Therefore, this mutual understanding would promote the partial reduction of the US armed forces originally directed at containing China, and in turn encouraged China's tacit admission of the US military presence in the Western Pacific region. Finally, the media described Nixon's meeting with Mao as "frank and serious" and as "the highlight of the week."[60]

3.2 The Nixon-Zhou talks

Following the Nixon-Mao meeting, the two sides held discussions at various official levels. The plenary session indicated the general direction of the summit and arranged for 1) a restricted principal talk between Nixon and Zhou on a wide

---

withdraw totally from the Pacific because it might "create a power vacuum that would be filled by another power," namely Japan, or the Soviet Union. Kissinger to Nixon, "Meeting with Mr. Andre Malraux," February 14, 1972 at 4:00pm to 5:30pm, pp. 4–8, Memoranda for the President, Records of Meetings, Box 87, POF, WHCF, NPMS, NA. In his memoirs, Nixon recorded his favorable impression of Malraux's "original and striking" assessments of the world outlook of the Chinese leaders. Nixon, *RN*, pp. 557–559. On the contrary, Kissinger is much more skeptical of Malraux's "grossly out of date" views. Kissinger, *White House Years*, pp. 1051–1052.

58   Memcon 21 February 1972, pp. 6–7.
59   Ibid., p. 8.
60   "Nixon Spends An Hour With Mao And Then, At A Banquet, Hears Chou Toast His Trip As 'Positive,'" *The New York Times*, February 22, 1972.

range of major issues[61] and 2) an assisting talk between Secretary of State William Rogers and Chinese Foreign Minister Chi Peng-fei on a series of steps to promote bilateral relations, such as trade, scientific and other exchanges.[62] The drafting of the joint communiqué was conducted between Zhou and Kissinger and between Chinese Deputy Foreign Minister Ch'iao Kuan-hua (Qiao Guanhua) and Kissinger.[63] Finally, Nixon reiterated to Zhou the importance of the preservation of secrecy.[64] Hereafter, this chapter examines the five major security issues addressed in the US-PRC talks: Taiwan, Indochina, Japan, India-Pakistan relations, and the Soviet Union.

3.2.1 The Taiwan issue
As President Nixon wrote before the departure for China, the Taiwan issue remained the "most crucial" issue between the two sides.[65] While reviewing the briefing books, Nixon was fully aware that Taiwan would be "the first item" on the Chinese agenda which would require him to "show flexibility in addressing it." [66] It was crucial for him to find a way to put the issue aside: "Neither of us should allow the Taiwan

---

61   CHINA – President's Talks with Mao and Chou En-lai February 1972, CF-Far East, NSCF, NPMS, NA. See also Nixon, *RN*, pp. 564–579; and Kissinger, *White House Years*, pp. 1070–1087. Among US officials, also present were Kissinger, Lord, and Holdridge.
62   MemCons Between Secretary Rogers and PRC Officials, POL Chicom, 1970–1973, Box 2699, Subject-Numeric Files (SNF), General Records of the Department of State, Record Group 59 (RG59), NA. Among US officials, also present were Marshall Green, John Scali, Ron Ziegler, Alfred le S. Jenkins, Charles W. Freeman Jr., and Commander John Howe (NSC staff).
63   Dr. Kissinger's Meetings in the People's Republic During the Presidential Visit February 1972, CF-Far East, HAKOF, NSCF, NPMS, NA.
64   Nixon assured Zhou that only five individuals (namely the President himself, Kissinger, Winston Lord, John Holdridge, and General Haig) would see the transcripts of their talks. Memorandum of conversation, February 22, 1972, 2:10–6:00pm (hereafter referred to as Memcon February 22, 1972), pp. 3–4, CHINA – President's Talks with Mao and Chou En-lai February 1972, CF-Far East, NSCF, NPMS, NA. Two Chinese interpreters, T'ang Wen-sheng and Chi Chao-chu interpreted the Nixon-Zhou talks. Kissinger arranged interpretation with Zhou in advance: "We will not use our interpreters but will rely on your interpreters. We will tell the press that we have Mr. Holdridge there to check on your interpreter." Memcon, Kissinger and Zhou, February 21, 1972, 4:15–5:30pm, p. 2, Dr. Kissinger's Meetings in the People's Republic During the Presidential Visit February 1972, CF-Far East, HAKOF, NSCF, NPMS, NA. Nixon later explained to Congressional leaders that Premier Zhou must have understood English because he "corrected the translator many times." Holdridge told the President that it was a disadvantage for the US side because every time the President spoke, while the translator translated it into Chinese, Zhou "had a great deal of time to think about his response." "Meeting with Bipartisan Leadership February 29, 1972, 10:00am The Cabinet Room, pp. 3–4, MemforP, ROM, Box 88, POF, WHCF, NPMS, NA.
65   Nixon's handwritten notations, February 15, 1972, p. 2, China Notes, Alpha/Subject File, Box 7, PPF, WHSF, NPMS, NA.
66   Taiwan, p. 3, underline by Nixon in original, Book V, The President, Briefing Papers for the China Trip, FPF/Lord, Box 847, NSCF, NPMS, NA.

<u>issue to color unduly our developing relationship</u> (Taiwan will be settled)."⁶⁷ At the beginning of the first restricted talk, Nixon proposed the so-called "five principles":

> Principle one. There is one China, and Taiwan is a part of China. There will be no more statements made – if I can control our bureaucracy – to the effect that the status of Taiwan is undermined.
>
> Second, we have not and will not support the Taiwan independence movement.
>
> Third, we will, to the extent we are able, use our influence to discourage Japan from moving into Taiwan as our presence becomes less, and also discourage Japan from supporting a Taiwan independence movement.
>
> The fourth point is that we will support any peaceful resolution of the Taiwan issue that can be worked out. And related to that point, we will not support any military attempts by the Government on Taiwan to resort to a military return to the Mainland.
>
> Finally, we seek the normalization of relations with the People's Republic.⁶⁸

These five principles, especially the "One China" premise was the central assurance for the Chinese in proceeding in the Sino-US normalization process. In addition, viewing Taiwan as "an irritant" and as having "a high emotional content," Nixon referred to the technical aspect of "language" for public presentation.⁶⁹ It was a question of the US domestic political situation, because there was a possibility that the critics might "gang up" and create "a danger to the whole initiative."⁷⁰ Thus, Nixon and Zhou decided to have some flexible "running room" which would reflect the remaining differences between the two sides in the joint communiqué.⁷¹

---

67   Ibid., p. 7. Underline by Nixon in original. Nixon's handwritten notations in parentheses.
68   Memcon 22 February 1972, p. 5; and Taiwan, pp. 4–5, Book V. Nixon's opening statement on the Taiwan issue was a crucial pre-condition for the Chinese to improve Sino-US diplomatic relations. While reviewing briefing books, Nixon wrote:
I restate what our policy is:
1. Status
One China, Taiwan is part of China –
2. Won't support Taiwan independence move
3. <u>Try</u> to restrain Japan –
4. Support peaceful resolution
5. Discuss –
Will seek normalization
Nixon's handwritten notations, February 21, 1972, p. 16, underline by Nixon in original, China Notes, Alpha/Subject File, Box 7, PPF, WHSF, NPMS, NA.
69   Memcon February 22, 1972, p. 6.
70   Ibid., p. 7.
71   Memorandum of conversation, February 24, 1972, 5:15–8:05pm (hereafter referred to as Memcon 24 February 1972), p. 10.

Regarding the methods of resolving the Taiwan issue, Nixon sought to clarify the US long-term position that Taiwan should be <u>settled peacefully</u>.[72] Nixon wrote the negotiating position:

> You must not listen to what I <u>say</u>. You must watch what I <u>do.</u>
> Coming to Peking has itself created a new reality.
> ... We want a peaceful resolution.[73]

As for the political timetable for the US-PRC diplomatic normalization, Nixon wrote: "Age: My life is 10 months or 5 years – then done – I have little time and will do it."[74] "Want RN reelected – ...Direction – must be pointed out –[.]"[75]

Hence, Nixon suggested to Zhou that the two sides should refrain from making Taiwan "a big issue" in the next two or three years which implied his second term in office.[76] Moreover, it was essential for the Nixon administration to "sell" the promotion of the US withdrawal from Taiwan "as step by step" to Congress, while persuading the public of the importance of normalization with the People's Republic.[77]

In response, Zhou made it clear that "[w]hile your armed forces are there our armed forces will not engage in military confrontation with your armed forces."[78] However, Zhou emphasized that China would still treat Taiwan as an "internal issue" and "liberate" it in its own way.[79] Thus, Zhou did not make any further commitment: "we would rather let the question of Taiwan wait for a little while."[80]

Regarding the US's withdrawal from Asia, Nixon sought to link the reduction of US armed forces in Taiwan and the promotion of the Vietnam settlement. He wrote his calculation:

> Taiwan – V. Nam [Vietnam] = trade off
> 1. You expect action on Taiwan
> 2. Our people expect action on V. Nam
> 3. Neither can act immediately
>   But both are inevitable – Let us not embarrass each other[81]

---

72 Taiwan, p. 7, Book V. Underline by Nixon in original.
73 Nixon's handwritten notations, in Ibid., p. 8. Underline by Nixon in original.
74 Nixon's handwritten notations, February 21, 1972, p. 16, China Notes, Alpha/Subject File, Box 7, PPF, WHSF, NPMS, NA. Nixon referred to his presidential terms.
75 Nixon's handwritten notations, February 24, 1972, China, Speech Files, Box 73, China Trip, PPF, WHSF, NPMS, NA.
76 Memcon 24 February 1972, p. 10.
77 Ibid., p. 12.
78 Memcon 24 February 1972, p. 6.
79 Memorandum of conversation February 28, 1972, 8:30–9:30am (hereafter referred to as Memcon 28 February 1972), p. 8.
80 Ibid.
81 Nixon's handwritten notations, February 23, 1972, 6am, p. 17, China Notes, Alpha/Subject File, Box 7, PPF, WHSF, NPMS, NA. Garver interprets that the Chinese leaders were hoping to drive a wedge between Washington and Taipei by opening to the United States.

In direct talks, Nixon gave assurance to Zhou that:

> [T]wo-thirds of our present forces on Taiwan are related to the support of our forces in Southeast Asia. These forces, regardless of what we may do will be removed as the situation in Southeast Asia is resolved.[82]

Finally, Nixon assured that once the military operation in Vietnam was completed, the US could reduce its "other forces," the remaining one-third, from Taiwan.[83]

On February 26, Secretary of State Rogers and Assistant Secretary Green were given the opportunity to read the communiqué approved by Nixon and Kissinger, and also by the Chinese Politburo. Importantly, Green immediately detected "a major flaw" in the draft.[84] First, while the communiqué stated that "all people" on either side of the Straits regarded Taiwan as part of China, Green objected to the word "people." He maintained that the inhabitants of Taiwan, who considered the island their home regardless of their ancestors' origin in China, and who regarded themselves as "Taiwanese," would not necessarily agree that Taiwan was a part of China.[85] Accordingly, Kissinger proposed to re-negotiate with Chinese Vice Foreign Minister Ch'iao Kuan-hua (Qiao Guanhua) to change the term "people" to "Chinese."[86]

Second, the draft communiqué reaffirmed the continuation of the US security commitment to its Asian allies such as Japan, South Korea, South Vietnam, the Philippines, the Southeast Asia Treaty Organization (SEATO), and the Australia-New Zealand-US treaty (ANZUS). Yet, it did not mention America's treaty obligation to the Republic of China on Taiwan.[87] Green estimated that this omission would

---

John W. Garver, *The Sino-American Alliance: Nationalist China and American Cold War Strategy* (New York: An East Gate Book: M.E. Sharpe, Inc., 1997), p. 274.

82   Memcon February 22, 1972, pp. 5–6.

83   Memcon February 24, 1972, p. 10.

84   Marshall Green, *Evolution of US-China Policy 1956–1973: Memoirs of An Insider*, pp. 37–38, Oral History Interview in *A China Reader*, Vol. II, January 1995, FAOHC. See also Marshall Green, John. H. Holdridge, and William Stokes, *War and Peace with China: First-Hand Experiences in the Foreign Service of the United States* (Maryland: Dacor-Bacon House, 1994), pp. 162–165; and Kissinger, *White House Years*, pp. 1082–1084. Nixon blamed the State Department's involvement as a failure to preserve secrecy, fearing the leak of the major points of the communiqué. In reality, however, during the early drafting of the communiqué for his October 1971 trip to Beijing, Kissinger brought in a China desk officer, Al Jenkins, to work with John Holdridge on the second and third round drafting. Jenkins also gave much of his drafting to his deputy Roger Sullivan.

85   Ibid.

86   Memcon, Kissinger and Ch'iao Kuan-hua, February 26–27, 1972, 10:20–1:40am, pp. 2–3, Dr. Kissinger's Meetings in the People's Republic During the Presidential Visit February 1972, CF-Far East, HAKOF, NSCF, NPMS, NA. However, Kissinger dropped Green's suggestion to change "all Chinese" to "the Chinese."

87   Green, *Evolution of US-China Policy*, Oral History Interview, pp. 37–38, FAOHC. Green recalls further that this omission of any reference to a treaty obligation toward Taiwan reminded him of former Secretary of State Dean Acheson's failure in the early 1950. Acheson, defining the "defensive perimeter" for the United States ranging from the Ryukyu islands in

almost certainly be seized by the opposition to the US-PRC summit, especially the US domestic critics charging the Nixon trip as unilaterally terminating the treaty obligation and "selling out" the Chinese Nationalists. It also posed a serious question for US reliability in terms of its willingness and capability to fulfill treaty obligations to its allies. As Kissinger told Ch'iao, 'every other ally in the Pacific will say "what about us?"'[88] After intense exchanges, they finally agreed to remove that particular section on defense treaty from the communiqué. On February 27, in a news conference in Shanghai, Kissinger orally re-confirmed the US commitment toward the Republic of China.[89]

Regarding strict secrecy, Lord recalls that: "We could have had more expertise. … I think it would have been worth running that risk."[90] Lord also admits that: "I still feel it would have been useful to have State there in dealing with the Chinese, and also it would have been much less messy at the end, where the State Department had to climb in on the communiqué at the last minute, for bureaucratic support."[91]

In the final version of the joint communiqué, China reiterated its long-term vital interest in the sovereignty over Taiwan:

> [T]he Government of the People's Republic of China is the sole legal government of China; Taiwan is a province of China which has long been returned to the motherland; the liberation of Taiwan is China's internal affair in which no other country has the right to interfere; and all US forces and military installations must be withdrawn from Taiwan. The Chinese Government firmly opposes any activities which aim at the creation of 'one China, one Taiwan,' 'one China, two governments,' 'two Chinas,' and 'independent Taiwan,' or advocate that 'the status of Taiwan remain to be determined.'[92]

In response, the US declared:

> The United States acknowledges that all Chinese on either side of the Taiwan Strait maintain there is but one China and that Taiwan is a part of China. The United States does not challenge that position. It reaffirms its interest in a peaceful settlement of the Taiwan question by the Chinese themselves. With this prospect in mind, it affirms the ultimate objectives of the withdrawal of all US forces and military installations from Taiwan. In the meantime, it will progressively reduce its forces as the tension in the area diminishes.[93]

Western Pacific to the Philippines in Southeast Asia, did not include South Korea, and thus might have induced the North Korean launching of the Korean War. Ibid.

88   Memcon, Kissinger and Ch'iao, February 26 to 27, 1972, p. 3. Ch'iao reacted furiously to Kissinger's proposals: "the sentiments of all Chinese are very strong on the Taiwan question. I am restraining myself to the utmost. … If you have to persist in this, let us not continue tonight." Ibid., p. 10.

89   Kissinger prepared a statement as follows: "we are here on the soil of a country with which we have no diplomatic relations and for which this is the most sensitive issue. Therefore do not keep asking this question. I will answer it once. We stated in the World Report our position on this, and the statement in the World Report remains intact. Then when the President goes back to Congress he will have to answer it again." Ibid., p. 11.

90   Lord, "The Nixon Administration National Security Council," p. 44, NSCP-OHR.

91   Ibid., p. 45.

92   *The New York Times*, February 28, 1972. Quotation marks in original.

93   Ibid.

After the summit, a China expert in the NSC staff, Richard Solomon, conducted a detailed comparative analysis of the English and Chinese versions of the joint communiqué. First, while the English version "<u>acknowledges</u>" "the legitimacy of Chinese declaration that Taiwan is part of China," the Chinese version conveyed that the U.S "<u>understands [is aware]</u>" that both Chinese states maintained this position.[94] Moreover, the Chinese version's use of a verb "understands" [jen-shih-tao] would imply diplomatic recognition [ch'eng-jen] or acceptance of the other side's point of view.[95]

Second, the English statement that the US "<u>does not challenge</u>" the Chinese position acquired an "even more hands-off implication" in the Chinese version. It implied a degree of involvement in the issue – "<u>does not raise a divergent opinion [an objection]</u>."[96] The Chinese version thus could mean that the US "does not wish to get involved in a dispute over the matter."

Third, where the English version "<u>reaffirms</u>" the US "interest" in a peaceful resolution of the Taiwan question, the Chinese phrase was better translated as "reiterate its concern" with a peaceful solution on the US part.[97] The likelihood of peaceful solution was thus stronger in the Chinese language version. Overall, each side interpreted the implications of the communiqué for its own advantage.

Regarding the US partial withdrawal, the US statement, "as the tension in the area diminishes" implied the final reassurance of the linkage between the US withdrawal from Taiwan and the progress of Vietnamization. In other words, the US would withdraw from Taiwan as the tension in the region eased with its military disengagement from the Vietnam War. One of the major purposes of the communiqué for the US, and especially for Kissinger, was "to put off the issue of Taiwan for the future."[98] Thus, the US statement was an indication of "One China, but not now."

3.2.2 Conflicts in Indochina

As President Nixon's comments on a yellow pad indicate, the conflicts in Indochina were the "most urgent" issue between the two sides.[99] While preparing for his trip to China, Nixon outlined his negotiating positions.

> V. Nam:
> 1. We are ending our involvement.
> 2. We had hoped you would help – but now it doesn't matter

---

94 Solomon to Kissinger, "Comparison of the Chinese and English Versions of the Sino-American Joint Communiqué," March 17, 1972, p. 1, Underline in original, Box 501, China Trip – February–March 1972 [Part 2], PTF, NSCF, NPMS, NA. On March 20, Kissinger transmitted a brief summary of Solomon's detailed memo to the President.
95 Ibid.
96 Ibid. Underline in original.
97 Ibid., p. 2. Underline in original.
98 Kissinger, *White House Years*, p. 1074.
99 Nixon's handwritten notations, February 15, 1972, p. 2, China Notes, Alpha/Subject File, Box 7, PPF, WHSF, NPMS, NA.

(Our lost offer – It doesn't matter to us –)[100]
1. We must end it honorably – it will –
2. S.V. Nam is stronger than you think –
You can't be expected to do anything –
Soviet would accuse you of colluding.
But it is in your interests for US to get out (2/3 of Taiwan)
It is in Soviet interests for US to stay[101]

Regarding the promotion of Vietnamization, Nixon was seriously concerned about the question of US reliability for its allies in the world. While preparing for the talks with Zhou, Nixon wrote:

Should take bold action in V. Nam –
Or others will benefit –[102]

Accordingly, Nixon explained to Zhou that: "if the US does not behave honorably, the US would cease to be a nation as a friend and which the people of the world could depend upon as an ally."[103] Nixon believed that the US should "react strongly if tested."[104] Finally, Nixon clarified that the US would never intend to "engage in unilateral withdrawal without accomplishing the objectives of our policy there."[105]

On the other hand, believing that the Vietnam problem should no longer be the division line between Washington and Beijing, Nixon wrote his comments on the NSC briefing book: "Reduces irritant to our relations"[106] Thus, Nixon gave assurance to Zhou:

I am removing this irritant as fast as anyone in my position could. My predecessor sent in 500,000 men into Vietnam, and I've taken 500.000 out. I will end American involvement – it's a matter of time. I can speak with certainty on this point.[107]

---

100 Ibid., p. 4. On January 30, the Chinese replied to Kissinger's message (dated on January 26) via Paris showing its continuing support for North Vietnamese and refusing to "exert pressure" on Hanoi on the behalf of Washington. On February 6, 1972, through the Paris backchannel, Nixon and Kissinger asked China to arrange a meeting with the North Vietnamese on Chinese soil during the Nixon visit. China refused to arrange a meeting with Le Duc Tho. Memo from Walters to Haig, February 16, 1972, Box 330, Policy Planning Staff (Director's File – Winston Lord), General Record of the Department of State, Record Group 59, NA. Tyler interprets that while asking the Chinese to help convince Hanoi to come to acceptable terms, Nixon was determined to get a breakthrough at almost any cost and as early as possible in the presidential campaign season. Patrick E. Tyler, *A Great Wall: Six Presidents and China, An Investigative History* (New York: Public Affairs, 1999), pp. 125–126.

101 Ibid.

102 Nixon's handwritten notations, February 22, 1972, China, Speech Files, Box 72, China Trip, PPF, WHSF, NPMS, NA.

103 Memcon February 22, 1972, p. 25.

104 Ibid., p. 26.

105 Memcon February 24, 1972, p. 17.

106 Indochina-Vietnam, Book V, p. 11.

107 Memcon February 22, 1972, p. 27.

Accordingly, Nixon stated further that: "you have no reason to believe that we have territorial designs in Southeast Asia."[108]

As for China's influence in Indochina, Nixon underlined the following specific points in the NSC briefing book:

> The US has recently been suggesting that the PRC exert pressure on its allies.
> (We don't ask –)[109]
> We would thus welcome Peking's constructive attitude.
> (But do not expect)[110]

Nixon also wrote his comments on the yellow pad:

> We would appreciate influence on Hanoi.
> We think it is in your interest
> But if you can't, we understand
> We shall chart our own course.[111]

Hence, Nixon was fully aware that the chances for any agreed statement on the conflicts in Indochina were slim. During the talk on February 22, while still maintaining "hopes," Nixon made it clear that he had "no illusions" about the promotion of a Vietnam settlement during his stay in Beijing: "I don't ask the Prime Minister to do anything about it, and certainly not do anything about it publicly."[112]

Regarding the danger of North Vietnamese expansion, while reviewing the NSC briefing books, Nixon underlined that the Chinese would "not want to see Hanoi control all of Indochina."[113] The NSC staff estimated that Beijing had no desire to "see an overwhelming North Vietnamese victory in Laos and Cambodia."[114] Nixon wrote his comments on the NSC briefing book:

> N.V.nam presence in Cambodia + Laos would mean expanded Soviet influence.
> All alien influence should be removed –
> Neutrality + non alignment our policy –[115]

In direct talks, Zhou repeatedly urged an earlier completion of the US military withdrawal from Indochina: "you went there by accident. Why not give this up?...

---

108 Ibid., p. 28.
109 Indochina-Vietnam, Book V, p. 10. Underline by Nixon in original. Nixon's handwritten notations in parentheses.
110 Ibid., p. 11. Underline by Nixon in original. Nixon's handwritten notations in parentheses.
111 Nixon's handwritten notations, Indochina-Vietnam, Point to Emphasize, p. 2, Book V-a, The President, Briefing Papers for the China Trip, FPF/Lord, Box 847, NSCF, NPMS, NA.
112 Memcon February 22, 1972, p. 29.
113 Indochina-Vietnam, Book V, p. 1, The President, Briefing Papers for the China Trip, FPF/Lord, Box 847, NSCF, NPMS, NA.
114 Indochina: Laos and Cambodia, Book V, p. 3, The President, Briefing Papers for the China Trip, FPF/Lord, Box 847, NSCF, NPMS, NA.
115 Nixon's handwritten notations, ibid.

It would be beneficial for the relaxation of tensions in the Far East to bring about a nonaligned Southeast Asia."[116] Thus, Zhou expressed China's continuing support for all Indochina states, "but we will not get involved unless, of course, you attack us."[117] Moreover, Zhou clarified that China only had an obligation to assist them but not the right to engage in negotiation on their behalf, for it respected "their sovereignty and independence."[118] Finally, Zhou stressed that China had "exerted great restraints" in Indochina since July 1971.[119]

Regarding the Soviet expansionism in Indochina, Nixon wrote his comments on the NSC briefing book: "Reduces Soviet hand there."[120] Nixon was thus seeking to enhance China's understanding of the US search for a negotiated settlement in Indochina by stressing the Soviet threat. During the direct talks, Nixon estimated that the Soviets expected the US to be "tied down" in Indochina, and consequently increased Moscow's influence on North Vietnam to be "the only gainer" from the prolonged US military operation.[121] On the other hand, Zhou urged that the United States should "take more bold action" because the delay of the US military withdrawal was likely to "facilitate the Soviets in furthering their influences."[122] In other words, the longer the US stayed, the more difficulty it would bring for the satisfactory completion of its military withdrawal from Indochina.

Finally, Nixon anticipated how his domestic political opponents would criticize the outcomes of his trip:

> Obviously what will be said, even with a skilful communiqué, is what the People's Republic of China wanted from us was movement on Taiwan and it got it; and what we wanted was help on Vietnam, and we got nothing.[123]

Nixon expressed appreciation to Zhou that China would "not try to discourage the North Vietnamese from negotiating."[124] In the joint communiqué, the US side stated: "the peoples in Indochina should be allowed to determine their destiny without outside intervention; its constant objective has been a negotiated solution."[125] In the "absence of a negotiated settlement," the United States "envisages the ultimate withdrawal of all US forces from the region consistent with the aim of self-determination for each country of Indochina."[126] On the other hand, with a strong opposition to "foreign aggression, interference and subversion," the Chinese side expressed "its firm support to the peoples of Vietnam, Laos, and Cambodia" in their continual efforts to

---

116   Memcon February 22, 1972, p. 28.
117   Ibid., p. 29.
118   Memcon February 28, 1972, pp. 9–10.
119   Ibid.
120   Indochina-Vietnam, Book V, p. 11.
121   Memcon February 24, 1972, p. 19.
122   Memcon February 22, 1972, p. 20.
123   Memcon February 24, 1972, p. 16.
124   Ibid., p. 24.
125   *The New York Times*, February 28, 1972.
126   Ibid.

achieve "freedom and liberation."[127] Lord assesses that the US rapprochement with China "generally helped to provide stability in Asia and the Pacific region. It was of some help on Vietnam."[128] In reality, however, it took another eleven months for the United States to achieve the Paris Peace Accords with the North Vietnamese, which took place on January 13, 1973.

3.2.3 Japan's future role

The NSC staff's briefing book explained that the Chinese traditionally had both "hated and feared the Japanese."[129] Thus, the Chinese would not want to "push Japan in the direction of a heavily-armed neutralism (including nuclear weapons) outside China's ability to control." The NSC staff recommended that the President should "focus the Chinese attention on this possibility and on the countervailing."[130] Nixon thus sought to exploit China's long-term fear of Japan's possible move in the future. Nixon wrote specific instructions to Kissinger:

> K – Japan –
> Don't say "we oppose rearmament of Japan."
> We oppose nuclear Japan[131]

Nixon further outlined his negotiating positions:

> Japan ready for take off commercially
> Best to provide nuclear shield –
> 1. To keep Japan from building its own.
> 2. To have influence from US.
> (1) We oppose Japan "stretching its hands" to Korea, Taiwan, Indochina –
> (2) But if we don't keep a truly [word] our recommendation would be like "empty cannon."
> Wild horse would not be controlled.[132]

Regarding the anticipated Chinese position, Nixon wrote: "You prefer neutral – (you should say it)[.]"[133] Nixon was aware that discussions on the Japan issue would be "very difficult."[134]

---

127 Ibid.
128 Lord, interview with the author, October 15, 2003.
129 Japan, p. 1, underline by Nixon in original, Book V, The President, Briefing Papers for the China Trip, FPF/Lord, Box 847, NSCF, NPMS, NA.
130 Ibid., p. 4. Underline by Nixon in original.
131 Nixon's handwritten notations, February 18, 1972, p. 8, Quotation marks in original, China Notes, Alpha/Subject File, Box 7, PPF, WHSF, NPMS, NA. The NSC staff originally recommended the following point that: "We oppose a rearmed Japan particularly with nuclear weapon. Nixon erased "particularly with nuclear weapon" and added "nuclear" in front of "rearmed." Japan, p. 6, Book V. Underline by Nixon in original.
132 Ibid., p. 10, Quotation marks in original.
133 Nixon's handwritten notations, February 21, 1972, p. 16, China Notes, Alpha/Subject File, Box 7, PPF, WHSF, NPMS, NA.
134 Ibid.

During the direct talks with Zhou, Nixon sought to justify the US-Japan Security Treaty by re-emphasizing the danger of US withdrawal from East Asia:

> The US can get out of Japanese waters, but others will fish there. And both China and the US have had very difficult experiences with Japanese militarism ... The Japanese, with their enormously productive economy, their great natural drive and their memories of the war they lost, could well turn toward building their own defenses in the event that the US guarantee were removed. That's why I say that where Taiwan is concerned, and I would add where Korea is concerned, the US policy is opposed to Japan moving in as the US moves out, but we cannot guarantee that. And if we had no defense arrangement with Japan, we would have no influence where that is concerned.[135]

In essence, as Nixon wrote, "It is a US Japan policy with a US veto."[136] On the other hand, as the NSC suggested, "[i]f Japan feels abandoned, it could follow a much more dangerous course."[137] There were basically two possible directions for Japan, either toward China or toward the Soviet Union "for nuclear protection."[138] During the direct talks, Nixon thus explained the essential implications of the US role in East Asia as: "the US will use its influence with Japan and those other countries where we have a defense relationship or provide economic assistance, to discourage policies which would be detrimental to China."[139] In other words, Nixon sought to persuade Zhou for the continuation of the US military presence, as he wrote: "Our friendship with Japan is in your interests – not against."[140]

Premier Zhou estimated that Japan, as an emerging economic great power, was "at the crossroads." Zhou thus warned: "Since their development has been at such a great rate the result is bound to be expansion abroad. Expanding in such a great way as they are toward foreign lands, the inevitable result will be military expansion."[141] Moreover, Zhou insisted that once reaching "a certain point," Japan would "cease listening to" the US and begin to pursue its own path.[142] In response, Nixon gave assurance that the US policy was, to the extent possible, to "restrain the Japanese from going from economic expansion to military expansion."[143]

Regarding Beijing's diplomatic relations with Tokyo, Zhou emphasized the remaining historical antagonism and "a state of war" between China and Japan.[144]

---

135 Memcon February 22, 1972, p. 12.
136 Nixon's handwritten notations, February 15, 1972, p. 5, China Notes, Alpha/Subject File, Box 7, PPF, WHSF, NPMS, NA.
137 Japan, Points to Emphasize, p. 1, Underline by Nixon in original, Book V-a, The President, Briefing Papers for the China Trip, FPF/Lord, Box 847, NSCF, NPMS, NA.
138 Nixon's handwritten notations, February 15, 1972, p. 5, China Notes, Alpha/Subject File, Box 7, PPF, WHSF, NPMS, NA.
139 Memcon February 22, 1972, p. 12.
140 Nixon's handwritten notations, February 21, 1972, p. 16, China Notes, Alpha/Subject File, Box 7, PPF, WHSF, NPMS, NA.
141 Memorandum of conversation February 23, 1972, 2:00–6.00pm (hereafter referred to as Memcon February 23, 1972), p. 18.
142 Ibid., p. 19.
143 Ibid., pp. 19–20.
144 Ibid.

However, Zhou also hinted that: "if China and Japan are able to restore diplomatic relations, Chinese-Japanese friendship [sic] should not hurt the relations between Japan and the United States."[145]

In the joint communiqué, the US side declared that:

> The United States places the highest value on its friendly relations with Japan; it will continue to develop the existing bonds.[146]

The phrase "the existing bonds" implied a broad relationship, including the US-Japan Security Treaty. It was a crucial reassurance for the maintenance of the US presence in the Asia-Pacific region. On the other hand, the Chinese side maintained that:

> It firmly opposes the revival of and outward expansion of Japanese militarism and firmly supports the Japanese people's desire to build an independent, democratic, peaceful and neutral Japan.[147]

The Chinese statement reflected its long-term opposition to the revival of Japanese military expansionism.

Overall, the US gave assurance that it would attempt to discourage the designs of the Japanese if they pursued an expansionist policy. In response, China gave its private approval of the US continuous presence in the Asia-Pacific region. For both sides, a Japan closely allied with the United States and diplomatically related to China was more preferable to its pursuit of an independent defense policy.

3.2.4 The India-Pakistan rivalry

The NSC staff's briefing book explained that Beijing had "wanted to strengthen Pakistan as a power rival to China's great opponent in the subcontinent, India."[148] Therefore, the US and the PRC had "parallel interests in coping with expanded Soviet influence in the subcontinent."[149] In his comments, Nixon wrote:

> Moscow seeks a dominant role in India –
> US help to India would blunt this role –[150]

On February 15, while reviewing the briefing books, Nixon wrote his concerns:

> Need for US to be strong as counter to Soviet –

---

145 Ibid. However, Zhou remained suspicious of the Sato Cabinet's pro-Taiwan attitude. Hence, the Chinese did not make any substantial diplomatic move until Kakuei Tanaka's new cabinet came to power in June 1972, as the Epilogue of this book later discusses.
146 *The New York Times*, February 28, 1972.
147 Ibid.
148 South Asia, p. 1, underline by Nixon in original, Book V, The President, Briefing Papers for the China Trip, FPF/Lord, Box 847, NSCF, NPMS, NA.
149 Ibid., p. 3. Underline by Nixon in original.
150 Ibid. Nixon's handwritten note on a paper between page 3 and page 4.

India shows – if a vacuum
They will fill it.[151]

During the direct talks, Nixon sought to stress the expansion of the Soviet military threat in the subcontinent: "India is no threat to China, but India supported by the Soviet Union is a very present threat to China."[152] Thus, Nixon explained that during the India-Pakistan war of December 1971, "we were speaking not just to India or Pakistan but also – and we made them well aware of it – to the Soviet Union."[153] Accordingly, Nixon sought to develop further cooperation with China in the subcontinent: "our policies in the subcontinent go together.... we don't want to make movement with respect to India and Pakistan unless you are fully informed, because we believe your interest here is greater than ours."[154] Finally, Nixon revealed to Zhou that during the December 1971 war, he was "prepared to warn the Soviet Union against undertaking an attack on China."[155]

In essence, while Nixon sought to re-affirm a get-tough policy against any further Soviet advancement in the subcontinent in order to protect US credibility in the world, Zhou still viewed the growth of the India-Soviet relationship as a major step toward the encirclement of China. Together, the two sides were principally concerned about the expansion of India's hegemonic aspiration to establish "a great Indian empire" backed by the Soviet Union.[156] Hence, the two sides would coordinate their policies and "go in tandem," in Nixon's words, to counterbalance the India-Soviet aspiration in South Asia.[157] Thereafter, the India-Pakistan rivalry became less of an urgent issue between the two sides.[158]

3.2.5 The Soviet military threat

The handling of the Soviet threat in the direct talks with the Chinese required diplomatic subtlety. While reviewing the NSC briefing book, Nixon underlined the following specific point of reality: "Although the Soviet Union is the PRC's major reason for seeking better relations with us (and although they know we know that), they will, of course, never acknowledge the fact."[159] Thus, Nixon anticipated that the Chinese leaders would still try to show their self-reliance against the Soviets.

---

151 Nixon's handwritten notations, underline by Nixon in original, February 15, 1972, p. 2, China Notes, Alpha/Subject File, Box 7, PPF, WHSF, NPMS, NA.
152 Memcon February 22, pp. 10–11.
153 Ibid., p. 11.
154 Ibid.
155 Memcon February 23, p. 21.
156 Ibid., p. 10. Kissinger provided intelligence reports on New Delhi's arms purchase from Moscow. Ibid., p. 9.
157 Nixon's handwritten notations, February 21, 1972, p. 16, China Notes, Alpha/Subject File, Box 7, PPF, WHSF, NPMS, NA.
158 During the rest of his term in office, President Nixon visited neither India nor Pakistan again. He also never visited Bangladesh.
159 The Soviet Union, p. 2, underline by Nixon in original, Book V, The President, Briefing Papers for the China Trip, FPF/Lord, Box 847, NSCF, NPMS, NA.

Regarding the deepening Sino-Soviet mutual hostility, Nixon wrote: "We will treat with even handedness[.]"[160] Before his arrival in Beijing, Nixon outlined his policy:

Russia:
1. Maintain balance of power –
2. Restrain their expansion (if our interests are involved)
3. Try to reduce tension between us
4. Not make them irritated at you –
5. Make no deal with them we don't offer to you
   Will inform you in all details[161]

While preparing talks with Zhou, Nixon wrote: "Can be no vacuum in the world[.]"[162] In the direct talks, Nixon thus stressed the importance of the continuing presence of the world's two superpowers: "in terms of the safety of these nations which are not superpowers in the world, they will be much safer if there are two superpowers, rather than just one."[163] Nixon warned that if the US fell into a position of weakness, it would raise a credibility problem in terms of its "shield of protection" for its allies.[164] Thus, the United States must maintain its military strength at least to be in a "position of equality" with the Soviets.[165]

In response, Zhou explained the danger of the full encirclement of China: "The worst possibility is… that you all would attack China – the Soviet Union comes from the north, Japanese and the US from the east, and India into China's Tibet."[166] Accordingly, Nixon sought to assure Zhou that the US "would oppose any attempt by the Soviet Union to engage in aggressive action against China."[167] Moreover, Nixon made it clear that while the US would continue arms control talks with the Soviets, it would put both China and the Soviets on "an absolutely equal footing."[168]

---

160 Nixon's handwritten notations, in Ibid., p. 6.
161 Nixon's handwritten notations, February 21, 1972, p. 16, China Notes, Alpha/Subject File, Box 7, PPF, WHSF, NPMS, NA.
162 Nixon's handwritten notations, February 22, 1972, China, Speech Files, Box 72, China Trip, PPF, WHSF, NPMS, NA.
163 Memcon 22 February 1972., p. 9.
164 Ibid., p. 10. Nixon offered Zhou a briefing by Kissinger on "very sensitive material" on the position of the Soviet forces against China. Ibid. Accordingly, "on a very restricted basis," Kissinger briefed Zhou with "a list of all the negotiations" which the US was conducting with the Soviet Union as well as "some information on dangers" the US and China might confront in "the military field." Memcon, Kissinger and Zhou, February 21, 1972, 4:15–5:30pm, p. 2, Dr. Kissinger's Meetings in the People's Republic During the Presidential Visit February 1972, CF-Far East, HAKOF, NSCF, NPMS, NA. In reality, the Soviets knew "as a fact" that when Kissinger visited Beijing for the first time, he handed over to the Chinese "American satellite pictures of Soviet installations along the Sino-Soviet border." Memo from John Scali to Kissinger, March 8, 1972, p. 1, Box 501, China Trip – February–March 1972 [Part 1], PTF, NSCF, NPMS, NA.
165 Ibid., p. 11.
166 Ibid., p. 18.
167 Memcon February 23, 1972, p. 21.
168 Ibid, p. 22.

More particularly, Nixon reiterated the US intention to respect China's interests vis-à-vis the Soviets: "under no circumstances will I negotiate about or discuss our relations with the People's Republic of China without his [Zhou's] approval or knowledge."[169]

Regarding the restoration of stability in the Asia-Pacific region, Nixon wrote on his yellow pad: "Neither seeks Hegemony."[170] In the direct talks, Nixon and Zhou discussed a new principle.

> Premier Zhou: ... [N]either of us should seek hegemony in the Asia-Pacific region. And that would not only imply our two countries should not seek hegemony in this region, but that Japan should not either.
>
> President Nixon: And the Soviet Union.
>
> Premier Zhou: That's right. Nor the Soviet Union.
>
> President Nixon: Nor India.
>
> Premier Zhou: That's right. Here implies that both will try to do good things, not do bad things.
>
> President Nixon: Let me clarify. It implies that neither of our two sides should seek hegemony. It also implies, to the extent that each of us can, that we will resist efforts of others to seek hegemony. In that what it means?
>
> Premier Zhou: Yes, that is, we oppose any efforts by another country.[171]

In other words, Nixon and Zhou sought to apply the so-called "anti-hegemony clause" not only to the United States and China, but also to the Soviet Union, Japan, and India in order to prevent any potential threat from expanding its influence in the Asia-Pacific region. Equally important, Zhou was fully aware of the Soviet sensitivity to the idea of Sino-US collusion: "They claim that our two sides are discussing how to oppose the Soviet Union, to conclude an anti-Soviet alliance."[172] Hence, Zhou clarified: "neither is prepared to negotiate on behalf of third countries or enter into agreements or understanding directed at other states."[173] Together, the US and China sought to impose restraints on the great powers in the Asia-Pacific region.

---

169   Ibid., p. 36; and The Soviet Union, Points to Emphasize, p. 1, Book V-a, The President, Briefing Papers for the China Trip, FPF/Lord, Box 847, NSCF, NPMS, NA.

170   Nixon's handwritten notations, February 24, 1972, China, Speech Files, Box 73, China Trip, PPF, WHSF, NPMS, NA.

171   Memcon February 24, 1972, pp. 3–4.

172   Ibid., p. 3.

173   Ibid., p. 4.

4. Reactions to the February 1972 Summit

4.1 The Shanghai communiqué

At the end of the February 1972 summit, the two sides released the so-called Shanghai Communiqué. Following the formula developed in the October 1971 talks, the joint communiqué took a unique approach in clarifying both the new common grounds and the remaining historical differences.[174] The two sides jointly declared the five principles of peaceful coexistence as the fundamental basis of state relations, namely "the principles of respect for the sovereignty and territorial integrity of all states, non-aggression against other states, non-interference in the internal affairs of other states, equality and mutual benefit, and peaceful coexistence."[175] Finally, both sides clarified the common interest in the materialization of diplomatic normalization.

While preparing his statement for the final banquet in Shanghai on February 27, Nixon wrote: "We have changed the world – But it is only a beginning[.]"[176] Upon his return to Washington, Nixon made a public statement:

> As a result of this trip, we have started the long process of building a bridge across that gulf of almost 12,000 miles and 22 years of non-communication and hostility … We have demonstrated that nations with very deep and fundamental differences can learn to discuss those differences calmly, rationally, and frankly, without compromising their principles.[177]

In essence, Nixon emphasized the new characteristics of the US relations with China, namely the beginning of the long process to establish substantial communication after two decades of mutual hostility.

4.2 Foreign reactions

Even while staying in China, Nixon and Kissinger developed concerns about possible reactions to the summit. On February 27, Haig, who stayed in Washington, sent a memo on initial reactions. In short, the traveling press corps and reports from foreign capitals had been "positive and objective."[178] Anticipating wide speculation

---

174 *The New York Times*, February 28, 1972. The communiqué was issued on February 27 at Chinese local time. For the full text of the Shanghai Communiqué, see Appendix.

175 Ibid.

176 Nixon's handwritten notations, February 27, 1972, Shanghai, Speech Files, Box 73, China Trip, PPF, WHSF, NPMS, NA. Nixon declared in his toast: "This was the week that changed the world," with a conviction that the two governments were committed to "build a bridge" across the Pacific after 22 years of mutual hostility. Max Frankel, "China Visit Ends: President Presents a Pledge to Build Pacific 'Bridge,'" *The New York Times*, February 28, 1972.

177 Return to Washington, February 28, 1972, *Weekly Compilation of Presidential Documents*, February 28, 1972, The President's Trip to China, pp. 483–484, Box 86, US China Policy 1969–1972 [2 of 2], CF-Far East, HAKOF, NSCF, NPMS, NA.

178 Haig to Kissinger, "Initial Reactions to Communiqué and briefing," February 27, 1972, p. 1, Box 88, China – President's Trip February 15–29, 1972, CF-Far East, HAKOF, NSCF, NPMS, NA.

especially in Asia, President Nixon decided to send Assistant Secretary of State for East Asian and Pacific Affairs Marshall Green, and NSC staff member John Holdridge to brief US allies in the Asia-Pacific region.[179] The main purpose of their mission was to assure allied leaders that "we will remain true to our commitments and have struck no secret deals."[180]

The Republic of China expressed its "surprise and shock" by the US statement in the communiqué on its future withdrawal from Taiwan.[181] Taipei also demonstrated "strong disapproval" of the Chinese positions in the joint communiqué. Importantly, however, the statement "avoided any invective" toward the United States or the Americans.[182] After the initial shock over the communiqué, Taipei was "still highly apprehensive" of US "long-term intentions."[183] The Green-Holdridge mission appeared to have "reassured" the ROC that the US defense commitment was "intact for the present." Nevertheless, the Chinese Nationalist officials still wondered whether the long-run US strategy might "not be to preserve the appearance of adherence to its commitment."[184]

In Japan, Foreign Minister Takeo Fukuda described the President's trip as "fruitful" and stated that it would serve as a "lubricant" for Japan to normalize its relations with China.[185] The Japanese Government, "fearful of being undermined" by the Nixon trip, reacted with an "almost visible relief" to the limited concrete achievement in the joint communiqué.[186] On the other hand, some Japanese critics called the trip a "betrayal" by the United States and blamed Prime Minister Eisaku Sato for having been "outstripped" by Washington in forming ties with Beijing.

---

179 Green, *Evolution of US-China Policy*, Oral History Interview, pp. 41–45, FAOHC. The Green-Holdridge mission included visits to Japan, South Korea, Taiwan, South Vietnam, the Philippines, Indonesia, Singapore, Malaysia, Thailand, Australia, and New Zealand. See also Holdridge, *Crossing the Divide*, pp. 97–102.

180 Haig to Nixon, "Summary of Foreign Reactions to Your Trip to China," March 24, 1972, p. 1, Box 501, China Trip – February–March 1972 [Part 2], PTF, NSCF, NPMS, NA.

181 Haig to Kissinger, "Initial Reactions to Communiqué and briefing," February 27, 1972, p. 1, Box 501, China Trip – February–March 1972 [Part 2], PTF, NSCF, NPMS, NA.

182 Tillman Durdin, "Taipei says Nixon's Trip Will Not Result in Peace," February 29, 1972, *The New York Times*.

183 Haig to Nixon, "Summary of Foreign Reactions," March 24, 1972, p. 1, Box 501, China Trip – February–March 1972 [Part 2], PTF, NSCF, NPMS, NA.

184 Ibid.

185 Haig to Kissinger, "Initial Reactions to Communiqué and briefing," February 27, 1972, p. 1, Box 88, China – President's Trip February 15–29, 1972, CF-Far East, HAKOF, NSCF, NPMS, NA.

186 John M. Lee, "Tokyo Is Relieved By Limited Result," February 28, 1972, *The New York Times*. Green gave assurance to the Japanese Government that President Nixon had made "no secret deals" with the Chinese leaders. Green conveyed Nixon's personal letter to Sato reassuring that Japan "remained a key ally" of the US Green also assured Fukuda that US delegation refused to accept Chinese charges of a "revival of Japanese militarism." Green, *Evolution of US-China Policy*, Oral History Interview, p. 41, FAOHC.

The Western media reported that the Soviets were "fearfully of some new power grouping directed against Moscow."[187] The Soviet press agency *Tass* reported that there remained "essential differences" between China and the United States on foreign policy issues and in their social systems. *Tass* also noted that the joint communiqué stated some of their views with "insufficient clarity." For nearly three weeks, the Soviet government itself withheld official comment, confining itself to a "cautious" and equivocal reaction expressing "suspicion of possible US-PRC secret arrangements."[188]

The general reaction in Saigon, in South Vietnam, appeared to be "cautious and favorable."[189] "We felt at ease," reportedly stated a senior official of South Vietnamese Foreign Ministry. On the contrary, despite Premier Zhou's trip to Hanoi immediately after Nixon's departure from China, the North Vietnamese were "bitter and disenchanted."[190] The most negative reaction came from India, where there was a "tendency to read the worst possible into the trip," namely a "new balance of forces" that would "circumscribe Indian freedom of action."[191] In contrast, Pakistani reaction to the trip was "strongly positive," and the communiqué was "welcomed."[192]

In sum, most Asian states were "publicly approving" of the trip and privately became "less apprehensive" as a result of the assurance given by the Green-Holdridge mission.[193] Many Asian capitals came to believe that they "must begin adapting their policies to a changing international context."[194] However, there was a wide-spread belief in Asia that there were "secret agreements or understanding" in Beijing that were "left out of the communiqué."[195] In particular, there still remained "uncertainty" among Asian states over whether the US had "loosened its commitment" to defend its allies.[196]

4.3 Briefing on the domestic front

After his return to Washington, President Nixon conducted extensive briefings on the trip. On February 29, 1972, Nixon met the bipartisan Congressional leaders in the Cabinet Room of the White House to discuss his trip to China. Nixon pointed out two lessons for the future. First, the Chinese had reiterated that they were "not a super

---

187 "Soviet Shows Relief At Results of Talks," February 29, 1972, *The New York Times*.

188 Haig to Nixon, "Summary of Foreign Reactions," March 24, 1972, p. 3, Box 501, China Trip – February–March 1972 [Part 2], PTF, NSCF, NPMS, NA.

189 Craig R. Whitney, "Saigon Pleased By Communiqué," February 28, 1972, *The New York Times*.

190 Haig to Nixon, "Summary of Foreign Reactions," March 24, 1972, p. 2, Box 501, China Trip – February–March 1972 [Part 2], PTF, NSCF, NPMS, NA.

191 Ibid., p. 4.

192 Ibid.

193 Ibid., p. 1.

194 Ibid.

195 *The New York Times*, February 29, 1972.

196 Ibid.

power."[197] However, the President stressed that: "750 million Chinese Communists are something to be reckoned with. Consequently, they are destined to become a major force."[198] Second, the US relationship with China was "a very delicate one," which required building upon "trust," assuring that: "We are reliable, we are strong and we will continue to build for the future."[199]

During a Cabinet meeting on the same day, Nixon emphasized: "[W]e both agreed we will not resort to the threat of force or the use of force in international relations and with each other. We agreed that no nation should dominate Asia. This is the heart of the communiqué."[200] Kissinger also explained that what the President had done was to "set a major new direction."[201] Finally, when asked a question about the most important thing to the Chinese, Nixon replied "[c]old blooded interest, [n]ot friendship":

> They see the Soviet Union, India, Japan – with all of them, each in its way, encircling them – so they need somebody who is not antagonistic. They know the Soviets have more men on the Chinese frontier than against Western Europe. As for Japan, history has to give them some pause. With India, they've had a little squabble. As for the United States, first, we're long way off; and second, while they would never state publicly that India, Russia and Japan have designs on them, they know very well, I think, that we don't."[202]

It was Nixon's realization of the Chinese perception of threat regarding full encirclement that drove the entire initiative of rapprochement.

Shambaugh argues that the Chinese were approaching the United States "not out of the question of balance of power but out of the self-survival."[203] The Chinese leaders believed that the Soviet Union would really attack them. Therefore, they thought that the United States could be a "counterweight and perhaps even help to defend China if it were attacked." Shambaugh thus assesses that the balance of power between the US, the Soviets and China was "the consequence rather than the motivation" of the opening.[204] Beijing's motivation was "very much fear of the military attack," and thus the Chinese wanted to "put pressure on the Soviet Union from another flank."[205]

As for the balancing dynamic in Asia, Solomon assesses that the United States, allied to various Asian countries, such as Japan, South Korea, and Taiwan, was checking the expansion of China." However, the Chinese at that point were

---

197 Tom C. Korologos (via, William E. Timmons), "Meeting with Bipartisan Leadership February 29, 1972, 10:00am The Cabinet Room," p. 3, MemforP, ROM, Box 88, POF, WHCF, NPMS, NA.

198 Ibid., p. 5.

199 Ibid.

200 Raymond K. Price, Jr., "Cabinet Meeting, February 29, 1972, 12:02pm–1:20pm," p. 7, MemforP, ROM, Box 88, POF, WHCF, NPMS, NA.

201 Ibid., p. 18.

202 Ibid., pp. 21–22. Underline in original.

203 David Shambaugh, interview with the author, October 15, 2003.

204 Ibid. Shambaugh argues further that balance of power relates to "shifting correlates and weights of power either in the region or in the globe." Ibid.

205 Ibid.

principally worried about the Soviet Union and did not see the United States as their primary threat.

Finally, Nixon and Kissinger viewed that "if we can not resolve our strategic difference with China, then a nuclear-armed China is going to be a big threat. We already got one threat from the Soviet Union. So, it was strategically important to neutralize the threat from China." In his meeting with Mao, Nixon clarified that there was no fundamental strategic conflict between China and the US, which became his way of saying "We do not want to have a confrontation with another nuclear power."[206]

---

206   Solomon, interview with the author, September 24, 2003.

Epilogue

Personalized Diplomacy

The February 1972 summit promoted dynamism and optimism in the relations between the US and China for the rest of the year and the first half of 1973.[1] One of the principal consequences of the pursuit of strict secrecy by Nixon and Kissinger was the development of a highly personalized diplomatic practice. A China specialist in the NSC staff, Richard Solomon, emphasized the importance of "personalized diplomacy" during the "transitional period" before the US relations with China were "institutionalised."[2] A highly significant factor was that Kissinger developed a "notable degree of personal rapport" with Premier Zhou. Thus, timing became very important, as "changes in key personnel" were likely to require "further visitations," and thus possibly delaying progress toward normalization.[3] In other words, to the US advantage, "the degree of mutual personal respect" was a key ingredient in "breaking down the distrust of the past," and in "generating a degree of confidence." Finally, therefore, Solomon suggested that it was in the US's vital interest to "consolidate the political gains" "before Mao and Chou pass from the scene."[4]

Kissinger "really was impressed" by Mao and Zhou for their "intelligence and charisma." During his trips to China from 1972 to 1975, Kissinger shared "a strategic view of international affairs" with the Chinese leaders and found it was "exciting and interesting to have encounters with them." [5] Thus, as a former State Department official, Donald Anderson recalls, Kissinger "retained a very direct interest in China" that set the tone that shaped the way the US interacted with China.[6] Within the US

---

1   As for the US relations with China in the mid 1970s, see Robert Ross, *Negotiating Cooperation: The United States and China 1969–1989* (Stanford, California: Stanford University Press, 1995), chapter 4; Patrick E. Tyler, *A Great Wall: Six Presidents and China, an Investigative History* (New York: Public Affairs, 1999), pp. 183–225; and James H. Mann, *About Face: A History of America's Curious Relationship with China from Nixon to Clinton* (New York: Alfled Knopf, 1999), chapter 3.

2   Solomon (via John Holdridge) to Kissinger, "Impressions of Peking and its Politics," June 28, 1972, Country Files (CF)–Far East, Box 97, Henry A. Kissinger Office Files (HAKOF), National Security Council Files (NSCF), Nixon Presidential Materials Staff (NPMS), National Archives (NA).

3   Ibid., p. 2.

4   Ibid.

5   Richard Solomon, interview with the author, September 24, 2003.

6   Donald Anderson (Talks with Chinese American Embassy Paris, France, 1972–1973, Political Officer, American Liaison Office Beijing, China, 1973–1975, Political Officer, American Consulate General Hong Kong, 1975–1977), Oral History Interview, p. 13, in *A*

government, there was an atmosphere that, as long as Kissinger was in charge of foreign policy decision-making in dealing with China, the US would focus on "the big picture and the strategic relationship" rather than the details of the bilateral relations. However, US officials, especially those in the State Department, were increasingly feeling that the US was "giving away things" that it did not need to give to China.[7]

Following Nixon's landslide re-election victory in November 1972, Kissinger and the NSC staff estimated that "we now had four years to deal with each other, building up a certain mutual trust. ...The Chinese knew that they would have four more years to deal with a strong leader."[8] Thus, Kissinger and the NSC staff anticipated that the Chinese leaders would be willing to "accelerate the normalization and institutionalisation" of the US-PRC bilateral relations.[9] Importantly, however, as Kissinger reported to Nixon, "we have no assurance that the PRC will continue its policy toward us when Mao and Chou depart."[10] In other words, US officials were aware that there was an opposition by the radical group in China toward the opening to the United States, and only that Mao and Zhou appeared to be capable of restraining the criticisms of those rebels.

By late 1973, the Watergate scandal was damaging Nixon's presidential authority, and, according to Lord, it had "tremendous impact on foreign policy in general."[11] The NSC staff came to perceive "greater aloofness and lack of cooperation" from the Chinese at the operational level.[12] Owing to "policy and philosophical differences," Beijing opposed Washington's attempt to improve the mere "appearance" of bilateral relations.[13] A former NSC staff member, Peter Rodman, recalls that Kissinger "did not see how he could function in any way at all without the presidential authority. He did not think he could survive, or the policies he believed in could survive, unless he had institutional base of the State Department."[14] Thus, after he was sworn-in as the

---

China Reader, Vol. III, January 1995, Foreign Affairs Oral History Collection (FAOHC), Association for Diplomatic Studies and Training, Lauinger Library, Georgetown University.

7 Ibid.
8 Winston Lord, interview with the author, October 15, 2003.
9 Kissinger to Nixon, "My Trip to China," March 2, 1973, p. 1, HAK China Trip – February 1973 Memcons and Reports (originals), Box 98, HAK Trip Files, HAKOF, NSCF, NPMS, NA.
10 Kissinger to Nixon, "My Visit to China," November 19, 1973, p. 3, China-Sensitive WL File Misc and Reports November 1974, Box 374, Records of Policy Planning Staff (PPS), Director's Files (Winston Lord), 1969–1977, General Record of the Department of State, Record Group 59 (RG59), NA. By late 1973, Zhou's health was declining. However, US officials were not yet sufficiently aware of Zhou's fatal illness. See, for example, Zhisui Li, *The Private Life of Chairman Mao: The Memoirs of Mao's personal physician* (London: Arrow Books, 1994), pp. 604–608.
11 Lord, interview with the author, October 15, 2003.
12 Solomon to Kissinger, "The PRC's Domestic Political Situation and Foreign Policy as a Context for Your Meeting with Deng Tsiao-p'ing and Ch'iao Kuan-hua," April 12, 1974, Box 376, China – Sensitive – February–April 1974, PPS-Lord, RG59, NA.
13 Ibid.
14 Peter Rodman, Oral History Interview, July 22, and August 22, 1994, p. 55, FAOHC.

Secretary of State in September 1973, Kissinger sought to pursue more personalized and secretive relations with the aging Chinese leaders.[15] It appeared, however, that the Watergate scandal "puzzled" the Chinese.[16] It was difficult for the Chinese to comprehend why the leader of a superpower could be so vulnerable to domestic criticisms. The NSC staff estimated that the Chinese leaders increased their doubt as to whether Nixon could still be in a position to "act in a strong manner in foreign policy" and to make "further major initiatives" in the normalization process.[17]

On August 8, 1974, President Nixon resigned from the Oval Office, elevating Gerald R. Ford to presidential power.[18] It was the pursuit of strict secrecy that materialized the US rapprochement with China; ironically, however, it was also the excessive secrecy that destroyed the Nixon presidency as a whole. During the Ford presidency, it was principally Secretary Kissinger who sought to negotiate with the aging Chinese leaders in order to explore "their continued presence on the scene as leaders, and to discuss in concrete terms which we have in mind."[19] In other words, Kissinger estimated that as long as Mao and Zhou and held a strong grip of power over foreign policy decision-making, it would be more manageable for the US to continue diplomatic communication with China toward full normalization.

Conflicts in Indochina

After the February 1972 summit, the Vietnam War remained the predominant issue that hindered US relations with China.[20] During Kissinger's visit to Beijing in June 1972, Zhou took a "hands-off attitude" regarding the military and in negotiating questions in Indochina.[21] Kissinger judged that while Beijing was not letting Vietnam block US-China bilateral relations, the Chinese would be "less willing" than the Russians to "exert actual pressure" on Hanoi to be reasonable at the negotiating table.[22] Although Beijing was putting the Vietnam issue aside in order to improve its diplomatic relations with Washington, it appeared that the Chinese leaders were not necessarily actively supporting the US leaders toward a negotiated settlement

---

15   Kissinger held his position as Assistant to the President for National Security Affairs until October 1975, when he was replaced by his deputy Brent Scowcroft.

16   Richard Solomon, interview with the author, September 24, 2003.

17   Solomon to Kissinger, "Peking Sends the US Some Warning Signals," February 16, 1974, China Exchanges 1 November 1973–March 31, Box 330, PPS-Lord, RG59, NA.

18   As for the fall of the Nixon presidency, see, for example, Richard Reeves, *President Nixon: Alone in the White House* (New York: Simon & Schuster, 2001), pp. 604–609; and Walter Isaacson, *Kissinger: Biography* (New York: McGraw-Hill, 1992), pp. 592–606.

19   Kissinger to Ford, "Commitments to the People's Republic of China," August 14, 1974, Box 371, PPS-Lord, RG59, NA. As for Kissinger's reassessment of the Ford Presidency, see Henry A. Kissinger, *Years of Renewal* (New York: Little Brown, 1999), pp. 169–191.

20   Kissinger to Nixon, "My Trip to Peking, June 19–23, 1972," June 27, 1972, p. 2, CF-Far East, Box 97, HAKOF, NSCF, NPMS, NA. As for the Nixon-Kissinger strategy toward the Vietnam settlement, see Jeffrey Kimball, *Nixon's Vietnam War* (Lawrence, Kansas: The University Press of Kansas, 1998), pp. 368–371.

21   Ibid., p. 3.

22   Ibid., pp. 3–4.

between the US and North Vietnam. Kissinger estimated further that while the Chinese would approve the US course of action toward a ceasefire, withdrawal, and "leaving the political solution to the Vietnamese alone," it was North Vietnam that was still "reluctant to rely upon it."[23] Therefore, in his report to Nixon, Kissinger concluded that the US could "not expect to solve the Vietnam issue" in Beijing.[24]

On January 17, 1973, the United States and North Vietnam finally agreed upon what became the Paris Peace Accords – US-Vietnamese Armistice Agreement.[25] Henceforth, the US and China came to share the principal interest in Indochina: neither side wished for North Vietnam to fulfill its regional hegemonic aspiration. Rodman recalls that Chinese leaders supported the Paris agreement because they were "happy to have Vietnam divided."[26] In reality, however, the radicals' criticisms of Zhou in China increased after the failure of a joint Sino-US agreement in Cambodia to establish a neutral coalition government under Prince Sihanouk bringing together the Lon Nol regime and the Khmer Rouge.[27] After the collapse of the Nixon presidency, the United States failed to prevent the fall of the Cambodian regime; Khmer Rouge captured Phnom Penh on April 17, 1975 and replaced the Lon Nol regime. On April 30, North Vietnamese troops captured Saigon, defeating the remaining South Vietnamese and expanding its aspiration in Indochina. In consequence, as Kissinger reported to Ford, the collapse of the Indochina policy had "created a context where any major change in our relationship with Taiwan which implied the abandonment of yet another ally would be unacceptable."[28]

The Soviet Military Threat

Winston Lord recalls that the opening to China "had a particularly strong short-term impact on the Soviet behavior."[29] As US-China diplomatic relations improved, the Soviet Union also sought to speed up its dialogue with the United States. Nixon's presidential trip to Moscow from May 22 to 29, 1972 symbolized détente – an era of negotiation, resulting in the SALT I Treaty and the Agreement and Declaration

---

23 Ibid., p. 5. Underline in original.
24 Ibid., p. 6.
25 Berman argues that despite the terms "peace with honor," Nixon and Kissinger never believed in the peace settlement. They expected North Vietnam to violate it, which would enable the US to continuing bombing without Congressional interference. Hence, Nixon and Kissinger reportedly believed that the US could return with air power in order to avoid being criticized for the "loss" of war. See Larry Berman, *No Peace, No Honor: Nixon, Kissinger, and Betrayal in Vietnam* (New York: The Free Press, 2001).
26 Peter Rodman, interview with the author, October 21, 2003.
27 Ross, *Negotiating Cooperation*, pp. 61–62; Henry A. Kissinger, *Years of Upheavals* (Boston: Little Brown, 1982), pp. 344–355, and pp. 678–681; and Qiang Zhai, *China and the Vietnam Wars, 1950–1975* (Chapel Hill, NC: The University of North Carolina Press, 2000), p. 221.
28 Kissinger to Ford, "Your Trip to the People's Republic of China: A Scope Analysis," November 20, 1975, Box 380, PPS-Lord, RG59, NA.
29 Lord, interview with the author, October 15, 2003.

on Basic Principles of US-USSR relations.[30] During his trip to Beijing in June 1972, Kissinger gave long briefings to Zhou on Nixon's recent talks with the Soviet leaders in Moscow. Kissinger particularly stressed that the US was "not joining in any agreements" that might be directed against China and was "keeping them [Chinese leaders] fully informed."[31] In his report to Nixon, Kissinger argued that the "existence of Soviet global ambitions" remained China's "main preoccupation and principal motive" for moving ahead with the United States.[32] Thus, Kissinger sought to "play the ominous Soviet themes" with the Chinese.[33]

Kissinger assessed that it was striking the degree to which the Chinese had moved from an "adversary posture" to one that could be described as a "tacit ally."[34] More particularly, Kissinger also interpreted that the Chinese were "trying to build walls around the Soviet Union" by opening to the US, encouraging a "united Europe as a counterweight" in the west, moving toward Japan in the east, and trying to "contain India" – a "tool of Soviet encirclement" – by supporting an "independent Pakistan" in the south.[35] Thus, Kissinger reminded Nixon that "only a strong United States" was of use to them, and that they would seek the balance which the US would provide.[36]

In his report to Nixon after his trip to Beijing in February 1973, Kissinger evaluated the current nature of US-PRC relations: "The Chinese leaders are among the very few in the world with a global and longer term perspective – and it now parallels ours in many important respects."[37] In November 1973, Kissinger and Zhou completed a new communiqué, which extended the joint opposition to hegemony to anywhere in the world, beyond the Asia-Pacific region.[38] As Kissinger reported to Nixon, the Chinese crucial calculation was "the steadiness and strength of America

---

30 In June 1973, Brezhnev visited Washington DC for the second summit, bringing about an agreement calling for the Prevention of Nuclear War. For the development of US-USSR relations, see William Bundy, *A Tangled Web: The Making of Foreign Policy in the Nixon Presidency* (New York: Hill and Wang, A Division of Farrar, Straus and Gioux, 1998), pp. 322–327.

31 Memcon, Kissinger and Zhou, June 20, 1972, 2:05–6:05pm, p. 20, p. 27, CF-Far East, Box 97, HAKOF, NSCF, NPMS, NA.

32 Kissinger to Nixon, "My Trip to Peking, June 19–23, 1972," June 27, 1972, p. 2, p. 8, CF-Far East, Box 97, HAKOF, NSCF, NPMS, NA. Following the Moscow summit of May 1972, Kissinger visited Beijing from June 19 to 23, 1972. Interestingly, however, Kissinger fails to refer to this trip in his memoirs.

33 Ibid.

34 Ibid., p. 2.

35 Ibid., p. 9, and p. 12; and Memcon, Kissinger and Zhou, p. 27, June 20, 1972, 2:05–6:05pm, Country Files – Far East, Box 97, HAKOF, NSCF, NPMS, NA.

36 Ibid.

37 Kissinger to Nixon, "My Trip to China," March 2, 1973, p. 3, HAK China Trip – February 1973 Memcons and Reports (originals), Box 98, HAK Trip Files, HAKOF, NSCF, NPMS, NA. Kissinger thus concluded: "For in plain terms, we have now become tacit allies." Ibid., p. 2, underline in original.

38 Kissinger to Nixon, "My Visit to China," November 19, 1973, p. 1, China-Sensitive WL File Misc and Reports November 1974, Box 374, PPS, RG59, NA. See also Kissinger, *Years of Upheaval*, p. 697.

as a counterweight."[39] Nixon commented: "K – the key."[40] From the mid-1970s, the promotion of the so-called "tacit alliance" would become one of the central issues in US relations with China.[41]

The Chinese leaders, however, still remained suspicious of the possible collusion between the two superpowers against the PRC. In February 1973, Mao warned Kissinger that the whole of the West intended "to push Russia eastward."[42] Mao and Zhou also criticized that the US wanted "to reach out to the Soviets by standing on Chinese shoulders."[43] By late 1973, the NSC staff saw an increasing sign that the Chinese leaders did not fully trust Kissinger, especially in terms of the issue of "who is using whom" against the Soviet Union, which was the "nature of the strategic triangle."[44] In November 1973, for example, Mao and Zhou "even intimidated Kissinger a bit" for the delay of Sino-US normalization process compared with the development of US-USSR relations.[45] The significant implication is that there was a clear contrast between the tense atmosphere of the November 1973 talks and the cordial mood of the February 1973 talks.

During the November 1974 Vladivostok summit, Ford and Brezhnev reached an interim agreement on the overall numbers of strategic nuclear weapons, leading to grain sales, technology transfers, and the signing of the Final Act at the Helsinki Conference on Security and Cooperation in Europe in August 1975. However, the Soviet adventurism continued in Third World conflicts, such as in the Middle East and Africa. The development of Eurocommunism in Italy, France, Portugal, and elsewhere – Communist parties in Western Europe's search for a more independent path – threatened to undermine the unity of the West.[46] It appeared that détente did not create the expected effect of self-restraint of the Soviets' external behavior.[47]

Equally important, the Nixon-Ford-Kissinger détente became the principal target of US domestic criticisms. While the liberals criticized them for its inadequate attention to human rights, the conservatives attacked the Nixon-Ford administrations

---

39   Ibid., p. 2, underline by Nixon in original.
40   Nixon's handwritten notations in ibid.
41   On the development of the US-PRC military and intelligence cooperation in the middle of the 1970s, see Mann, *About Face*, pp. 56–60; Jussi Hanhimaki, *The Flawed Architect: Henry Kissinger and American Foreign Policy* (New York: Oxford University Press, 2004); and Michael P. Pillisbury, "US-Chinese Military Ties?" *Foreign Policy*, No. 20, Fall 1975.
42   Kissinger to Nixon, "My Trip to China," March 2, 1973, HAK China Trip – February 1973 Memcons and Reports (originals), Box 98, HAK Trip Files, HAKOF, NSCF, NPMS, NA.
43   Ibid.
44   Solomon, interview with the author, September 24, 2003.
45   Ibid.
46   See Bundy, *A Tangled Web*, pp. 428–472; and Isaacson, *Kissinger*, pp. 673–692.
47   The Soviet desk officers in the State Department often disagreed with Kissinger: "the errors he made were in areas with which he was not familiar. He was making assumptions about the Soviets, that they would let economic incentives influence their political actions." William Dyess (Assistant Administrative Officer, Embassy Moscow, 1966–1968; Political Officer, Bureau of European Affairs, Department of State, 1970–1979), Oral History Interview, p. 3, Russia, Country Collection, 1996, FAOHC.

for being soft on the Soviet global threat, and the neo-conservatives stressed the importance of American traditional moral values underlining foreign policy, instead of Kissinger's focus on the promotion of arms control talks with the adversary, the Soviets, based on the practice of balance of power.[48] During Kissinger's visit to Beijing in November 1974, Vice Premier Deng Xiaoping criticized détente: "[W]e don't think there is any agreement that can bind the hands of Russia."[49] As Solomon reassesses, Deng felt that Kissinger was rather "manipulating intelligence information to make them more nervous about the Soviet Union than they felt."[50] Kissinger himself believed that only the continuing sense of a common adversary could preserve "a strictly unsentimental relationship."[51]

On October 21, 1975, Mao criticized Kissinger: "We see that what you are doing is leaping to Moscow by way of our shoulders, and these shoulders are now useless."[52] The Chinese thus would not "let itself be used" because détente was "in trouble."[53] The NSC staff described this situation as "a cooling of our relationship linked to the Chinese perception of the US as a fading power in the face of Soviet advance."[54] Kissinger and his advisers became very doubtful of whether Washington was still "capable of playing the kind of major world role" which would provide "an effective counterweight" to Moscow's attempt to encircle Beijing.[55] US officials estimated further that the Chinese would keep their relations with the US at the "present level – alive enough to suit their geopolitical purposes" but not more than that.[56] In the short term, therefore, as Kissinger reported to Ford before his presidential trip to China in December 1975, "appearances were everything" in the US relations with China.[57] In the long term, however, the US remained China's "only real option as a counterweight" to the growing "Soviet menace."[58] Thus, despite the collapse of the Nixon presidency and the decline of détente, the strategic triangle between the

---

48 On the US domestic controversy on détente, see Kissinger, *Years of Renewal*, pp. 92–112; and Isaacson, *Kissinger*, pp. 607–611.

49 Memcon, Kissinger and Deng, November 27, 1974, 9:45–11:32am, Secretary Kissinger's Talks in China, November 25–29 1974, Box 372, PPS-Lord, LORD PRC NOV 1974, RG59, NA.

50 Solomon, interview with the author, September 24, 2003.

51 Scowcroft to Ford, November 29, 1974, Secretary Kissinger's Talks in China November 25–29, 1974, Box 372, PPS-Lord, LORD PRC NOV 1974, RG 59, NA. See also Kissinger, *Years of Renewal*, p. 138.

52 "Analysis/Highlights of Secretary Kissinger's Meeting with Chairman Mao, October 21, 1975," October 25, 1975, pp. 2–3, Underline in original, Attached to Kissinger to Ford, "Possible Approaches to Your China Trip," October 24, 1975, Sec. Kissinger's Trip to China October 1975, Box 374, PPS-Lord, RG59, NA.

53 Ibid.

54 Ibid., p. 1. Underline in original.

55 Kissinger to Ford, "Your Trip to the People's Republic of China: A Scope Analysis," November 20, 1975, CHINA NOTES, Box 380, PPS-Lord, RG 59, NA.

56 Ibid; and Kissinger Ford, "Possible Approaches to Your China Trip," October 24, 1975, China Sensitive Chron October-December 1975, PPS-Lord, RG59, NA.

57 Ibid.

58 Kissinger to Ford, "Possible Approaches to Your China Trip," November 24, 1975, Sec. Kissinger's Trip to China October 1975, Box 374, PPS, RG 59, NA.

Japan's Future Role

The US rapprochement with China paved the way for the restoration of Sino-Japanese relations. It appeared that Japan was prepared to abandon Taiwan for normalization with China. From the US point of view, however, it raised the problem of Zhou's three principles for Sino-Japanese normalization: "recognition of the PRC as the sole legal government of China"; "recognition of Taiwan as an integral part of China"; and "abrogation of the Japan-ROC peace treaty of 1952."[59] The NSC staff was concerned that Japan's "<u>unqualified</u>" acceptance of these three principles would be that: 1) the international status of the ROC would be "seriously undercut"; 2) the US-ROC mutual defense treaty would become "more difficult to justify"; and 3) from the Japanese standpoint, the US bases within Japan could no longer be used to defend Taiwan against a PRC effort to "liberate" it.[60]

The US vital interest was that Tokyo's moves toward Beijing would "not inhibit" the US use of its bases within Japan in fulfilment of its "<u>defense commitments to Taiwan and South Korea.</u>"[61] Kissinger and his NSC staff were concerned that the new cabinet of the Japanese Prime Minister, Kakuei Tanaka, might "<u>haste</u>" to normalize Tokyo's relations with Beijing, which would give its recognition of the settlement of the Taiwan issue as China's internal problem.[62] Thus, Kissinger recommended to Nixon that he "<u>encourage Japan to preserve its economic and cultural ties with Taiwan.</u>"[63]

On August 31, 1972, during a two-day summit at Hawaii, Nixon emphasized to Tanaka the "overriding importance" that the US and Japan "not get into a conflict over China policy."[64] Nixon cautioned that while the two sides "need not have identical

---

59   Holdridge to Kissinger, "Your Meeting with Tanaka and Ohira," August 10, 1972, China Policy, p. 1, Tanaka Visit (Hawaii) August 31–September 1 (1972), Box 926, VIP Visits, NSCF, NPMS, NA.

60   Ibid. Underline in original.

61   Kissinger, to Nixon "Your Meeting with Japanese Prime Minister Tanaka in Honolulu on August 31 and September 1," August 29, 1972, p. 1 and p. 4. Underline by Nixon in original, Tanaka Visit (Hawaii) August 31–September 1 (1972), Box 926, VIP Visits, NSCF, NPMS, NA. The NSC staff referred to the Nixon-Sato communiqué of November 1969 which stated that the defense of Taiwan as a "most important factor" for Japan's security. Ibid. See Chapter 6, Section 2.3 of this book (p. 174). State Department officials also recommended that the effective area of US-Japan Security Treaty to "maintain peace and stability" in East Asia "must continue to encompass Taiwan." Rogers to Nixon, "Your Meeting with Japanese Prime Minister Tanaka and Foreign Minister Ohira," August 18, 1972, Issues and Talking Points, p. 5, Briefing Paper, Department of State, Box 926, VIP Visit, NSCF, NPMS, NA.

62   Ibid., p. 2. Underline by Nixon in original.

63   Ibid., p. 1. Underline by Nixon in original.

64   Memcon, Nixon and Tanaka, August 31, 1972, 1:00pm, p. 9, Box 926, VIP Visit, NSCF, NPMS, NA. The State Department's memorandum for the President recommended that the President stress that the US did not regard itself "in a race or competition" with Japan

positions," "neither should we allow antagonism to develop between us."⁶⁵ Finally, Nixon cautioned again that Tokyo's normalization with Beijing "should not be done at the expense of Japan's friends," particularly implying the Republic of China.⁶⁶

On September 29, Premier Zhou and Prime Minister Tanaka finally achieved Sino-Japanese rapprochement ending the state of war situation and resuming diplomatic relations between the two old Asian rivals.⁶⁷ Japan closed down its embassy in Taiwan while maintaining a non-governmental office for trade and cultural relations.⁶⁸ In the joint communiqué, Beijing and Tokyo declared their opposition to hegemony in the Asia-Pacific region. The combination of Sino-Japanese rapprochement and Sino-American rapprochement thus brought Japan into broader triangular relations with the United States and China in order to contain Soviet expansionism.⁶⁹ Consequently, in Kissinger's interpretation, the Chinese came to regard the US-Japan Security Treaty as a "brake on Japanese expansionism and militarism."⁷⁰ Equally, the Chinese leaders viewed Japan as an "incipient ally" "to counter Soviet and Indian designs."⁷¹ The Washington-Beijing-Tokyo strategic triangle against Moscow became one of the major features of the Cold War in Asia during the 1970s and the 1980s.

The Taiwan Issue

The February 1972 summit enhanced a more regular and direct communication between Washington and Beijing. As Solomon explains, the rapprochement with China meant "initiating and broadening a political dialogue" that would ultimately lead to the US diplomatic recognition of the People's Republic of China.⁷²

---

to improve its relations with China. Rogers to Nixon, "Your Meeting with Japanese Prime Minister Tanaka and Foreign Minister Ohira," August 18, 1972, Issues and Talking Points, p. 3, Briefing Paper, Department of State, Box 926, VIP Visit, NSCF, NPMS, NA.

65   Ibid.
66   Ibid., p. 12.
67   See Akira Iriye, *Japan and the Wider World: From the Mid-Nineteenth Century to the Present* (New York: Addison Wesley Publishers, 1997), pp. 165–166; and James Babb, *Tanaka: The Making of Postwar Japan* (Essex: Pearson Education Limited, 2000), pp. 77–78.
68   The so-called "Japan formula" thus set a restrictive framework for the US in normalizing with China.
69   However, Japan was still reluctant to make a substantial military-security role in East Asian geopolitical term. On the inter-relationship between Sino-Japanese rapprochement and Sino-American rapprochement, see, for example, Michael Schaller, 'Détente and the Strategic Triangle: Or "Drinking Your Mao Tai and having Your Vodka, Too,"' in Robert Ross and Jiang Changbin (eds), *Re-examining the Cold War: US-China Diplomacy, 1954–1973* (Cambridge, Massachusetts: Harvard University Press, 2001); Sadako Ogata, *Normalization with China: A Comparative Study of US and Japanese Process* (Berkeley: Institute of East Asian Studies, University of California, 1988).
70   Kissinger to Nixon, "My Trip to China," March 2, 1973, p. 1, HAK China Trip – February 1973 Memcons and Reports (originals), Box 98, HAK Trip Files, HAKOF, NSCF, NPMS, NA.
71   Ibid.
72   Solomon, Oral History Interview, September 13, 1996, pp. 55–56, FAOHC.

In February 1973, Kissinger and Zhou agreed to establish liaison offices in Washington and Beijing, which Kissinger saw as "embassies in everything but name."[73] Importantly, Kissinger offered an explicit timetable for normalization: in the first two years of Nixon's second term, the US would remove all the remaining armed forces from Taiwan; and in the second two years, it would complete full diplomatic normalization with China. Normalization would be achieved along the same line as Sino-Japanese normalization, namely the so-called "Japan formula" – terminating formal diplomatic relations with Taiwan and preserving only an unofficial tie with the Taipei government. Finally, the US would "abolish its defense treaty" with the Republic of China.[74]

In reality, however, the Chinese opening of the Liaison Office in Washington in May and the American opening of the Liaison Office in Beijing in July 1973 marked the last major official developments in the US relations with China during the middle of the 1970s. Thereafter, Nixon and Kissinger came to further realize the seriousness and complexity of China's persistence on the Taiwan issue, which was greater than they had estimated before the February 1972 summit. The Chinese leaders were in no rush to resolve the Taiwan issue. In November 1973, Mao indicated to Kissinger that: "[W]e can do without Taiwan for the time being, and let it come after one hundred years."[75] Kissinger estimated that the US normalization of relations with China could be achieved "only on the basis of confirming the principle of one China," to which Nixon commented: "K very significant."[76] By mid-1974, however, the NSC staff estimated that "[o]ur China policy is drifting without a clear sense of how we will move toward normalization, or indeed what the shape of a future normalized relationship with the PRC will look like," particularly regarding Taiwan.[77] "We are in danger of losing a sense of momentum in our dealing with Peking."[78]

After Nixon's resignation in August 1974, the Chinese leaders "put a lot of pressure on Kissinger" because they wanted him to get President Ford to "fulfill Nixon's commitment to normalize relations" with them and to make them to "break relations with Taiwan" before the end of Nixon's second term.[79] However, the Chinese did not run risk of seriously damaging the newly established direct communication with the United States. The Chinese were patient on Taiwan and confident of its

---

73 Kissinger to Nixon, "My Trip to China," March 2, 1973, HAK China Trip – February 1973 Memcons and Reports (originals), Box 98, HAK Trip Files, HAKOF, NSCF, NPMS, NA.

74 "Peking's Current Posture Towards Normalization," pp. 5–6, Attached to Memo from Habib, Lord and Solomon to Kissinger, "Partial Steps Toward Normalization of US/PRC Relations," August 4, 1975, Box 332, PPS-Lord, RG59, NA.

75 Memcon, Mao and Kissinger, November 12, 1973, Secretary Kissinger's Conversations in Peking, Box 100, HAK Trip Files, HAKOF, NSCF, NPMS, NA.

76 Kissinger to Nixon, "My Visit to China," November 19, 1973, p. 4, Nixon's handwritten notations in original, China-Sensitive WL File Misc&Reports November 1974, Box 374, PPS, RG59, NA.

77 Hummel, Lord, and Solomon, to Kissinger, "Imperatives for Planning and Action on the China Issue," May 24, 1974, p. 1, China Exchanges April 1–August 8 1974, Box 331, PPS-Lord, RG59, NA.

78 Ibid.

79 Solomon, interview with the author, September 24, 2003.

ultimate resolution.[80] In October 1975, Mao downplayed the Taiwan issue: "The small issue is Taiwan, the big issue is the world." Taiwan was "unwantable." Mao argued further, "It is better for the US to maintain control over Taiwan for the time being" because it was "filled with counter-revolutionaries," and also in order to prevent an independence movement or the influence from the Soviet Union.[81] Lord recalls that the October 1975 trip was very "unpromising. ... When we got back, we were so annoyed."[82] A great deal of momentum from the Nixon trip in February 1972 was "declining" by the Ford trip in December 1975.[83] Therefore, as State Department officials estimated, it appeared that the Chinese "want to put us under psychological pressure by maneuvering us into a position where we want the relationship with them more than they with us."[84] Overall, Kissinger believed that although the pro-Nationalist Taiwan lobby became a "vocal minority" rather than a majority, the US still needed a transitional period to persuade its public.[85] In reality, however, without a strong presidential authority, it was "impossible" for Kissinger, even with his great diplomatic skills, to proceed in full diplomatic normalization with China before the 1976 presidential election.[86]

After the death of Chinese key leaders, Premier Zhou and Chairman Mao, and the arrest of the radical leaders, namely the so-called "Gang of Four" in 1976, the moderate leaders named Hua Guofeng as Party Chairman, and sought to determine the timing of Deng Xiaoping's return to power.[87] In the November 1976 presidential election, Ford was defeated by Democrat candidate Jimmy Carter. Hence, the completion of full normalization had to wait until January 1979 when it was undertaken by President Carter and Vice Premier Deng.[88]

---

80   Ibid.
81   Kissinger to Ford, "Your Meeting with Chairman Mao," November 28, 1975, p. 6, Pres. Ford's Visit to Peking-International Issues December 1–5, 1975 (1 of 2), Box 372, PPS-Lord, RG 59, NA; "Analysis/Highlights of Secretary Kissinger's Meeting with Chairman Mao, October 21, 1975," October 25, 1975, p. 6, Sec. Kissinger's Trip to China October 1975, Box 374, PPS-Lord, RG59, NA.
82   Lord, interview with the author, October 15, 2003.
83   Ibid.
84   The State Department, Briefing Paper, "Normalization," November 1975, Pres. Ford's Visit to Peking-Bilateral Issues December 1–5, 1975, Box 372, PPS-Lord, RG59, NA.
85   Memcon, Kissinger and Zhou, June 22, 1972, 11:03pm–12:55am, p. 20, CF-Far East, Box 97, HAKOF, NSCF, NPMS, NA.
86   Memcon, Kissinger and the NSC staff, July 6, 1975, p. 1, Box 331, Box 330, PPS, RG59, NA.
87   The Gang of Four consisted of Jiang Qing, Wang Hongwen, Yao Wenyuan, and Zhang Chunqiao. On the final stage of political situation in Mao's China, see, for example, Philipe Short, *Mao: A Life* (New York: Henry Holt & Company, 1999), chapter 16 and epilogue; Ross Terrill, *Mao: A Biography* (Stanford, California: Stanford University Press, 1999), chapter 22 and epilogue.
88   On US full normalization with the PRC, see Tyler, *A Great Wall*, pp. 229–285; Mann, *About Face*, chapter 4; and Ross, *Negotiating Cooperation*, chapter 5.

Conclusion

This book has focused on the advantages and disadvantages of the pursuit of strict secrecy by Nixon and Kissinger as a key feature in the foreign policy decision-making leading to the US rapprochement with China in the early 1970s. Within that fundamental framework, it has examined three major elements of the US rapprochement with China: Conception – the presidential leadership, and the revitalization of the NSC system as the principal foreign policy decision-making machinery; Implementation – the evolution of policy option studies, and the public and private signal exchange from January 1969 to June 1971; and Direct Talks – major security issues in Kissinger's trips to Beijing in July and October 1971 and Nixon's trip to China in February 1972.

Conception

This study has analyzed the similarities and differences between Nixon and Kissinger regarding the development of their respective views on China. The origin of Nixon's personal interest in China could be traced back to the late 1940s and the early 1950s. While maintaining the political stance of an anti-Communist cold warrior in public, Nixon privately took great interest in the development of domestic and international situations surrounding Communist China. By the late 1950s, he came to believe that the PRC was there to stay, rather than being a passing phenomenon, and realized the advantage of trade as a possible means of promoting an initial dialogue with China and widening the split between Moscow and Beijing. However, he remained cautious, principally because of the danger of conservative backlash from the pro-Chinese Nationalists in Congress.

During the 1960s, crucial changes gradually took place in the American view of China. First, academic experts took a lead in the debate on the China policy in American domestic politics. There was a long-term development of an underlining willingness to have better relations with China, which was less strategic than idealistic. The academic contribution to the development of what became solid public support for a new China initiative in the long term was much more important than was previously thought.

At the same time, the State Department's middle ranking officials were examining a number of possible policy options, such as the easing of trade and travel restrictions, as a means of developing a new dialogue with China. The Warsaw Ambassadorial Talks played a crucial role as a channel of communication between Washington and Beijing, which helped to prevent any miscalculation of the respective intentions during the Vietnam War. Therefore, there was already some fundamental consideration on the China policy by the bureaucracy and also by academic experts in America.

As a private citizen, Nixon became more aware of changes in the threat posed by China in terms of the decreasing danger of its entry into the Vietnam War. During foreign trips to Europe and Asia, Nixon reassessed China's geopolitical importance. He concluded that China with its influence prevailing in Asia could no longer be excluded in the international scene. Thus, Nixon, who was a political pragmatist, came to realize the utility of China for the restoration of the US strategic centrality in the post-Vietnam world. In his *Foreign Affairs* article of October 1967, Nixon advocated that China should be pulled back into the community of nations, implying that its external behavior should be modified in the long term. Nixon believed that a new China initiative should be developed to make China's re-emergence safe for the restoration of stability in Asia. Simultaneously, however, he was still concerned about the remaining danger of conservative backlash, and thus carefully avoided providing open-ended support for the idea of a new China initiative.

As this study emphasized, Kissinger was much more skeptical about the necessity and possibility of the rapprochement with China than was previously estimated. The development of Sino-Soviet border clashes from March to September 1969 certainly provided a crucial opportunity for Kissinger to assess the necessity of a new China policy. Even in its weakened state, China was imposing some form of constraint on the Soviet Union, tying down a large number of Soviet forces along the Sino-Soviet borders. Thus, Kissinger came to view the China policy as a part of the broader US Soviet policy. However, Kissinger remained uncertain about the possibility of a new initiative toward Beijing until late 1969. He was pessimistic about the danger of a Soviet military attack on China. Despite his underestimation of the bureaucratic contribution of the Warsaw Ambassadorial Talks to the US China policy, it was the resumption of these talks in January and February 1970 that finally convinced him that the Chinese were seriously interested in a new dialogue with the United States. Details of unilateral public steps, such as the removal of trade and travel restrictions toward Beijing did not really interest Kissinger, and what was much more important for him was to go to Beijing to lay out the broad picture of what the US-China relations could be. Kissinger enhanced his negotiation skills and emerged as a great diplomat on largely as a result of his substantial talks with Premier Zhou in July and October 1971.

In essence, Nixon's presidential authority for the political credibility of a new China initiative was even more important than was previously assessed. With his strong willingness for bold action, Nixon articulated the US rapprochement policy, viewing an isolated China as a great threat to peace and stability in Asia and the world. He sought to seize the political opportunity to demonstrate a dramatic opening aimed at the easing of great tensions in the world, especially the ending of the Vietnam War and the promotion of arms control talks with the Soviet Union. In contrast, Kissinger's role in the early period of the opening toward China in 1969 and 1970 was less important than was previously pointed out. As the chief theorist within the Nixon administration, Kissinger examined the structural aspects of the international system in terms of the restoration of its stability. He developed a strategic perspective to formulate a triangular balance of power relationship between the United States,

China, and the Soviet Union in which the US exploited the escalation of Sino-Soviet mutual hostility and played the central role of pivot between the two communist giants. This study argues that it was Nixon's presidential leadership that drove the new China initiative, and Kissinger was more of a skillful negotiator with strategic vision.

Regarding the materialization of their conception for a new China initiative, Nixon and Kissinger still relied on the foreign policy decision-making machinery in order to obtain expert advice from the bureaucracy. The revitalization of the NSC system by Nixon and Kissinger was a "diplomatic coup." The exclusion of the State Department from the direct decision-making process was much more systematic than has previously been discussed in the existent literature. The revitalized NSC system was planned to conduct a systematic policy study by obtaining a wide range of policy alternatives from departments and agencies without necessarily informing them of the real objectives of the White House. As former NSC staff member Peter Rodman recalls, Nixon and Kissinger used the interagency process for policy studies "to get what they thought was the best of the wisdom of the bureaucracy."[1] Owing to this excessive secrecy, however, they did not make sufficient use of the expert advice that was available in the State Department. Instead, they relied on policy analysis papers filtered through the perceptions of Kissinger and of his selected NSC staff members. Ironically, however, even State Department officials believed that some secrecy was needed to protect the evolution of a new China initiative from the conservative backlash. Thus, Nixon and Kissinger could have consulted a limited number of senior officials in the State Department in a highly confidential way in order to make use of their expertise more effectively.

President Nixon took the lead in the new China initiative by sending very confidential memoranda to Kissinger, such as a broad review of the US China policy on February 5, 1969, and the lifting of trade and travel restrictions and the reassessment of the Chinese UN representation issue on November 22, 1970. Nixon had only a handful of senior officials in his inner circle, such as Kissinger, Haig, and Haldeman. In Nixon's confidential meetings with foreign leaders, such as De Gaulle, Yahya, and Ceauşescu during 1969, even Kissinger was not present. Nixon used these meetings to test his views on US China policy. Kissinger thus became much more eager to ensure that he would be included in every important meeting between the President and foreign leaders, while his attempt to exclude Secretary of State William Rogers increased. Paradoxically, however, Nixon was personally reluctant to have a face-to-face meeting with the heads of departments and agencies. Thus, the communication between the Oval Office and the rest of the administration was conducted principally through memoranda, which escalated further the pursuit of secrecy by the White House.

As the National Security Adviser, Kissinger recruited his NSC staff from a variety of backgrounds, such as the State Department, the Defense Department, the CIA, and academia, in order to develop diversity and flexibility in policy studies. Regarding the China policy, Kissinger pursued highly personalized secrecy by using the limited

---

1   Peter Rodman, Oral History Interview, July 22, and August 22, 1994, p. 13, Foreign Affairs Oral History Collection (FAOHC), Lauinger Library, Georgetown University.

number of NSC staff members, such as Alexander Haig Jr., John Holdridge, Winston Lord, Peter Rodman, and Richard Solomon. The NSC staff provided expertise and developed policy options for a new China initiative, taking short, medium, and long term perspectives. Simultaneously, however, as Solomon recalls, Kissinger was "very jealous of who got credit, and of the visibility that resulted from all facets of the China issue."[2]

While the NSC staff functioned as the mini and "operational State Department," the State Department itself continued to manage most of the routine things.[3] Importantly, despite the pursuit of strict secrecy by Nixon and Kissinger, State Department officials and NSC staff members had informal and private exchanges with each other on the background information of policy studies. In particular, on the basis of past efforts in the earlier administrations, the State Department's Bureau of East Asian and Pacific Affairs and the Bureau of Intelligence and Research prepared a number of basic materials for policy studies on possible steps towards China. The State Department's principal interest was the Taiwan issue, such as the language of the "One China" principle, the renouncement of the use of force between Beijing and Taipei, and the Chinese representation issue in the UN. Former Assistant Secretary for East Asian and Pacific Affairs Marshall Green confirms, "The focus was so much on Taiwan. China almost meant Taiwan in those days."[4]

The NSC sub-committees provided very important occasions on which to examine a wide range of policy options to promote a new China initiative. At Review Group meetings (1969–1970) and Senior Review Group meetings (1971) on NSSM studies (such as NSSM 14: Initial review of US China Policy, NSSM 63: Sino-Soviet differences, and NSSMs 106 and 107: the Chinese representation issue in UN), Kissinger encouraged broader discussions for a new China initiative without necessarily revealing his true views. China experts in the State Department urged a friendly dialogue with China in order to encourage its participation in the world community and promote a stable environment in Asia. These experts still thought that Taiwan was a crucial issue that would prevent the US from having a contact with Beijing without giving up its formal diplomatic relations with Taipei. On the contrary, Soviet experts opposed any quick move toward China which might provoke Moscow because of its sensitivity to the danger of the Washington-Beijing collusion. In reality, however, as a result of the opening to China, the US became a balancer in Sino-Soviet mutual hostility. Thus, the regional experts who were "too close to a subject" misjudged possible policy alternatives in a broader strategic context.[5]

Implementation

From January 1969 to June 1971, selectively adopting the recommendations from the interdepartmental policy studies, Nixon and Kissinger sent a series of unilateral

---

2 Richard Solomon, Oral History Interview, September 13, 1996, p. 28, FAOHC.
3 Solomon, interview with the author, September 24, 2003.
4 John Holdridge and Marshall Green, Oral History Interview in *A China Reader*, Vol. II, p. 9, January 1995, FAOHC.
5 Peter Rodman, interview with the author, October 21, 2003.

public signals toward Beijing, such as lifting trade and travel restrictions. Nixon used press conferences, media interviews, and speeches to clarify his personal interest in promoting a new dialogue with the Chinese leaders. Kissinger and his NSC staff drafted the President's annual Foreign Policy Reports to Congress in order to promote a positive political atmosphere and to encourage China's participation in the community of nations. Importantly, sending these unilateral public signals did "not require Chinese reaction."[6]

Simultaneously, owing to their distrust of the State Department, Nixon and Kissinger developed a very closely guarded communication with the Chinese through the backchannels, such as Pakistan, Romania, and France. These channels were based on Nixon's long-term personal connections with foreign leaders. Nixon and Kissinger privately conveyed to the Chinese leaders that: "We're the ones you should talk to, and don't pay much attention to these others."[7] In every confidential message until June 1971, they stressed that the US was "serious about moving toward them."[8] In reality, however, owing to excessive secrecy, Nixon and Kissinger occasionally missed subtle signals from the Chinese and had difficulty in comprehending complex regional problems, especially the Taiwan issue and the India-Pakistan rivalry.

In military-security terms, while the Chinese insisted on the US total withdrawal from Asia, the Nixon administration sought to justify the continuing US presence in that area of the world. In the short term, realizing China's physical weakness, Nixon and Kissinger sought to exploit the deepening Sino-Soviet mutual hostility. While seeking a new dialogue with China, the Nixon administration also sought to promote détente – the global relaxation of tensions through arms control talks with the Soviet Union. Equally important, it was the reduction of China's direct threat in Southeast Asia that enabled the US retrenchment of military deployment in the Asia-Pacific region. The Nixon Doctrine of July 1969 thus demanded much more burden sharing among allies in order to promote military withdrawal from the Vietnam War. In the long term, it was China's potential strength, especially its geopolitical importance in East Asia with nuclear capability, that persuaded Nixon and Kissinger to seek new diplomatic relations with Beijing. In other words, it was too dangerous to leave a nuclear-armed China outside of state interactions.

During the early period of the opening in 1969 and 1970, because of the pursuit of strict secrecy by Nixon and Kissinger, a highly complex bureaucratic rivalry emerged between the White House and the State Department. While the White House focused on promoting US relations with its adversaries, namely China and the Soviet Union, State Department officials were more concerned with maintaining regular US diplomatic relations with its allies, such as the Republic of China and Japan. In contrast to Kissinger's underestimation in his memoirs, the resumption of the Warsaw Ambassadorial Talks in January and February 1970 was crucial. It was the first major breakthrough during the US opening to China. As this study demonstrated, from December 1969 to May 1970, the White House and the State Department were

---

6 Rodman, interview with the author, October 21, 2003.
7 Rodman, Oral History Interview, July 22, and August 22, 1994, p. 15, FAOHC.
8 Rodman, interview with the author, October 21, 2003.

respectively testing how far the Chinese were prepared to move forward in a new dialogue with the United States. The bureaucratic preparations for the Warsaw talks revealed the growing difference between the White House and the State Department regarding the timing, agenda, and channel of direct communication with the Chinese. The State Department took an initial lead by preparing detailed instructions to Ambassador Stoessel in Warsaw. Importantly, it was State Department officials, such as the Director of the Office of Asian Communist Affairs, Paul Kreisberg and a China expert Alfred Jenkins, who originally prepared the draft language on Taiwan. At the February 1970 Warsaw talks, Ambassador Stoessel made clear the US intention to withdraw its armed forces from Taiwan in accordance with the development of the Vietnam settlement. Nixon and Kissinger adopted the same expression in their direct talks with the Chinese leaders in July and October 1971, and in February 1972.

After the January and February 1970 talks, however, the White House became increasingly irritated by the time-consuming nature of the bureaucratic preparations for the Warsaw meetings. As for the materialization of sending a special envoy to Beijing, the State Department's Bureau of East Asian and Pacific Affairs remained cautious, still seeking to hold one additional Warsaw talk in order to obtain more practical and substantial concessions on the Taiwan issue, in particular the agreement on the renunciation of the use of force in the Taiwan Strait. Also of great importance, Nixon and Kissinger became much more sensitive to the danger of leaks because of the State Department's continuing briefing to US allies on the Warsaw talks. Thus, Nixon and Kissinger wanted to move faster by sending a special envoy to Beijing to hold a direct and secret meeting with the Chinese leaders. From late 1970, seeking to materialize the opening to China before the 1972 presidential election, Nixon and Kissinger thus decided to exclude the State Department from involvement in the China issue and relied on the Pakistan and Romanian backchannels to communicate with the Chinese.

Direct Talks

The bureaucratic preparations for the presidential meetings with the Chinese leaders in February 1972 were much more systematic and substantial than discussed in the existing writings on this subject. The State Department prepared and sent over the "Books" to the NSC in advance. The NSC staff also wrote their own "Books," which had more confidential information on the backchannel communications as well as Kissinger's trips to Beijing in July and October 1971. Thus, as Solomon recalls, "we had a double track system."[9] These briefing books included the President's talking points, the anticipated Chinese positions as well as background information about the Chinese leaders' biographical sketches, Chinese history, philosophy, and culture. Nixon reviewed the briefing books as well as Kissinger's confidential memoranda carefully and took extensive notes (including comments, questions, and new directives), which reflected the development of his own thoughts on major security issues. Despite the initial secrecy characterizing the China initiative, Nixon and

---

9   Solomon, interview with the author, September 24, 2004.

Kissinger also came to realize the importance of holding briefings in order to calm the anxiety held by US allies as well as conservative politicians in the US Congress. In his meetings with Cabinet members and Congressional leaders in July 1971 and February 1972, Nixon illustrated the essence of his China initiative, namely the importance of pulling China back into the international community before it became too powerful for the US to manage.

Regarding the great powers encircling China, Nixon and Kissinger assessed that the Chinese feared the Soviets as the most urgent threat, disdained an India backed by the Soviets, and suspected Japan as being a long-term potential threat. Nixon and Kissinger concluded that Beijing would view new relations with Washington as the beginning of a long process for its re-emergence in the international scene. Thus, Nixon and Kissinger sought to convince the Chinese leaders of the advantage of the US's continuous presence in the Asia-Pacific region in order to prevent the emergence of any expansive states. In February 1972, Mao and Nixon agreed that there was no direct threat between the US and China. As a result of this realization, the two parties were then able to discuss five major issues of concern between the two sides during the July and October 1971 talks and the February 1972 talks, such as Taiwan, Indochina, Japan, South Asia, and the Soviet Union.

The Taiwan issue was the most sensitive and difficult obstacle in restoring relations between the US and China. There was long-term disagreement between China's insistence on the use of force to resolve the Taiwan question as a part of its internal concern and the US persistence on a peaceful resolution between Beijing and Taipei. As a historic remainder of the Chinese civil war, the Chinese leaders kept insisting that the Sino-US diplomatic communication could progress only after the Taiwan question was substantially discussed. On the other hand, Nixon and Kissinger tended to perceive Taiwan through the lens of US domestic politics, namely the remaining danger of the conservative backlash from pro-Taiwan conservatives in Congress rather than through the lens of the Nationalist-Communist Chinese civil war. The handling of the Taiwan issue for the Nixon administration was also related to the question of US reliability to its allies in the world. Owing to the excessive secrecy by the White House, however, Washington's rapid move towards Beijing significantly shocked Taipei. In October 1971, Washington failed to preserve Taipei's membership in the United Nations. This was a serious flaw in the Nixon-Kissinger China initiative, and therefore the successive US administrations had to reassure Taipei of its continuing commitment to Taiwan.

In the February 1972 summit, Nixon gave a crucial assurance to Zhou, admitting to the "One China" principle and pledging a future commitment to withdraw the US armed forces from the islands and to achieve normalization with the People's Republic. Moreover, Nixon gave an assurance that the remaining US armed forces in Taiwan would discourage the Chinese Nationalists from creating an independence movement, especially launching a military action against the mainland. By adopting the State Department's draft, Nixon and Kissinger sought to link the Taiwan issue with the issue of Vietnam's settlement. The joint communiqué thus stated that the US withdrawal of its armed forces from Taiwan would be conducted as the tensions in the area diminished, which principally implied the ending of the US military operation in Indochina. Nixon and Kissinger attempted to defer the Taiwan issue in order to concentrate on the US-Soviet-China triangular relations.

In reality, however, Nixon and Kissinger still underestimated the complexity of the Taiwan issue, especially the importance of the Chinese long-term persistence on its sovereignty on Taiwan. In February 1972, because of the pursuit of strict secrecy, the drafting of the joint communiqué caused a serious flaw, namely the failure to refer to the US defense commitment to the Republic of China. Nixon and Kissinger also failed to obtain Chinese agreement on the renunciation of the use of force in the Taiwan Strait. Overall, by excluding the State Department's expertise and by rushing to the rapprochement to meet the 1972 presidential election, Nixon and Kissinger made the handling of the Taiwan issue more difficult. The opening of the Liaison Offices in the respective capitals in 1973 was the only official development in the normalization process during the mid 1970s. The Chinese demanded three vital conditions for a full diplomatic normalization, namely: 1) formal recognition by the US of Beijing as the sole government of China and the end of official Washington-Taipei diplomatic relations; 2) the US military withdrawal from Taiwan; and 3) the termination of the US-Republic of China Security Treaty. After the fall of the Nixon presidency as a result of the Watergate scandal and the damaging of the US reliability to its allies as a result of the collapse of Indochina policy, the fulfillment of the official diplomatic normalization became impossible during the mid 1970s.

The conflicts in Indochina were the most urgent problem for the US in its new dialogue with China. Nixon and Kissinger sought to reduce tensions in Indochina by promoting the US's withdrawal and by inducing a cooperative attitude in Beijing toward a negotiated settlement between Washington and Hanoi. Nixon and Kissinger also attempted to develop common ground with the Chinese leaders in order to prevent the emergence of North Vietnam's regional hegemonic aspirations in Indochina backed by the Soviet Union. For the State Department, the Vietnam factor existed principally in terms of the danger of China's entry into the Vietnam War. Thus, State Department officials continued to use the Warsaw Ambassadorial Talks to reassure the Chinese that the US had no intention to expand the Vietnam War. Importantly, both the White House and the State Department came to share the view that China was not as dangerous as it had previously been estimated.

The Chinese leaders, however, were not necessarily willing to cooperate with the US in a search for a negotiated settlement in the Vietnam War. Moreover, China's influence over North Vietnam was more limited than it was previously estimated among US officials. Both the White House and the State Department underestimated the degree of Hanoi's independence from Beijing and Moscow. Moreover, the linkage between the US withdrawal from Taiwan and the US negotiated settlement with North Vietnam allowed the Chinese to pressure the US for the delay of its withdrawal from Indochina as well as from Taiwan. Overall, Nixon and Kissinger were unsuccessful in obtaining Chinese active assistance in Indochina.

Regarding the future of Japan, State Department officials were principally concerned about Japan's anxiety over the US move toward China. The State Department thus sought to reassure Tokyo by briefing Japanese leaders on the Warsaw Ambassadorial Talks. On the other hand, Nixon and Kissinger focused on the possibility of a more independent Japanese defense policy. In direct talks with

Chinese leaders, Nixon and Kissinger over-exaggerated the danger of the revival of Japan's military expansionism in order to exploit China's long-term anxiety. Nixon and Kissinger sought to convince the Chinese leaders that Japan's independent defense policy should be contained by the preservation of the US-Japan Security Treaty. In essence, Nixon and Kissinger gave assurance to the Chinese leaders that the US-Japan Security Treaty would play multiple roles to prevent Japan from expanding its influence over Taiwan, Korea, and Indochina. In return, Nixon and Kissinger acquired the Chinese leaders' tacit acknowledgement of US military bases in Asia. Thus, the US rapprochement with China led to Sino-Japanese rapprochement and the formulation of the US-China-Japan strategic triangle against the Soviet Union.

In the long term, however, the combination of the Nixon Doctrine's pressure on Japan for further burden sharing in military and economic terms and the rapid development of the US opening to China brought about a functional fragmentation in US relations with Japan. The US secretive initiative toward China, done single-handedly without the knowledge of Japanese officials, shocked Japan and led to Japan's more independent economic policy and its diplomatic initiative to normalize with China. Nixon and Kissinger calculated that the emergence of diversity between Washington and Tokyo could be contained under its restored credibility in world politics. However, a fragmentation within US-Japan relations continued to remain as a potential source of uncertainty for the regional security in East Asia, creating an imbalance in the US relations with China and Japan respectively in the long term.

It was the India-Pakistan rivalry over which the perception gap between the White House and the State Department significantly widened in 1971. Without substantially knowing of Pakistan's role as a crucial intermediary between the White House and Beijing from late 1970, the State Department's Bureau of Near Eastern and South Asian Affairs believed that Pakistan had principally increased tensions and caused the war with India. In contrast, Nixon and Kissinger believed that they had to prove their reliability in the eyes of the Chinese leaders by supporting China's friend, Pakistan. On the other hand, Nixon and Kissinger also sought to exploit Chinese anxiety by exaggerating the danger of the emergence of India's Soviet-backed regional hegemony. In reality, however, the Chinese leaders showed little interest in any active involvement in the India-Pakistan conflicts of December 1971. Overall, it was the pursuit of excessive secrecy by Nixon and Kissinger that over-simplified and even distorted the complexity of India-Pakistan regional rivalry. After the February 1972 summit, the India-Pakistan rivalry decreased in its importance as a major security issue between the US and China.

Regarding the deepening Sino-Soviet hostilities, Nixon and Kissinger attempted to induce China's tacit cooperation against the growing Soviet military threat. In essence, Nixon and Kissinger were fully aware that the US's position toward the Soviet Union and to China was closer than they were with each other. Nixon and Kissinger thus sought to improve US diplomatic flexibility by pursuing an even-handed approach toward the two states. For the State Department, however, the Soviet factor was not enough to promote a new dialogue with the Chinese; the Soviet factor existed as one of the major issues rather than the principal dominant issue. The State Department thus underestimated the geopolitical dynamism in the short term, especially the US leverage in the Sino-Soviet rivalry and the impact of the US opening to China on the Soviets as a patron of North Vietnam.

Nixon and Kissinger tended to view the China policy in global terms rather than regional terms. They concentrated on the promotion of a strategic triangle between the US, the USSR, and China, and then handled regional problems in terms of how they enhanced or interfered with the overall stability in the international system. Their primary concern with local conflicts was "when a big power attempts to exploit them for its own ends."[10] Thus, Nixon and Kissinger over-exaggerated the Soviet threat and essentially imposed the simplified measures that developed from global security on the complex regional security. Equally important, owing to the pursuit of the strategic triangle, Washington tended to be highly sensitive to the possible reactions from Beijing in both global and regional security. After the fall of the Nixon presidency, Kissinger calculated that the continuation of a China policy would sustain the imagery of the US's commitment in international affairs. The fundamental framework of the strategic triangle continued to remain crucial in the relations between the US and China.

In conclusion, the pursuit of strict secrecy brought about surprise as well as imagery in the US rapprochement with China, restoring the US credibility in world politics in the short term. It appeared that Nixon and Kissinger anticipated that the overwhelming impacts of the historic opening justified its highly secretive means and processes. However, the rapid and dramatic US opening to China made the international and domestic audiences over-expectant for further developments. In other words, Nixon and Kissinger over-sold the ending of mutual hostility and the easing of tensions with China. Moreover, there was a wishful thinking among US officials that China could be brought to accept restraints in regional security to facilitate the overall easing of tensions in global security. Certainly, Nixon and Kissinger never expected that a single summit would eliminate many conflicting issues in the US relations with China. However, Nixon and Kissinger still underestimated the depth of the perception gap between the two sides over the respective worldviews. The Chinese leaders would not allow the US to continue to use its new relations with China for the improvement of US centrality in the world. Moreover, by pursuing the highly secret diplomacy with Mao and Zhou, Kissinger placed himself in the front position of direct US negotiation with China. The Chinese leaders sought to exploit this personalized relationship to pressure and even intimidate Kissinger, criticizing the delay of the US diplomatic normalization with China.

Overall, the US rapprochement with China in the early 1970s was a substantial learning process between the two governments and subsequently characterized Washington's diplomatic communication with Beijing in the long term, namely in the pursuit of highly personalized diplomacy with the Chinese leaders. After the February 1972 summit, neither side allowed the remaining conflicting interests to jeopardize the newly established communication. US officials realized that they could disagree with the Chinese leaders and that, despite intervals, negotiations could be resumed at a later date as long as the diplomatic communication line itself was preserved. Thus, the US rapprochement marked the beginning of the long process to pursue pragmatic co-existence with China – neither as a friend nor an enemy.

---

10   Memcon, Kissinger and Zhou, June 20, 1972, 2:05–6:05pm, p. 27, Country Files – Far East, Box 97, HAKOF, NSCF, NPMS, NA.

Appendix

The Joint Communiqué between the United States of America and the People's Republic of China – Shanghai, February 27, 1972

President Richard Nixon of the United States of America visited the People's Republic of China at the invitation of Premier Chou En-lai of the People's Republic of China from February 21 to February 28, 1972. Accompanying the President were Mrs. Nixon, US Secretary of State William Rogers, Assistant to the President Dr. Henry Kissinger, and other American officials. President Nixon met with Chairman Mao Tse-tung of the Communist Party of China on February 21. The two leaders had a serious and frank exchange of views on Sino-US relations and world affairs.

During the visit, extensive, earnest and frank discussions were held between President Nixon and Premier Chou En-lai on the normalization of relations between the United States of America and the People's Republic of China, as well as on other matters of interest to both sides. In addition, Secretary of State William Rogers and Foreign Minister Chi Peng-fei held talks in the same spirit.

President Nixon and his party visited Peking and viewed cultural, industrial and agricultural sites, and they also toured Hangchow and Shanghai where, continuing discussions with Chinese leaders, they viewed similar places of interest.

The leaders of the People's Republic of China and the United States of America found it beneficial to have this opportunity, after so many years without contact, to present candidly to one another their views on a variety of issues. They reviewed the international situation in which important changes and great upheavals are taking place and expounded their respective positions and attitudes.

The US side stated: Peace in Asia and peace in the world requires efforts both to reduce immediate tensions and to eliminate the basic causes of conflict. The United States will work for a just and secure peace: just, because it fulfills the aspirations of peoples and nations for freedom and progress; secure, because it removes the danger of foreign aggression. The United States supports individual freedom and social progress for all the peoples of the world, free of outside pressure or intervention. The United States believes that the effort to reduce tensions is served by improving communication between countries that through accident, miscalculation or misunderstanding. Countries should treat each other with mutual respect and be willing to compete peacefully, letting performance be the ultimate judge. No country should claim infallibility and each country should be prepared to re-examine its own attitudes for the common good. The United States stressed that the peoples of Indochina should be allowed to determine their destiny without outside intervention; its constant primary objective has been a negotiated solution; the eight-point proposal put forward by the Republic of Vietnam and the United States on January 27, 1972 represents a basis for the attainment of that objective; in the absence of a negotiated settlement the United States envisages the ultimate withdrawal of all US forces from the region consistent with the aim of self-determination for each country of Indochina. The United States will maintain its close ties with and support for the Republic of Korea; the United States will support efforts of the Republic of Korea to seek a relaxation of tension and increased communication in the Korean peninsula. The United States places the highest value on its friendly relations with Japan; it will continue to develop the existing close bonds. Consistent with the United Nations Security Council Resolution of December 21, 1971, the United States favors the continuation of the ceasefire between India and Pakistan and the withdrawal of all military forces to within their own territories and to their own sides of the ceasefire line in Jammu and Kashmir; the United States supports the right of the peoples of South Asia to shape their own future in peace, free of military threat, and without having the area become the subject of great power rivalry.

The Chinese side stated: Wherever there is oppression, there is resistance. Countries want independence, nations want liberation and the people want revolution – this has become the irresistible trend of history. All nations, big or small, should be equal; big nations should not bully the small and strong nations should not bully the weak. China will never be a superpower and it opposes hegemony and power politics of any kind. The Chinese side stated that it firmly supports the struggles of all the oppressed people and nations for freedom and liberation and that the people of all countries have the right to choose their social systems according to their own wishes and the right to safeguard the independence, sovereignty and territorial integrity of their own countries and oppose foreign aggression, interference, control and subversion. All foreign troops should be withdrawn to their own countries. The Chinese side expressed its firm support to the peoples of Vietnam, Laos and Cambodia in their efforts for the attainment of their goal and its firm support to the seven-point proposal of the Provisional Revolutionary Government of the Republic of South Vietnam and the elaboration of February this year on the two key problems in the proposal, and to the Joint Declaration of the Summit Conference of the Indochinese Peoples. It firmly supports the eight-point program for the peaceful unification of Korea put forward by the Government of the Democratic People's Republic of Korea on April 12, 1971, and the stand for the abolition of the "UN Commission for the Unification and Rehabilitation of Korea." It firmly opposes the revival and outward expansion of Japanese militarism and firmly supports the Japanese people's desire to build an independent, democratic, peaceful and neutral Japan. It firmly maintains that India and Pakistan should, in accordance with the United Nations resolutions on the India-Pakistan question, immediately withdraw all their forces to their respective territories and to their own sides of the ceasefire line in Jammu and Kashmir and firmly supports the Pakistan Government and people in their struggle to preserve their independence and sovereignty and the people of Jammu and Kashmir in their struggle for the right of self-determination.

There are essential differences between China and the United States in their social systems and foreign policies. However, the two sides agreed that countries, regardless of their social systems, should conduct their relations on the principles of respect for the sovereignty and territorial integrity of all states, non-aggression against other states, non-interference in the internal affairs of other states, equality and mutual benefit, and peaceful coexistence. International disputes should be settled on this basis, without resorting to the use or threat of force. The United States and the People's Republic of China are prepared to apply these principles to their mutual relations.

With these principles of international relations in mind the two sides stated that:

- progress toward the normalization of relations between China and the United States is in the interests of all countries:
- both wish to reduce the danger of international military conflict;
- neither should seek hegemony in the Asia-Pacific region and each is opposed to efforts by any other country or group of countries to establish such hegemony; and
- neither is prepared to negotiate on behalf of any third party or to enter into agreements or understandings with the other directed at other states.

Both sides are of the view that it would be against the interests of the peoples of the world for any major country to collude with another against other countries, or for major countries to divide up the world into spheres of interest.

The two sides reviewed the long-standing serious disputes between China and the United States. The Chinese reaffirmed its position: The Taiwan question is the crucial question obstructing the normalization of relations between China and the United States; the Government of the People's Republic of China is the sole legal government of China; Taiwan is a province of China which has long been returned to the motherland; the liberation of Taiwan is China's internal affair in which no other country has the right to interfere; and all US forces and military installations must be withdrawn from Taiwan. The Chinese Government firmly opposes any activities which aim at the creation of "one China, one Taiwan," "one China, two governments," "two Chinas," and "independent Taiwan" or advocate that "the status of Taiwan remains to be determined."

The US side declared: The United States acknowledges that all Chinese on either side of the Taiwan Strait maintain there is but one China and that Taiwan is a part of China. The United States Government does not challenge that position. It reaffirms its interest in a peaceful settlement of the Taiwan question by the Chinese themselves. With this prospect in mind, it affirms the ultimate objective of the withdrawal of all US forces and military installations from Taiwan. In the meantime, it will progressively reduce its forces and military installations on Taiwan as the tension in the area diminishes.

The two sides agreed that it is desirable to broaden the understanding between the two peoples. To this end, they discussed specific areas in such fields as science, technology, culture, sports and journalism, in which people-to-people contacts and exchanges would be mutually beneficial. Each side undertakes to facilitate the further development of such contacts and exchanges.

Both sides view bilateral trade as another area from which mutual benefit can be derived, and agreed that economic relations based on equality and mutual benefit are in the interest of the peoples of the two countries. They agree to facilitate the progressive development of trade between their two countries.

The two sides agreed that they will stay in contact through various channels, including the sending of a senior US representative to Peking from time to time for concrete consultations to further the normalization of relations between the two countries and continue to exchange views on issues of common interest.

The two sides expressed the hope that the gains achieved during this visit would open up new prospects for the relations between the two countries. They believe that the normalization of relations between the two countries is not only in the interest of the Chinese and American peoples but also contributes to the relaxation of tension in Asia and the world.

President Nixon, Mrs. Nixon and the American party expressed their appreciation for the gracious hospitality shown them by the Government and people of the People's Republic of China.

Bibliography

I. Archives and Manuscript Collections

Manuscript Division, Library of Congress, Washington DC.

> Elliot Richardson Papers
>
> Papers of the Nixon White House, Part 5, H.R. Haldeman: Notes of White House Meetings, 1969–1973

National Archives and Records Administration, Archives II, College Park, Maryland.

The General Records of the Department of State, Record Group 59 (RG59)

> Subject-Numeric Files
> POL, Chicom, Chicom-US., Chicom-USSR, 1967–1969
> POL, Chicom, Chicom-US., Chicom-USSR, 1970–1973
> Records of the Secretaries of State and the Principal Offices of the Department of State
> Records of Policy Planning Staff, Director's Files (Winston Lord), 1969–1977
> Record of Administrative Offices
> Record of the NSC 1961–1972
> Correspondence of Richard Nixon and American Ambassadors, 1969–1971
> Central Files of NSC Matters, 1969–1972
> President's Evening Reading Reports, 1964–1974
> Summary of the Undersecretary's Meeting with the National Security Adviser, 1970–1972
> Special Correspondence of Secretary Kissinger
>
> Lot Files
> Records of Offices Responsible for Far Eastern and Pacific Affairs
> Office of Assistant Secretary of State for East Asian and Pacific Affairs (Marshall Green), 1969–1973
> Far East Asia (China, Korea, Japan)

Nixon Presidential Materials Staff

    The National Security Council Files
      Subject Files
      President's Trip Files
      Country Files
      Name Files
      For the President Files (Winston Lord) – China Trip/Vietnam
      VIP Visits
      Alexander M. Haig Special Files
      Presidential/HAK Memcons
      For the President Files – China/Vietnam Negotiations
      Henry A. Kissinger Office Files
        HAK Administrative and Staff Files
        HAK Trip Files
        Country Files

    National Security Council Institutional Files
      Senior Review Group Meeting Minutes
      National Security Council Meeting Minutes
      Washington Special Action Group Meeting Minutes

    White House Central Files
      Subject Files
      Confidential Files
      Countries Files
      Foreign Affairs Files
      Staff Members and Office Files

    White House Special Files
      President's Office Files
      President's Personal Files

    The Nixon White House Tapes

    H.R. Haldeman Diaries (Tapes and CD-ROMs)

US Department of State, Declassified State Department and Other Agency Documents, FOIA Released Documents

II. Published Governmental Sources

The Central Intelligence Agency.

——, *The China Collection.*
——, *Tracking the Dragon: Selected National Intelligence Estimates on China, 1948–1976*, National Intelligence Council, CD-ROM, Washington DC: US Government Printing Office, 2004.
Congressional Record. "Communist China Policy," Hon. John Rousselot, August 6, 1971, 30765–30767.
——, *US Policy with Respect to Mainland China.* Hearings Before the Committee on Foreign Relations, US Senate, Eighty-Ninth Congress Second Session, March 8, 10, 16, 18, 21, 28, 30, 1966, Washington DC Government Printing Office, 1966.
——, *United States Relations with the People's Republic of China.* Hearings before the Committee on Foreign Relations United States Senate Ninety Second Congress First Session on S.J. Res. 48, S. Res. 37, S. Res. 82, and S. Res.139 June 24, 25, 28, and, July 20, 1971, Washington DC: US Government Printing Office, 1972.
——, *United States-China Relations.* Committee on Foreign Relations United States Senate Ninety Second Congress First Session on The evolution of US Policy toward Mainland China (Executive hearing held July 21, 1971; made public December 8, 1971) and Hearings before the Committee on Foreign Relations United States Senate Seventy-Ninth Congress First Session on The Situation in the Far East, Particularly China, December 5, 6, 7, and 10, 1945, Washington DC: US Government Printing Office, 1971.
Nixon, Richard M. "United States Foreign Policy for the 1970s: A Strategy for Peace," President Nixon's Report to Congress, Vol. 1. February 18, 1970, Washington DC: Government Printing Office.
——, "United States Foreign Policy for the 1970's: Building for Peace," President Nixon's Report to Congress, Vol. 2, February 25, 1971, Washington DC: Government Printing Office.
——, "United States Foreign Policy for the 1970s: The Emerging Structure of Peace," President Nixon's Report to Congress, Vol. 3, February 9, 1972, Washington DC: Government Printing Office.
——, "United States Foreign Policy for the 1970s: Shaping a Durable Peace," President Nixon's Report to Congress, Vol. 4. May 3, 1973, Washington DC: Government Printing Office.
Public Papers of the Presidents of the United States: Richard M. Nixon 1969–1974. Washington DC: Government Printing Office, 1969–1974.
US Department of State. *Bulletins of the Department of State, 1969–1972.* Washington DC: Government Printing Office, 1969–1972.
——, *Foreign Relations of the United States 1948–1972.* Washington DC: United States Government Printing Office.

1948 Vol. VII, *The Far East: China* (1973)
1948 Vol. VIII, *The Far East: China* (1973)
1949 Vol. VIII, *The Far East: China* (1978)
1949 Vol. IX, *The Far East: China* (1974)
1950 Vol. VI, *East Asia and the Pacific* (1976)
1950 Vol. VII, *Korea* (1976)
1951 Vol. VI, *Asia and the Pacific, Part 1* (1978)
1951 Vol. VI, *Asia and the Pacific, Part 2* (1978)
1951 Vol. VII, *Korea and China* (1983)
1952–54 Vol. XIV, *China and Japan* (1985)
1955–57 Vol. II, *China* (1986)
1955–57 Vol. III, *China* (1986)
1958–60 Vol. XIX, *China* (1996)
1961–63 Vol. XXII/XXIV, *Northeast Asia* (1997)
1964–68 Vol. XXX, *China* (1998)
1964–68 Vol. VI, *Vietnam, 1968* (2002)
1964–68 Vol. VII, *Vietnam, 1968* (2003)
1964–68 Vol. XIV, *Soviet Union* (2001)
1969–72 Vol. I, *Foreign Policy Foundations of the Nixon Administration 1969–1972* (2003)
1969–72 Vol. V, *United Nations* (2004)
1969–72 Vol. XI, *South Asia Crisis, 1971* (2005)
——,*United States Relations with China*. Publications 3573, Far Eastern Series. Washington DC: Government Printing Office, 1949.

III. Oral Histories

Foreign Affairs Oral History Collection (FAOHC)
Association for Diplomatic Studies and Training (ADST), Arlington, Virginia
Special Collections Division, Lauinger Library, Georgetown University, Washington DC.

Individual Files

> ANDERSON, Donald
> BARNETT, Robert
> CLOUGH, Ralph
> FREEMAN Jr., Charles W
> GREEN, Marshall
> HOLDRIDGE, John
> HUMMEL, Jr., Arthur
> JOHNSON, U. Alexis
> LILLEY, James R
> LORD, Winston
> NICHOLAS, Robert L

OSBORN, David
SOLOMON, Richard
THAYER, Harry E.T

Country Files

Cambodia
Cambodia Reader
China Reader
India
Japan
Korea
Pakistan
Russia
Vietnam Reader

Interviews and Correspondence by the Author

BARMAN, Fredrick Barman Jr. Manuscript Reference Librarian, Manuscript Division, Library of Congress, 10/07/2003.
FOOT, Rosemary. Professor, St. Antony's College, Oxford University, 04/29/2004, 07/13/2004, 08/30/2004, 09/01/2004.
GIRVAN, Anna. Information Resource Center, US Embassy, London 02/11/2003.
GOH, Evelyn. then Assistant Professor, The Institute of Defence and Strategic Studies, Nanyang Technological University, Singapore, 08/02/2004, 08/03/2004.
GUSTAFSON, Milton O. Senior Archivist, Civilian Records Textual Archives Services Division, National Archives, 06/25/2003, 08/05/2003.
HALPERIN, Morton. Senior NSC staff member (1969), 05/11/2004, 06/10/2004.
HARDING, Harry. Professor, The Elliot School of International Affairs, George Washington University, 09/24/2003.
KENNEDY, Charles Stuart. Oral History Director, The Foreign Affairs Oral History Program of the Association for Diplomatic Studies and Training, Arlington, Virginia, 09/15/2004, 10/10/2003.
KIRBY, Bruce. Manuscript Reference Librarian, Manuscript Division, Library of Congress, 10/07/2003.
KIRSTIN, Julian. Archivist, The Richard Nixon Library & Birthplace, 05/11/2004.
LORD, Winston. Senior NSC staff member (1969–1973), 10/14/2003, 10/15/2003.
RASMUSEEN, Kathleen. Office of the Historian, Department of State 02/11/2003.
RODMAN, Peter. NSC staff member (1969–1976), 10/21/2003, 09/24/2004.
SAMTAMARIA, Daniel. Public Policy Papers Project Archivist, Seeley G. Mudd Manuscript Library, Princeton University, 09/03/2004.
SHAMBAUGH, David. Professor, The Elliot School of International Affairs, George Washington University, 10/08/2003, 10/15/2003.

SMYSER, Richard. NSC staff member (1969–1973), 10/02/2003, 10/05/2003.
SOLOMON, Richard. Senior NSC staff member (1971–1975), 09/24/2003, 09/22/2004.
TEPPERMAN, Jonathan. Senior Editor, *Foreign Affairs*, 05/11/2004.
TUCKER, Nancy Bernkopf. Professor, Department of History, School of Foreign Service, Georgetown University, 10/01/2003, 10/14/2003.
WHITING, Allen S. Regents' Professor of Political Science, University of Arizona, 09/30/2003, 10/19/2003, 04/07/2004, 04/13/2004.

IV. Published Documentary Materials on Websites

ABC News Productions, The Discovery Times Channel

> *History Declassified: Nixon in China*
> (http://hnn.us/readcomment.php?id=49237)

The Brookings Institution, Washington DC and Center for International and Security Studies, Maryland

> The National Security Council Project, Oral History Roundtables
>
> *The Nixon Administration National Security Council*, December 8, 1999
> (http://www.brookings.org/fp/research/projects/nsc/transcripts/19981208.htm)
>
> *The Roles of the National Security Adviser*, October 25, 1999
> (http://www.brookings.org/fp/research/projects/nsc/transcripts/19991025.htm)
>
> *China Policy and the National Security Council*, November 4, 1999
> (http://www.brookings.org/fp/research/projects/nsc/transcripts/19991104.htm)

CNN. The Cold War: Episode Scripts. 1999
(http://www.cnn.com/SPECIALS/cold.war/)

> Episode Script 15: *China 1949–1972*.
> Episode Script 16: *Détente*.

Cold War International History Project, The Woodrow Wilson International Center for Scholars, Washington DC.

> CWIHP Document Library. (http://cwihp.si.educwihp.nsf)
> Keywords: *Rise and Fall of Détente (1962–1980)*.
> Geographic Subject: *China, Vietnam, Cambodia, Laos, USA*.

The National Security Archive, Gelman Library, The George Washington University, Washington DC.

——, CNN. The Cold War: Interviews and Documents (http://www.seas.gwnu.edu/nsarchive/coldwar/interviews/)

BOGGAN, Tim
BOWIE, Robert
DAVIES, John Paton
EHRLICHMAN, John
FORD, Gerald
GREEN, Marshall
KISSINGER, Henry
LAIRD, Melvin
NEGROPONTE, John
NINGKUN, Wu
LORD, Winston

——, *The United States, China, and the Bomb*, Electronic Briefing Book No.1 1998 (http://www.gwu.edu/~nsarchiv/NSAEBB/NSAEBB1/nsaebb1.htm).
——, *Presidential Directives on National Security from Truman to Clinton*,1994 (http://www.gwu.edu~nsarchiv/nsa/publications/presidentusa/presidential.html).
——, *US-Japan Project: Diplomatic, Security, and Economic Relations since 1960*, 1997 (http://www.gwu.edu/~nsarchiv/japan/usjhmpg.htm).
——, Working Paper No. 2, SCHALLER, Michael. "The Nixon 'Shocks' and US-Japan Strategic Relations, 1969–1974."
——, Working Paper No. 4, TUCKER, Nancy Berhkopf. "US-Japan Relations and the Opening to China."
——, Working Paper No. 5, SOETA, Yoshihide. "US-Japan-China Relations and The Opening To China: The 1970s."
——, *Record of Historic Richard Nixon-Zhou Enlai Talks in February 1972 Now Declassified*, 1999 (http://www.seas.gwu.edu/~nsarchiv/nsa/publications/DOC_leaders/kissinger/nixzhou/).
——, *Kissinger Transcripts and Related Material*, 1999 (http://www.gwu.edu/~nsarchiv/nsa/publications/DOC_readers/kissinger/docs/index.html).
——, *The United States and China: From Hostility to Engagement 1960–1998*, 1999, RICHELSON, Jeffrey T. (ed.) (http://www.gwu.edu/~nsarchiv/nsa/publications/china-us/index.htm).
——, *The United States and the Chinese Nuclear Program, 1960–1964*. BURR, William and RICHELSON, Jeffrey T. (eds) (http://www.gwu.edu/~nsarchiv/NSAEBB/NSAEBB38).
——, *The Sino-Soviet Borders Conflicts, 1969: US Reactions and Diplomatic Maneuvers*, 2001, BURR, William (ed.) (http://www.gwu.edu/~nsarchiv/NSAEBB/NSAEBB49).
——, *The Secret History of the ABM Treaty, 1969–1972*, Electronic Briefing Book No. 60, BURR, William (ed.) (http://www.gwu.edu/~nsarchiv/NSAEBB/NSAEBB60/index2.html).

——, *Archive Hails Final Turnover of Kissinger Telecons: GWU Group Persuades Archives to Recover Telephone Transcripts* (http://www.gwu.edu/~nsarchiv/news/20020211/index2.html).

——, *The Beijing-Washington Back-Channel and Henry Kissinger's Secret Trip to China September 1970–July 1971*, Electronic Briefing Book No. 66, BURR William (ed.) (http://www.gwu.edu/~nsarchiv/NSAEBB/NSAEBB66/).

——, *Negotiating US-Chinese Rapprochement: New American and Chinese Documentation Leading Up to Nixon's 1972 Trip*, Electronic Briefing Book No. 70, BURR, William (ed.) (http://www.msarchive.org/NSAEBB/NSAEBB70).

——, *New Documentary Reveals Secret US, Chinese Diplomacy Behind Nixon's Trip*, Electronic Briefing Book No. 145, BURR William (ed.) (http://www2.gwu.edu/~nsarchiv/NSAEBB/NSAEBB145/index.htm).

PBS. *American Experience: Nixon's China Game* (http://www.pbs.org/wgbh/amex/china/index.html).

    Enhanced Transcript.
    Interview Transcripts: HAIG, Alexander Jr.
    Special Features: Interview, KISSINGER, Henry.

Published Memoirs, Diaries, and Biographies

AMBROSE, Stephen E. *NIXON, Volume I, The Education of a Politician 1913–1962*. London: Simon & Schuster, 1987.

——, *NIXON, Volume II, The Triumph of a Politician 1962–1972*. London: Simon & Schuster, 1989.

BABB, James. *Tanaka: The Making of Postwar Japan*. Essex: Pearson Education Limited, 2000.

BRESLIN, Shaun. *Mao*. London and New York: Longman, 1998.

BRZEZINSKI, Zbigniew. *Power and Principle: Memoirs of the National Security Adviser 1977–1981*. London: Weidenfeld and Nicolson, 1983.

BUNDY, William. *A Tangled Web: The Making of Foreign Policy in the Nixon Presidency*. New York: Hill and Wang A Division of Farrar, Straus and Giroux, 1998.

CHANG, Jung and HALLIDAY, Jon. *Mao: The Unknown Story*. New York: Random House, 2005.

CHEEK, Timothy (ed.), *Mao Zedong and China's Revolutions: A Brief History with Documents*. Boston, New York: Bedford/St. Martin's, 2002.

DALLECK, Robert. *Nixon and Kissinger: Partners in Power*. New York: HarperCollins, 2007.

EVANS, Richard. *Deng Xiaoping and the Making of Modern China*. London: Penguin Books, 1995.

FORD Gerald R. *A Time To Heal: The Autobiography of Gerald R. Ford*. New York: Harper & Row Publishers and the Reader's Digest Association, Inc., 1979.

GARDNER, Lloyd C. *The Great Nixon Turnaround*. New York: A Division of Franklin Watts, Inc., 1973.

GRAUBARD, Stephen. *Kissinger: Portrait of a Mind*. New York: McGraw-Hill, 1973.
GREEN, Marshall, HOLGRIDGE, John H., STOKES, William N. *War and Peace with China: First-Hand Experiences in the Foreign Service of the United States*. Maryland: Dacor-Bacon House, 1994.
HAIG Jr., Alexander M. *Caveat: Realism, Reagan, and Foreign Policy*. London: Weidenfeld and Nicolson, 1984.
———, with McCARRY, Charles. *Inner Circle: How America Changed the World, A Memoir*. New York: Warner Books, 1992.
HALDEMAN, H.R. with DIMONA Joseph. *The Ends of Power*. New York: Times Books, 1978.
———, *The Haldeman Diaries: Inside The Nixon White House*. New York: G.P. Putnam's Sons, 1994.
HAMBURG, Eric. (ed.), *Nixon: An Oliver Stone Film*. London: Bloomsbury, 1995.
HAN, Suyin. *Eldest Son: Zhou Enlai and the Making of Modern China*. London: Pimlico An imprint of Random House, 1994.
HANHIMAKI, Jussi. *The Flawed Architect: Henry Kissinger and American Foreign Policy*. New York: Oxford University Press, 2004.
HERSH, Seymour. *The Price of Power*. New York: Summit Books, 1983.
HOLDRIDGE, John H. *Crossing the Divide: An Insider's Account of the Normalization of US-China Relations*. Lanham, Boulder, New York, Oxford: Rowman & Littlefield Publishers, Inc., 1997.
ISAACSON, Walter. *Kissinger: A Biography*. New York: McGraw-Hill, 1992.
JOHNSON, U. Alexis. *The Right Hand of Power*. Englewood Cliffs, New Jersey: Prentice-Hall, 1984.
KALB, Marvin and KALB, Bernard. *KISSINGER*. London: Hutchinson, 1974.
KEITH, Ronald. *The Diplomacy of Zhou Enlai*. New York: St. Martin's Press, 1989.
KISSINGER, Henry A. *White House Years*. Boston: Little Brown, 1979.
———, *Years of Upheaval*. Boston: Little Brown, 1982.
———, *Diplomacy*. London: Simon & Schuster, 1994.
———, A. *Years of Renewal*. New York: Little Brown, 1999.
KUTZER, Stanley I. *Abuse of Power: The New Nixon Tapes*. New York: The Free Express, 1997.
LANDAU, David. *Kissinger: The Use of Power*. Boston: Houghton Mifflin, 1972.
LI, Zhisui. *The Private Life of Chairman Mao: The Memoirs of Mao's personal physician*. Arrow Books: London, 1994.
MACMILLAN, Margaret. *Seize the Hour: When Nixon Met Mao*. London: John Murrey, 2006.
MORRIS, Roger. *Uncertain Greatness*. New York: Harper & Row Publishers, 1977.
NIXON, Richard M. *RN*. New York: Grssett & Danlap, 1978.
———, *Leaders*. London: Sidgwick & Jackson, 1982.
NUTTER, G. Warren. *Kissinger's Grand Design*. Washington DC: American Enterprise Institute, 1975.
OUDES, Bruce (ed.), *From: President: Richard Nixon's Secret Files*. London: Andre Deutsch, 1989.

PRICE, Raymond. *With Nixon.* New York: Viking, 1977.
REEVES, Richard. *President Nixon: Alone in the White House.* New York: Simon & Schuster, 2001.
ROSS, Terrill. *Mao: A Biography.* New York: Harper & Row, Publishers, 1980.
SAFIRE, William. *Before the Fall.* New York: Doubleday, 1975.
SALISBURY, Harrison E. *The Long March: The Untold Story.* London: Pan Books Ltd., 1986.
——, *The New Emperors Mao and Deng: A Dual Biography.* London: HarperCollins Publishers, 1993.
SCHUIZINGER, Robert. *Henry Kissinger: Doctor of Diplomacy.* New York: Columbia University Press, 1989.
SHEN, James C.H. *The US and Free China: How the US Sold Out Its Ally.* Washington DC Acropolis Books LTD, 1983.
SHORT, Philipe. *Mao: A Life.* New York: Henry Holt & Company, 1999.
SMALL, Melvin. *The Presidency of Richard Nixon.* Lawrence, Kansas: University Press of Kansas, 1999.
SNOW, Edgar. *Red Star Over China.* First revised and enlarged edition. London: Victor Gollancz Ltd., 1973.
——, *The Long Revolution.* London: Hutchinson & Co Publishers Ltd., 1973.
SPENCE, Jonathan D. *Mao* Zedong. New York: Viking, Penguin, 1999.
STROBER, Gerald S. and STROBER Deborah Hart. *Nixon: An Oral History of His Presidency.* New York: Harper Collins Publishers, 1994.
SUMMERS, Anthony with SWAN, Robbyn. *The Arrogance of Power: The Secret World of Richard Nixon.* London: Victor Gollancz, 2000.
SZULC, Tad. *The Illusion of Peace: Foreign Policy in the Nixon Years.* New York: Viking, 1978.
TERILL, Ross. *Mao: A Biography.* Stanford, California: Stanford University Press, 1999.
TUCKER, Nancy Bernkopf (ed.), *China Confidential: American Diplomats and Sino-American Relations, 1945–1996.* New York: Columbia University Press, 2001.
WILSON, Dick, *Zhou Enlai: A Biography.* New York: Viking, 1984.
YOUNG, Kenneth T. *Negotiating with the Chinese Communists: The United States Experience, 1953–1967.* New York: McGraw-Hill, 1968.
ZHABG, Shu Guang. "In the Shadow of Mao: Zhou Enlai and New China's Diplomacy," in CRAIG, Gordon A. and LOEWENHEIM, Francis L. (eds), *The Diplomats 1939–1979.* Princeton, New Jersey: Princeton University Press, 1994.

Books

AIJAZUDDIN, F.S. (ed.), *The White House and Pakistan: Secret Declassified Documents, 1969–1974.* Oxford, New York: Oxford University Press, 2002.
ALEXANDER, Bevin. *The Strange Connection: US Intervention in China, 1944–1972.* Westport Connecticut: Greenwood Press, 1999.
ALLISON, Graham Allison. *Essence of Decision: Explaining the Cuban Missile Crisis.* Boston: Little Brown, 1971.

Bibliography

ALLISON, Graham Allison and ZELIKOW Philipe. *Essence of Decision: Explaining the Cuban Missile Crisis*. Second edition. New York: Longman, 1999.
AMBROSE, Stephen E. *Rise to Globalism*. New York: Penguin Books, 1993.
ARMSTRONG, David. *Revolutionary Diplomacy: Chinese Foreign Policy and the United Front Doctrine*. Berkley: University of California Press, 1977.
——, *Revolution and World Order: The Revolutionary State in International Society*. Oxford: Clarendon Press, 1993.
ARUGA, Tadashi. "Japanese Scholarship in the History of US-East Asian Relations," in COHEN (ed.), *Pacific Passage*. New York: Columbia University Press, 1996.
ASHTON, S.R. *In Search of Détente*. London: Macmillan, 1989.
BARNETT, Doak A. *Communist China and Asia: Challenge to American Policy*. New York: Council on Foreign Relations by Harper & Brothers, 1960.
——, *China and the Major Powers in East Asia*. Washington DC: The Brookings Institution, 1977.
BELL, Coal. *The Diplomacy of Détente*. New York: St. Martin's, 1977.
BORG, Dorothy and HENNETH, Waldo. (eds), *Uncertain Years: Chinese American Relations, 1947–1950*. New York: Columbia University Press, 1980.
BROWN, Seyom. *The Faces of Power*. New York: Columbia University Press, 1994.
BURR, William. (ed.), *The Kissinger Transcripts: The Top Secret Talks with Beijing and Moscow*. New York: The New Press, 1999.
CHAFE, William H. *The Unfinished Journey*. Oxford: Oxford University Press, 1995.
CHANG, Gordon H. *Friends and Enemies: The United States, China, and the Soviet Union, 1948–1972*. Stanford, California: Stanford University Press, 1990.
CHEN, Edward K.Y. *Sino-American Relations Since 1900*. Hong Kong: The Centre of Asian Studies, The University of Hong Kong, 1991.
CHEN Jian. *Mao's China and the Cold War*. Chapel Hill, NC: University of North Carolina Press, 2001.
COHEN, Warren I. *America's Response to China: A history of Sino-American Relations*. Third edition. New York: Columbia University Press, 1990.
——, (ed.), *Pacific Passage: The Study of American-East Asian Relations on the Eve of the Twenty-First Century*. New York: Columbia University Press, 1996.
CRAIG, Gordon A. and LOEWENHEIM, Francis L. (eds), *The Diplomats 1939–1979*. Princeton, New Jersey: Princeton University Press, 1994.
DALLEK, Robert. *The American Style of Foreign Policy: Cultural Politics and Foreign Affairs*. New York: Knopf, 1983.
DEGROOT, Gerald D. *Noble Cause? American and the Vietnam War*. New York: Longman, 1999.
DICKSON, Peter. *Kissinger and the Meaning of History*. New York: Cambridge University Press, 1979.
DIETRICH, Craig. *People's China: A brief history*. Second edition. Oxford: Oxford University Press, 1994.
DITTMER, Lowell and KIM, Samuels. *China's Quest for National Identity*. London: Cornell University Press, 1993.

DOCKRILL, Saki. *Eisenhower's New-Look National Security Policy, 1953–1961*. New York: St. Martin's Press, 1996.

DOUGHERTY, James E. and PFALTZGRAFF Jr., Robert L. *Contending Theories of International Relations: A Comprehensive Survey*. Third edition. New York: HarperCollins Publishers, 1990.

ETZOLD, Thomas H. and GADDIS John Lewis. (eds), *Containment: Documents on American Policy and Strategy*. New York: Columbia University Press, 1978.

FAIRBANK, John King. *The United States and China*. Cambridge, Massachusetts: Harvard University Press, 1965.

——, *The Chinese World Order*. Cambridge, Massachusetts: Harvard University Press, 1968.

——, *China Watch*. Cambridge, Massachusetts and London: Harvard University Press, 1987.

——, *China: A New History*. Cambridge, Massachusetts and London: Harvard University Press, 1992.

FAIRBANK, J.K and MACFARQUHAR, R. (eds), *The Cambridge History of China, Volume 15*. Cambridge: Cambridge University Press, 1991.

FAIRBANK, John King, REISCHAUER, Edwin O., and CRAIG, Albert M. *East Asia: Tradition and Transformation*. Boston: Houghton Mifflin, 1970.

FOOT, Rosemary. *The Practice of Power: US Relations with China since 1949*. Oxford New York: Clarendon Press, 1995.

FREEMAN, Charles. W. Jr. *The Diplomat's Dictionary*. Revised edition. Washington DC: United States Institute of Peace Press, 2006.

GADDIS, John Lewis. *Strategies of Containment*. Oxford: Oxford University Press, 1982.

——, *The United States and the End of the Cold War*. Oxford: Oxford University Press, 1992.

——, *Now We Know: Rethinking Cold War History*. Oxford: Oxford University Press, 1998.

GALLICCHIO, Marc. "Recovery through Dependency: American-Japanese Relations, 1945–1970," in COHEN (ed.), *Pacific Passage*. New York: Columbia University Press, 1996.

GARTHOFF, Raymond L. *Détente and Confrontation*. Washington DC: The Brookings Institution, 1985.

GARVER, John. W. *China's Decision for Rapprochement with the United States, 1968–1971*. Colorado: Westview Press, Inc., 1982.

——, *The Sino-American Alliance: Nationalist China and American Cold War Strategy*. New York: An East Gate Book M.E. Sharpe, Inc., 1997.

GEORGE, Alexander. *Presidential Decision Making in Foreign Policy: The Effective Use of Information and Advice*. Boulder: Westview Press, 1980.

GOH, Evelyn. *Constructing the US Rapprochement with China, 1961–1974: From 'Red Menace' to 'Tacit Ally'* New York: Cambridge University Press, 2004.

GOLDSTEIN, Steven M. "Nationalism and Internationalism: Sino-Soviet Relations," in ROBINSON, T.W. and SHAMBAUGH, D. (eds), *Chinese Foreign Policy: Theory and Practice*. London: Clarendon Press, 1994.

GOODMAN, David S.G., and SEGAL, Gerald. *China Rising: Nationalism and Interdependence*. New York: Routledge, 1997.

GOTTLIEB, Thomas M. *Chinese Foreign Policy Factionalism and the Origins of the Strategic Triangle*. Santa Monica, California: The Rand Corporation, 1977.

HALPERIN, Morton H. *Bureaucratic Politics and Foreign Policy*. Washington DC: The Brookings Institution, 1974.

HALPERIN, Morton H. and CLAPP Priscilla with KANTER Arnold. *Bureaucratic Politics and Foreign Policy*. Second edition. Washington DC: The Brookings Institution, 2007.

HALPERIN, Morton H. and KANTER, Arnold. (eds), *Readings in American Foreign Policy: A Bureaucratic Perspective*. Boston: Little Brown, 1973.

HAMLIN, Carol Lee. "Elite Politics and the Development of China's Foreign Relations," in ROBINSON, Thomas W. and SHAMBAUGH, David. *Chinese Foreign Policy: Theory and Practice*. Oxford, New York: Oxford University Press Clarendon Paperbacks, 1994.

HANDEL, Michael. *The Diplomacy of Surprise: Hitler, Nixon, Sadat*. Massachusetts: Center for International Affairs, Harvard University, 1981.

HARDING, Harry. (ed.), *Chinese Foreign Relations in the 1980s*. New Haven: Yale University Press, 1985.

——, *A Fragile Relationship: The United States and China since 1972*. Washington DC: The Brookings Institutions, 1992.

HOFFMANN, Stanley. *Stanley Gulliver's Troubles, Or the Setting of American Foreign Policy*. New York: McGraw-Hill, 1968.

——, *Primary or World Order*. New York: McGraw-Hill, 1978.

HOWE, Christopher. (ed.), *China and Japan: History, Trends, and Prospects*. Oxford: Clarendon Press, 1996.

HSIUNG, James C. (ed.), *Asia Pacific in the New World Politics*. Boulder & London: Lynne Rienner Publishers, 1993.

HSU, Immanuel C.Y. *The Rise of Modern China*. Third edition. New York: Oxford University Press, 1983.

INOGUCHI, Takashi. *Japan's International Relations*. London: Pinter Publishers, 1991.

IRIYE, Akira. *Japan and the Wider World: From the Mid-Nineteenth Century to the Present*. New York: Addison Wesley Publishers, 1997.

IRIYE, Akira and COHEN, Warren. (eds), *American, Chinese, and Japanese Perspectives on Wartime Asia 1931–1949*. Wilmington, Delaware: A Scholarly Resources Imprint, 1990.

JISI, Wang. "International Relations Theory and the Study of Chinese Foreign Policy: A Chinese Perspective," in ROBINSON, T.W. and SHAMBAUGH, D. (eds), *Chinese Foreign Policy: Theory and Practice*. Oxford: Clarendon Press, 1994.

JOHNSTON, A.I. *Cultural Realism: Strategic Culture and Grand Strategy in Chinese History*. Princeton, New Jersey: Princeton University Press, 1995.

——, "Cultural Realism and Strategy in Maoist China" in KUTZENSTEIN, K.J. (ed.), *The Culture of National Security: Norms and Ideology in World Politics*. New York: Columbia University Press, 1996.

KEGLEY Jr., Charles W. and WITTKOPF, Eugene R. *American Foreign Policy: Pattern and Process*. Fifth edition. New York: St. Martin's Press, 1996.

KENNAN George F. *American Diplomacy 1900–1950*, Chicago: University of Chicago Press, 1985.

KENNETH, Lieberthal and OKSENBURG, Michel. *Policy Making in China: Leaders, Structures, and Processes*. New Jersey: Princeton University Press, 1988.

KEOHANE, Robert O. (ed.), *Neorealism and its Critics*. New York: Columbia University Press, 1986.

KEOHANE, Robert O. and NYE, Joseph. S. *Power and Interdependence*. New York: HarperCollins, 1989.

KIM Samuel S. (ed.), *China and the World: Chinese Foreign Relations in the Post-Cold War Era*. Third edition. Boulder, Colorado and Oxford: Westreview Press, 1994.

KIMBALL, Jeffrey. *Nixon's Vietnam War.* Lawrence, Kansas: The University Press of Kansas, 1998.

KIRBY, William C. "Traditions of Centrality, Authority, and Management in Modern China's Foreign Relations," in ROBINSON, T.W. and SHAMBAUGH, D. (eds), *Chinese Foreign Policy: Theory and Practice*. Oxford: Clarendon Press, 1994.

KISSINGER, Henry A. *A World Restored*. Boston: Houghton Mitflin, 1957.

——, *Nuclear Weapon and Foreign Policy*. New York: Harper & Brothers, 1957.

——, *The Necessity for Choice*. New York: Harper & Brothers, 1961.

——, *The Troubled Partnership: A Reappraisal of the Atlantic Alliance*. New York: McGraw-Hill, 1965.

——, "Bureaucracy and Policymaking: The Effects of Insiders and Outsiders on the Policy Process," in HALPERIN, Morton H. and KANTER, Arnold (eds), *Readings in American Foreign Policy: A Bureaucratic Perspective*. Boston: Little Brown, 1973.

——, *American Foreign Policy: Three Essays*. London: Wedenfeld and Nicolson, 1969.

KUTZENSTEIN P.J. (ed.), *The Culture of National Security: Norms and Ideology in World Politics*. New York: Columbia University Press, 1996.

KUX, Dennis. *The United States and Pakistan, 1947–2000: Disenchanted Allies*. Washington DC: Woodrow Wilson Center Press, 2001.

LEVINE, Steven I. "Perception and Ideology in Chinese Foreign Policy," in ROBINSON, T.W. and SHAMBAUGH, D. (eds), *Chinese Foreign Policy: Theory and Practice*. Oxford: Clarendon Press, 1994.

LIEBERTHAL, Kenneth and DICKSON, Bruce J. *A Research Guide to Central Party and Government Meetings in China 1949–1986*. New York: An East Gate Book, M.E. Sharpe, Inc., 1989.

LIEBERTHAL, Kenneth and OKSENBURG, Michael. *Policy Making in China Leaders, Structures, and Process*, Princeton. New Jersey: Princeton University Press, 1988.

LITWAK, Robert S. *Détente and Nixon Doctrine: American Foreign Policy, 1969–76*. New York: Cambridge University Press, 1986.

LONGMAN. *Longman Dictionary of Contemporary English*. New edition. Essex: Longman, 1991.
MACFARQUHAR, Roderick. *Sino-American Relations, 1949–1971*. Newton Abbot: David & Charles, 1972.
MADSEN, Richard. *China and the American Dream: A Moral Inquiry*. Berkeley/ Los Angels/ London: University of California Press, 1995.
MANN, James H. *About Face: A History of America's Curious Relationship with China, from Nixon to Clinton*. New York: Alfred Knopf, 1999.
MAO, Tse-tung. *Selected Military Writings of Mao Tse-tung*. Peking: Foreign Language Press, 1966.
——, *Selected Works of Mao Tse-tung Volume 1–4*. Peking: Foreign Language Press, 1967.
MOORSTEEN, Richard and ABRAMOWITZ, Morton. *Remaking China Policy*. Cambridge Massachusetts: Harvard University Press, 1971.
MORGENTHAU, Has J. *Truth and Power: Essays of a Decade, 1960–70*. New York: Praeger Publishers, 1970.
——, *Politics among Nations: The Struggle for Power and Peace*. Sixth edition (brief edition). Revised by THOMPSON, Kenneth W. New York: Knopf, 1993.
MCGREW, Anthony and BROOK, Christopher (eds), *Asia-Pacific in the New World Order*. London and New York: Routledge, 1998.
NAGAI, Yonosuke and IRIYE, Akira. (eds), *The Origins of the Cold War in Asia*. New York: Columbia University Press, 1977.
NYE, Joseph S. Jr. *Bound to Lead: The Changing Nature of American Power*. New York: Basic Books, 1990.
POLLACK, Jonathan D. "The Opening to America," in FAIRBANK, J.K and MACFARQUHAR, R. (eds), *The Cambridge History of China, Volume 15*. Cambridge: Cambridge University Press 1991.
PRADOS, John. *Keepers of the Keys: A History of the National Security Council from Truman to Bush*. New York: William Morrow and Company, Inc., 1991.
QIANG, Zhai. *China and the Vietnam Wars, 1950–1975*. Chapel Hill, NC: University of North Carolina Press, 2000.
QIU, Jin and PERRY Elizabeth. *The Lin Biao Incident and the Cultural Revolution*. Stanford, California: Stanford University Press, 1999.
ROBINSON, Thomas W. and SHAMBAUGH, David. (eds), *Chinese Foreign Policy: Theory and Practice*. London: Clarendon Press, 1994.
ROSS, Robert. S. *After the Cold War: Domestic Factors and US-China Relations*. New York: M.E. Sharpe, 1998.
——, *Negotiating Cooperation: The United States and China 1969–1989*. Stanford, California: Stanford University Press, 1995.
——, *The United States, and The Soviet Union: Tripolarity and Policy Making in the Cold War*. New York: An East Gate Books, 1993.
ROSS, Robert S. and JIANG Changbin. (eds), *Re-examining the Cold War: US-China Diplomacy, 1954–1973*. Cambridge, Massachusetts: Harvard University Press, 2001.

ROY, Denny. *China's Foreign Relations*, London: Macmillan Press Ltd., 1998.
SCHALLER, Michael. *The United States and China in the Twentieth Century*. Second edition. New York, Oxford: Oxford University Press, 1990.
SHAMBAUGH, David. *Beautiful Imperialist: China Perceives America, 1972–1990*. Princeton, New Jersey: Princeton University Press, 1991.
——, "Pattern of Interaction in Sino-American Relations" in ROBINSON, T.W. and SHAMBAUGH, D. (eds), *Chinese Foreign Policy: Theory and Practice*. Oxford: Clarendon Press, 1994.
SHERRY, Michael. *In the Shadow of War*. Yale University Press, 1995.
SOLOMON, Richard H. *Chinese Negotiating Behavior: Pursuing Interests Through 'Old Friends'*. Washington DC: United States Institute of Peace Press, 1999.
SPANIER, John and USLANER, Eric M. *American Foreign Policy Making and the Democratic Dilemmas*. Fifth edition. Belmont, California: Wadsworth, Inc., 1989.
SUN TZU. *The Art of War*. London: Hodder & Stoughton, 1981.
TANG, Tsou. *America's Failure in China 1941–50*. Chicago: University of Chicago Press, 1963.
TOW, William T. "China and the International Strategic System," in ROBINSON, T.W. and SHAMBAUGH, D. (eds), *Chinese Foreign Policy: Theory and Practice*. Oxford: Clarendon Press, 1994.
TUCKER, Nancy Bernkopf. *Patterns in the Dust: Chinese-American Relations and the Recognition Controversy, 1949–1950*. New York: Columbia University Press, 1983.
——, "Continuing Controversies in the Literature of US-China Relations since 1945," in COHEN (ed.), *Pacific Passage*, New York: Columbia University Press, 1996.
TURABIAN, K.L. *Manual for Writing of Term Papers, Theses, and Dissertations*. Sixth edition. Chicago: University of Chicago Press, 1996.
TYLER, Patrick E. *A Great Wall: Six Presidents and China, an Investigative History*. New York: Public Affairs, 1999.
VIOTTI, Paul R. and KAUPPI, Mark V. *International Relations Theory*. New York: Macmillan Publishing Company, 1993.
WALTZ, Kenneth N. *Man the State and War: A Theoretical Analysis*. New York: Columbia University Press, 1959.
——, *Theory of International Politics*. New York: McGraw-Hill, 1979.
WHITING, Allen S. *China Crosses the Yalu the Decision to Enter the Korean War*. Stanford, California: Stanford University Press, 1960.
——, *The Chinese Calculus of Deterrence: India and Indochina*. Michigan: The University of Michigan Press, 1975.
YAHUDA, Michael. "The Significance of Tripolarity in China's Policy Toward the United States Since 1972," in ROSS, R. (ed.), *China, The United States, and The Soviet Union: Tripolarity and Policy Making in the Cold War*. New York: An East Gate Books, 1993.
——, *The International Politics of the Asia-Pacific, 1945–1995*. New York: Routeledge, 1996.
ZHAI, Qiang. *China and the Vietnam Wars, 1950–1975*. Chapel Hill, NC: University of North Carolina Press, 2000.

——, *The Dragon, the Lion, and the Eagle: Chinese-British-American Relations, 1949–1958*. Kent, Ohio: The Kent University Press, 1994.

Articles and Working Papers

BALL, George W. "Japan Urged to Reassess its Attitude," *Pacific Community*, October 1970.
BARNETT, Doak A. "Peking and the Asian Power Balance," *Problems of Communists*, July–August 1976.
BEISNER, Robert L. "History and Henry Kissinger," *Diplomatic History*, Fall 1990.
BERGER, Thomas U. "From Sword to Chrysanthemum: Japan's Culture of Antimilitarism" *International Security*, Vol. 17, No. 4, Spring 1993.
BRANDS, Jr., H.W. "Testing Massive Retaliation: Credibility and Crisis Management in the Taiwan Strait," *International Security*, Vol. 12, No. 4, Spring 1988.
BRIDGHAM, Philip. "The Fall of Lin Biao," *The China Quarterly*, 55, July–September, 1973.
BROWN, R.G. "Chinese Politics and American Policy: A New Look at the Triangle," *Foreign Policy*, 23, 1976.
BRZEZINSKI, Zbigniew. "US Foreign Policy: The Search for Focus," *Foreign Affairs*, July 1973.
BULL, Hedley. "The New Balance of Power in Asia and the Pacific," *Foreign Affairs*, Vol. 49, No. 4, July 1971.
BUNDY, William. "The Nixon Politics in Asia and the Pacific," *Pacific Community*, October 1970.
BURR, William. "Sino-American Rapprochement, 1969: The Sino-Soviet Border War and Steps towards Rapprochement," *Cold War History*, Vol. 1, No. 3, April 2001.
BUZAN, Barry and SEGAL, Gerald. "Rethinking of East Asian Security," *Survival*, Vol. 36, No. 2, Summer 1994.
CARPENTER, Ted Galen. "Rolling Asia: US Coziness with China Upsets the Neighbors," *Foreign Affairs*, November/December 1998.
CHANG, Gordon H. "To the Nuclear Brink: Eisenhower, Dulles, and the Quemoy-Matsu Crisis," *International Security*, Vol. 12, No. 4, Spring 1988.
——, Feature Review, "Who Benefited? Forty Five Years of US-China Relations," *Diplomatic History*, Vol. 21, No. 2, Spring 1997.
CHANG, Gordon H. and HE, Di. "The Absence of War in the US-China Confrontation over Quemoy and Matsu in 1954–1955: Contingency, Luck, Deterrence?" *American Historical Review*, Vol. 98, No. 5, December 1993.
CHEN Jian. 'The Myth of America's "Lost Chance" in China: A Chinese Perspective in Light of New Evidence,' *Diplomatic History*, Vol. 21, No. 1, Winter 1997.
CHEN Jian, and WILSON, David. (eds), *"All Under the Heaven is Great Chaos"— Beijing, the Sino-Soviet Border Clashes, and the Turn Toward Sino-American Rapprochement, 1968–69*. Bulletin 11. Cold War International History Project, The Woodrow Wilson International Center for Scholars.

CHRISTENSEN, Thomas J. "Threats, Assurances, and the Last Chance for Peace: The Lessons of Mao's Korean War Telegrams," *International Security* Vol. 17, No. 1, Summer 1992.

——, "Chinese Realpolitik," *Foreign Affairs*, Vol. 75, No. 5, September/October 1996.

CLAPP, Priscilla "Okinawa Reversion: Bureaucratic Interaction in Washington 1966–1969," *Kokusai seiji*, 1974.

COHAN, Jerome A. "A China Policy For The Next Administration," *Foreign Affairs*, Vol. 55, No. 1, October 1976.

COHEN, Warren I. "Conversation with Chinese Friends: Zhou Enlai's Associates Reflect on Chinese American Relations in the 1940s and the Korean War," *Diplomatic History*, Summer 1987.

——, 'Symposium: Rethinking the Lost Chance in China: Introduction: Was there a "Lost Chance" in China?' *Diplomatic History*, Vol. 21, No. I, Winter 1997.

CRANMER-BYNG, J. "The Chinese View of Their Place in the World: An Historical Perspective," *The China Quarterly*, 53, 1973.

DESTLER, I.M. "Can One Man Do?" *Foreign Policy*, No. 5, Winter 1971–72.

DIBB, Paul. "Towards a New Balance of Power in Asia," Oxford University Press, *Adelphi Paper*, 295, 1995.

DINGMAN, Roger. "Atomic Diplomacy During the Korean War," *International Security*, Vol. 13, No. 3, Winter 1988/89.

DITTMER, L. 'Bases of Power In Chinese Politics: An Analysis of the Fall of the "Gang of Four",' *World Politics*, 31, 1978.

——, "The Strategic Triangle: An Elementary Game-Theoretical Analysis," *World Politics*, 33, 1981.

FAIRBANK, John King. "China's Foreign Policy in Historical Perspective," *Foreign Affairs*, February 1969.

——, "The New China and the American Connection," *Foreign Affairs*, October 1972.

——, "Has China Changed?" *Foreign Policy*, Summer 1973.

FOOT, Rosemary. "Nuclear Coercion and the Ending of the Korean Conflict," *International Security*, Vol. 13, No. 3, Winter 1988/89.

GADDIS, John Lewis. "The Rise and Fall of Détente," *Foreign Affairs*, Winter 1983/84.

GARVER, J. "Chinese Foreign Policy in 1970: The Tilt toward the Soviet Union," *The China Quarterly*, No. 82, 1980.

——, "Little Chance," *Diplomatic History*, Vol. 21, No. 1, Winter 1997.

GELB, Leslie H. "Arms Sales," *Foreign Policy*, No. 25, Winter 1976.

GELMAN, H. "The Rise and Fall of Détente," *Problems of Communism*, March/April 1985.

HALLORAN, Richard. "The US, Asia and Japan; A Proposal For the '70s," *Pacific Community*, October 1970.

HAMLIN, Carol Lee. "China reassess the superpowers," *Pacific Affairs*, Vol. 56, No.2, Summer 1983.

HANHIMAKI, Jussi. "'Dr. Kissinger' or 'Mr. Henry': Kissingerology, Thirty Years and Counting," *Diplomatic History*, Vol. 27, No. 5, November 2003.

——, "Selling the 'Decent Interval': Henry Kissinger, Triangular Diplomacy, and the End of the Vietnam War, 1971–1973," *Diplomacy & Statecraft*, Vol. xiv, No. 1, March 2003.

——, "Some more 'Smoking Guns'? The Vietnam War and Kissinger's Summitry with Moscow and Beijing, 1971–1972," *SHAFR Newsletter*, Vol. 32, No. 4, December 2001.

——, "A Prize-Winning Performance? Henry Kissinger, Triangular Diplomacy, and the End of the Vietnam War, 1969–1973," *Norwegian Nobel Institute Series*, No. 7. Oslo: Norwegian Nobel Institute, 2001.

HAO, Yufan and Zhai Zhihai. "China's Decision to Enter the Korean War: History Revised," *China Quarterly*, 121, March 1990.

HARDING, Harry. "From China With Disdain: New Trends in the Study of China," *Asian Survey*, Vol. xii, No. 10, October 1982.

HE, Di. "The Most Respected Enemy: Mao Zedong's Perception of the United States," *The China Quarterly*, 1994.

HENDRICKSON, David C. Review Essay "All the President's Acumen: The Paradox of Nixon's Foreign Policy," *Foreign Affairs*, May/June 1998.

HERMANN, M.G. "Explaining Foreign Policy Behaviour Using the Personal Characteristics of Political Leaders," *International Studies Quarterly*, 24, 1980.

HOFFMANN, Stanley. "Weighing the Balance of Power," *Foreign Affairs*, Summer 1972.

——, "Will the Balance Balance at Home?" *Foreign Policy*, Summer 1972.

——, "Choices," *Foreign Policy*, No. 12, Fall 1973.

——, "No Choices No Illusions," *Foreign Policy*, Winter 1976/77.

HUNT, Michael H., and WESTAD, Odd Arne. "The Chinese Communist Party and International Affairs: A Field Report on New Historical Sources and Old Research Problems," *The China Quarterly*, No. 122, June 1990.

HUNT, Michael H. "Beijing and the Korean Crisis, June 1950–June 1951," *Political Science Quarterly*, Fall 1992.

IKLE, Fred Charles and NAKANISHI, Terumasa. "Japan's Grand Strategy," *Foreign Affairs*, 1991.

KENNAN George F. "Is Détente worth Saving?" *Saturday Review*, 6, March 1976.

KISSINGER, Henry A. "White Revolutionary: Reflection on Bismarck," *Daedelus*, xcvii, Summer 1968.

LEACACOS, John P. "Kissinger's Apparatus," *Foreign Policy*, No. 5, Winter 1971–1972.

LEVINE, Steven I. "A New Look at American Mediation in the Chinese Civil War: The Marshall Mission and Manchuria," *Diplomatic History*, Fall 1979.

LIAO, K. "Linkage Politics in China: Internal Mobilization and Articulated External Hostility in the Cultural Revolution 1967–1969," *World Politics*, 27, 1976.

LIEBERTHAL, Kenneth. "The foreign policy debate in Peking as seen through allegorical articles, 1973–1976" *The China Quarterly*, No. 71, September 1977.

——, "A New China Policy," *Foreign Affairs*, Vol. 74, No. 6, 1995.

LITWAK, Robert S. "Henry Kissinger's Ambiguous Legacy," *Diplomatic History*, 1990.

LIU, Melinda. "In Love With A Vision" in Special Report "Standing Up," *Newsweek*, September 20, 1999.

MAGA, Timothy P. "'Golf Ball Diplomacy:' Richard Nixon and Japan, 1969–1974," *Diplomacy and Statecraft*, Vol. 9. No. 1, March 1998.

MCLEAN, David. "American Nationalism, the China Myth, and the Truman Doctrine: The Question of Accommodation with Peking, 1949–1950," *Diplomatic History*, Winter 1988.

MCMAHON, Robert J. "The Cold War in Asia: Toward a New Synthesis," *Diplomatic History*, Summer 1988.

MONROE, Jr. J.G. "Garver's Pro-Soviet Tilt: Do the Data Tell the Truth?" *The China Quarterly*, No. 88, 1981.

MORGENTHAU, Has J. "Détente: The Balance Sheet," *The New York Times*, March 28, 1974.

NATHAN Andrew. "A Factionalism Model for CCP Politics," *The China Quarterly*, No. 53, January–March 1973.

NG-QUINN, Michael. "The Analytic Study of Chinese Foreign Policy," *International Studies Quarterly*, 1983.

NIXON, Richard M. "Asia After Viet Nam," *Foreign Affairs*, October 1967.

OKSENBERG, Michel. "Mao's policy commitments, 1921–1976," *Problems of Communism*, No. 6, November–December 1976.

——, "A Decade of Sino-American Relations," *Foreign Affairs*, 1982.

——, "China's Confident Nationalism," *Foreign Affairs*, Winter 1986–1987.

——, "The China Problem," *Foreign Affairs*, 1991.

OKSENBERG, Michel and GOLDSTEIN Steven. "The Chinese Political Spectrum," *Problems of Communism*, Vol. 23, No. 2, March–April 1974.

PFALTZGRAFF, R.L. "Multipolarity, Alliances, and US-Soviet-Chinese Relations," *Orbis*, 17, 1973.

PILLISBURY, Michael P. "US-Chinese Military Ties?" *Foreign Policy*, No. 20, Fall 1975.

——, "Future Sino-American Security Ties: The View from Tokyo, Moscow, and Peking," *International Security*, Spring 1977.

PYE Lucian W. "Mao Tse-tung's Leadership Style," *Political Science Quarterly*, Summer 1976.

——, "China: Erratic State, Frustrated Society," *Foreign Affairs*, Vol. 69, No. 4, Autumn 1990.

RAVENAL, Earl C. "The Nixon Doctrine and our Asian Commitments," *Foreign Affairs*, January 1971.

——, "The Case for Strategic Disengagement," *Foreign Affairs*, October 1972.

——, "Large-Scale Foreign Policy Change: The Nixon Doctrine as History and Portent," Policy Papers in International Affairs, No. 35, California, Berkeley: Institute of International Studies, University of California, 1989.

REISCHAUER, Edwin O. "Japanese-American Relations in the 1970s," *Pacific Community*, April 1971.

——, "The Sinic World in Perspective," *Foreign Affairs*, January 1974.

ROSS, Robert. S. "International bargaining and domestic politics: US-China relations since 1972," *World Politics*, Vol. xxxviii, No. 2, January 1986.

——, "From Lin Biao to Deng Xiaoping: Elite Instability and China's US policy," *The China Quarterly*, June 1989.

ROY, Denny. "Hegemon on the Horizon? China's Threat to East Asian Security," *International Security*, Vol. 19, No. 1, Summer 1994.

RUSELL, Greg. "Kissinger's Philosophy and Kantian Ethics," *Diplomacy and Statecraft*, Vol. 7, No. 1, March 1996.

SCALAPINO. Robert A. "China and the Balance of Power," *Foreign Affairs*, January 1974.

——, "Asia and the United States: The Challenging Ahead," *Foreign Affairs*, 1989/90.

SCHRAM, Stuart. "Mao Zedong a Hundred Years On: The Legacy of a Ruler," *The China Quarterly*, No. 137, March 1994.

SCHWARTZ, Benjamin I. "The Maoist Image of World Order," *Journal of International Affairs*, 1967.

SEGAL, Gerald. "China and the Great Power Triangle," *The China Quarterly*, No. 83, September 1980.

——, "China Changes Shape: Regionalism and Foreign Policy," *Adelphi Paper*, 287, March 1994.

——, 'East Asia and "Constrainment" of China,' *International Security*, Vol. 20, No. 4, Spring 1996.

SERVICE, John S. "Edgar Snow: Some Personal Reminiscences," *The China Quarterly*, No. 50, April/June 1972.

SHAMBAUGH, David L. "China's National Security Research Bureaucracy," *The China Quarterly*, No. 109, March 1987.

——, "China's America Watchers," *Problem of Communism*, May-August 1988.

——, "China's Security Policy in the Post Cold War Era," *Survival*, Vol. 34, No.2, Summer 1992(a).

——, "Peking's Foreign Policy Conundrum since Tiananmen: Peaceful Coexistence vs. Peaceful Evolution," *Issues and Studies*, 28, No. 11, November 1992(b).

——, "Growing Strong; China's Challenge to Asian Security," *Survival*, Vol. 36, No. 2, Summer 1994.

——, "Containment or Engagement of China," *International Security*, Vol. 21, No. 2, Fall 1996.

SHENG, Michael. "The Triumph of Internationalism: CCP-Moscow Relations before 1949," *Diplomatic History*, Vol. 21, No. 1, Winter 1997.

SHIMODA, Takeso. "Approach to China Problem," *Pacific Community*, April 1971.

SPENCE, Jonathan. "Kissinger and Emperor," *The New York Review of Books*, March 4, 1999.

——, "Mao Tse-Tung and Peaceful Coexistence," *Orbis*, Spring 1964.

TANG, Tsou and HALPERIN, Morton. "Mao's Revolutionary Strategy and Peking's International Behavior," *American Political Science Review*, 59, 1965.

THOMSON Jr., James C. "Will the Nixon Administration recognize Communist China?" *Pacific Community*, October 1970.

——, "On the Making of US China Policy, 1961–1969: A Study in Bureaucratic Politics," *The China Quarterly*, No. 50 (April/June) 1972.

TUCHMAN, Barbara W. "If Mao Had Come to Washington: An Essay in Alternatives," *Foreign Affairs*, October 1972.

TUCKER, Nancy Bernkopf. "China and America, 1941–1991," *Foreign Affairs*, Vol. 70, No. 5, Winter 1991–92.

———, "No Common Ground: America-Chinese-Soviet Relations 1948–1972," *Diplomatic History*, Spring 1992.

WARNKE, Paul C. "We Don't Need A Devil," *Foreign Policy*, No. 25, Winter 1976.

WEITZ, Richard. "Henry Kissinger's Philosophy of International Relations," *Diplomacy and Statecraft*, Vol. 2, No. 1, March 1991.

WESTAD, Odd Arne. "Losses, Chances, and Myths: The United States and the Creation of the Sino-Soviet Alliance, 1945–1950," *Diplomatic History*, Vol. 21, No. 1, Winter 1997.

WHITING, Allen S. "Sino-American Détente," Review Article, *The China Quarterly*, No. 82, June 1980.

WORTZEL, Larry M. "China and Strategy: China Pursues Traditional Great-Power Status," *Orbis*, Summer 1994.

YAHUDA, Michael "Kremlinology and Chinese Strategic Debate 1965–66," *The China Quarterly*, 149, January–March 1972.

YANG, Kuisong. "The Sino-Soviet Border Clash of 1969: From Zhenbao Island to Sino-American Rapprochement," *Cold War History*, Vol. 1, No. 1, August 2000.

ZHAI, Qiang. "Dulles, Wedge and the Sino-American Ambassadorial Talks 1955–1957," *Chinese Historians*, June 1989.

Newspapers and Periodicals

The Boston Globe
Newsweek
The New York Times
Philadelphia Bulletin
Time
The Times
The Washington Post

Unpublished PhD Theses

GARRETT, Banning N. 'The "China card" and Its Origins: US Bureaucratic Politics and the Strategic Triangle' Unpublished PhD thesis, Brandeis University MA 1983.

GOH, Evelyn. "From 'Red Menace' to 'Tacit' Ally: Constructing the Rapprochement with China, 1961–1974" PhD thesis, Nuffield College, Oxford University, 2001.

———, "Re-representations: Competing images and the recovery of US relations with China, 1961–1968" M.Phil thesis, Faculty of Social Studies, Nuffield College, Oxford University, 1999.

JUNG, H.S. US Alliance Policy toward Japan, 1969–1982: George Kennan's Prescription for Indirect Control of Japan and Its Legacy to US-Japanese Security Relations. PhD thesis, Lancaster University, 1993.

KOMINE, Yukinori. US Foreign Policy Toward Sino-US Rapprochement in the early 1970s: A Study of Secrecy in Bureaucratic Politics. PhD Thesis, Lancaster University, 2005.

POPE, Philipe. "Foundation of Nixonian Foreign Policy: The Pre-Presidential Years of Richard Nixon, 1946–1968" University of Southern California, August 1988.

SPEER, Glenn. "Richard Nixon's Position on Communist China, 1949–1960: The Evolution of a Pacific Strategy," PhD thesis, City University of New York, 1992.

Index

Acheson, Dean, 16, 211
Adenauer, Konrad, 24
Allison, Graham, 2
Amur River Incidents. *See* Sino-Soviet border clashes
Anderson, Donald, 22, 168–169, 193, 229
"Asia After Viet Nam." *See* Nixon: *Foreign Affairs* article, October 1967
Asia-Pacific region, 182, 206, 219, 222, 224, 233, 237, 245, 247. *See also* specific countries

backchannel (US-China secret communications), 5, 85, 181, 221
   France as, 81
   Pakistan as, 98, 120–121, 141–143, 146, 151–155
   Paris as, 137–138, 140
   Romania as, 100, 144
balance of power
   Chinese view of, 226
   in practice, 33–35
   in theory, 31–33
   Kissinger on, 9, 31–35, 85–86, 235, 242
   Nixon on, 19, 34, 163–164, 226
   realist school and, 32
   strategic triangle between the U.S., China, and the Soviets based on, 1, 3–4, 9, 234–235, 237, 243, 250
   strategic triangle between the US, China, and Japan against the Soviets based on, 237, 249
Barnett, A. Doak, 22–23, 104–105
Barnett Robert, 92
Books (NSC briefing papers). *See also* specific countries
   Kissinger's trips to Beijing (July and October 1971) and, 161, 165
   Nixon's trip to China (February 1972) and, 200–204

Brezhnev, Leonid, 189, 233–234
   Asian Collective Security proposal and, 86, 100–101
Brown, Winthrop, 86, 92
Bureau of East Asian and Pacific (US State Department), 7–8, 10, 65, 82, 86–87, 89, 113, 115, 121, 123, 128–129, 155, 187, 244, 246
Bureau of Intelligence and Research (INR: US State Department), 7–8, 63, 79, 83, 87, 89, 102, 104, 106–107, 112–113, 122, 130, 133, 136, 144, 150, 190, 244
bureaucratic politics, 2–3, 45–46, 59, 126
   National Security Council and, 2–3, 46
   problems, 6–8
   State Department and, 2, 8, 60–63
Bush, George H.W., 169–170

Cambodia, 8, 81, 136, 146, 171, 215–216, 232, 252
   Khmer Rouge, 232
   Lon Nol-Sirik Matak, 171, 232
   US military operations (May 1970), 8, 130–135
Carter, Jimmy, 239
Ceaușescu, Nicolae
   as intermediary in US-China secret communications, 24
   Nixon's talks with (August 1969), 98–99
   Nixon's talks with (October 1970), 139–140
Chennault, Anna, 29
Central Intelligence Agency (CIA)
   briefing papers for Nixon's trip to China and, 201–202
   cables used by Nixon and Kissinger and, 61
   contact in Hong Kong, 111
   contact in New York, 193
   Laird and, 59

Laos and, 146
NSC system and, 56, 243
NSSM 63 and, 87
policy studies by, 141
situational analyses of US-China-Soviet relations by, 80, 85, 102, 130
Chenpao Island Incidents. *See* Sino-Soviet border clashes
Chiang Ching-kuo, 129
Chiang Kai-shek, 29, 149, 167, 186
China. *See* People's Republic of China (PRC)
China experts
  academics, 3–4, 22–23
  Kissinger's criticisms of, 9, 33–34
  State Department (Sinophile group), 4, 8, 22, 65, 147, 244
Chinese Ministry of Foreign Affairs (PRC), 80, 108, 143, 165
CIA. *See* Central Intelligence Agency
Cold War, 20, 34
Communists, Chinese, 18–19, 226
Congress, 131, 210, 212, 245
  hearings on US policy toward China, 23
  Nixon's briefings to Congressional leaders, 79, 92, 98, 146, 191, 205, 208, 225–226, 247
  pro-Chinese Nationalist lobby, 5, 17, 29, 65, 239, 241
Cultural Revolution, 20–22, 27, 63, 75, 95–96, 183
Czechoslovakia, 28, 75

Damansky Island Incidents. *See* Sino-Soviet border clashes
Defense Department. *See* US Defense Department
De Gaulle, Charles, 24, 36, 243
  Nixon's talks with (June 1963), 23–24
  Nixon's talks with (March 1969), 77–79, 81
Democratic People's Republic of Korea (North Korea), 130, 212
Democratic Republic of Vietnam (DRVN: North Vietnam), 1, 9, 22–23, 66–67, 75, 133, 146, 171–172, 198–199, 216, 232, 248–249. *See also* Indochina; and Vietnam War
Deng Xiaoping, 235, 239

détente (US-USSR/Soviet relations), 24, 232, 234–235, 245
diplomacy, 1, 3, 6, 9, 36, 80, 183, 229, 250. *See also* secrecy
triangular diplomacy, 35, 103, 151, 180
Dobrynin, Anatoly, 38, 65, 74, 111, 119–120, 125, 137, 189, 194

East Asia, 22, 25, 62, 75, 142, 161, 174–176, 182, 184, 218, 227. *See also* specific countries
East Asian and Pacific Interdepartmental Group (NSC), 62, 83, 160
Ehrlichman, John, 57
Eisenhower, Dwight D.
  NSC system under the presidency of, 43–45
  Taiwan Strait crises and the administration of, 17–19

Fairbank, John King, 22–23, 104
Farland, Joseph, 57, 152–154, 192
Ford, Gerald, 231, 234, 238
  Kissinger and, 232
  Mao and, 239
  trip to China (December 1975), 235, 239
Foreign Affairs. *See* Nixon: "Asia After Viet-Nam"
Foreign Ministry. *See* Chinese Ministry of Foreign Affairs (PRC)
France, 24, 36, 245

Gandhi, Indira, 191–192, 194
Gang of Four, 239
Goodpaster, Andrew, 44–45, 48, 53, 58
Green, Marshall, 7, 10, 24–25, 61–62, 64
  trip to Asia (March–April 1969), 82
  briefings to Asian leaders after Nixon's trip to China, 224–225
  China and, 110–112, 118, 224
  Japan and, 173–174, 188
  Kissinger and, 62, 82–83
  as liaison between State and NSC staff, 165
  Nixon and, 24–25, 62, 87, 99
  Nixon Doctrine and, 99
  on secrecy, 62
  Shanghai Communiqué and, 211–212
  Taiwan and, 186, 244

Warsaw ambassadorial talks and, 122–123, 125, 128–129
Gromyko, Andre, 110, 189–190
Guam Doctrine. *See* Nixon Doctrine

Haig, Alexander M., Jr., 7, 54, 137, 155, 166, 193, 208, 223, 243–244
　Defense Department and, 59
　Kissinger and, 74
　on Nixon, 38
　NSC and, 58
　trip to China (January 1972), 197–200
Haldeman, Harry, R., 7, 94, 155, 243
　Kissinger and, 57–58, 99, 185
　Nixon and, 57–58, 96, 153, 184
Halperin, Morton, 2, 7, 45–46, 53, 85
hegemony. *See also* Shanghai Communiqué: anti-hegemony clause
　Chinese view of, 28, 199, 249
　Kissinger-Zhou talks on, 182, 233
　Nixon-Zhou talks on, 222
　Sino-Japanese rapprochement and, 237
　western interpretation of, 182
Helm, Richard, 87–88
Hilaly, Agha, 97, 111, 120–121, 127, 142, 151–154
Ho Chi Minh, 106
Ho Chi Minh Trail, 81, 145–146
Holdridge, John H., 8, 53, 55, 97, 112, 130, 155, 161, 208, 244
　briefings to Asian leaders after Nixon's trip to China, 224–225
　cable to the Chinese (July 1969), 94
　on Cambodia, 131
　Japan and, 187
　Kissinger and, 54
　on Laos, 146
　on Nixon Doctrine, 92
　on NSC staff, 56
　on NSC staff-State relationship, 54
　on the Soviet Union, 181–182
　on Taiwan, 166–167
　on Vietnam, 170
　Whiting and, 104–105
Hong Kong. *See* US Consulate General in Hong Kong
　CIA contact with China in, 111–112
Hua Guofeng, 239
Huang Hua, 193, 197

India, 9, 20, 22, 84, 86. *See also* Indira Gandhi
　Kissinger on India-China rivalry, 233, 247
　Pakistan, conflict with, 191–194, 249
India-Pakistan relations, 8, 12, 95, 98, 100, 176–180, 245
　Haig-Zhou talks on, 198–199
　Kissinger-Zhou talks on, 178–180
　Nixon on, 219
　Nixon-Zhou talks on, 220–222
　NSC staff on, 178, 219
　State Department on, 176–178, 192–193, 249
Indochina, 9, 20, 66, 132, 145, 248. *See also* specific countries
　Haig-Zhou talks on, 198–200
　Kissinger on, 231–232
　Kissinger-Zhou talks on, 167, 170–173
　Nixon on, 213
　Nixon-Zhou talks on, 215–217
　NSC staff on, 170, 172
　State Department on, 66–67, 129, 248
intelligence, 7–8, 47, 53–53. *See also* Bureau of Intelligence and Research (INR: US State Department)

Japan, 8–9, 20, 26, 34, 84–85, 93, 150, 160–161, 236–237, 249
　Kissinger on, 173, 237
　Kissinger-Zhou talks on, 175–176, 233
　Nixon on, 174, 194, 204, 217, 226
　Nixon Doctrine and, 249
　Nixon-Kissinger talks on, 162–163, 247, 249
　Nixon-Mao talks on, 206–207
　Nixon-Sato joint communiqué (November 1969) and, 174
　Nixon-Zhou talks on, 175–176, 233
　normalization/rapprochement with China (September 1972), 237, 249
　NSC staff on, 174–175, 217
　reactions to Kissinger's trip to Beijing (July 1971: Nixon Shock/shokku), 187–188, 249
　reactions to Nixon's trip to China (February 1972), 224
　State Department on, 174, 248
Jenkins, Alfred, 165, 208, 211, 246
Johnson, Lyndon B., 44

Johnson, U. Alexis, 174, 187
  on Nixon Shock/shokku, 188
Joint Chiefs of Staff, 138

Kansas City address (Nixon: July 1971), 163–164, 191
Keating, Kenneth, 178
Kennedy, John F., 19, 44
Khmer Rouge. *See* Cambodia
Kissinger, Henry A., 1–2, 30, 242. *See also* diplomacy; and specific countries
  on balance of power in practice, 9, 33–35, 85–86
  on balance of power in theory, 31–33
  trips to Beijing (July and October 1971), 5, 164–184
  China, early views, 4, 35–37
  China policy, skeptical views, 7, 74, 80, 86
  on legitimacy in the international order, 30–31
  Mao and, 37
  on multipolarity, 30–31
  Nixon on, 39
  Nixon, first meeting with, 29, 41–42
  Nixon, leadership with, 37–39
  NSC system and, 41–43
  NSC staff and, 56–59
  on secrecy, 6–7
  as Secretary of State, 34, 230–231
  on Sino-Soviet relations, 36, 81, 85
  State Department and, 5, 42, 46–48
  on State Department's contributions to China policy, 61, 168
  as strategic thinker, 37, 39, 226–227, 229
  Warsaw ambassadorial talks and, 8, 75–76, 118–119, 126, 129, 132
  Zhou and, 37
Korea. *See* Democratic People's Republic of Korea (North Korea); and Republic of Korea (South Korea)
Korean War, 1, 4, 17, 43, 89, 111, 136, 155, 212
Kosygin, Alexei, 106–107, 109
Kreisberg, Paul, 66–67, 116, 121, 128, 168–169, 246

Laird, Melvin R., 87–88
  Cambodia and, 131
  Japan and, 187
  Kissinger and, 58–59
  NSC system and, 46–47
Laos, 81
  Kissinger-Zhou talks on, 171
  Nixon on, 215
  Nixon-Zhou talks on, 216
  NSC staff on, 215
  US military operation (February 1971), 145–146
leak/leakage, 52, 88. *See also* secrecy
  Kissinger's concern about NSC staff, 191
  Nixon's concern about NSC staff, 141
  Nixon's concern about the State Department, 42, 60, 211
  Nixon and Kissinger on, 61, 89
  Nixon's and Kissinger's concern about Japan, 187
Lin Biao, 81, 138, 144, 190, 194
Lord, Winston, 8, 244
  Books (NSC briefing books) and, 161
  on Kansas City address (Nixon), 164
  on Kissinger, 57, 59
  on Mao and Zhou, 205
  on Nixon, 27, 29, 74, 202
  on Nixon Doctrine, 92
  on NSC procedure, 49–50, 52
  on secret trip to Beijing, 152
  on Sino-Soviet border clashes, 103, 232
  as special assistant of Kissinger, 54–55, 155, 205–206
  on State Department, 168, 212
  on Vietnam War, 217
  on Watergate, 230

Malraux, Andre, 206–207
Mao Zedong (Mao Tse-tung), 1, 10, 30, 80, 239. *See also* specific countries
  Cambodia and, 133
  CIA briefing paper to Nixon on, 201
  on encirclement of China, 20, 199
  Kissinger and, 37–38, 229–231, 250
  Kissinger's briefing paper to Nixon on, 202, 230–231
  on Lin Biao incident, 190
  Nixon and, 166, 203, 205–207, 227, 247
  on Nixon's *Foreign Affairs* article, 27
  on Nixon's Inaugural address, 72
  North Vietnam and, 131

NSC briefing book to Nixon on, 202, 229
Pakistan and, 95–96, 141–142, 154
ping pong diplomacy and, 150
Romania and, 136, 144
Shanghai Communiqué and, 168, 182
Sino-Soviet border clashes and, 80, 234–235
on Sino-US relations, 138, 165, 234–235
Snow and, 138, 143
Taiwan and, 206, 238–239
Zhou and, 80, 96, 202, 205, 229–231, 234, 250
Morgenthau, Hans J., 32
multipolarity, 3, 34
  Kissinger on, 30–31, 33
  Nixon on, 163
  NSC staff on, 34

National Intelligence Estimate (CIA), 102, 133, 146
Nationalists, Chinese, 17–18, 20, 169, 212, 241, 247
National Security Council (NSC) system, 6–8, 41–67
  Goodpaster's memoranda, 44–45
  Halperin's memorandum, 45–46
  objections from Defense and State, 46–48
  State Department downgraded by Nixon and Kissinger in, 60–61
  structure and procedure under the Nixon presidency, 49–52
  problems of the previous NSCs, 41–44
National Security Council (NSC) staff, 6–8, 53–59. *See also* specific individuals
  drafting of policy papers by, 54–56
  relations with Kissinger, 56–59
  procedures, 53–54
  relations with State Department officials, 63–63
National Security Decision Memorandum (NSDM), 52
  NSDM 1: "Establishment of NSC Decision and Study Memoranda Series," 49
  NSDM 2: "Reorganization of National Security Council System," 49, 62
  NSDM 17: "China Trade," 88, 117
  NSDM 13: "Policy Toward Japan," 173–174

NSDM 85: "The National Security Council Senior Review Group," 50
National Security Study Memorandum (NSSM), 7, 46, 49, 62
  NSSM 9: "Review of International Situation," 73
  NSSM 14: "United States China Policy," 73–74
  NSSM 35: "US Trade Policy Toward Communist Countries," 88
  NSSM 63: "US Policy on Current Sino-Soviet Differences," 87–88, 108–110
  NSSM 69: "US Nuclear Policy in Asia," 87–88
  NSSSM 106: "China Policy," 141, 148–149
  NSSM 107: "Study of Entire UN Membership Question: US-China Policy," 141, 148–149
  NSSM 124: "Next Steps Toward the People's Republic of China," 159–161
New China News Agency, 28, 72, 107, 131
Nixon, Richard M., 1–2, 15, 205, 243. *See also* specific countries
  "Asia After VietNam" (*Foreign Affairs* article, October 1967), 25–27, 29, 72, 164, 194, 242
  announcement of trip to China (July 1971), 1, 185–186
  China, early views of, 4, 15–19, 23–25
  Foreign Policy Reports to Congress, 55, 64, 126, 146
  Inaugural address (January 1969), 71–72
  Kissinger, first meeting with, 29, 41–42
  Kissinger, leadership with, 37–39
  Kissinger on, 38
  Mao and, 166, 203, 205–207, 227, 247
  memorandum to Kissinger on China policy (February 1, 1969), 73–74
  memorandum to Kissinger on China policy and the Chinese representation issue at the UN (November 22, 1970), 141
  NSC system and, 41–43
  operating style, 7, 38, 57–58, 77, 162
  presidential campaign and China (1960), 19
  presidential campaign and China (1968), 27–28

re-election concern, 5–6, 210
on secrecy, 6–7, 191
Time magazine interview with, 139, 144
trip to China (February 1972), 5, 205–223
trips to Europe (1963, 1967), 23–24
trip to France (March 1969), 77–79
trip to Pakistan (July 1969), 95–98
trip to Romania (August 1969), 98–100
as vice president of the Eisenhower administration, 4, 17–18, 42–43, 95
Yahya Khan and, 95–98
Zhou and, 27, 207–222
Nixon Doctrine, 9, 26, 91–93, 122, 136, 149, 163, 174, 245. *See also* Vietnam War; and Vietnamization
Nixon Shock/shokku. *See* Japan: reactions to Kissinger's trip to Beijing (July 1971)
North Korea. *See* Democratic People's Republic of Korea
North Vietnam. *See* Democratic Republic of Vietnam (DRVN)
NSC. *See* National Security Council

One-China principle, 168, 198, 200, 244, 247. *See also* United Nations: Chinese representation issue at the UN

Pakistan. *See also* India-Pakistan relations
as backchannel in US-China secret communications, 5, 59, 95–96, 98, 100, 121, 141, 146, 179, 246
India, conflict with, 191–194, 249
Paris Peace Accords (January 1973), 217, 232
People's Daily, 72, 145, 175
People's Republic of China (PRC), 1, 4, 8, 16, 20, 29, 83, 124, 140–141, 146–147, 150, 153–154, 168, 212
five principles of peaceful coexistence, 29, 76, 108, 122
Ninth Congress, 81–82, 138
Soviet invasion of Czechoslovakia and, 28
ping pong diplomacy, 149–150
Poland, 57, 115
PRC. *See* People's Republic of China
Price, Raymond, 24–25
Qiao, Guanhua, 208, 211

Radford, Charles, 138, 186
Republic of China (ROC: Taiwan), 8, 17, 20, 65, 73, 83, 86, 112, 122, 148–149, 160–161, 191, 237, 247–248. *See also* United Nations: Chinese representation issue at the UN
Defense department on, 149
Haig on, 198
Japan formula, 237–238
Kissinger on, 142, 162, 184, 247–248
Kissinger-Mao talks on, 239
Kissinger-Zhou talks on, 166–170, 238
Nixon on, 18, 147, 163, 204, 214, 216–217, 247–248
Nixon-Zhou talks on, 208–211, 218
NSC staff on, 167–168, 208–209
PRC's attitude toward, 29, 84, 110–111, 126–127, 136, 141–142, 144–145, 154–155, 248
reactions to Kissinger's trip to Beijing (July 1971), 186
reactions to Nixon's trip to China (February 1972), 224
Sato on, 174
Shanghai Communiqué and, 168–169, 211–213
State Department on, 8, 65–66, 76, 81, 84, 113, 123, 125, 127–130, 132, 136, 141, 152, 155, 244–246
Taiwan Independence Movement, 167, 209, 239, 247
Vietnam and, 172, 210, 247–248
Warsaw ambassadorial talks and, 119, 124–125, 246
Republic of Korea (South Korea), 8, 20, 136, 161, 174, 199, 211–212, 224, 226, 236, 249
Kissinger-Zhou talks on, 175
Nixon-Mao talks on, 207
Nixon-Zhou talks on, 217–218
Republic of Vietnam (South Vietnam), 131, 146, 163, 171, 199, 211, 224–225, 252. *See also* Indochina; and Vietnam War
Review Group (NSC), 46, 48, 50–51, 67, 108, 244
on NSSM 14, 83–86, 102–103
on NSSM 63, 108–110, 112–113
on NSSMs 106 and 107, 147–149

Richardson, Elliot L., 48, 61, 88, 108, 119, 126
　address on China in New York (September 1969), 106–107
ROC. *See* Republic of China
Rockefeller, Nelson, 35, 56
Rodman, Peter, 8, 244
　as assistant of Kissinger, 54–55,
　on Haldeman, 57
　on Japan, 174
　on Kissinger, 36, 54, 61, 230
　on Nixon, 27,
　on Nixon Doctrine, 93
　on NSC staff, 55
　on NSM system, 243
　on Sino-Soviet relations, 106
　on Taiwan, 65
　on Vietnam War and China, 232
Rogers, William P., 76, 95, 101, 131, 136, 152–153, 187, 205, 208
　address on China in New York (April 1969), 81
　briefing to Japan (July 1971), 187
　briefing to Taiwan (July 1971), 186
　Haldeman and, 57–58
　Kissinger's trip to Beijing and, 184–185
　Nixon and Kissinger, relations with, 60–61
　NSC system and, 46–47
　as Secretary of State, 60
　Shanghai Communiqué and, 211
　Warsaw ambassadorial talks and, 119, 125–126, 128, 131–132, 137
Romania, 98–100
　as backchannel in US-China secret communications, 5, 144, 151, 245
Rusk, Dean, 21, 26

Safire, William, 24–25
SALT. *See* Strategic Arms Limitation Talks (US-USSR)
Sato, Eisaku, 219, 224
　Nixon-Sato joint communiqué (November 1969), 136, 174, 236
　Nixon Shock/shokku and, 187–188
Saunders, Harold, 97, 178, 192
secrecy, 1–3, 6–8, 98, 153, 229, 241, 250. *See also* leak/leakage
　bureaucratic politics and, 60

Chinese view of, 153
　Kissinger on, 43, 137, 165, 191, 246
　NSC system and, 6–7, 52
　Nixon and Kissinger on, 6
　problems of, 138, 151, 186, 188, 231, 245–249
　special envoy/representative to Beijing and, 76, 123, 125, 127, 142, 144, 151–152, 155, 246
　State Department excluded by Nixon and Kissinger and, 7–8, 52, 60–63, 67, 211, 243–244
　Warsaw ambassadorial talks and, 168–169, 212, 223
Senior Review Group (NSC), 244
　on India-Pakistan crisis, 179
　on NSSMs 106 and 107, 147–149
Shanghai Communiqué, 168–169, 212, 223
　anti-hegemony clause, 182, 222. *See also* hegemony
Shen, James, 186
Sino-Indian conflict, 20
Sino-Soviet borders clashes, 79–80, 86–89, 101–106, 113, 194, 242. *See also* NSSM 63: "US Policy on Current Sino-Soviet Differences"
　Amur River Incidents, 83, 87
　Chenpao/Damansky Island Incidents, 79–80
　Ussuri River Incidents, 79–80
Sino-Soviet relations, 1, 9, 20–21, 89, 109, 112, 118, 137, 201
　India-Pakistan crisis and, 176, 191–194
　Kissinger on, 4, 35–37, 66, 81, 85, 105, 137–138, 179–180
　Nixon on, 9, 25, 78, 98, 103, 162, 206, 221, 226
　NSC staff on, 180–181, 220
　State Department on, 65–66, 112, 122
Sisco, Joseph, 97, 192
Smyser, Richard, 8, 53, 140, 161, 170
Sneider, Richard L., 34, 53, 75, 86, 174, 187
Snow, Edgar, 38
　Mao and, 138, 143
　Zhou and, 145
Solomon, Richard, 8, 15, 19, 25
　as China expert, 53, 244
　on Chinese leadership, 229
　on Haig's trip to China, 200

on Kissinger, 54, 244
on Kissinger-Deng relationship, 235
on NSC procedure, 51, 56, 64, 246
on Nixon, 15–16, 19, 25, 27, 37
on Nixon Doctrine, 93
on Nixon's Kansas City speech, 164
on Romanian backchannel, 100, 151
on Shanghai Communiqué, 213
on US-China normalization, 237
on Zhou, 205
South Asia, 8, 177–178, 180–181, 191–194, 200. *See also* specific countries
Southeast Asia, 122–123, 131, 161, 172, 211, 215, 245. *See also* specific countries
South Korea. *See* Republic of Korea
South Vietnam. *See* Republic of Vietnam
Soviet experts (Kremlinologists/Slavopile group: US State Department), 8, 85–86, 244
Soviet-Indian Treaty of Peace, Friendship, Cooperation, 179
Soviet Union, 8–9, 20–21, 65, 124, 139, 145, 180, 200, 232, 234, 245, 248–249. *See also* Sino-Soviet relations
  arms control talks, 1, 9, 242, 245. *See also* Strategic Arms Limitation Talks (SALT: US-USSR)
  Chinese view of, 20, 118, 193, 199, 207, 233
  India and, 177
  Indochina and, 216
  Kissinger on, 33–34, 36, 83, 113, 193, 233, 242
  Kissinger-Deng talks on, 233
  Kissinger-Mao talks on, 233, 239
  Kissinger-Zhou talks on, 181–184
  Nixon on, 24, 36, 103, 163, 194, 226
  Nixon-Mao talks on, 206–207
  Nixon-Zhou talks on, 218, 220, 221–222
  NSC staff on, 180–181, 200, 220
  reactions to Kissinger's trip to Beijing (July 1971), 188–190
  reactions to Nixon's trip to China (February 1972), 225
  State Department on, 66, 112
State Department. *See* US State Department

Strategic Arms Limitation Talks (SALT: US-USSR), 111, 117–118, 153–154, 181, 232
Stoessel, Walter J., Jr., 115–122, 129, 132
  Warsaw ambassadorial talks (January and February 1970) and, 123–124, 127, 246

Taiwan. *See* Republic of China
Tanaka, Kakuei, 237
Thieu, Nguyen Van, 81, 87, 171
Truman, Harry S., 16, 43

Under Secretaries Committee (NSC), 48, 52, 88
United Nations (UN), 78, 85, 99, 110, 140, 142, 147–149, 162, 169–170, 193, 243–244
  Chinese representation issue at the UN, 141, 169–170
  Nixon's public statement on, 28
Ussuri River Incidents. *See* Sino-Soviet border clashes
United States, 1, 5–6, 26, 30–31, 37, 73, 91, 147, 163–164, 169, 185, 212, 219
US-China relations, 1, 4, 16–17, 39
  liaison offices (Washington, Beijing), 238, 248
  trade and travel, 5, 18, 86, 88–89, 100, 110, 113, 120, 122, 164, 241–243, 245
  normalization, 2, 27, 66, 75–76, 83, 150, 164, 167, 185, 209–210, 223, 229–231, 234, 236–239, 247–248, 250
  rapprochement, 1–2, 4, 33–35, 73, 103, 127, 182, 204, 207, 217, 226, 231, 237, 242, 248–250
  tacit alliance, 233–234
US Consulate General Hong Kong, 63, 74, 118, 136, 145,
US Defense Department, 45, 53–54, 80, 123, 149, 243
  NSC staff and, 58–59
  NSC system under Nixon and Kissinger and, 46–47
US-Japan Mutual Security Treaty, 173, 218, 236–237, 249. *See also* Japan
US-Republic of China Mutual Defense Treaty, 149, 236. *See also* Republic of China (ROC: Taiwan)

Index 287

US State Department. *See also* specific countries; and Warsaw ambassadorial talks
 earlier initiatives toward China, 21–22
 geopolitical perspective, 64–67
 intelligence sources, 8, 63
 NSC staff, relations with, 63–64
 NSC system under Nixon and Kissinger and, 2–3, 7–8
 secrecy by Nixon and Kissinger and, 7–8, 60–61
 senior officials responsible for US policy toward China, 7–8, 61–62
US-USSR/Soviet relations, 74, 103, 109, 119, 153, 233

Vietnam. *See* Democratic People's Republic of Vietnam (North Vietnam); Republic of Vietnam (South Vietnam); and Vietnam War
Vietnam War, 1, 4, 9, 20–27, 36–37, 65, 81, 100, 106, 122, 127, 133, 143, 162–163, 231–232, 242, 245, 248
 Kissinger and NSC staff on, 66
 Kissinger-Zhou talks on, 170–173
 Nixon-Zhou talks on, 213–217
 State Department on, 66–67
 Vietnamization, 9, 51, 58, 131, 171, 213–214

Walsh, James Edward, 136, 139
Walters, Vernon A., 131, 137–138, 190, 214
Waltz, Kenneth, 32
Watergate, 6, 230–231, 248
Warsaw ambassadorial talks, 4–5, 8, 115–134
 as breakthrough in US-China relations, 126–127
 Cambodian military operation (May 1970) and the collapse of, 130–134
 cancellation (February 1969) of, 74–77
 Kissinger's earlier views of, 75–76
 Kissinger-State Department differences over, 126, 128–130
 resumption (January 1970) of, 123–125
 State Department's earlier initiatives toward, 22, 28, 66–67, 76
 State Department's policy studies toward, 110–111, 116–123, 125–126, 128–130
Washington Special Action Group (WSAG) (NSC), 67, 108, 192
Whiting, Allen, 23, 60, 86
 Kissinger's consultation with, 104–105

Yahya, Kahn, 95, 97, 111, 120–121, 127, 141–142, 153–154, 176–177, 192, 243
 Kissinger and, 96
 Nixon's talks with (August 1969), 95–96
 Nixon's talks with (October 1970), 139

Zhenbao Island Incidents. *See also* Damansky Island incidents
Zhou Enlai (Chou En-lai), 1, 239. *See also* specific countries
 Kissinger and, 164–169, 171–172, 175–176, 178–183
 on Kissinger, 38–39
 Mao and, 80, 96, 202, 205, 229–231, 234, 250
 Nixon and, 27, 207–211, 214–222
 ping pong diplomacy and, 150
Zumwalt, Elmo, 59, 152

Made in the USA
Monee, IL
17 November 2022